Reproductive Justice

**Recent Titles in
Women's Psychology**

"Intimate" Violence against Women: When Spouses, Partners,
or Lovers Attack
Paula K. Lundberg-Love and Shelly L. Marmion, editors

Daughters of Madness: Growing Up and Older with
a Mentally Ill Mother
Susan Nathiel

Psychology of Women: Handbook of Issues and Theories, Second Edition
Florence L. Denmark and Michele Paludi, editors

WomanSoul: The Inner Life of Women's Spirituality
Carole A. Rayburn and Lillian Comas-Diaz, editors

The Psychology of Women at Work: Challenges and Solutions for
Our Female Workforce
Michele A. Paludi, editor

Feminism and Women's Rights Worldwide, Three Volumes
Michele A. Paludi, editor

Single Mother in Charge: How to Successfully Pursue Happiness
Sandy Chalkoun

Women and Mental Disorders, Four Volumes
Paula K. Lundberg-Love, Kevin L. Nadal, and Michele A. Paludi, editors

Reproductive Justice

A Global Concern

Joan C. Chrisler, Editor

Foreword by Joy K. Rice, PhD

Women's Psychology
Michele A. Paludi, Series Editor

 PRAEGER

AN IMPRINT OF ABC-CLIO, LLC
Santa Barbara, California • Denver, Colorado • Oxford, England

Library of Congress Cataloging-in-Publication Data

Reproductive justice : a global concern / Joan C. Chrisler, editor.
   p. cm. — (Women's psychology)
   Includes index.
   ISBN 978-0-313-39339-6 (hardcopy : alk. paper) — ISBN 978-0-313-39340-2 (ebook)
1. Human reproduction—Law and legislation.   2. Reproductive health—Law and legislation.   3. Reproductive rights.   4. Women—Legal status, laws, etc.
I. Chrisler, Joan C.
   K2000.R47   2012
   342.08'78—dc23   2011038703

ISBN: 978-0-313-39339-6
EISBN: 978-0-313-39340-2

16   15   14   13   12   1   2   3   4   5

This book is also available on the World Wide Web as an eBook.
Visit www.abc-clio.com for details.

Praeger
An Imprint of ABC-CLIO, LLC

ABC-CLIO, LLC
130 Cremona Drive, P.O. Box 1911
Santa Barbara, California 93116-1911

This book is printed on acid-free paper ∞

Manufactured in the United States of America

This book is dedicated to the women of the world, too many of whom lack reproductive justice, and to all of those individuals, agencies, and organizations that are engaged in the struggle to achieve and ensure it.

Contents

Contents

Series Foreword

Because women's work is never done and is underpaid or unpaid or boring or repetitious and we're the first to get fired
and what we look like is more important than what we do
and if we get raped it's our fault and if we get beaten we must
have provoked it and if we raise our voices we're nagging
bitches and if we enjoy sex we're nymphos and if we don't
we're frigid and if we love women it's because we can't get
a "real" man and if we ask our doctor too many questions
we're neurotic and/or pushy and if we expect childcare we're
selfish and if we stand up for our rights we're aggressive and
"unfeminine" and if we don't we're typical weak females and
if we want to get married we're out to trap a man and if we
don't we're unnatural and because we still can't get an adequate safe contraceptive but men can walk on the moon and
if we can't cope or don't want a pregnancy we're made to feel
guilty about abortion and . . . for lots of other reasons we are
part of the women's liberation movement.

Author unknown, quoted in *The Torch,* September 14, 1987

These sentiments underlie the major goals of Praeger's book series, Wom-
en's Psychology:

1. Valuing women. The books in this series value women by valuing
   children and working for affordable child care; valuing women by
   respecting all physiques, not just placing value on slender women;
   valuing women by acknowledging older women's wisdom, beauty,

aging; valuing women who have been sexually victimized and viewing them as survivors; valuing women who work inside and outside
of the home; and valuing women by respecting their choices of careers, of whom they mentor, of their reproductive rights, their spirituality, and their sexuality.
2. Treating women as the norm. Thus the books in this series make up
   for women's issues typically being omitted, trivialized, or dismissed
   from other books on psychology.
3. Taking a non-Eurocentric view of women's experiences. The books in
   this series integrate the scholarship on race and ethnicity into wom-
   en's psychology, thus providing a psychology of *all* women. Women
   typically have been described collectively, but we are diverse.
4. Facilitating connections between readers' experiences and psychological theories and empirical research. The books in this series offer
   readers opportunities to challenge their views about women, feminism, sexual victimization, gender role socialization, education, and
   equal rights. These texts thus encourage women readers to value
   themselves and others. The accounts of women's experiences as
   reflected through research and personal stories in the texts in this
   series have been included for readers to derive strength from the
   efforts of others who have worked for social change on the interpersonal, organizational and societal levels.

A student in one of my courses on the psychology of women once
stated:

> I learned so much about women. Women face many issues: dis-
> crimination, sexism, prejudices . . . by society. Women need to work
> together to change how society views us. I learned so much and
> talked about much of the issues brought up in class to my friends
> and family. My attitudes have changed toward a lot of things. I got
> to look at myself, my life, and what I see for the future. (Paludi, 2002)

It is my hope that readers of the books in this series also reflect on the
topics and look at themselves, their own lives, and what they see for the
future.

Dr. Joan Chrisler's book, *Reproductive Justice: A Global Concern,* provides readers with the opportunity to accomplish this goal and offers us
understanding of reproductive justice, including female genital cutting,
infertility and reproductive technologies, pregnancy and prenatal care,
female feticide and infanticide, and sexual assault as reproductive justice.
Dr. Chrisler has taken an international perspective to these important issues and has addressed public policy for reproductive justice. She has included contributors, all scholars and advocates for women's reproductive

justice, who share her concern of reaching out to women in the general public to inform them about their reproductive health and reproductive rights.

Dr. Chrisler has served as Chair of the International Committee for Women of Div 52 and has served as President of the American Psychological Association's division on the Psychology of Women as well as the Society for Menstrual Cycle Research. She has published extensively on gender research in psychology, psychology of women, menarche, and menstruation.

This book envisions the complete psychological, physical, and spiritual well being of women of all ages. As Dr. Chrisler and her contributors note, reproductive justice will only be achieved when women have political, economic, and social power to make healthy decisions about their bodies, reproduction, and sexuality. With this publication, Dr. Chrisler has edited a major work in women's psychology. I am proud to have her book as part of the women's psychology series.

Michele A. Paludi

REFERENCE

Paludi, M. (2002). *The psychology of women* (2nd ed.). Upper Saddle River, NJ: Prentice Hall.

Foreword

This exciting book is the culmination of years of advocacy and collaborative work by women psychologists and active members of the International Committee for Women (Division 52—International Psychology) and the Global Issues Committee (Division 35—Society for the Psychology of Women) within the American Psychological Association (APA). A decade ago the collaborative efforts of these two groups blossomed in parallel with the effort to infuse a greater international feminist focus within APA. Whether there are social justice concerns, as in the aftermath of apartheid or ethnic civil wars, or economic concerns, as in the proliferation of new markets and multinational corporations, international events, trends, and issues have become increasingly relevant not only to psychology's interests and involvement, but to all fields and disciplines. Women's issues, however, have not been specifically singled out for study or attention in the internationalization of psychology within APA until more recent times. In contrast, issues related to gender and the psychology of women and gender within the U.S. have long been integrated into the concerns, policies, and activities of the American Psychological Association. APA itself has a Women's Programs Office and a Committee on Women in Psychology (CWP) within the Public Interest Directorate, and Division 35—the Society for the Psychology of Women (SPW) is one of the largest and most active divisions in APA.

In recent years a groundswell of interest has resulted in several initiatives and newly formed organizations that have expanded the horizons of the area of psychology of women in terms of a global perspective. In 1990 Division 35 formed The Global Issues Committee (GIC), which is now a standing committee of the Society of the Psychology of Women. The general mission of the committee is to develop and update an agenda of issues that affect the psychology of women and girls across a global context and to explore linkages between women psychologists in various countries.

Initial projects included the development of a Resource Directory of International Feminist Psychologists; a bibliography; an electronic network to facilitate information exchange; informative articles in the Division's newsletter; and symposia, round tables, and invited addresses at the APA convention. Through the work and contacts of the various committee members, collaboration and updates on UN special projects on women, such as the 1995 UN Fourth World Conference on Women (held in Beijing), was also accomplished.

The Global Issues Committee of Division 35 asked women psychologists to consider to what extent their work was connected to and informed by realities of the world's women and girls. This question also inspired and informed the formation and mission of the International Committee for Women (ICfW). The goal of developing a psychology of women that integrates the diversity of women's experiences challenged existing theory and practice. Economic and political events at the international level also made it clear that American women's lives are inextricably linked with the lives of the world's women, and reproductive issues, the theme of this book, are at the heart of women's lives.

Bearing these important questions in mind, in 1999 I convened a small group of women who met at APA to discuss how we could infuse these questions and issues into the fabric of the brand new international division and, even more ambitiously, into the international efforts of the APA itself. The newly formed International Committee for Women sparked the immediate interest of women across divisions in APA. As a result, ICfW became the first standing committee of Division 52 and remains its most active committee. I was privileged to serve as ICfW's first chair, and our initial task was to forge a mission statement that today continues to serve as the guiding light for the ICfW:

> The primary mission of the International Committee for Women (ICfW) will be to identify substantive issues that affect the welfare of women globally and to recommend action to the Division. The committee will promote research, education, symposia, and projects that advance equality for women internationally and will encourage the awareness and infusion of gender equity issues throughout the activities of the division.

Recognizing the similarity of their respective missions and concerns, the *Global Issues Committee* and the *International Committee for Women* soon joined forces and now hold their annual meetings at APA together. Our mutual goals and many subsequent achievements have centered around four areas: communication, awareness, advocacy, and collaborative research, of which this book is a part.

Ongoing active communication is a key part of any collaboration, and we update our members through annual meetings at APA, electronic announcements on our list serv, and articles in the divisional newsletters and websites. The importance of a discussion list serv includes not only posting information, but identifying issues and sharing information about interesting developments relevant to international women's issues. We have shared internet resources with our membership and circulated lists of international websites on women in psychology. ICfW also has liaisons with other APA divisions and organizations who are encouraged to publicize our activities, recruit membership, and promote collaborative efforts in their respective divisional newsletters or other venues.

We have become a very active voice for women within our divisions and the greater APA through newsletter announcements, annual and midwinter meetings, and the mounting of symposia and conversation hours at the APA convention. Our strategic planning efforts always include infusing awareness about international gender issues into APA committees, initiatives, and concerns.

In line with our aim to foster broader awareness of women's issues internationally and to increase consciousness about avoiding cultural nepotism in exporting Western psychology, in 2000 an ambitious project was born, and an ICfW subcommittee was formed to write an APA position paper. This position paper took 4 years to write, undergo review, and gain APA endorsement. The 2004 *APA Resolution on Culture and Gender Awareness in International Psychology* was widely disseminated and endorsed by many social justice divisions of APA. The resolution recognizes the positive impact of U.S. psychology on world psychology, but was written to reflect a more sensitive understanding and appreciation of the cultural and gender implications of the wholesale exportation of the goals, values, outlook, and methodology of Western psychology to the rest of the world. The *APA Resolution on Culture and Gender Awareness in International Psychology* was a high point on the road to achieving our original mission awareness objective.

Another high point was helping to launch a mentoring match project through the International Psychology Division. Many of our members served as initial mentors to emerging women leaders, students, and early career psychologists throughout the world, and that collaborative project continues today. In addition we identified the need for individual mentoring for international women psychologists who are required to publish in English-language journals in order to earn tenure and promotion at their universities. Additional mentoring efforts at our annual meetings have included division suite presentations, conversation hours, and round tables designed to help women to understand the ins and outs of publishing international research. An emphasis has been on practical issues in publishing, especially the publishing challenges experienced by women and the needs of newcomers and early career psychologists.

From its inception, advocacy has been another integral part of our mission, and we cooperate and work with other APA divisions and external organizations, both U.S.-based and international, to help and support women globally. Thus in the past decade we have sponsored projects and raised funds to help support the Fatima Jinnah Women's University in Pakistan; the Revolutionary Association of the Women of Afghanistan (RAWA); the Half the Sky Orphanage for Girls in China; the Coalition against Sex Trafficking (CAST); and MADRE, which works with women in Latin America.

Advocacy is a part of our efforts, but collaborative research is the heart. Since the inception of our group we have promoted collaborative research, networking opportunities in the international psychology of women, and the dissemination and publicizing of members' research on global women's issues. Over the past decade our collaboration has led to the organization and presentation of dozens of APA convention symposia on highly relevant topics, such as Transracial Adoption; Sex Trafficking; Leadership Development for Women; International Media Depictions of Women; Reproductive Justice for Women Internationally; Psychotherapy with Women Internationally; Teaching the Psychology of Women from a Global Perspective; Collaboration and Partnerships in International Research; Internationalizing the Teaching of Health Psychology; Global Women's Health; Process and Practice Issues in Mentoring Women Internationally; Education and Attitudes towards International Women's Rights; Feminist Perspectives on International Collaboration; Cross-national Comparative Experiences of Women Psychologists; Translating Feminist Research into the Public Sphere; Cross-cultural Perspectives on Feminist Therapy and Research; Gender Issues in Immigration; and Internationalizing the Psychology of Women within the American Psychological Association.

In addition we encourage the infusion of highly relevant gender issues into the annual APA addresses of the division presidents (e.g., Rice, 2006). Even more important, we have worked to integrate women's issues within the curriculum in a manner consistent with the 2004 *Resolution on Culture and Gender Awareness in International Psychology* by collaborating with the APA Committee on Internationalizing the Psychology Curriculum. Key questions/issues include: how we examine and critique Western gender constructs that are often presumed to be universal and how non-Western women's experiences and perspectives can inform the curriculum.

Many of our sponsored symposia have become articles in the *Feminist Psychologist* (Division 35's newsletter) and the *International Psychology Bulletin* (Division 52's newsletter), as well as in many other venues of publication in psychology. Our long-term goal, however, has been always to mount a more ambitious research project beyond publishing individual journal and newsletter articles. Thus, early on, we discussed a book of readings on women in international psychology or a supplementary text-book that would incorporate the voices of women psychologists around the world. However, it was our past ICfW chair, Joan C. Chrisler, who took the ball and led us to realize our goal with a book on global reproductive justice issues for women. Reproductive justice is critical to equality for women. It is basic to women's physical and mental health, and it is also essential to ensure their children's healthy development and welfare.

This book broadens the view of what reproductive justice and equality mean in different countries. Furthermore, it offers us a comprehensive overview of the meaning of reproductive justice and focuses on a wide range of aspects of reproductive justice, from basic personal issues, such as contraception and family planning, to societal issues, such as violence against women, and it concludes with a discussion of international public policy. This book should be in the library of everyone who is concerned with the goal of achieving basic global gender parity. Speaking now not only for myself, but for everyone who, over the past two decades, was directly or indirectly connected with the many projects and experiences that made this book possible, we are extremely proud to be a small part of this important project and achievement.

Joy K. Rice, PhD

REFERENCES

APA Resolution on Culture and Gender Awareness in International Psychology. Adopted July 28, 2004. Retrieved from http://www.apa.org/about/gover nance/council/policy/gender.aspx.

Rice, J. K. (2006). What is family? Global changes in family structure and life cycle. *International Psychology Bulletin, 10*(4), 4–12.

Acknowledgments

The editor would like to thank Michele Paludi for suggesting a book on the topic of reproductive justice; Debbie Carvalko and all the staff at Praeger for our beautiful cover and for their advice and assistance throughout the publication process; and the members of the International Committee for Women (American Psychological Association Division 52—International Psychology) and the Global Issues Committee (American Psychological Association Division 35—Psychology of Women) for their enthusiastic encouragement, support, and participation in this project.

Introduction

What Is Reproductive Justice?

Joan C. Chrisler

For almost two decades, some women's health activists (e.g., Asian Communities for Reproductive Justice [ACRJ], n.d.; SisterSong, n.d.) have been making the case that the conventional rhetoric of the reproductive rights movements is culture bound; the framing of family planning as a woman's *choice* fits best the situation of relatively privileged women in Western, industrialized nations with an individualistic culture. The framework of choice assumes that all women can, and do, decide for themselves whether and when to have children. It also assumes that all women have the resources to obtain and pay for any medical or counseling services they need in order to follow through with their family planning. Even more basic to this framework is the assumption that a woman's body is *her own*—that she owns it, controls it, and makes her own decisions about her body, her health, and her relationships. Furthermore, the framework requires that a woman know that she has reproductive rights, that her nation and her community acknowledge those rights, and that she is able to exercise them. Many, if not most, of the world's women—even many in Western, developed nations—lack reproductive rights, have limited choices, or cannot access the services they need to in order to choose. Reproductive rights denied—whether by law, custom, ignorance, or access—is injustice.

The movement toward *reproductive justice* began in the United States and emerged from discussions among a group of women of color who had attended the 1994 International Conference on Population and Development, which was sponsored by the UN and held in Cairo (ACRJ, n.d.). The group realized, as Loretta Ross (as cited in Silliman, Fried, Ross, & Gutiérrez, 2004, p. 4) wrote, that "[o]ur ability to control what happens to our bodies is constantly challenged by poverty, racism, environmental degradation, sexism, homophobia, and injustice in the United States." This is unquestionably the case in the United States, which does not have universal health care and where reproductive rights have been under constant assault for decades by the religious right (i.e., conservative politicians, the Catholic Church, and evangelical and fundamentalist Christian churches). Although abortion is technically legal in the United States during the first and second trimesters, federal and state laws have narrowed its accessibility in various ways (e.g., no funding for poor women; no abortion services for the military, Peace Corps volunteers, and Native Americans who use Indian Health Services; parental consent for minors; mandatory ultrasounds and counseling—sometimes even the provision of information that is medically incorrect—followed by a waiting period). Antiabortion activists have assaulted, murdered, and terrorized physicians, nurses, and other clinic staff. As a result of these activities, 87 percent of counties in the United States have no clinics, hospitals, or private physicians who provide abortion services (Guttmacher Institute, 2011). The religious right has also curtailed curricula and funding for sex education (i.e., the abstinence-only movement), and many activists are also against contraception. Recently, the U.S. Congress attempted to end all subsidies for Planned Parenthood, even though none of the federal government's money currently goes to provide abortion services and Planned Parenthood is often the only affordable place for low-income women (and students) to obtain gynecological health care and other medical screening. Most private insurance plans in the United States do not fund assisted reproductive technologies (ARTs) for infertile couples, and neither does Medicaid (i.e., government assistance for the poor). The United States also has higher maternal and infant mortality rates than most other industrialized nations do, and as many as one in four American women (one in three African American and Native American women) do not receive the recommended prenatal care (Amnesty International, 2010).

The rhetoric of "choice" suggests a "marketplace of options" (Silliman et al., 2004, p. 5), much like the array of goods presented to consumers in a shopping mall, where many options are appealing. In reality, reproductive decisions are often painful and difficult. For example, if a woman uses contraceptives or seeks abortion because she cannot afford to raise a child, because of her own ill health (or a serious medical condition of the fetus), or because of insecurity due to war or natural disaster, does she experience her decision as a choice? What if women choose to become parents but cannot get pregnant (e.g., no partner, partner resistance, infertility, forced sterilization), are prevented from utilizing adoption services (e.g., by economic status, by discrimination), or lose their children to early death or revocation of custody as a result of divorce or government action (e.g., substance abuse, physical or mental illness, disability)? Many women have been forced or coerced (by partners, kin, or courts) to use contraceptives or terminate pregnancies that they wanted. In a world where many women cannot even select their own sexual partners, where rape and other violence against women are endemic, where trafficking and forced prostitution are among the fastest growing segments of criminal activity (Orhant, 2002), "the choice before the choice" (see chapter 1, "The Choice before the Choice") is denied to too many. Thus, even in individualistic cultures, such as the United States, where personal agency and control are expected, reproductive rights can be elusive, and choices are not always experienced as such (Silliman et al., 2004). In collectivist cultures, especially in poverty-stricken developing nations, where women have little self-efficacy and few opportunities to control their lives or their bodies, reproductive justice is a "dream deferred" (Hughes, 1995, p. 426).

Justice implies that people are treated fairly, equitably, and respectfully. Thus, the term *reproductive justice* situates the work in the context of the greater social justice movement. Activists who work for social justice are concerned with issues such as peace, prejudice and discrimination, poverty, human rights, employment conditions, health care, and educational equity. All of these issues are fundamental to the achievement of reproductive justice. For example, if girls and women do not have access to menstrual hygiene supplies (e.g., tampons, pads), they cannot go to school or work. It is estimated that 60 percent of girls and women in Kenya have little or no access to these supplies; 800,000 girls miss several days of school each month, which affects their ability to keep up with their class and is a barrier to graduation for many (Mukuria, 2011). Girls who leave school early will have less knowledge about their bodies, lower income to support themselves and their families, and less power to negotiate with their future partners about family planning; they are more likely to live in poverty in rural areas with little health care infrastructure.

The movement for reproductive justice has also been influenced by global (e.g., Morgan, 1996) and transnational feminism (e.g., Mohanty, 2003). Global feminists emphasize the importance of solidarity with women around the world and our need to work together to solve systemic problems. They recognize that patriarchal structures and customs affect women's health, well-being, and social and economic rights in different ways everywhere in the world. Transnational feminists emphasize the fact that people and problems transcend borders and make it impossible, as well as undesirable, to divide women into *us* and *them*. They emphasize the intersectionality of oppression (i.e., the ways that aspects of social status [e.g., gender, race, ethnicity, age, sexual orientation, religion, age, income, and educational level] affect individual women's experiences and perspectives), and they encourage feminists in developed countries to support the efforts of feminists in developing countries rather than to try to impose solutions on them. Cultural attitudes and practices are often best changed by movements that arise within the culture; what works in one country may not work in another. The authors of this volume describe a number of such indigenous movements, and information about how readers can support women's efforts to promote reproductive justice can be found in the afterword.

The authors of this book are an interdisciplinary group of scholars who work at the nexus of research, clinical practice, and activism. Our goal in writing this volume was to provide a comprehensive view of the barriers to women's reproductive rights and the challenges that face the movement for reproductive justice. Editing the chapters of this book was like taking a ride on an emotional roller coaster. I was, at times, horrified by the violent situations women face, angry at the unfairness women and girls experience, dismayed by the neglect of girls and women, disgusted by the ways that politicians and other leaders put their own preferences and beliefs ahead of women's needs, sad to hear about the unsanitary conditions in which women give birth and experience genital cutting, amazed at the persistence and resilience women and girls show in stressful circumstances, happy to learn about progress being made, and proud of the girls and women who resist injustice and insist upon their rights. Readers should prepare themselves for a similar range of emotional reactions.

To being our exploration of this complex topic, Makiko Kasai and S. Craig Rooney discuss the importance of partner selection, and they question whether reproductive justice can exist if women lack the right to choose their own partner and coparent. The chapter begins with a consideration of the legal status of lesbians, same-sex marriage, and coadoption in countries around the world. The authors then discuss heterosexual arranged marriages, which may or may not involve the consent of the intended spouses. In some places (e.g., Afghanistan), even today, a father has the right to give his daughter in marriage to whomever he chooses, and a daughter has no right to resist, even if her intended husband is prone to violence, has other wives, or is decades older than she is. Honor killings are one way that families punish women who engage in premarital or extramarital sex; practices such as widow cleansing (i.e., forcing a widow to have sex with a designated "cleanser" or a relative of her late husband), levirate (i.e., passing a widow on to a male relative of her late husband), and sati (i.e., the ritual burning of a Hindu widow on her husband's funeral pyre; now against the law in India) are still reported in Asia and Africa (Murthy, 2010).

Next, Virginia Braun provides a comprehensive and thought-provoking discussion of female genital cutting. Traditional genital cutting is performed in at least 28 countries, most of them in Africa. The practice is medically unnecessary (but can produce medical complications at the time of the cutting or later during childbirth), usually takes place in childhood, and often is done without the consent of the girl. It is easy for most Westerners to see this practice as injustice, but Braun challenges us to consider unnecessary genital cutting that is sanctioned in Western cultures, such as the "repair" of ambiguous genitalia in intersex infants, which is also performed without the consent of the child. She then discusses cosmetic genital surgery (known as designer vaginas), which is a growing fad in the West. Although cosmetic surgeries are elected by adults and never performed without consent, cultural constructions of beauty that damage women's body image to such an extent that they choose genital surgery are considered by many feminists to be a form of oppression. In cultures that practice traditional genital cutting *and* those that practice cosmetic genital surgery, women believe that their natural bodies are abnormal, ugly, disgusting, and make them unlovable without improvement.

Kathryn L. Norsworthy, Margaret A. McLaren, and Laura D. Waterfield discuss the ways that women's unequal power in their intimate relationships can form a barrier to shared decision making about family planning. Women's social status is lower than men's in most cultures, and heterosexual women tend to marry up, that is, to marry men who are older and better educated than they are and who earn more money than they do. Thus, men tend to have considerably more social power than women do, and that allows them to control decision making about when to have sex and whether to use condoms (or other forms of birth control). Women whose partners are prone to anger and violence have even less power and influence than the average woman does.

Violence is the subject of the chapter by Thema Bryant-Davis, Shaquita Tillman, and Pamela A. Counts. They discuss the prevalence of sexual assault around the world, with a focus on the use of rape as a weapon in wartime and as a threat to control women at any time. Not only is rape another way in which women's agency to choose their own sexual partners is curtailed, but women often become pregnant as a result of rape. In some recent civil wars (e.g., Bosnia, Rwanda), rape was explicitly used with the goal of impregnating women for the purposes of "ethnic cleansing." Women who lack access to abortion are expected to bear, raise, and even love their rapists' children. The authors describe the physical and mental health consequences of rape, and they situate violence against women in the context of a public health crisis.

Next, Nancy M. Sidun discusses the growing global phenomenon of human trafficking and its use for the sexual exploitation of women and girls. She describes common ways that girls and women are sold, tricked, and coerced into entering the modern-day slave trade. Although human trafficking is recognized as a human rights violation by the UN, and as a crime by many countries, trafficking is a transnational problem, and virtually every country in the world is involved as a location of origin, transit, or destination for trafficked individuals. Work conditions in the brothels are deplorable, and the trafficked victims' physical and mental health suffers. Not only do the victims lack the ability to consent to sexual activity, they often cannot insist that their partners use condoms. Unwanted pregnancy is not uncommon.

Sexually transmitted infections (STIs) are frequently passed from one lover to another, but they are also commonly experienced by victims of rape and trafficking. Dionne P. Stephens, Vrushali Patil, and Tami L. Thomas discuss the global prevalence of HIV and other STIs and show how unequal access to sex education, prevention services, and medical treatment affects the world's women. Although medical advancements mean that, with proper care, HIV+ people can live a long time, in many poor countries there is little access to the necessary drugs; thus contraction of HIV is still a death sentence for many today. Women who lack the power to insist that their partners use condoms, and girls in countries where men believe the myth that sex with a virgin can cure AIDS, are particularly vulnerable to STIs. Untreated STIs can result in sterility, thus preventing women from conceiving when they desire to become mothers.

Nancy Felipe Russo and Julia R. Steinberg discuss contraception and abortion—the centerpiece issues of reproductive justice. The authors describe obstacles to reproductive rights and barriers to contraception and abortion services, and they explain the importance of family planning for women's physical, mental, social, and economic health and well-being. Closely spaced births are not good for the health of women or children, and large family sizes are more likely to be the result of the "motherhood mandate" (Russo, 1976) or lack of knowledge about, and access to, contraception than they are the result of women's choice. Furthermore, legal restriction of abortion services does not mean the end of abortion, but it does mean higher rates of death, disability, sterility, and ill health in women who end up in the hands of untrained practitioners who use unsafe procedures.

Family planning is not just about avoiding unwanted pregnancies; it is also about achieving wanted pregnancies. Lisa R. Rubin and Aliza Phillips discuss the psychosocial aspects of infertility and ARTs, and they consider the ways that infertility and ARTs affect couples' relationships. ARTs remain controversial, even as couples who can afford these expensive treatments have embraced them. Do ARTs reinforce the motherhood mandate and further medicalize women's reproductive health? Do they echo old ideas of the eugenics movement by producing "perfect" infants and eliminating infants with disabilities? Does the lack of funding for these technologies through insurance plans and government sources mean that only privileged women are encouraged to have children? These are among the thought-provoking questions raised in this chapter.

Medicalization is also discussed in Lynda M. Sagrestano and Ruthbeth Finerman's chapter on pregnancy and prenatal care. The authors show how medical advances have saved women's lives but also limited their ability to control one of the most important experiences of their lives. It is ironic that women in developed nations often experience too much medical attention (e.g., the decline of midwifery, unnecessary cesarean sections and fetal monitoring), and women in developing nations often receive too little. The authors show the effects of poverty, stress, social support, and medical and spiritual advice on women's and infants' health.

Healthy pregnancies are essential to reproductive justice, as are safe and supportive birthing experiences. Too many women give birth in unsanitary conditions, and too many women with high-risk pregnancies lack the medical care they need to birth their children safely. Yet, in other parts of the world, women tend to give birth in depersonalized, medicalized situations that increase their stress and anxiety and decrease their control. Sayaka Machizawa and Kayoko Hayashi describe the movement for birth justice and the humanization of childbirth, and they show the importance of the role that experienced birth attendants (e.g., midwives, doulas, grandmothers) play in supporting and comforting women during childbirth. Yet culture and economics prevent many women from achieving a humanized birthing experience.

Women's poor health and nutritional status during pregnancy and unsafe and unsanitary practices during childbirth result in high levels of maternal and infant mortality around the world. Rates are so alarming in some countries that the UN has named maternal health as one of its Millenium Development Goals. Perhaps nothing is as unjust as a motherless infant or a mother grieving the loss of her newborn baby. Ramaswami Mahalingam and Madeline Wachman discuss another form of injustice—the use of technology for fetal sex selection. In countries where poverty or law (e.g., China's one-child policy) make small families a necessity and lack of access to contraceptives makes abortion a major tool for family planning, couples may seek ultrasounds to discover the sex of the fetus and then determine whether to maintain the pregnancy. The strong cultural preference for sons in many cultures has led to large sex imbalances, as millions of missing girls are lost to their societies as a result of extreme neglect, infanticide, and feticide.

Reproductive justice does not end with the birth of a child. Ingrid Johnston-Robledo and Allison Murray discuss the challenges women face due to postpartum morbidity. In developed nations, women are most likely to be concerned about postpartum mental health (e.g., depression, stress, lack of social support), but in developing nations, physical health concerns (e.g., postpartum hemorrhage, obstetric fistula) are a greater threat for many women. Furthermore, in both developing nations (where bottle-feeding seems to be more modern) and developed nations (where short maternity leaves make breastfeeding inconvenient and where popular culture emphasizes the role of breast for physical attraction rather than for nurturing infants), the rate of breastfeeding has decreased. Public health advocates are concerned about the effects the choice to bottle-feed may have on both infants and their mothers.

Finally, Janet Sigal, Florence L. Denmark, Amy Nadel, and Rebecca A. Petrie describe and discuss some of the international initiatives that the United Nations, the World Health Organization (WHO), and other agencies have taken to improve the opportunity women have to achieve reproductive justice. Among the major UN initiatives are the Millenium Development Goals (e.g., improve maternal health, end poverty, universal education, gender equality), which are supposed to be achieved by 2015 (readers can check member nations' progress at http://www.un.org/millenniumgoals/), and the 1949 UN Declaration of Human Rights, which asserts the rights to education and health care; equal dignity and rights for all; the right to life, liberty, and security; the right to enter marriage only with free and full consent; and that "no one shall be held in slavery or servitude" (http://www.un.org/events/humanrights/2007/hrphotos/declaration%20_eng.pdf). The 1979 Convention on the Elimination of All Forms of Discrimination Against Women (CEDAW) affirms reproductive rights as necessary for women's equality in political, economic, social, cultural, and civil arenas, and, at the 1994 International Conference on Population and Development (Cairo), representatives of 180 nations declared that reproductive rights are basic human rights and agreed to protect women's ability to control their reproductive lives (Center for Reproductive Rights, n.d.). International courts of justice have begun to hold governments accountable for infringing upon women's reproductive rights (Chrisler & Garrett, 2010), and WHO, UNICEF, and other agencies are working to help governments to end trafficking and curb HIV infections within their borders. These are very helpful developments, but much remains to be done.

Reproductive justice will remain elusive as long as large groups of the world's women are unable to make knowledgeable decisions about their sexuality and family planning and attain the support and medical services they need. Women who are particularly likely to be underserved are poor women, rural and inner-city women, refugees and homeless women, incarcerated and trafficked women, women with physical disabilities, women with mental retardation and learning disabilities, and women with HIV and other chronic illnesses. Many nonprofit groups are working to help these women and to support indigenous movements for reproductive justice. There is much to do; see the afterword to learn about ways that you can help. Remember, "sisterhood is global" (Morgan, 1996); we are responsible for each other's welfare. We must not rest until there is reproductive justice, not just for some, but for all of the women of the world.

REFERENCES

Amnesty International. (2010). *Deadly delivery: The maternal health care crisis in the USA* [summary]. Retrieved from http://amnest.org/en/library/info/AMR51/019/2010/en.

Asian Communities for Reproductive Justice. (n.d.). *What is reproductive justice?* Retrieved June 1, 2011, from http://repoductivejustice.org/what-is-reproductive-justice.

Center for Reproductive Rights. (n.d.). *Are reproductive rights human rights?* Retrieved from http://reproductiverights.org/en/feature/are-repro-rights-human-rights.

Chrisler, J. C., & Garrett, C. (2010). Women's reproductive rights: An international perspective. In M. A. Paludi (Ed.), *Feminism and women's rights worldwide* (Vol. 3, pp. 129–146). Santa Barbara, CA: Praeger.

Guttmacher Institute. (2011, May). *Facts on induced abortion in the United States.* Retrieved from http://www.guttmacher.org/pubs/fb_induced_abortion.html.

Hughes, L. S. (1995). Harlem 2: A dream deferred. In A. Rampersad & D. Roessel (Eds.), *The collected poems of Langston Hughes* (p. 426). New York: Vintage.

Mohanty, C. (2003). *Feminism without borders: Decolonizing theory, practicing solidarity.* Durham, NC: Duke University Press.

Morgan, R. (1996). *Sisterhood is global.* New York: Feminist Press.

Mukuria, M. W. (2011, June). *Cycles of life: Protecting the planet and alleviating poverty through sustainable menstruation management.* Paper presented at the meeting of the Society for Menstrual Cycle Research, Pittsburgh, PA.

Murthy, P. (2010). Violence against women and girls: A silent global pandemic. In P. Murthy & C. L. Smith (Eds.), *Women's global health and human rights* (pp. 11–24). Sudbury, MA: Jones and Bartlett.

Orhant, M. (2002). Human trafficking exposed. *Population Today, 30,* 1–4.

Russo, N. F. (1976). The motherhood mandate. *Journal of Social Issues, 32,* 143–154.

Silliman, J., Fried, M. G., Ross, L., & Gutiérrez, E. R. (2004). *Undivided rights: Women of color organize for reproductive justice.* Boston: South End Press.

SisterSong. (n.d.). *Mission statement.* Retrieved from http://www.sistersong.net.

Chapter 1

The Choice before the Choice: Partner Selection Is Essential to Reproductive Justice

Makiko Kasai and S. Craig Rooney

A comprehensive conceptualization of reproductive justice begins well before a woman's intention of becoming a parent and includes consideration of the individual liberties that are available to her and that define her rights and obligations as a potential mother. This broader viewpoint asks the question of whether reproductive freedom can even exist if a woman does not first have the right to choose her own partner or coparent. This chapter explores issues that relate to reproductive justice for populations of women who are frequently denied the basic cultural and legal right of partner choice: lesbian couples and women in arranged heterosexual marriages. These groups represent large and diverse populations, and a comprehensive review of the issues that face women in these different groups, particularly from an international perspective, is obviously beyond the scope of a single book chapter. Nonetheless, we highlight some of the unique challenges of some of the women in these groups as they pertain to concepts of reproductive justice.

SAME-SEX MARRIAGES AND LESBIAN MOTHERS

Worldwide, statutory responses to homosexuality are varied and wide ranging. For instance, 7 countries have death penalty punishments for homosexual behaviors (i.e., Iran, Mauritania, Nigeria, Saudi Arabia, Sudan, United Arab Emirates, and Yemen), and 10 countries have legalized same-sex marriages and codified the legal right for gay individuals to adopt children (i.e., Argentina, Canada, Belgium, Iceland, the Netherlands, Norway, Portugal, South Africa, Spain, and Sweden) (Corrales & Pecheny, 2010; International Lesbian, Gay, Bisexual, Trans, and Intersex Association [ILGA], 2010; O'Flaherty & Fisher, 2008; South African Society of Psychiatrists, 2005). The statutory and case law actions of many other nations fall well between these two situations and reflect the disparate conceptualizations of what lesbian, gay, and bisexual (LGB) marriages and LGB parents mean to the culture at large in each country.

In the Americas, a wide range of statutory and case law practices exist. Court cases and legal challenges can alter the landscape of the legal rights of sexual minorities rapidly and dramatically. For instance, in 1999, the case *M. v. H.* challenged the assumption of heterosexual marriage in the Ontario Family Law Act of 1990 and was heard by the Canadian Supreme Court (Judgments of the Supreme Court of Canada, 2010). The case involved the legal rights and responsibilities of a lesbian couple who had dissolved their relationship. The Canadian Supreme Court ruled that all Canadian family law had to be rewritten in order to include same-sex unions (Judgments of the Supreme Court of Canada, 2010).

In the United States, however, no sweeping federal court decision or legislation has made progress toward allowing individuals the right to choose their own romantic partner or to become parents in the context of a same-sex union. Thus, inclusion and protection of lesbian parents and their children is unfolding in a piecemeal and nuanced, state-by-state manner. Given the fact that legislation and legal action on LGBT issues is unfolding week by week, traditional printed sources on the topic of LGBT legal issues become quickly outdated.

In 1996, the U.S. Congress passed the Defense of Marriage Act (DOMA), which was signed into law by then president Bill Clinton (Human Rights Campaign, 2010). In essence, this piece of national legislation gave each state the right not to recognize a same-sex marriage from another state. It also legally defined marriage as existing between one man and one woman and defined a spouse as a member of the "opposite sex" (Human Rights Campaign, 2010). Thus, in addition to allowing states to decide for themselves if they would perform same-sex marriages, DOMA clarified that even if they did, the federal government would not recognize those marriages or extend federal benefits, such as Social Security, to partners in same-sex marriages (Human Rights Campaign, 2010). As we write this,

litigation is underway in U.S. federal courts to challenge the constitution-
ality of DOMA (Human Rights Campaign, 2010). Clearly, the very title of
this federal law reflects the worldview of many Americans that LGB marriage is an attack, or affront, on heterosexual marriage; how, specifically,
same-sex marriage hurts traditional marriage is seldom articulated.

In 2003, the U.S. Supreme Court invalidated any remaining sodomy
laws, which had criminalized specific real or perceived homosexual behaviors, by finding the Texas sodomy law unconstitutional (Kane, 2010).
However, with respect to those issues directly pertinent to reproductive
justice, namely, LGB marriage and the right to adopt and raise children,
DOMA is the only relevant piece of federal legislation in the United States,
and it was unaffected by that court decision. This has left the issues of LGB
marriage and adoption in the hands of each state. The website of Lambda
Legal is a source that allows for timely tracking of these issues and provides detailed information about the specific legalities of LGBT issues for
each state in the United States (Lambda Legal, 2010).

Although some states simply forbid same-sex marriages through statute, 21 states have gone the extra step of passing constitutional amend-
ments that define marriage as existing between one man and one woman
and that invoke their DOMA-instituted right to refuse to recognize same-
sex marriages from other states (Lambda Legal, 2010).

Six states (i.e., Connecticut, Iowa, Massachusetts, New Hampshire, New
York, and Vermont) and the District of Columbia, however, currently do
issue same-sex marriage licenses. Of those, all but New Hampshire explicitly allow for second-parent adoptions by LGB partners (Lambda Legal,
2010). Two additional states (i.e., California and New Mexico) have previously issued marriage licenses for same-sex couples but have uncertain
legal futures for the practices. In California, the issue became polarized and
was voted out through a statewide referendum. In New Mexico, a judge
in a single county has issued the same-sex marriage licenses, and no other
judges in the state have as yet weighed in on the issue (Lambda Legal, 2010).

Other states have taken the approach of providing some type of domestic partner registry that affords limited rights to members of cohabitating, same-sex couples (including some of the states that allow same-sex
marriage; i.e., in those states, one does not have to get married in order
to enjoy some legal protections). California, Connecticut, Hawaii, Iowa,
Maine, Massachusetts, New Hampshire, Oregon, Vermont, Washington,
Wisconsin, and the District of Columbia all recognize some type of domestic partnership (Lambda Legal, 2010). As we discuss later in this chapter,
such recognition of domestic partnership, although not a legal marriage,
can still have important ramifications for the rights and responsibilities of
lesbian parents (Hare & Skinner, 2008).

Regarding adoption of children by LGBT individuals in the United
States, most states now allow any adult the legal opportunity to try to

adopt children. Twenty-six states allow for a second parent to adopt a child either by statute or by lower court decisions (Lambda Legal, 2010). Mississippi and Florida expressly prohibit adoption by LGB couples, and Utah has refused to approve adoption for any couples living in nonlegally valid unions, which disqualifies LGB couples because Utah is one of the states that constitutionally defines marriage as existing between a man and a woman (Lambda Legal, 2010).

Thus, the current status of reproductive justice for LGB couples in the United States, as represented by the right to marry, formal recognition of partnerships, and the right to adopt children jointly, is inconsistent. In the absence of federal guarantees in the form of statutory or binding court decisions, LGBT individuals in the United States face environments that vary from quite supportive to openly hostile and that are vulnerable to change, as has happened in California and might be in the process of happening in Iowa (Lambda Legal, 2010). Antigay activists targeted the three Iowa Supreme Court justices who were up for reelection during the 2010 midterm elections: all three lost their elections (Taylor, 2010).

In Latin America, LGBT individuals have made the most significant gains in Argentina. In 2009, several court rulings allowed same-sex marriages to proceed on the finding that banning them was unconstitutional (Corrales & Pecheny, 2010). In May 2010, the lower house in Argentina passed legislation to allow for same-sex marriage, and the Senate followed in July 2010. The president did not move to block the legislation, and thus the first Latin American country joined the handful of nations that have legalized same-sex marriage and have explicitly protected the right of LGB individuals to adopt children as a couple (Corrales & Pecheny, 2010).

Corrales and Pecheny (2010) offered several reasons why Argentina became the first Latin American country to approve same-sex marriage and adoption. Although Argentina is a predominantly Catholic country, only 22 percent of Catholics attend church on a weekly basis, and the religious makeup of the country is only 2 percent evangelical Christian. Infrequent church attendance and low numbers of evangelicals may be predictive of those nations that recognize same-sex marriage and adoption. Argentina is different in this regard from Brazil, Mexico, the United States, and many countries in Central America.

Corrales and Pecheny (2010) also noted that Argentina promotes a separation of churches and political parties, a practice, again, quite different than traditions in Brazil, Chile, Colombia, Mexico, Venezuela, and even the United States, where there is a formal separation of church and state, but where political parties actively court the support of religious groups. Individuals who back LGBT legal rights conceptualized these rights within the context of "a broader agenda on behalf of feminism, gender, reproduction, health, and sexuality" (Corrales & Pencheny, 2010). In order to avoid the referendum problems faced by LGBT activists in places like California, Argentina's largest LGBT organization (i.e., Federación Argentina de Lesbianas, Gays, Bisexuales y Trans) encouraged its members to seek marriage licenses so the group would have a specific basis upon which to build a legal challenge. This approach avoided referendum democracy and appears to have worked, as lower-court judges married 12 couples prior to passage of the federal legislation (Corrales & Pencheny, 2010). The populist referendum approach to democracy that is popular in the United States often works against minority populations:

> Submitting to a majority vote questions of minority rights is inherently a biased process—against the minority group naturally—and this makes it undemocratic despite its reliance on the popular vote. (Corrales & Pencheny, 2010

On the other side of the Atlantic Ocean, the legality of same-sex marriage and adoption is also developing in an inconsistent manner. According to ILGA, the European Union has a directive that member states must introduce legislation that bans workplace discrimination on the basis of sexual orientation and gender identity (ILGA, 2010). Furthermore, the decriminalization of homosexual behaviors is ubiquitous in EU countries (ILGA, 2010). Nonetheless, much disparity remains in specific countries' approaches to the legal rights and responsibilities of LGBT individuals and their families.

Belgium, Iceland, the Netherlands, Norway, Portugal, Spain, and Sweden have legalized same-sex marriage. Twenty European countries (i.e., Andorra, Austria, Belgium, Croatia, Czech Republic, Denmark, Finland, France, [FYR] Macedonia, Germany, Hungary, Ireland, Luxembourg, the Netherlands, Norway, Portugal, Slovenia, Sweden, Switzerland, and the United Kingdom) have registered partnerships for cohabiting same-sex couples that afford them various degrees of legal rights and protections (ILGA, 2010). Latvia has a statutory same-sex marriage ban. The Netherlands has signed on to the Yogykarta Principles (http://www.yogyakartap rinciples.org), a document created at an international meeting of human rights legal experts that proposes full and complete legal membership of LGBT persons (ILGA, 2010).

There is not a direct correlation between those countries that recognize same-sex marriage and those that afford legal rights to LGB persons who wish to become parents. Belgium, Denmark, Iceland, the Netherlands, Norway, Spain, Sweden, and the United Kingdom allow for LGB couples to adopt children jointly, become the second parent in the adoption of one partner's biological child(ren), and provide for medically supported insemination of lesbian or bisexual women (ILGA, 2010). Finland allows an LGB partner to become the second parent in the adoption of another LGB person's biological child(ren) and allows for medically supported insemination, and Germany allows second parent adoptions (ILGA, 2010). In a manner similar to the patchwork of opinions found among the states in the United States, member nations of the European Union represent various attitudes and legal responses to LGBT individuals.

A wide range of attitudes exists among the nations of Africa, as well. As previously mentioned, Nigeria is one of the countries that can execute an individual for same-sex sexual behaviors (O'Flaherty & Fisher, 2008). Uganda is considering a death penalty for homosexual behavior, and recently, a prominent gay rights activist was murdered there (Gettleman, 2011). South Africa, however, represents the other end of the spectrum, as it gave LGBT people full citizenship when the country ratified a new constitution following the fall of apartheid. The text of their constitution is straightforward and bold, including the right of *everyone* to have control over their bodies and to make decisions about reproduction; it also specifically includes sexual orientation in its nondiscrimination clause (Constitution of the Republic of South Africa, 1996). The South African Society of Psychiatrists (SASOP, 2005) published a position paper in support of the decision of the South African Constitutional Court to follow through on the promises of the constitution by legalizing same-sex marriages and the legal right for LGB couples to adopt children (SASOP, 2005).

Other countries in Africa and the Middle East represent a spectrum of viewpoints toward homosexuality and highly disparate legal approaches to sexual minorities. A number of countries in Africa have criminalized homosexual behaviors. Imprisonment penalties that range from 3 to 25 years can be applied in Algeria, Botswana, Cameroon, Cape Verde, Ethiopia, Gambia, Guinea, Kenya, Liberia, Mauritius, Morocco, Mozambique, Senegal, Somalia, Swaziland, Tanzania, Togo, Tunisia, Zambia, and Zimbabwe (ILGA, 2010). Israel has had a registered partnership program since 1994 (ILGA, 2010), but none of the surrounding Muslim countries have legalized, or recognized, the relationships of LGBT people.

No Asian countries have legally accepted same-sex marriage. Like every other continent previously reviewed, however, there is a wide range of perspectives and approaches to same-sex relationships and parenting. Currently, a number of Asian countries have statutes that criminalize the sexual behaviors of LGBT people (i.e., Bangladesh, Bhutan, Brunei, China, India, Indonesia, Malaysia, Maldives, Myanmar, Nepal, Pakistan, Singapore, Sri Lanka, Turkmenistan, and Uzbekistan), although China is currently reexamining the issue of same-sex marriage (ILGA, 2010). Japan and Thailand offer no official protections and have no antidiscrimination laws for LGBT individuals. Ironically (considering the lack of formal legal protections for LGB people there), Thailand is a center for sex-reassignment surgery, and it is relatively tolerant of transgender people in terms of their public, day-to-day treatment on the streets of the larger cities (Thailand Law Forum, 2010). In 2002, Thailand's Department of Mental Health declassified homosexuality as a mental illness; in 2005, the Thai military agreed to stop discharging gay and transgender soldiers due to a severe mental disorder, and the First International Conference of Asian Queer Studies was held in Bangkok (Khor & Kamano, 2006; Thailand Law Forum, 2010). In 2007, Thailand expanded the definition of rape to include perpetrators and survivors of either sex, thus raising the penalty for the rape of trans-men, a criminal act that had formerly fallen under a lesser charge because the survivor and perpetrator were typically both biologically male. In 2008, the Thai military added a third category for the inclusion of transgender soldiers so that their military dismissals would not carry the stigma of a mental disorder (Thailand Law Forum, 2010).

For approximately 20 years, the Asian Lesbian Network has been hold-ing conferences so that lesbian activists could gather and share informa-tion with one another. This has led to networking among lesbian scholars in China, Hong Kong, Japan, and South Korea, and their work has pro-vided information about the sexual and reproductive lives of lesbian women in these countries (Khor & Kamano, 2006).

Advancement of reforms in China in recent years has facilitated more openness for lesbian women living in China's mainland, who have been able to come out more frequently, live their lives more openly, and start to be recognized by the masses (Chen & Chen, 2006). Shanghai, for example, has become a place wherein a vibrant and robust lesbian community is beginning to flourish (Park-Kim, Lee-Kim, & Kwon-Lee, 2006). The In-ternet is a convenient and safe place for Chinese lesbians to voice their opinions and feelings and to obtain relevant information and knowledge (Chen & Chen, 2006). The first lesbian organization in mainland China, the Beijing Sisters, was founded in 1998; as a result of the Internet, many more lesbian organizations have been founded in China in recent years (Chen & Chen, 2006).

Despite this progress, most lesbians must still live relatively restricted lives in Chinese society. The Danwei system of morality has effective con-trol of many aspects of people's lives, including the preferential provision of more economic rewards and social recognition to married people than to unmarried people (Kam, 2006). In this tradition, being married means being an adult and, thus, having social responsibility and being produc-tive. Having children is seen as evidence of one's value in society and also of one's physical and psychological well-being (Kam, 2006). Obvi-ously, lesbians outside of the institution of marriage are not recognized as fully adult, productive, valuable, and healthy. In fact, women who reach middle age without being married are called *Lao Gu'niangs* (i.e., old girls) and are stereotyped as physically unattractive and as having poor social skills, ill health, and personality defects (Kam, 2006). In China there is a hierarchy of social recognition related to marital status: married (at the top), single, divorced, and homosexual (Kam, 2006). In this system, unmarried lesbians are stigmatized and marginalized by the normative heterosexual discourse. As one might imagine in such a society, parents play a significant role in their daughters' marriages. At times this has led to forced, arranged marriages in an attempt to keep daughters from facing the stigma and stereotype of remaining unwed (Kam, 2006). Arranged marriages are becoming rare in Chinese cities, but semiarranged marriages are common (i.e., parents introduce their offspring to potential partners but leave the choice to them; Kam, 2006).

Japan is frequently portrayed as culturally and historically more tolerant of homosexuality than many of its Asian counterparts (Horie, 2006). *Rezubian,* the Japanese term for lesbian, became widely known in Japan during the 1960s and served as a means of lexically articulating an awareness of self and/or others of similar affections (Sugiura, 2006). In the 1960s, the term captured a broader and more diverse group of people, including masculinized women and FTM transgender individuals. During the 1990s, the definition of *rezubian* began to narrow into "women whose gender identity consists of regarding others of the same sex as objects of sexual love" (Sugiura, 2006, p. 128). Although this definition translates rather clumsily into English and uses gender identity in a different manner than is usual in the scholarly literature, readers may note that this narrower definition of lesbian is more similar to a Western notion of sexual orientation. In the 1990s in Japan, court action regarding discrimination cases against LGBT people occurred concurrently with more frequent open representations of LGBT individuals in the mass media and with more direct appeals from LGBT people for recognition by larger Japanese society (OCCUR, 2000).

In 1992 a group called Remaza Kansai was created for lesbian mothers living in the Kansai region of the country (Arita, 2006). This group has remained active since that time in its support of lesbian mothers through workshops and activities, such as group camping trips for mothers and their children (Arita, 2006). This organization was formed because Japanese culture does not recognize same-sex parents; therefore, their children are often isolated and feel unable to share about their home lives with their peers. Remaza Kansai has informally reported several issues that face the lesbian mothers they serve. First, because educational institutions in Japan do not imagine that any of their students have same-sex parents, lesbian mothers feel that they have to educate their children's teachers. Second, lesbian mothers in Japan face a legal system that does not recognize their existence and, therefore, does not extend them any legal protections. No second parent adoption exists in Japan, so, in lesbian couples, only one woman can legally be the children's parent. The legal parent in a lesbian couple can sign a notarized deed that will transfer the children to the other woman in the event of the legal mother's death, but this does not guarantee custody should a family member of the legal parent challenge that custody (Arita, 2006). Children of lesbian couples typically come from a previous heterosexual union, as single women in Japan are not allowed to adopt or to receive reproductive medical treatments (Kasuya, 2003).

In Japanese scholarship on sexual orientation, Kazama (1996, 2002) and Horie (2006) have pointed out problems both with the term *sexual preference* and also with a sole focus on the sexual behaviors of LGBT individuals. As Kazama (2002, pp. 107–108) noted, "homosexuality as a sexual preference is an argument premised on the assumption of asymmetry of heterosexuality and homosexuality because it does not consider that heterosexuality itself is a preference." He also aptly pointed out that, by conceptualizing homosexuality in Japanese culture as an issue of preference and by associating it strictly with sexual behaviors, sexual minorities have been considered an issue of privacy among Japanese people rather than one that is welcomed in public discourse (Kazama, 2002). Finally, Horie (2006, p. 147) has noted that efforts to increase tolerance of homosexuality have often only considered the lives and experiences of gay men, thus rendering invisible the "lesbian existence."

Historically, Korean culture has been an expression of conservative patriarchy that informed the subordination of women's sexuality to men and conservatism in sexuality in general. The Confucianism tradition of Korea has a norm of heterosexuality that was passed on and maintained by traditional, nuclear families, which has resulted in a family system built on paternal, monogamous, and heterosexual marriage in a culture that discriminates against anyone who lives outside the system. This stigmatizes LGBT people as "abnormal" and "deviant" (Joe-Lee, 2003). Homosexuality was not publicly acknowledged in mainstream Korean society until the early 1990s when a homophobic ideology began to form around the idea that "AIDS is the plague of homosexuals" (Park-Kim et al., 2006, p. 162). Since that time, the existence of LGBT people has become increasingly recognized in South Korean culture. According to Park-Kim et al. (2006), Korean students are not openly taught about homosexuality in their first 12 years of education. Furthermore, LGBT youth who seek services at counseling centers or from psychiatrists are often told that their sexuality is perverted or that their sexual feelings are abnormal and will only be temporary. This message has led many sexual minority Korean youth to deny their sexual identity or to commit suicide.

Prior to the 1990s, Korean lesbians had to network through informal groups in order to combat isolation and insecurity. Since the 1990s, a number of lesbian groups have developed and are fostering an increased level of lesbian consciousness and identity as an oppressed minority. The first lesbian rights group, Kirikiri, was formed in 1994 (Park-Kim et al., 2006). Kirikiri has provided lesbians not only with a place to communicate with one another, affirm their identities, and network with one another, but also a place to find personal consultations and counseling services to help them deal with various forms of social discrimination.

After the 1990s, as discourses about Western sexual politics represented by scholars such as Foucault began to be studied in Korean universities, the topic of homosexuality frequently entered the intellectual discourse in higher education. Such discourse was fertile ground for the development of feminist identity on Korean college campuses and allowed lesbian students to develop a feminist identity that encouraged them to come out. This was seen as a "symbol of progressiveness" because such identities represent a departure from the sexual restraints of Korean Confucianism (Park-Kim et al., 2006, p. 165). Increased openness has facilitated the identity of college-educated Korean lesbians, but it has remained difficult for noneducated lesbian women to be open about their sexuality in other quarters of Korean society.

In 2004, the Lesbian Institute for Lesbians and the Lesbian Counseling Center in South Korea conducted one of the first scholarly studies of the experiences of Korean lesbians (Park-Kim et al., 2006). The data, which included the responses of 561 lesbian women in their 20s and 30s, indicate that 74.7 percent of respondents felt pain with respect to their "relationship with family," and 34.8 percent struggled with the notion of "marriage to the opposite sex." Fifty percent of the women reported that they had difficulty "when they had to hide their relationship," and 19 percent expressed frustration "when they did not have any institution or person to get advice from." Many respondents (37.6%) reported not being able to come out as lesbian easily because "they already knew well how deeply and firmly homophobia is rooted in Korean society" (Park-Kim et al., 2006, p. 166). According to the group Kirikiri, cultural homophobia and the fear of "outing" (i.e., nonconsensual revelation of one's sexual identity to the public) makes it difficult to account fully for the difficulties faced by Korean lesbians (Kirikiri, 1999, 2005).

Currently, a number of organizations have been founded by and for lesbian women in this region: the Lesbian Counseling Center in South Korea, the Center for Women's Sexual Minority Rights in Busan, the Ewha University lesbian rights organization called Flyinggurl, and the Lesbian Institute for Lesbians. Nonetheless, lesbian rights organizations are often excluded from coalitions by both gay rights groups and by feminist organizations (Park-Kim et al., 2006). For example, Park-Kim et al. (2006) noted that most feminist organizations in South Korea remain either homophobic or ignorant about lesbians and often do not consider the lesbians' issues a part of their agenda.

Transgender Rights

In this chapter, we have attempted to include transgender issues in our considerations of the legal rights of lesbians throughout the world. Transgender issues, however, are unique, and several issues will be discussed in more detail here. When sex is defined legally, it may be defined by any one of several criteria: the chromosomal determination system, the type of gonads a person possesses, the type of external sexual features a person possesses, or the person's social identification. Consequently, both transsexuals (i.e., persons who desire to live as the other gender) and intersexed individuals (i.e., those born with the sexual organs, or part of the sexual organs, of both sexes, or with ambiguous genitalia; see chapter 2, "Female Genital Cutting around the Globe") may be legally categorized into confusing gray areas, and this may prohibit them from marrying. In any legal jurisdiction where marriages are defined without distinction of the requirement of one man with one woman, these complications do not occur. Legal jurisdictions that recognize a legal change of one's sex may allow transsexual individuals to be married in accordance with their adopted gender identity (Walter, Benner, & Coleman, 2009).

The degree of legal recognition provided to transsexualism varies widely throughout the world. Many countries now extend legal recognition to sex reassignment by permitting a change of sex on one's birth certificate (Currah, Juang, & Minter, 2006). Many transsexual people surgically or medically (e.g., hormone treatment) modify their bodies to be more consistent with their adopted gender identity. Some countries require such modifications before they will legally recognize the gender transition (Currah et al., 2006).

In 2003, the Parliament of South Africa enacted the Alteration of Sex Description and Sex Status Act, which allows postoperative transsexual people (as well as intersex people) to apply to the Department of Home Affairs to have the sex description altered on their birth records (Phahlane, 2003). Once the birth record is altered, these individuals can be issued a new birth certificate and identity document, and they are then considered to be the new sex. Some transgender activists have criticized the law because it requires sex-reassignment surgery to be completed before records can be changed (Phahlane, 2003). Also in 2003, the National Diet (i.e., Japan's legislative body) unanimously approved a new law that enables transsexual people to change their legal sex. The law, effective in 2004, has been controversial because it demands that applicants be unmarried and childless (http://www.courts.go.jp/naha). On July 28, 2004, the Naha Family Court in the Okinawa Prefecture allowed the first recognized sex change to a transwoman (Naha Family Court, 2004). In Japan, sex-reassignment surgery is also required for a legal sex change, but neither sex-change surgeries nor hormone therapies are covered under the Japanese national health insurance program (Japanese Society of Psychiatry and Neurology, 2006).

In South Korea, it is possible for individuals to change their legal sex, but each case depends upon the decision of a judge. Since the 1990s, the courts have approved most legal sex-change petitions. Once people have changed their sex, they are allowed to marry an individual of the other sex under Korean law. In 2006, the Supreme Court of Korea ruled that trans-sexuals have the right to have their legal papers altered to reflect their reassigned sex, including the designation that they were born as their re-assigned sex ("Recognition of Transgender Rights," 2006).

The Role of Religion

As suggested by Corrales and Pecheny (2010), the religious beliefs and backgrounds of a nation often affect, if not outright dictate, that country's response to LGBT individuals. In Argentina, for example, the infrequent church attendance of Catholics and the low percentage of evangelical Christians in the culture at large may have facilitated the legalization of same-sex marriage (Corrales & Pencheny, 2010).

Christian churches do not unanimously condemn homosexuality and are not the only spiritual communities to address the issue of homosexuality for their believers. Most world religions have sought to address the moral issues that arise from sexuality and intimate relationships. Each major re-ligion has developed moral codes covering issues of sexuality, morality, and ethical behavior. Though not all religions address issues of sexuality directly, most seek to regulate situations in which sexual interests arise and to influence people's sexual activities and practices. The views of the world's religions and religious believers vary widely—from the belief that sex, flesh, and physical bodies are sinful to the belief that sexuality is the highest expression of the divine. Some religions distinguish between those sexual activities that bring about biological reproduction and those activities that are pursued purely for physical pleasure. Often, great variation exists even among adherents to the same religious sect.

Buddhism does not always explicitly address details about what is right and wrong within the mundane activities of day-to-day life (Sad-dhatissa, 1987). Details about acceptable and unacceptable sexual practices are not specifically mentioned in any of the religious scriptures. The most commonly accepted formulation of Buddhist ethics are the Five Precepts and the Eightfold Path, which say that one should neither be attached to or crave sensual pleasure (Harvey, 2000). The third of the Five Precepts is to refrain from committing sexual misconduct. Sexual misconduct, however, is a broad term that has been subjected to many interpretations relative to the social norms of a particular set of followers (Harvey, 2000). Buddhist monks and nuns in most traditions are expected to refrain from all sexual activity (Japanese Buddhism is a notable exception), and the Buddha is said to have admonished his followers to avoid unchaste behavior "as if it were a pit of burning cinders" (Saddhatissa, 1987, p. 88).

Due to the ambivalent language about homosexuality in Buddhist teachings, there has been no official stance regarding the issue of same-sex marriage (Bhikkhu, 2005). Buddha gave no rule or advice as to whether LGB individuals should be allowed to marry or not; he simply posited himself as the one who shows the way. Given that he did not insist that he had any right to enforce the behavior of others, many Buddhists do not believe the Buddha's teachings cover social ceremonies or rituals (Bhikkhu, 2005).

Among Hindus, views of sexual morality differ widely depending upon region and sect. Hindu scriptures are often vague about sexuality. Although there are temples that openly depict images of sexual activity and sexual imagery is not sacrilegious, sexual self-restraint is often considered an essential part of a Hindu's well-being and his or her dharmic/karmic duties (Vanita & Kidwai, 2001). In Hindu society, there are no restrictions on particular kinds of consensual sex among adults, but public displays of romantic affection are viewed as distasteful (Narrain & Bhan, 2005; Shakuntala, 1977; Vanita, 2006). Indian law, influenced by the highest concentration of Hindus in the world, has not legalized same-sex marriage (Vanita & Kidwai, 2001).

The majority of Islamic legal scholars cite the rulings of Muhammad and the story of Lot in Sodom as official condemnations of homosexuality (Wafer, 1997). Given that Islam views marriage as an exchange between two parties for the protection and security of exclusive sexual *and* reproductive rights, same-sex marriages are not considered legal within a Muslim framework (Wafer, 1997). There are many sexually related behaviors that are prohibited or forbidden under Islamic Hadiths. Homosexuality is one of them, and acts of sodomy (presumably interpreted as anal sex among men) are explicitly punishable by death in accordance with the Hadith, a ruling that has been upheld by the four Caliphs as well as the Prophet's companions (Wafer, 1997). As previously mentioned, this has led to making homosexuality a capital offense in some Muslim countries.

ARRANGED HETEROSEXUAL MARRIAGES

The inclusion of lesbian women and heterosexual women in arranged (and sometimes forced) marriages in the same chapter occurred out of our interest in discussing the two largest populations of women who are often not extended the basic right of partner choice by the societies in which they live. Arranged marriages are most common in south Asia, India, and parts of Africa and the Middle East (Ghimire, Axinn, Yabiku, & Thornton, 2006; Madathil & Benshoff, 2008). More than 90 percent of all Indian marriages are arranged (Gautam, 2002). Arranged marriages are rare in the West unless they involve individuals transplanted from cultures that practice this tradition (Madathil & Benshoff, 2008).

Given the many cultures in which arranged marriages occur, it is difficult to make sweeping statements about the practice. Many variations exist among different ethnic groups, but the marriages often involve some transfer of wealth, real or symbolic, between the families of the bride and the groom (Ghimire et al., 2006). Many Hindu traditions explicitly, or historically, forbid the involvement of young people in the choice of their mate (Batabyal, 2001; Ghimire et al., 2006; Skolnick, 1987). Nonetheless, in some parts of India, young people are increasingly involved in the process, and there is some evidence that the more involved they are, the happier their relationships are (Madathil & Benshoff, 2008).

Bhopal (1999) explained that arranged marriages are seen as a contract between two families rather than between two individuals; both sides of the contract hold the parties to specific behaviors that fulfill their obligations. Arranged marriages are considered ritual and sacramental unions and have been customary for centuries among many south Asian, African, and Middle Eastern peoples. As previously stated, many forms of arranged marriage exist, including traditional (i.e., the parents and elders within a family choose the spouse), cooperative traditional (i.e., the young person and the parents together make the selection), and more autonomous formats (i.e., the young person makes the choice but seeks parental consent) (Stopes-Roe & Cochrane, 1990). In these traditions, romantic love is often viewed as impractical, unnecessary, and even dangerous, whereas companionate, practical love is seen as a more legitimate form of affection and bonding between spouses (Desai, McCormick, & Gaeddert, 1989).

Forced arranged marriages are still commonplace in some parts of the world (Chantler, Gangoli, & Hester, 2009), and this tradition prevents reproductive justice at its most basic level. When women—or, as is often the case, girls—are sold or otherwise forced into marriage, they often face a higher risk of disease, pregnancy at a young age, and pregnancy-and-childbirth-related death or serious health risks (e.g., obstetric fistulas; see chapter 12, "Reproductive Justice for Women and Infants") (Chantler et al., 2009; Hampton, 2010; Samad, 2010). Forced arranged marriages are generally assumed to take place in primarily Muslim communities (e.g., Afghanistan), but recent studies suggest that the practice is seen in a wide variety of countries, and there are reports of the practice in African, European, Middle Eastern, and Asian nations (Chantler et al., 2009; Samad, 2010).

The United Nations (Hampton, 2010) reported that more than 64 million women between 20 and 24 years of age were married before they were 18 years old, which is often a sign of traditional arranged marriage. This number includes 43 percent of Afghan women, 51 percent of Nepalese women, 44.5 percent of Asian Indian women, and more than 70 percent of the women in Mali, Chad, and Niger (Hampton, 2010). Medical studies have shown that young women and girls in forced marriage situations are at higher risk for malnutrition, physical abuse, and HIV infection, and they are more likely to have miscarriages, premature births, and infants with high mortality rates (Hampton, 2010). Reproductive justice cannot be achieved when women and their infants suffer ill health, risk early death, and have low well-being.

Arranged marriages are particularly difficult for Westerners to understand because they confront the assumption of individualism. In the West, falling in love and selecting a mate is considered a hallmark of normal development for late adolescents and young adults (Medora, Larson, Hortacsu, & Dave, 2002), and love is the primary cultural requisite for marriage (Simpson, Campbell, & Berscheid, 1986). Nonetheless, the issue is not a simple one, and members of individualist cultures ought to evaluate this tradition with caution and consider the context. For example, one study of marital satisfaction (Madathil & Benshoff, 2008) showed that Asian Indians in arranged marriages who lived in the United States were happier than both Indians in arranged marriages in India and Americans in marriages of choice in the United States (Madathil & Benshoff, 2008). Of course, this is only one measure in a specific comparison and does not address the broader issues of women and girls being forced into marriages without their consent.

CONCLUSION

In this review of the legal rights of lesbians, as well as this brief exploration of the experiences of women in arranged heterosexual marriages, we have attempted to provide information to highlight the experiences of women who are denied the right to choose their spouse or, at least, face great personal risk and social stigmatization in order to do so. Readers may notice that much of the discussion about lesbians is focused upon their legal right to marry. This issue is of particular concern in any consideration of the broader concept of reproductive justice for the ironic reason that, without marriage, there can be no legal dissolution of a relationship, and, without a legal dissolution, any children of that union are left vulnerable. In their analysis of California Supreme Court decisions regarding the children of lesbian couples who split up, Hare and Skinner (2008, p. 367) deftly noted that "in the absence of marriage and civil unions, families do not have the established dissolution means to ensure that the child's network of care is protected." In other words, when a nonbiological parent is not given a legal parental status (or when second parent adoption is not legal, and, thus, only one woman is granted legal parental status), "the child's connection to the nonlegal parent is insecure" (Hare & Skinner, 2008, p. 367). Hare and Skinner's (2008) article is a must-read for anyone seriously considering the legal challenges of lesbian parenthood. These scholars advanced the concept of *moral parenthood* wherein children are considered persons with rights rather than as property. Moral parenthood, then, dictates that we begin legislating policy that is designed to protect the interests of the children of any union rather than becoming preoccupied with the nature of the union itself.

The notion of children's rights is also important to protect children from being sold to traffickers (see chapter 5, "Reproductive Injustice") by parents in poverty and to protect girls from being forced into early, arranged marriages to which they object. It is not uncommon, in some parts of the world, for girls to be given to men much older than they are, sometimes to men who already have other wives. This creates a power imbalance in the relationship (see chapter 3, "Women's Power in Relationships") that sets the stage for the abuse and neglect of women and their children. Thus, reproductive justice can seem like an unattainable ideal for the women discussed in this chapter who are not able to choose their own partners and decide whether and when to give birth to, or adopt, children.

REFERENCES

Arita, K. (2006). Lesbian mothers in Japan: An insider's report. *Journal of Lesbian Studies, 10,* 105–112.

Batabyal, A. A. (2001). On the likelihood of finding the right partner in an arranged marriage. *Journal of Socio-Economics, 30,* 273–280.

Bhikkhu, M. (2005, July 13). Religion and same-sex marriage. The Buddhist Channel: Bringing Buddha dharma home—Issues. *The Bangkok Post.* Retrieved from http://www.buddhistchannel.tv/index.php?id=70,1429,0,0,1,0.

Bhopal, K. (1999). South Asian women and arranged marriages in east London. In R. Barot, H. Bradley, & S. Fenton (Eds.), *Ethnicity, gender, and social change* (pp. 117–134). New York: St. Martin's Press.

Chantler, K., Gangoli, G., & Hester, M. (2009). Forced marriage in the UK: Religious, cultural, economic, or state violence? *Critical Social Policy, 29,* 587–612.

Chen, Y. & Chen, Y. (2006). Lesbians in China's mainland: A brief introduction. *Journal of Lesbian Studies, 10,* 113–125.

Constitution of the Republic of South Africa. (1996). Retrieved from http://www. info.gov.za/documents/constitution/1996/96cons2.htm.

Corrales, J., & Pecheny, M. (2010). *Six reasons why Argentina legalized gay marriage first.* Retrieved from http://www.americasquarterly.org/node/1753.

Currah, P., Juang, M. R., & Minter, P. S. (2006). *Transgender rights.* Minneapolis, MN: University of Minnesota Press.

Desai, S. R., McCormick, N. B., & Gaeddert, W. P. (1989). Malay and American undergraduates beliefs about love. *Journal of Psychology and Human Sexuality, 2,* 93–116.

Gautam, S. (2002). Coming next: Monsoon divorce. *New Statesman, 131*(4574), 32–33.

Gettleman, J. (2011, January 11). Ugandan who spoke up for gays is beaten to death. *New York Times.* Retrieved from http://www.nytimes.com/2011/01/28/ world/africa/28uganda.html.

Ghimire, D. J., Axinn, W. G., Yabiku, S. T., & Thornton, A. (2006). Social change, premarital nonfamily experience, and spouse choice in an arranged marriage society. *American Journal of Sociology, 111,* 1181–1218.

Hampton, T. (2010). Child marriage threatens girls' health. *Journal of the American Medical Association, 304*, 509–510.

Hare, J., & Skinner, D. (2008). "Whose child is this?" Determining legal status for lesbian parents who used assisted reproductive technologies. *Family Relations, 57*, 365–375.

Harvey, P. (2000). *An introduction to Buddhist ethics.* New York: Cambridge University Press.

Horie, Y. (2006). Possibilities and limitations of "lesbian continuum": The case of a Protestant church in Japan. *Journal of Lesbian Studies, 10*, 145–159.

Human Rights Campaign. (2010). *What the Defense of Marriage Act does.* Retrieved from http://www.hrc.org/issues/5443.htm.

International Lesbian, Gay, Bisexual, Trans, and Intersex Association (ILGA). (2010). Retrieved from http://www.ilga-europe.org.

Japanese Society of Psychiatry and Neurology. (2006). *Guidelines for diagnosis and treatment of gender identity disorder* (3rd ed.). Tokyo: Author.

Joe-Lee, Y. (2003). Yusungjoouiran Mooutinga? [What is feminism?]. *Ilda* (Feminism Online Journal). Retrieved from http://www.ildaro.com/Scripts/news/index.php?menu=ART&sub=View&idx00004&art_menu=7&art_sub=10.

Judgments of the Supreme Court of Canada. (2010). M. v. H. [1999] 2 S. C. R. 3. Retrieved from http://scc.lexum.umontreal.ca/en/1999/1999scr2–3/1999scr2–3.html.

Kam, L. (2006). Noras on the road: Family and marriage of lesbian women in Shanghai. *Journal of Lesbian Studies, 10*, 87–103.

Kane, M. D. (2010). You've won, now what? The influence of legal change on gay and lesbian mobilization, 1974–1999. *Sociological Quarterly, 51*, 255–277.

Kasuya, N. (2003). Lesbian mother. *Josei-gaku Nenpo* [Women's Studies Report], *24*, 132–143.

Kazama, T. (1996). Undou to Chousa no Aida [Between activism and research]. In K. Satou (Ed.), *Toshi no Dokkairyoku* [Reading ability in cities] (pp. 65–102). Tokyo: Keisou Shobo.

Kazama, T. (2002). Douseiaisha wo Mosshou suru Bouryoku [Violence that erases gays]. In H. Yoshii & T. Yamada (Eds.), *Jissen no Fiiludo Waaku* [Field work practices] (pp. 97–120). Tokyo: Serika Shobo.

Khor, D., & Kamano, S. (2006). *"Lesbians" in east Asia: Diversity, identities, and resistance.* New York: Harrington Park Press.

Kirikiri. (1999). Hankook Lesbian Inkwonoondongui yucksa [History of the lesbian rights movement in South Korea]. *Ttodarum Sesang* [Another world]. Seoul: Trodarun Sesang.

Kirikiri. (2005). Hankook Lesbian Inkwonoondongui Sipnyunsa [Ten year history of lesbians' rights movement in South Korea]. *Woorisidaeui Sosoofa Undong* [Minority's movement in this/our age]. Seoul: Ihaksa.

Lambda Legal. (2010). Retrieved from http://www.lambdalegal.org.

Madathil, J., & Benshoff, J. M. (2008). Importance of marital characteristics and marital satisfaction: A comparison of Asian Indians in arranged marriages and Americans in marriage of choice. *Family Journal, 16*, 222–230.

Medora, N. P., Larson, J. H., Hortacsu, N., & Dave, P. (2002). Perceived attitudes towards romanticism: A cross cultural study of American, Asian Indian, and Turkish young adults. *Journal of Comparative Family Studies, 33*, 183–190.

Naha Family Court. (2004). After the first time I allowed to change the gender of the family registration law enforcement, fire Naha (translated from Japanese). http://www.47news.jp/CN/200407/CN2004072901000849.html.

Narrain, A., & Bhan, G. (Eds.). (2005). *Because I have a voice: Queer politics in India.* New Delhi, India: Yoda Press.

OCCUR. (2000). http://www.occur.or.jp/info.html.

O'Flaherty, M., & Fisher, J. (2008). Sexual orientation, gender identity and international human rights law: Contextualising the Yogyakarta Principles. *Human Rights Law Review, 8,* 207–248.

Park-Kim, S., Lee-Kim, S., & Kwon-Lee, E. (2006). The lesbian rights movement and feminism in South Korea. *Journal of Lesbian Studies, 10,* 161–190.

Phahlane, C. (2003, September 10). Transgender group calls for more time to consider "inhumane" bill on sex status. *Cape Times.* Retrieved from http://dictionary.sensagent.com/legal+aspects+of+transsexualism/en-en/#cite_note-4.

Recognition of transgender rights: Compassion and logic. (2006, July 5). *Korean Herald.* from http://www.koreanherald.com/common/List.jsp?ListId=020101000000.

Saddhatissa, H. (1987). *Buddhist ethics: The path to nirvana.* Boston: Wisdom Publications.

Samad, Y. (2010). Forced marriage among men: An unrecognized problem. *Critical Social Policy, 30,* 189–207.

Shakuntala. (1977). *The world of homosexuals.* New Delhi, India: Vikas.

Simpson, J., Campbell, B., & Berscheid, E. (1986). The association between romantic love and marriage: Kephart (1967) twice revisited. *Personality and Social Psychology Bulletin, 12,* 363–372.

Skolnick, A. S. (1987). *The intimate environment: Exploring marriage and the family.* Boston: Little, Brown.

South African Society of Psychiatrists. (2005, December 1). *Press statement on homosexuality.* Retrieved from http://www.sasop.co.za/C_ftpsyc_Positionstat5.asp.

Stopes-Roe, M., & Cochrane, R. (1990). *Citizens of this country: The Asian British.* Clevedon, UK: Multilingual Matters.

Sugiura, I. (2006). Lesbian discourses in mainstream magazines of post-war Japan: Is Onabe distinct from Rezubian? *Journal of Lesbian Studies, 10,* 127–144.

Taylor, C. (2010). *What happened in Iowa.* Retrieved from http://www.lambdalegal.org/publications/factsheets/fs_what-happened-in-iowa.html.

Thailand Law Forum. (2010). *Transsexuals and Thai law.* Retrieved from http://www.thailawforum.com/Transsexuals-and-Thai-Law.html.

Vanita, R. (2006). *Love's rite: Same-sex marriage in India and the West.* New Delhi, India: Penguin Books.

Vanita, R., & Kidwai, S. (2001). *Same-sex love In India: Readings from literature and history.* London: Palgrave.

Wafer, J. (1997). Muhammed and male homosexuality. In S. O. Murray & W. Roscoe (Eds.), *Islamic homosexualities: Culture, history, and literature* (pp. 88–90). New York: New York University Press.

Walter, B., Benner, A., & Coleman, E. (2009). Gay and bisexual identity development among female-to-male transsexuals in North America: Emergence of a transgender sexuality. *Archives of Sexual Behavior, 38,* 688–701.

Chapter 2

Female Genital Cutting around the Globe: A Matter of Reproductive Justice?

Virginia Braun

Women's natural genitalia are troublesome—to society and to women themselves. The trouble they invoke can relate to social order and patriarchal dominance; to ideas and practices about gender, sexuality, race, and ethnicity, about culture and belonging; to the psychology of the woman, if she experiences genital distress. Women's genital/reproductive organs are not just flesh. They are a rich and potent source of symbolic meanings, which are culturally located, (re)produced and practiced, solidified within cultures, but also subject to change, as cultures themselves are constantly changing. Globally, diverse practices of female genital cutting (FGC) attest to our trouble with women's genitalia.

The intersection of different rights, contexts, laws, and (cultural) values, as well as constructions of the individual, the subject, the body, and the social, means FGC is a practice certain women are entitled to choose, other women are precluded from choosing, and yet other women are compelled to choose (for themselves or their daughters). Dominated by traditional forms of cutting, debates about FGC have sometimes been fraught, caught up questions of culture, tradition, gender, sexuality, agency, ethnocentrism, cultural imperialism, neocolonialism, and cultural relativism. There has been far less (Western) interest in FGC as it takes place *in the West,* unless on the bodies of girls/women from those countries where it is traditional, or on those deemed "ambiguously" sexed. This chapter is not about FGC as it happens to *the other:* It is about FGC as a culturally located global practice that needs to be analyzed contextually as well as critically.

POSITIONING MYSELF

Everyone has positions in relation to FGC. As a privileged, White Western feminist who has never experienced FGC, it is important that I make clear my position(s). Ultimately, I want a world in which women and girls are under *no* compulsion, either from self or others, to cut or alter healthy genital tissue, and thus I fully support the elimination of such practices. However, not all FGC is created equal, as FGC can range from the very minor and impermanent to extreme and permanent. Talking about it as if it is one thing is not necessarily helpful (Walley, 2002). Although FGC is a useful blanket label, more precision is needed, both in analysis and to clarify the basis of objections to (any or all) FGC.

I *am* sympathetic to critics who argue that work against FGC needs to come from those within a culture; I feel most secure in my critique of Western practices for this reason. In writing on FGC, I have endeavored not to fall prey to arrogant ethnocentrism (James & Robertson, 2002a), yet my analysis—the points I find compelling—are inevitably shaped by my location(s). My broader cultural context is not one in which a collective sense of identity and action takes precedence over the individual. At the same time, it is heavy with culture-bound mandates that women be "thin (White) and attractive" (and now also sexually agentic; Gill, 2008) to experience full citizenship; most women are subject to these mandates, some even to the point of death. In this context, the cutting of women's genitals has emerged as a (market driven) "solution" to female genital distress. Much of my recent scholarship (and activism) has involved critiquing solution (Braun, 2005, 2009a, 2009b, 2010; Braun & Tiefer, 2010).

WHAT IS FGC?

Typically used to refer to traditional practices of cutting and often removal of genital tissue for nonmedical reasons, the term *FGC* allows the inclusion of a far *wider* range of practices, such as female genital cosmetic surgery procedures and medical interventions to resex the genitals of infants born with visually ambiguous genitalia—those not clearly female *or* male.[1] Although historically Western medicine has clitorectomized women (Green, 2005), my focus is more contemporary. Likewise, *male* genital cutting (MGC) is not discussed here.[2]

We cannot access the physical act of cutting in a pure form, only through the evocative imaginary that language constructs (Rogers, 2009). Language is important and, yet, problematic. I use *traditional* to describe practices associated in some way with broader *cultural* identity or practices: Regardless of the length of their existence, these FGCs typically occupy a rhetorical status *as* traditional and/or a marker of culture. The other FGCs have been framed within a discourse of modern (Western) medicine, and I identify these in relation to the "problem" they "fix": vulval aesthetics or genitally ambiguous bodies. Each domain has been subject to diverse scholarship; a chapter like this can barely touch on the issues.

Traditional FGC (TFGC)

TFGC covers an incredibly diverse range of cuttings (Walley, 2002) practiced in at least 28 countries in sub-Saharan Africa and a few in Asia, the Middle East, and South America (Clarence-Smith, 2008; Merli, 2008; OHCHR et al., 2008). Practices range from a prick to the clitoris or clitoral hood to the removal—and reorganization—of most external genital tissue. The most widely used categorization system is from the World Health Organization (WHO):[3] *Type I*—partial or total removal of the clitoris and/or the prepuce; *Type II*—partial or total removal of the clitoris and the labia minora, with or without excision of the labia majora; *Type III*—narrowing of the vaginal orifice with creation of a covering seal by cutting and appositioning the labia minora and/or the labia majora, with or without excision of the clitoris (Types I–III contain subtypes); *Type IV*—unclassified, which includes all other harmful procedures to the female genitalia for nonmedical purposes, for example pricking, piercing, incising, scraping, and cauterization. Exactly which practices are included in Type IV is contested (OHCHR et al., 2008). Certain practices that do not involve cutting, such as labial stretching or vaginal inserts, as well as some that do, are not always defined as TFGC (Bagnol & Mariano, 2008; Koster & Price, 2008; Martin-Hilber et al., 2009; Scorgie et al., 2010).

The cutting, which typically takes place sometime between infancy and the transition to adulthood, serves no medical need, and it may or may not involve the consent of the individual who is cut. It can be understood as a *socially* sustained practice, performed for one or more of a wide range of reasons (for quick summaries see Committee on Bioethics, 2010; WHO, 2010a) related to national, cultural, religious, or gender identity; social organization; ideas about appropriate female sexuality; and genital aesthetics or hygiene (Abusharaf, 2001; Anuforo, Oyedele, & Pacquiao, 2004; Budiharsana, Amaliah, Utomo, & Erwinia, 2003; Clarence-Smith, 2008; Fahmy, El-Mouelhy, & Ragab, 2010; Gruenbaum, 2001, 2006; Jirovsky, 2010; Khaja, Barkdull, Augustine, & Cunningham, 2009; Mandara, 2004; Newland, 2006; Putranti, 2008; Smith, 2008; Yount & Abraham, 2007).[4]

Although associated often with Islam, there is no necessary correspon-
dence. Many who practice TFGC are not Muslim; many Muslims do not
condone the practice (Berkey, 1996; Clarence-Smith, 2008); some religious
authorities are starting to issue fatwa against TFGC (Khalife, 2010; "Muslim Leaders Ban Female Circumcision," 2010).

Meanings correspond somewhat to type, age, and context of TFGC
(James & Robertson, 2002a). More extreme cuttings, which tend to take
place at the youngest ages, without the child's consent, in an individual,
largely private context, are typically associated with meanings that intersect cultural and gender identity and constructions of female sexual
desire—but not necessarily *pleasure*—as in need of controlling, for her
own chastity (Fahmy et al., 2010) and/or to maintain the social order—
both often linked to marriageability. Less extreme cuttings, which tend to
take place in adolescence, often with the girl's consent, in a (public) group
context, tend to be associated with (wider) rites of passage into womanhood and to link gendered identity with cultural/national identity (e.g.,
Njambi, 2004b). Female sexuality may be seen as controlled through this
process (Smith, 2008; Walley, 2002).

Every year, 2–3 million girls/women are at risk of TFGC, and global total
estimates suggest 100–140 million girls/women have had TFGC (OHCHR
et al., 2008; Yoder & Khan, 2008). The most robust African estimates suggest 91.5 million girls and women *over the age of 10* have experienced TFGC
(Yoder & Khan, 2008).[5] Prevalence across Africa ranges from more than
95 percent (e.g., Guinea, Somalia) to less than 5 percent (e.g., Cameroon,
Ghana); prevalence for non-African countries is less known, but rates in
Indonesia are high (Budiharsana et al., 2003; Clarence-Smith, 2008). The
extensive work against TFGC across Africa suggests it *should* be declining,
but that has not always been evidenced (Toubia & Sharief, 2003); it seems
to be *increasing* in frequency and severity in some Muslim Asian countries
(Clarence-Smith, 2008).

Questions of agency and cultural influence in TFGC have been points of
contention. Even beyond childhood, decisions about TFGC are likely rarely
individual as understood by a Western analytic lens; they may involve extended family and take place within a context of "extensive social pressure
and strong expectations to comply" with community norms related to TFGC
(Shell-Duncan & Johansen, 2010, p. 1). It has been easy for Westerners to
frame (others') culture as a totalizing, static, essential marker of beliefs about
and practice of TFGC (Walley, 2002), but culture and cultural traditions are
diverse, sometimes contradictory, and always changing (Berkey, 1996). Culture is vital (Gruenbaum, 2005b), and it should not be reified as unchanging
or all-determining for anyone. Although "cultural values are indeed powerful influences in structuring through an action, human actors regularly critique their backgrounds, making choices that reinterpret their cultural and
religious values and add new elements" (Gruenbaum, 2005b, p. 430).

What to call TFGC has been contentious at the international level; communities that practice it have their own terms (Walley, 2002). After the term *circumcision* was critiqued for being euphemistic and invoking a *minor* process, the language of female genital *mutilation* (FGM) was adopted to emphasize seriousness and harm (Rahman & Toubia, 2000). Still preferred by international agencies such as the WHO and the Inter-African Committee on Traditional Practices Affecting the Health of Women and Children, the term *FGM* has been critiqued as offensive, denying (some) women's lived experience, stigmatizing individuals and communities, imposing a sadistic intent onto parents, and imposing an external frame of reference, thus alienating communities (Khaja et al., 2009; Obermeyer, 2005; Walley, 2002). To ameliorate such concerns, the neutral descriptive term *FGC* is often used (Rahman & Toubia, 2000). Both FGC and FGM are understood by WHO (2010a) to situate the act as a violation of human rights. Use of *different* language to talk about FGC in different contexts may offer some solution (Gunning, 2002; Obermeyer, 2005). Given that a reproductive rights and justice framework for FGC emphasizes the importance of contextualized, localized knowledge and the development of interventions with/in communities, concern over precision of, and evocation through, language is an important one, but not one the language of FGC can necessary resolve.

Cosmetic FGC (FGCS)

FGCS removes or changes genital tissue for aesthetic and other non-medical reasons. It is typically performed by gynecologists or plastic surgeons on the body of adult women who have given their informed consent. Every part of the female genitalia is "treatable." Particularly relevant here are labiaplasty (the removal of labia minora tissue, apparently the most common procedure), alterations to labia majora (through tissue removal or fat injections), clitoral procedures (hood reduction/removal), and hymenoplasty (hymen reconstruction).

FGCS emerged in the West but has spread globally. Based on *very* limited and partial data from the United Kingdom (Hospital Episode Statistics, 2009), the United States (American Society for Aesthetic Plastic Surgery, 2009, 2010), and Australia (Robotham, 2010), which put FGCS procedures per year in the thousands, and the short time span of widespread availability, it may be that less than 100,000 women worldwide have, so far, undergone some form of FGCS. However, FGCS is often claimed to be *increasing*. Despite U.S. statistics that show a reduction between 2007 and 2009, it is plausible this could the case, but far better statistics are needed to determine the actual frequency.

More is known about women's motivations for seeking FGCS: aesthetic dislike, physical discomfort, desire for a better sex life, (genital) self esteem and confidence issues (Braun, 2010), and, in the case of hymenoplasty, the need to comply with cultural mandates for physical evidence of virginity at marriage (Essén, Blomkvist, Helström, & Johnsdotter, 2010), which is situated *differently* than other FGCS. FGCS is heavily marketed, and advertising often evokes feminist rhetoric of empowerment, framing it as about increasing self-confidence and sexual pleasure. The marketing has been critiqued for creating both demand (Braun, 2009a) and a new medical problem for women (Braun & Tiefer, 2010).

Intersex Genital Cutting (IGC)

IGC refers to a range of procedures performed by surgeons on ambiguous genitalia—a short vagina, a clitoris larger than 0.9 cm, a penis smaller than 2.5 cm (Kessler, 1998)—often in infancy without the child's consent. *Intersex*[6] conditions are those where different aspects (e.g., gonads, phenotype) of an individual's sexed body are not discrete and/or aligned. A very narrow definition of intersex puts it at 0.018 percent of the population (Sax, 2002); more inclusive estimates for *any* nonconformity suggest 1–2 percent (Blackless et al., 2000). *Visibly* ambiguous genitalia likely occur in 1 in 2,000 people (de María Arana, 2005).[7] Frequency of IGC is impossible to determine. Although challenged, estimates of up to 5 infants per day in the United States (Chase, 2002) or 1–2 per 1,000 births (http://www.isna.org/faq/frequency) have been offered.

Genital surgery became standard (Western) practice in the treatment of intersex from the 1970s (see Karkazis, 2008; Kessler, 1990), the (medically) *moral* course of action to correct the defectively gendered body/child (Dreger, 2006; Murray, 2009) and produce a (normal) gendered subject— more often female (Minto, Liao, Woodhouse, Ransley, & Creighton, 2003). Feminizing genital procedures routinely performed include removal of gonads, clitorectomy (later replaced by clitoriplasty, to retain the glans clitoris), and construction of a (neo)vagina (Crouch, Liao, Woodhouse, Conway, & Creighton, 2008), often accompanied by hormonal treatments. The tendency was to operate as early as possible, to remove *uncertainty* about sex in the eyes of the family (and world), which can be experienced as confusing and distressing (Gough, Weyman, Alderson, Butler, & Stoner, 2008), and to create better psychosocial outcomes for the individual (Minto et al., 2003). Treatments were often accompanied by secrecy and silence: The child often denied knowledge; the parents also sometimes did (Dreger, 2006; Karkazis, 2008).

IGC is *socially* rather than *medically* necessary;[8] it reflects cultural values about gender dimorphism (Dreger, 2006). Although IGC is not aimed *at* female bodies, it is often aimed at female *subjects:* Disorders of sexual development (DSD) guidelines recommend that a gender be assigned (Lee et al., 2006),[9] which IGC confirms. As it is intended to create a properly genitally gendered body, it is often characterized as normalizing (Diamond, 1999; Hegarty & Chase, 2000).

Diversity and Similarity

FGCs are diverse but all are "entangled with cultural norms and ideology" (Johnsdotter & Essén, 2010, p. 35). Two other key factors unite different FGCs: (1) the tissue removed is not medically harmful—it is removed for other (cultural, social, psychological) reasons; (2) FGC is typically about conformity to a (perceived) norm of what female genitalia should *look* like or what female identity and sexuality should *be* like. However, a number of factors create divisions between different FGCs that span the different categories discussed. Materially, there are questions of: (1) age—whether those whose genitals are cut are children, youth, or adults; (2) agency—whether the person chooses and/or consents to the procedure; (3) cutting context—whether the procedure takes place in a medical setting or a community context; and (4) the cutter—what qualifications/ expertise, status, or authority the cutter has. Although answers to these questions may be locally situated, and the legitimacy of the answers contested, these are mostly matters of fact. Divisions are also created by different *voices* on FGC, which derive from politics, ideology, and interpretation, and relate to the rhetorical. The two most common rhetorical tropes at play are choice/coercion and harm/benefit. Claims of harm/benefit or choice/coercion are not just recordings of the truth; they (also) serve the function of legitimizing or delegitimizing different forms and contexts of FGC. To recognize this rhetorical element is not to deny material reality, but to provide a more thoughtful analysis.

THE HARMS/BENEFITS OF FGC

Impacts of FGC—whether physical, psychological/emotional, or sexual—are not necessarily cohesive nor permanent. Genitals are not *one* thing, with *one* purpose; they have multiple meanings and significations for individuals, and those around them, as does cutting. The same event can produce very different experiences, meanings, and stories, depending on *who* is telling *which* story about genitals and (which) FGC is involved (e.g., Kessler, 1998). It is important to acknowledge that many stories about FGC are framed around, and motivated by, benefits—to create better psychosocial outcomes for the person; to reduce genital distress; to create "normal" genitals, a marriageable girl, or a "properly" enculturated woman. Some women report positive stories about FGC; for many, it may be neither *purely* positive nor negative (Bramwell, Morland, & Garden, 2007; Njambi, 2004a, p. 326; Walley, 2002). And there is no doubt that FGC has caused many women intense trauma, harm, and even death. The widespread nature of FGC and the harms it can cause situate it as a *global* physical and mental health concern.

This concern has primarily been applied to TFGC, and a swathe of literature has reported diverse harms (WHO, 2000a, 2000b).[10] *Certain* forms of TFGC are associated with increased adverse obstetrical outcomes, including increased cesarean sections, fetal distress, and perinatal death.[11] Problems related to a range of gynecological and sexual health issues (STIs), menstruation, urination, scarring, and sex and sexual pleasure have been reported, as have psychological impacts, including posttraumatic stress disorder (PTSD; Banks et al., 2006; Behrendt & Moritz, 2005; Elnashar & Abdelhady, 2007; Klouman, Manongi, & Klepp, 2005; Obermeyer, 2005). Potential impacts vary with the severity of the cutting, but not always in an obvious or linear way. The early representation of female sexual pleasure as *universally* ablated by TFGC appears to be wrong, even for Type III (Ahmadu, 2007; Catania et al., 2007; Obermeyer, 2005; Smith, 2008).

A body of evidence similarly demonstrates that substantial harm often follows IGC, as its physical and emotional outcomes can be similar to those of TFGC (de María Arana, 2005). Outcomes have often been poor, both aesthetically and functionally, including sensitivity, scarring, pain, urological problems, a diminished or eliminated sexual response, and varied psychological/emotional impacts including depression; suicidality; shame; rage; a sense of having been damaged, mutilated, or violated; PTSD; and gender "confusion" (Chase, 1998a, 2002; Creighton, 2001, 2004; Crouch & Creighton, 2007; Crouch et al., 2008; de María Arana, 2005; Diamond, 1999; Hegarty & Chase, 2000; Minto et al., 2003). Evidence of long-term impact is limited (Lee et al., 2006). Some have suggested that IGC is potentially *more* harmful than TFGC (Ehrenreich & Barr, 2005) as additional surgery includes the risk of death from anesthesia.

In contrast, benefit dominates reports of FGCS outcomes, which are said to include improvements in self-esteem, physical and psychological comfort, and sexual pleasure, and overall high levels of "satisfaction" (typically > 90%). Such data are, however, limited in quantity but, more important, in quality (see Braun, 2010; Liao, Michala, & Creighton, 2010). Risks include altered sensation, dyspareunia, adhesions, scarring ("ACOG Committee Opinion No. 378," 2007), and worse: Anecdotal accounts indicate that FGCS *can* cause significant distress and severe/permanent harm (e.g., http://www.steadyhealth.com/Labiaplasty_Nightmare_t112049.html; http://www.experienceproject.com/groups/Had-Labiaplasty/106234). Nothing is known of long-term impact, including obstetrical experiences.

RESPONDING TO FGC

All forms of FGC have evoked responses, whether local, national, or international: critique, activism, intervention, policy development, and legislation (Boyle, 2002). Many are oriented to change, but in different ways. TFGC dominates; responses to it tend to be criminalizing or educational (Ehrenreich & Barr, 2005), and the Western response is predominantly one of zero tolerance (Johnsdotter & Essén, 2010). But the West's engagement with TGFC has not been uncontroversial; it has evoked (justified) critiques including homogenization, arrogant ethnocentrism, and neocolonialism (see Dustin, 2010; Gruenbaum, 2001; James & Robertson, 2002b; Lane & Rubinstein, 1996; Njambi, 2004b; Nnaemeka, 2005). Responses are determined by what, and where, the crux of the problem is seen to be.

Medicalization of FGC

If harm is seen as the crux of the problem with FGC, harm reduction/elimination becomes an obvious desire. Harm reduction has been one response to TFGC, whereby ritual and symbolism are maintained but harm is minimized (Shell-Duncan, 2001) through substituting a more minor procedure (e.g., a ritual nick of the clitoral hood). Another strategy, the use of health professionals to perform TFGC (i.e., the medicalization of TFGC; WHO, 2010a) has been supported for harm reduction reasons and as a step toward elimination (Committee on Bioethics, 2010; Shell-Duncan, 2001) but critiqued for *not* eliminating harm, for adding *legitimacy* to TFGC, and for condoning the (problematic) values and beliefs that the tradition of TFGC reflects (Budiharsana et al., 2003; Johnsdotter & Essén, 2010; WHO, 2010a; WHO, UNFPA, & UNICEF, 2009). In Egypt, a rapid transition to medicalized TFGC was not associated with much overall reduction (El-Mouelhy & Johansen, 2010; WHO et al., 2009); medicalized TFGC was specifically banned in Egypt along with all TFGC in 2008 (Hassanin, Saleh, Bedaiwy, Peterson, & Bedaiwy, 2008). Medicalization is associated with increases in frequency and severity of TFGC in Indonesia (Budiharsana et al., 2003; Clarence-Smith, 2008; Putranti, 2008). Medicalized TFGC is strongly condemned by organizations such as WHO, UNICEF, and international medical organizations such as the International Federation of Gynecology and Obstetrics (Ford, 2001; Serour & Faúndes, 2006).[12] The question of reinfibulation after childbirth is more thorny (Serour & Faúndes, 2006; WHO, 2010a), but some have argued that it violates medical ethics to do no harm (Cook & Dickens, 2010; Serour, 2010).[13]

In contrast, both ICG and FGCS are *already* medicalized procedures, situated within a discourse of health: The solution to social or psychological issues is located within, and resolved on, the body of an individual, for the individual's *well-being*. The medical context itself provides legitimacy. Within the logic of medicine, all procedures contain risk: The balance of risk/benefit is what needs to be considered. If IGC and FGCS are deemed not to be (too) harmful, this framework allows no objection; if they are, it does. Objection to IGC, in particular, has been related to *ethics* and to *rights,* rather than *just* to harm, to provide a platform for change.

An Ethical Analysis

Medical ethics provides another useful framework for responding to FGC, particularly in relation to medicalized FGC. Key overriding principles are do no harm (nonmaleficence) and autonomy, but ethical principles may work against each other. Ethics are interpretable, living, not static (Goodman et al., 2007). Although *do no harm* might seem simple, it can also be interpreted as *minimizing* harm (Cook, 2008), a subjective judgment. Based on the principle of autonomy, the question of consent appears simple: Did the patient agree or not? In many cases with children, the answer is clearly no. The right of parents to consent to IGC has been contested. IGC has been deemed to "violate most medical standards of informed consent" (de María Arana, 2005, p. 18) because it is normalizing, it carries serious risk of harm, and *full* information was often withheld from parents (Dreger, 2006). Even if information is provided, inadequate evidence of (long term) impacts may mean parents *cannot* give *informed* consent to IGC (Diamond, 1999). This same logic can apply to adult women who want FGCS, as long-term impacts are not known.

Commercialization in medicine, and the valorization of the "choosing consumer" has created new issues, as concerns about medical ethics may be "bendable and subject to the 'law' of the market" (de Andrade, 2010, p. 81). With FGCS, patient autonomy provides an ethical rationale for surgeons,[14] but choice is complex (see Braun, 2010), and

> where decisions to operate on healthy sex organs are triggered by a perceived defect informed by commercial pressure, where reliable information on risks and benefits is unavailable and where there is no provision of alternatives because there is no concerted effort to develop them, the ethics behind informed consent are vastly compromised (Liao et al., 2010, p. 23).

An Issue of Rights and Justice

Rights has been a dominant framework for responding to FGC, and it moves from questions of harm to questions of entitlements and protections. Human rights are those inherent in personhood, *fundamental* and inalienable, and those rights include life, health, physical integrity, and freedom from abuse and discrimination. Protections of these are provided by various international treaties, of which all nations have ratified at least one (Cottingham & Kismodi, 2009). A rights framework invokes a relationship between individuals and their government; governments are obligated to ensure and protect individuals' rights, and to modify customs that impinge on them (Gunning, 2002; Rahman & Toubia, 2000), *especially* when the impacts are not applied equally to all citizens (Chambers, 2008). The concept of *harmful cultural/traditional practices,* which marries both health and human rights (Ras-Work, 2006), has been used to describe such practices, and TFGC is the most evocative symbol (Gunning, 2002). A rights framework seeks the elimination of FGC as a violation of human rights; it has been explicitly and implicitly used against both TFGC and ICG (Chase, 2002; de María Arana, 2005; Diamond, 1999; Dreger, 2006; Dreger & Herndon, 2009; Ehrenreich & Barr, 2005; Ford, 2001; Greenberg, 2006; Haas, 2004; Johnsdotter & Essén, 2010; Murray, 2009; Shell-Duncan, 2008; Toubia & Sharief, 2003).

Major international summits in the 1990s saw the emergence and solidification of concepts of reproductive/sexual *rights* (Corrêa, 1997; WHO, 2010b) and the location of TFGC as a reproductive rights violation[15] based on concepts of gender-based discrimination and physical integrity, and as a form of (de facto) gender-based violence (de facto, as it is not intended as violence; WHO, 2010a). TFGC is seen to violate girls'/women's rights to bodily/physical integrity (Rahman & Toubia, 2000), regardless of how much cutting is done or whether complications arise. It has been argued that "speaking of [TFGC] as a human rights issue is a critical tool for social justice" (Rahman & Toubia, 2000, p. 13).[16] This framework supports moves to protect girls' bodily integrity, certainly until they are old enough to consent (Johnsdotter & Essén, 2010), and it has proved fruitful for moving toward the elimination of FGC (Khaja et al., 2009). Where questions remain they primarily relate to adult women, when rights protections may *clash* with individual choice and autonomy. However, choices are both individual and contextual, and as contexts enable certain choices and preclude others, not all choice is free (e.g., certain choices may be mandated by economic necessity; Feder, 2006; Petchesky, 2000; Silliman, Freid, Ross, & Gutierrez, 2004).

A reproductive *justice* framework is useful in bringing political analyses of economic justice, race, class, and so forth to reproductive rights and, thereby, recognizing the diverse *constraints* on rights and choices (Gilliam, Neustadt, & Gordon, 2009; Gruenbaum, 1996; Silliman et al., 2004). This framework also offers a critical analysis of the influence of *development,* broadly conceived, which is particularly pertinent to FGC as it relates to developing nations. An overall development agenda tied to a globalized world economy linked to world trade and the capitalist demands of growth and wealth, which involves economic exploitation of developing nations, and particularly the women within them, is problematic (Gruenbaum, 1996; Robertson, 2002). As empowerment of women must be part of a reproductive justice response to TFGC, such factors need to be considered.

For ICG, a rights analysis has been a central framework for scholarship and activism toward elimination (e.g., Dreger, 2006; Dreger & Herndon, 2009), and it has been used to highlight inconsistencies in responses to FGC: "If we are to consider the African girl's genital integrity as a matter of human (universal) rights, then the only way to cut the intersex girl's genitals for social reasons is to exempt her from human rights" (Dreger, 2006, p. 79). A key event in cementing the rights framework was the 2004 San Francisco Human Rights Commission hearings regarding IGC, which concluded that, without patient consent, ICG constituted "inherent human rights abuses" (de María Arana, 2005, p. 17).

As for FGCS, the concept of *rights* appears primarily in assertions of women's *unquestionable* "right to choose" (http://www.janakrasmussen mdfacs.com/procedures/labia-reduction-palm-beach-fl/) FGCS. A clear rhetorical distinction is made between FGCS and FGM, which is framed as *without* choice (see Braun, 2009b); indeed, legislative prohibition as a harmful cultural practice overrides choice/consent in the case of TFGC (Berer, 2010). One exception is Jeffreys's (2005) application of the harmful cultural practices framework to FGCS; she argued that, far from signaling liberation and freedom, such choices not only damage women's health but also reinforce gendered divisions and inequalities.

Legislating FGC

A response closely tied to rights is legislation; different forms of FGC are subject to different legal status. FGCS is not considered illegal anywhere. The legality of IGC is partly restricted only in Colombia (where *informed* consent is mandated, and parents may not be entitled to give it for children under 5 years old [Greenberg, 2006; Haas, 2004]). Although some argue *for* legal prohibition against IGC (Haas, 2004), that position has relatively little support (Creighton, Greenberg, Roen, & Volcano, 2009; de María Arana, 2005; Ehrenreich & Barr, 2005; Greenberg, 2006), but specific legislative rulings (e.g., mandating minimum requirements for consent) might be useful (Ehrenreich & Barr, 2005): The Colombia decision effectively operates in this way (Greenberg, 2006). In contrast, TFGC is illegal in many countries (Leye & Deblonde, 2004; Rahman & Toubia, 2000), and its legal status is evolving (Boyle & Preves, 2000). Currently 12 Western and 19 African nations ban it, and there are calls for a pan-Africa ban ("Push for Continent-wide Ban on Female Genital Mutilation," 2010). Some see laws as important tools for strengthening advocacy work for change (Gruenbaum, 2005a; Rahman & Toubia, 2000). Others argue that criminalization is not helpful, potentially counterproductive (James & Robertson, 2002a; Khaja et al., 2009; Toubia & Sharief, 2003), and (alone) does not necessarily reduce TFGC (Ako & Akweongo, 2009; Boddy, 2008; Serour & Faúndes, 2006).

Anti-FGC laws vary in which forms of cutting/modification are included (e.g., some exclude genital piercing, which fits WHO Type IV; Leye & Deblonde, 2004). In some places (e.g., United States), these laws apply only to minors (Rahman & Toubia, 2000); in some places (e.g., United Kingdom) "mental and physical health" offer an "out" clause (Berer, 2010); some (e.g., Sweden) have clarified that FGCS *is* "cosmetic surgery" and thus legal (Johnsdotter & Essén, 2010). But trenchant questions have been raised about to whom and how these anti-FGC laws, which typically were developed with TFGC in mind, are applied. In Western countries, such laws are typically applied to migrants *from* African countries where TFGC is practiced, who *may* wish to continue the practice in their new home (or may not; see Hussein, 2008; Johnsdotter, Moussa, Carlbom, Aregai, & Essén, 2009). Yet in what the laws describe, they often potentially prohibit FGCS (Berer, 2010; Leye & Deblonde, 2004) *and* IGC, although they are not taken to apply there. Although not legally tested, the differential interpretation and application of such laws according to the body at stake has been deemed cultural hypocrisy (Allotey, Manderson, & Grover, 2001; Berer, 2010; Davis, 2002; Essén & Johnsdotter, 2004; Sullivan, 2007):

> How can it be that extensive genital modifications, including reduction of labial and clitoral tissue, are considered acceptable and perfectly legal in many European countries, while those same societies have legislation making [FGC] illegal, and the [WHO] bans even the "pricking" of the female genitals? (Johnsdotter & Essén, 2010, p. 29).

Johnsdotter and Essén have argued that, to be ethically sustainable, laws need to apply to *all* FGC, regardless of the body/culture of the woman and the type of FGC, or they clearly need to apply *just* to those under a certain age. Questions about legislation include: What justice would be served by precluding *any* adult FGC, or by allowing it? Should we determine some tissue as vital (and hence *always* illegal to remove)?

Change

These different domains provide frameworks for responding to FGC, but many interventions draw on more than one (as well as some others). In relation to TFGC, for instance, legislation cannot be the only approach (Toubia & Sharief, 2003) but must exist alongside (or behind) educational and other locally based interventions for change (Ako & Akweongo, 2009). Contemporary thinking about TFGC elimination is that it is a multidimensional problem, not only related to health/gender education and change in gendered social roles, but tied to issues of development and governance (Asekun-Olarinmoye & Amusan, 2008; Donors Working Group on Female Genital Mutilation/Cutting, 2008; Toubia & Sharief, 2003; WHO, 2010a).

Interventions against TFGC were bolstered by the inclusion of (the elimination of) FGM in agendas such as the program of action from the 1994 International Conference on Population and Development (ICPD) in Cairo (Cottingham & Kismodi, 2009) and the UN Millennium Development Goals (MDGs) related to girls' and women's health (WHO, 2010a). The MDGs provide an international basis for action. However, any agenda for cultural change, even if externally *supported*, needs to be community motivated, owned, and driven, using localized, contextualized understandings of TFGC (Gruenbaum, 2005a, 2005b; Toubia & Sharief, 2003). Key components include community engagement, ownership, and empowerment. Such integrated, community-owned and based, social development–based approaches, with TFGC one of a collection of social justice issues such as health, literacy, and economic development, are proving successful (Toubia & Sharief, 2003).

An example of a successful "from the ground-up" intervention that produces rapid social change[17] is provided by TOSTAN (http://www.tostan. org), an NGO that uses democracy and human rights (Gillespie & Melching, 2010) analyses for social and community development to empower women. TFGC was not one of the organization's original objectives; however, after TOSTAN had engaged with women on the ground, it became a focal point for intervention. After taking part in a TOSTAN program, more than 4,500 villages in five countries *publicly* abandoned their tradition of TFGC, including 85 percent of the Senegalese communities practicing TFGC (Diop & Askew, 2009; http://www.tostan.org/web/page/586/ sectionid/547/parentid/585/pagelevel/3/interior.asp). The public commitment element is vital to declare "a new social order that no longer accepts the practice of cutting women's genitals" (Toubia & Sharief, 2003, p. 256). Other places, such as Egypt, Nigeria, and Somalia (e.g., Ford, 2001; Gulaid, 2008; Khaja et al., 2009; Rahlenbeck & Mekonnen, 2009; Snow, Slanger, Okonofua, Oronsaye, & Wacker, 2002; Tag-Eldin et al., 2008; Yount, 2004), have shown less dramatic patterns of change.

In contrast, (feminist) responses to the exposure of "morally outrageous" (Dreger, 2006, p. 74) IGC in the 1990s were quite different (Chase, 2002; Ehrenreich & Barr, 2005) and did not lead to rapid widespread intervention for change. Intensive critique and activism by intersex activists (Chase, 1998) and organizations such as the (former) Intersex Society of North America (ISNA; http://www.isna.org/), as well as scholars (e.g., Diamond, 1999; Diamond & Sigmundson, 1997; Dreger, 1998; Kessler, 1998), has resulted in changes, notably the development of guidelines for what could be better, more integrative, and patient/family-centered practice (e.g., Lee et al., 2006): full disclosure; delaying *most* surgery from infancy; prioritizing *function* over aesthetics in determining surgical practice; the implication that the child *should* have a say in IGC. Yet this new model of care is subject to critique (e.g., http://www.intersexualite.org/Response_

to_Intersex_Initiative.html) and has not yet fully been taken up *as practice:* Some surgeons still claim appearance as an indicator of the *success* of early IGC and advocate for early intervention as associated with positive outcomes (Crawford, Warne, Grover, Southwell, & Hutson, 2009).[18] So how *best* to treat children with ambiguous genitalia—if indeed they *need* treating—is far from agreed. Furthermore, such change is often limited to medical practice, rather than challenges to dominant Western ideas of gender dimorphism (e.g., Ozar, 2006).[19]

FGCS remains largely excluded from debates about FGC (OHCHR et al., 2008), but it has been critiqued by individual gynecologists and by professional organizations (Borkenhagen, Brähler, & Kentenich, 2009; Renganathan, Cartwright, & Cardozo, 2009; Royal Australian and New Zealand College of Obstetricians and Gynaecologists, 2008); the American College of Obstetricians and Gynecologists determined that FGCS "is not medically indicated, and the safety and effectiveness of these procedures have not been documented" ("ACOG Committee Opinion No. 378," 2007). Yet professional sanctions have not been applied to surgeons (Tiefer, 2010), and change appears to involve more advertising and more genital anxiety (Braun, 2010). Activism has been small scale: The New View Campaign (http://www.newviewcampaign.org/fgcs.asp) has had some success in attracting media attention (Tiefer, 2010) and caused possible shifts to more critical commentary in the *mainstream* media (e.g., Triffin, 2010). The agenda for change regarding FGCS is not prohibition. It includes education (e.g., about the diversity of genital appearance) to change culturally based mistaken beliefs and a ban on FGCS advertising (Tiefer, 2008).

CONCLUSION: IS *ALL* FGC A REPRODUCTIVE JUSTICE ISSUE?

FGC covers a vast spectrum of practices and contexts. TFGC has been characterized as the gender oppression to end all oppressions (Dawit & Mekuria, as cited in Walley, 2002); it would be a stretch to describe FGCS thus. Taking FGC as a whole, both TFGC and IGC clearly constitute reproductive justice issues. The case of FGCS is more complex, not least because it affects (relatively) privileged women, who are framed as liberated rather than oppressed by the practice. It could be argued that the provision of private, for-profit FGCS, even in wealthy developed countries, violates principles of social justice, as it shifts health resources that are notoriously limited (Berer, 2010) away from larger scale problems.[20] Furthermore, many of the same mechanisms that operate to produce TFGC and IGC also apply to FGCS. Women who choose to have FGCS do so in response to a cluster of cultural logics informed by gendered, culturally located constructions about what a woman is, what women's sexuality *should* be like, and how it should be valued.[21] Thus, this framework can prove useful for interrogating *all* FGC.

Control over one's reproductive and sexual life and body are important rights for *all* women. Yet the *enactment* of these rights by an individual woman is not always straightforward: Choices and practices are always context bound; some choices, rightfully or not, are precluded; others are mandated. In the case of FGC, the situation is complex: Materially similar practices carry vastly different meanings, in different contexts, on different bodies, and potentially at different ages, and the balance of harm and benefit varies greatly. Fundamentally important questions are whether we think that *any* nonmedically indicated genital cutting is ever acceptable, and, if so, when and what? Partly this question is about seeking clarity about the basis for objections to, or support for (different types of, or all), FGC, so that our responses to these various issues can be just and consistent.

NOTES

1. Intersex is of course about *much more* than just genitals. The focus on genitals can itself be seen as voyeuristic, reinforcing the problem as one of ambiguous genitalia. Yet genitals do get cut, with consequences.

2. Widespread normalized male circumcision has been subject recently to substantial Western critique, including reframing *as* genital *mutilation* (e.g., Denniston, Hodges, & Milos, 2010; Johnson, 2010) and within a discourse of human rights (Delaet, 2009). Concurrently, evidence of circumcision as a protective factor against heterosexual HIV transmission to men (e.g., Williams et al., 2006) has led to its inclusion and scaling up as a key HIV prevention strategy in certain African countries since 2007 (WHO & UNAINDS, 2010). That evidence and practice are also disputed (e.g., Green et al., 2010; Svoboda, 2010).

3. Typologies are not necessarily discrete and do not necessarily map onto what women report they have had done (Elmusharaf, Elkhidir, Hoffmann, & Almroth, 2006).

4. Local meanings of different TFGC practices often differ from Western/international analyses, which needs to be recognized in interventions (Khaja et al., 2009).

5. Self-reports of TFGC and clinical judgments don't always match (both can be wrong) (Klouman et al., 2005; Mandara, 2004).

6. Intersex has been (not uncontroversially; e.g., Feder & Karkazis, 2008; Reis, 2007) renamed as disorders of sex development (DSD; Lee et al., 2006). Debates continue (e.g., Aaronson & Aaronson, 2010).

7. Such statistics are derived from *mainly* White/Western surveys; DSD conditions are distributed differently in different populations (Blackless et al., 2000).

8. Some DSDs have health risks that do require medical attention (Dreger, 1998).

9. Assignment of gender is itself contentious (Karkazis, 2008).

10. The methodological rigor of some early research is questionable, that is, it is not possible to attribute impacts *entirely* to TFGC; some harms of TFGC could (also) be attributable to other issues (Obermeyer, 2005; Shell-Duncan, 2001).

11. Adverse obstetrical outcomes may continue to affect women who migrate to the West (Johnson, Reed, Hitti, & Batra, 2005; Small et al., 2008).

12. Medicalization as a general practice is frequently critiqued (e.g., Conrad, 2007).

13. Another recent (not uncontroversial) medical intervention is *clitoral reconstruction,* which is offered in Burkina Faso by the Raelian organization Clitoraid (Jirovsky, 2010).

14. Hymenoplasty is often seen as reflecting cultural values and as needed to *protect* women from harm; it thus raises slightly different ethical issues (Cook & Dickens, 2009).

15. The International Conference on Population and Development's framing of TFGC as a reproductive rights violation was not without protest (Winkel, 1995): The human rights framework overall has been critiqued as reflecting liberal Western cultural conceptions (Kalev, 2004) and, thus, a form of cultural imperialism. Transnational, transcultural, multicultural, and indigenous perspectives offer alternative voices about (and beyond) human rights and TFGC (Abusharaf, 2006; Hernlund & Shell-Duncan, 2007a; James & Robertson, 2002b; Nnaemeka, 2005).

16. Others offer a cautious analysis of this framework, pointing to potential perils and pitfalls (Hernlund & Shell-Duncan, 2007b; Shell-Duncan, 2008).

17. Rapid change in a tradition of FGC may occur even in the absence of targeted interventions (Halila, Belmaker, Rabia, Froimovici, & Applebaum, 2009).

18. In 2010, a U.S. pediatric urologist, who practiced early IGC surgery, caused controversy because his follow-up involved annual clitoral stimulation to test for responsiveness (see Dreger & Feder, 2010).

19. Other interesting—especially queer—discussions about intersex are taking place that I have not been able to do justice to in this chapter (e.g., Holmes, 2009; Roen, 2008).

20. In contexts of limited health resources, *justice* is an ethical principle that potentially applies to FGCS (Goodman et al., 2007).

21. We should, however, be cautious about providing an analysis that simply draws attention to the sameness of different culturally located practices without attending to specificities of difference (see Pedwell, 2007, 2008).

REFERENCES

Aaronson, I. A., & Aaronson, A. J. (2010). How should we classify intersex disorders? *Journal of Pediatric Urology, 6,* 443–446.

Abusharaf, R. M. (2001). Virtuous cuts: Female genital circumcision in an African ontology. *Differences, 12*(1), 112–140.

Abusharaf, R. M. (Ed.). (2006). *Female circumcision: Multicultural perspectives.* Philadelphia: University of Pennsylvania Press.

ACOG Committee Opinion No. 378: Vaginal "rejuvenation" and cosmetic vaginal procedures. (2007). *Obstetrics & Gynecology, 110,* 737–738.

Ahmadu, F. (2007). "Ain't I a woman too?" Challenging myths of sexual dysfunction in circumcised women. In Y. Hernlund & B. Shell-Duncan (Eds.), *Transcultural bodies: Female genital cutting in global context* (pp. 278–310). New Brunswick, NJ: Rutgers University Press.

Ako, M. A., & Akweongo, P. (2009). The limited effectiveness of legislation against female genital mutilation and the role of community beliefs in Upper East Region, Ghana. *Reproductive Health Matters, 17*(34), 47–54.

Allotey, P., Manderson, L., & Grover, S. (2001). The politics of female genital surgery in displaced communities. *Critical Public Health, 11*(3), 189–201.

American Society for Aesthetic Plastic Surgery. (2009). Statistics 2008. Retrieved from http://www.surgery.org/press/statistics-2008.php.

American Society for Aesthetic Plastic Surgery. (2010). Statistics 2009. Retrieved from http://www.surgery.org/sites/default/files/2009stats.pdf.

Anuforo, P. O., Oyedele, L., & Pacquiao, D. F. (2004). Comparative study of meanings, beliefs, and practices of female circumcision among three Nigerian tribes in the United States and Nigeria. *Journal of Transcultural Nursing, 15*(2), 103–113.

Asekun-Olarinmoye, E. O., & Amusan, O. A. (2008). The impact of health education on attitudes towards female genital mutilation (FGM) in a rural Nigerian community. *European Journal of Contraception and Reproductive Health Care, 13,* 289–297.

Bagnol, B., & Mariano, E. (2008). Elongation of the labia minora and use of vaginal products to enhance eroticism: Can these practices be considered FGM? *Finnish Journal of Ethnicity and Migration, 3*(2), 42–63.

Banks, E., Meirik, O., Farley, T., Akande, O., Bathija, H., & Ali, M. (2006). Female genital mutilation and obstetric outcome: WHO collaborative prospective study in six African countries. *Lancet, 367,* 1835–1841.

Behrendt, A., & Moritz, S. (2005). Posttraumatic stress disorder and memory problems after female genital mutilation. *American Journal of Psychiatry, 162,* 1000–1002.

Berer, M. (2010). Labia reduction for non-therapeutic reasons vs. female genital mutilation: contradictions in law and practice in Britain. *Reproductive Health Matters, 18*(35), 106–110.

Berkey, J. P. (1996). Circumcision circumscribed: Female excision and cultural accommodation in the medieval Near East. *International Journal of Middle East Studies, 28*(1), 19–38.

Blackless, M., Charuvastra, A., Derryck, A., Fausto-Sterling, A., Lauzanne, K., & Lee, E. (2000). How sexually dimorphic are we? Review and synthesis. *American Journal of Human Biology, 12,* 151–166.

Boddy, J. (2008). Clash of selves: Gender, personhood, and human rights discourse in colonial Sudan. *Finnish Journal of Ethnicity & Migration, 3*(2), 4–13.

Borkenhagen, A., Brähler, E., & Kentenich, H. (2009). Ein gefährlicher trend. *Deutsches Ärzteblatt, 106*(11), A500–A502.

Boyle, E. H. (2002). *Female genital cutting: Cultural conflict in the global community.* Baltimore: Johns Hopkins University Press.

Boyle, E. H., & Preves, S. E. (2000). National politics as international process: The case of anti-female-genital-cutting laws. *Law & Society Review, 34,* 703–737.

Bramwell, R., Morland, C., & Garden, A. S. (2007). Expectations and experience of labial reduction: a qualitative study. *British Journal of Obstetrics and Gynaecology, 114,* 1493–1499.

Braun, V. (2005). In search of (better) female sexual pleasure: Female genital "cosmetic" surgery. *Sexualities, 8,* 407–424.

Braun, V. (2009a). Selling the "perfect" vulva. In C. Heyes & M. Jones (Eds.), *Cosmetic surgery: A feminist primer* (pp. 133–149). Farnham, UK: Ashgate.

Braun, V. (2009b). "The women are doing it for themselves": The rhetoric of choice and agency around female genital "cosmetic surgery." *Australian Feminist Studies, 24,* 233–249.

Braun, V. (2010). Female genital cosmetic surgery: A critical review of current knowledge and contemporary debates. *Journal of Women's Health, 19,* 1393–1407.

Braun, V., & Tiefer, L. (2010). The "designer vagina" and the pathologisation of female genital diversity: interventions for change. *Radical Psychology, 18*(1). Retrieved from http://www.radicalpsychology.org/vol8–1/brauntiefer. html.

Budiharsana, M., Amaliah, L., Utomo, B., & Erwinia. (2003). *Female circumcision in Indonesia: Extent, implications, and possible interventions to uphold women's health rights.* Jakarta: Population Council.

Catania, L., Abdulcadir, O., Puppo, V., Verde, J. B., Abdulcadir, J., & Abdulcadir, D. (2007). Pleasure and orgasm in women with female genital mutilation/cutting (FGM/C). *Journal of Sexual Medicine, 4,* 1666–1678.

Chambers, C. (2008). *Sex, culture, and justice: The limits of choice.* University Park: Pennsylvania State University Press.

Chase, C. (1998). Hermaphrodites with attitude: Mapping the emergence of intersex political activism. *GLQ, 4*(2), 189–211.

Chase, C. (2002). "Cultural practice" or "reconstructive surgery"? U.S. genital cutting, the intersex movement, and medical double standards. In S. M. James & C. C. Robertson (Eds.), *Genital cutting and transnational sisterhood: Disputing U.S. polemics* (pp. 126–151). Urbana: University of Illinois Press.

Clarence-Smith, W. G. (2008). Islam and female genital cutting in southeast Asia: The weight of the past. *Finnish Journal of Ethnicity and Migration, 3*(2), 14–22.

Committee on Bioethics. (2010). Ritual genital cutting of female minors. *Pediatrics, 125,* 1088–1093.

Conrad, P. (2007). *The medicalization of society.* Baltimore: Johns Hopkins University Press.

Cook, R. J. (2008). Ethical concerns in female genital cutting. *African Journal of Reproductive Health, 12*(1), 7–11.

Cook, R. J., & Dickens, B. M. (2009). Hymen reconstruction: Ethical and legal issues. *International Journal of Gynecology & Obstetrics, 107,* 266–269.

Cook, R. J., & Dickens, B. M. (2010). Special commentary on the issue of reinfibulation. *International Journal of Gynecology & Obstetrics, 109,* 97–99.

Corrêa, S. (1997). From reproductive health to sexual rights: Achievements and future challenges. *Reproductive Health Matters, 5*(10), 107–116.

Cottingham, J., & Kismodi, E. (2009). Protecting girls and women from harmful practices affecting their health: Are we making progress? *International Journal of Gynecology & Obstetrics, 106,* 128–131.

Crawford, J. M., Warne, G., Grover, S., Southwell, B. R., & Hutson, J. M. (2009). Results from a pediatric surgical centre justify early intervention in disorders of sex development. *Journal of Pediatric Surgery, 44,* 413–416.

Creighton, S. M. (2001). Surgery for intersex. *Journal of the Royal Society of Medicine, 94,* 218–220.

Creighton, S. M. (2004). Long-term outcome of feminization surgery: The London experience. *BJU International, 93,* 44–46.

Creighton, S. M., Greenberg, J. A., Roen, K., & Volcano, D. L. (2009). Intersex practice, theory, and activism: A roundtable discussion. *GLQ, 15,* 249–260.

Crouch, N. S., & Creighton, S. M. (2007). Long-term functional outcomes of female genital reconstruction in childhood. *BJU International, 100,* 403–407.

Crouch, N. S., Liao, L-M., Woodhouse, C.R.J., Conway, G. S., & Creighton, S. M. (2008). Sexual function and genital sensitivity following feminizing genitoplasty for congenital adrenal hyperplasia. *Journal of Urology, 179,* 634–638.

Davis, S. W. (2002). Loose lips sink ships. *Feminist Studies, 28*(1), 7–35.

de Andrade, D. D. (2010). On norms and bodies: Findings from field research on cosmetic surgery in Rio de Janeiro, Brazil. *Reproductive Health Matters, 18*(35), 74–83.

Delaet, D. L. (2009). Framing male circumcision as a human rights issue? Contributions to the debate over the universality of human rights. *Journal of Human Rights, 8,* 405–426.

de María Arana, M. (2005). *A human rights investigation into the medical "normalization" of intersex people.* Retrieved from http://www.glhv.org.au/files/san_fran_intersex_report.pdf.

Denniston, G. C., Hodges, F. M., & Milos, M. F. (Eds.). (2010). *Genital autonomy: Protecting personal choice.* New York: Springer.

Diamond, M. (1999). Pediatric management of ambiguous and traumatized genitalia. *Journal of Urology, 162,* 1021–1028.

Diamond, M., & Sigmundson, H. K. (1997). Management of intersexuality: Guidelines for dealing with persons with ambiguous genitalia. *Archives of Pediatric & Adolescent Medicine, 151,* 1046–1050.

Diop, N. J., & Askew, I. (2009). The effectiveness of a community-based education program on abandoning female genital mutilation cutting in Senegal. *Studies in Family Planning, 40,* 307–318.

Donors Working Group on Female Genital Mutilation/Cutting. (2008). *Toward the abandonment of female genital mutilation/cutting (FGM/C).* Retrieved from http://www.fgm-cdonor.org/publications/dwg_platform_action.pdf.

Dreger, A. D. (1998). *Hermaphrodites and the medical invention of sex.* Cambridge, MA: Harvard University Press.

Dreger, A. D. (2006). Intersex and human rights: the long view. In S. E. Sytsma (Ed.), *Ethics and intersex* (pp. 73–86). Dordrecht, the Netherlands: Kluwer.

Dreger, A. D., & Feder, E. K. (2010). Bad vibrations. *Bioethics Forum.* Retrieved from http://www.thehastingscenter.org/Bioethicsforum/Post.aspx?id=4730&blogid=140.

Dreger, A. D., & Herndon, A. M. (2009). Progress and politics in the intersex rights movement: Feminist theory in action. *GLQ, 15,* 199–224.

Dustin, M. (2010). Female genital mutilation/cutting in the UK: Challenging the inconsistencies. *European Journal of Women's Studies, 17*(1), 7–23.

Ehrenreich, N., & Barr, M. (2005). Intersex surgery, female genital cutting, and the selective condemnation of "cultural practices." *Harvard Civil Rights-Civil Liberties Law Review, 40*(1), 71–140.

El-Mouelhy, M. T., & Johansen, R. E. B. (2010). *Men's and women's perceptions of the relationship between female genital mutilation and women's sexuality in three communities in Egypt.* Geneva: World Health Organization, Department of Reproductive Health and Research.

Elmusharaf, S., Elkhidir, I., Hoffmann, S., & Almroth, L. (2006). A case-control study on the association between female genital mutilation and sexually transmitted infections in Sudan. *British Journal of Obstetrics and Gynaecology, 113,* 469–474.

Elnashar, A., & Abdelhady, R. (2007). The impact of female genital cutting on health of newly married women. *International Journal of Gynecology & Obstetrics, 97,* 238–244.

Essén, B., Blomkvist, A., Helström, L., & Johnsdotter, S. (2010). The experience and responses of Swedish health professionals to patients requesting virginity restoration (hymen repair). *Reproductive Health Matters, 18*(35), 38–46.

Essén, B., & Johnsdotter, S. (2004). Female genital mutilation in the West: traditional circumcision versus genital cosmetic surgery. *Acta Obstetricia et Gynecologica Scandinavica, 83,* 611–613.

Fahmy, A., El-Mouelhy, M. T., & Ragab, A. R. (2010). Female genital mutilation/cutting and issues of sexuality in Egypt. *Reproductive Health Matters, 18*(36), 181–190.

Feder, E. K. (2006). "In their best interests": Parents' experience of atypical genitalia. In E. Parens (Ed.), *Surgically shaping children: Technology, ethics, and the pursuit of normality* (pp. 189–210). Baltimore: Johns Hopkins University Press.

Feder, E. K., & Karkazis, K. (2008). What's in a name? The controversy over "disorders of sex development." *Hastings Center Report, 38*(5), 33–36.

Ford, N. (2001). Tackling female genital cutting in Somalia. *Lancet, 358,* 1179–1179.

Gill, R. (2008). Empowerment/sexism: Figuring female Sexual agency in contemporary advertising. *Feminism & Psychology, 18,* 35–60.

Gillespie, D., & Melching, M. (2010). The transformative power of democracy and human rights in nonformal education: The case of TOSTAN. *Adult Education Quarterly, 60,* 477–498.

Gilliam, M. L., Neustadt, A., & Gordon, R. (2009). A call to incorporate a reproductive justice agenda into reproductive health clinical practice and policy. *Contraception, 79,* 243–246.

Goodman, M. P., Bachmann, G., Johnson, C., Fourcroy, J. L., Goldstein, A., Goldstein, G., et al. (2007). Is elective vulvar plastic surgery ever warranted, and what screening should be conducted preoperatively? *Journal of Sexual Medicine, 4,* 269–276.

Gough, B., Weyman, N., Alderson, J., Butler, G., & Stoner, M. (2008). "They did not have a word": The parental quest to locate a "true sex" for their intersex children. *Psychology & Health, 23,* 493–507.

Green, F. J. (2005). From clitoridectomies to "designer vaginas": The medical construction of heteronormative female bodies and sexuality through female genital cutting. *Sexualities, Evolution & Gender, 7*(2), 153–187.

Green, L. W., Travis, J. W., McAllister, R. G., Peterson, K. W., Vardanyan, A. N., & Craig, A. (2010). Male circumcision and HIV prevention: Insufficient evidence and neglected external validity. *American Journal of Preventive Medicine, 39,* 479–482.

Greenberg, J. A. (2006). International legal developments protecting the autonomy rights of sexual minorities: Who should determine the appropriate treatment for an intersex infant? In S. E. Sytsma (Ed.), *Ethics and intersex* (pp. 87–102). Dordrecht, the Netherlands: Kluwer.

Gruenbaum, E. (1996). The cultural debate over female circumcision: The Sudanese are arguing this one out for themselves. *Medical Anthropology Quarterly, 10,* 455–475.

Gruenbaum, E. (2001). *The female circumcision controversy: An anthropological perspective.* Philadelphia: University of Pennsylvania Press.

Gruenbaum, E. (2005a). Feminist activism for the abolition of FGC in Sudan. *Journal of Middle East Women's Studies, 1*(2), 89–111.

Gruenbaum, E. (2005b). Socio-cultural dynamics of female genital cutting: Research findings, gaps, and directions. *Culture, Health, & Sexuality, 7,* 429–441.

Gruenbaum, E. (2006). Sexuality issues in the movement to abolish female genital cutting in Sudan. *Medical Anthropology Quarterly, 20*(1), 121–138.

Gulaid, U. J. (2008). The challenge of female genital mutilation in Somaliland. *Finnish Journal of Ethnicity and Migration, 3*(2), 90–91.

Gunning, I. R. (2002). Female genital surgeries: Eradication measures at the Western local level—A cautionary tale. In S. M. James & C. C. Robertson (Eds.), *Genital cutting and transnational sisterhood: Disputing U.S. polemics* (pp. 114–125). Urbana: University of Illinois Press.

Haas, K. (2004). Who will make room for the intersexed? *American Journal of Law and Medicine, 30*(1), 41–68.

Halila, S., Belmaker, R., Rabia, Y. A., Froimovici, M., & Applebaum, J. (2009). Disappearance of female genital mutilation from the Bedouin population of southern Israel. *Journal of Sexual Medicine, 6*(1), 70–73.

Hassanin, I.M.A., Saleh, R., Bedaiwy, A. A., Peterson, R. S., & Bedaiwy, M. A. (2008). Prevalence of female genital cutting in upper Egypt: 6 years after enforcement of prohibition law. *Reproductive Biomedicine Online, 16,* 27–31.

Hegarty, P., & Chase, C. (2000). Intersex activism, feminism, and psychology: Opening a dialogue on theory, research, and clinical practice. *Feminism & Psychology, 10,* 117–132.

Hernlund, Y., & Shell-Duncan, B. (2007a). *Transcultural bodies: Female genital cutting in global context.* New Brunswick, NJ: Rutgers University Press.

Hernlund, Y., & Shell-Duncan, B. (2007b). Transcultural positions: Negotiating rights and culture. In Y. Hernlund & B. Shell-Duncan (Eds.), *Transcultural bodies: Female genital cutting in global context* (pp. 1–45). New Brunswick, NJ: Rutgers University Press.

Holmes, M. (Ed.). (2009). *Critical intersex.* Farnham, UK: Ashgate.

Hospital Episode Statistics. (2009). Number of labial reductions. Retrieved from http://www.hesonline.nhs.uk.

Hussein, F-H. M. (2008). Changing attitudes towards FGM in the Somali community in London. *Finnish Journal of Ethnicity and Migration, 3*(2), 92–95.

James, S. M., & Robertson, C. C. (2002a). Introduction: reimaging transnational sisterhood. In S. M. James & C. C. Robertson (Eds.), *Genital cutting and transnational sisterhood: Disputing U.S. polemics* (pp. 5–15). Urbana: University of Illinois Press.

James, S. M., & Robertson, C. C. (Eds.). (2002b). *Genital cutting and transnational sisterhood: Disputing U.S. polemics.* Urbana: University of Illinois Press.

Jeffreys, S. (2005). *Beauty and misogyny: Harmful cultural practices in the West.* London: Routledge.

Jirovsky, E. (2010). Views of women and men in Bobo-Dioulasso, Burkina Faso, on three forms of female genital modification. *Reproductive Health Matters, 18*(35), 84–93.

Johnsdotter, S., & Essén, B. (2010). Genitals and ethnicity: The politics of genital modifications. *Reproductive Health Matters, 18*(35), 29–37.

Johnsdotter, S., Moussa, K., Carlbom, A., Aregai, R., & Essén, B. (2009). "Never my daughters": A qualitative study regarding attitude change toward female genital cutting among Ethiopian and Eritrean families in Sweden. *Health Care for Women International, 30,* 114–133.

Johnson, E. B., Reed, S. D., Hitti, J., & Batra, M. (2005). Increased risk of adverse pregnancy outcome among Somali immigrants in Washington state. *American Journal of Obstetrics and Gynecology, 193,* 475–482.

Johnson, M. (2010). Male genital mutilation: Beyond the tolerable? *Ethnicities, 10,* 181–207.

Kalev, H. D. (2004). Cultural rights or human rights: The case of female genital mutilation. *Sex Roles, 51,* 339–348.

Karkazis, K. A. (2008). *Fixing sex: Intersex, medical authority, and lived experience.* Durham, NC: Duke University Press.

Kessler, S. J. (1990). The medical construction of gender: Case management of intersexed infants. *Signs, 16,* 3–26.

Kessler, S. J. (1998). *Lessons from the intersexed.* New Brunswick, NJ: Rutgers University Press.

Khaja, K., Barkdull, C., Augustine, M., & Cunningham, D. (2009). Female genital cutting African women speak out. *International Social Work, 52*(6), 727–741.

Khalife, N. (2010, September 18). A fatwa on FGM is only part of the solution. *Awene.* Retrieved from http://www.hrw.org/en/news/2010/09/18/fatwa-fgm-only-part-solution.

Klouman, E., Manongi, R., & Klepp, K. I. (2005). Self-reported and observed female genital cutting in rural Tanzania: Associated demographic factors, HIV, and sexually transmitted infections. *Tropical Medicine & International Health, 10*(1), 105–115.

Koster, M., & Price, L. L. (2008). Rwandan female genital modification: elongation of the *labia minora* and the use of local botanical species. *Culture, Health, & Sexuality, 10,* 191–204.

Lane, S. D., & Rubinstein, R. A. (1996). Judging the other: Responding to traditional female genital surgeries. *Hastings Center Report, 26*(3), 31–40.

Lee, P. A., Houk, C. P., Ahmed, S. F., Hughes, I. A., & in collaboration with the participants in the International Consensus Conference on Intersex organized by the Lawson Wilkins Pediatric Endocrine Society and the European Society for Paediatric Endocrinology. (2006). Consensus statement on management of intersex disorders. *Pediatrics, 118*(2), e488–500.

Leye, E., & Deblonde, J. (2004). *Legislation in Europe regarding female genital mutilation and the implementation of the law in Belgium, France, Spain, Sweden, and the UK.* Ghent, Belgium: International Centre for Reproductive Health.

Liao, L-M., Michala, L., & Creighton, S. M. (2010). Labial surgery for well women: A review of the literature. *British Journal of Obstetrics & Gynaecology, 117*(1), 20–25.

Mandara, M. U. (2004). Female genital mutilation in Nigeria. *International Journal of Gynecology & Obstetrics, 84,* 291–298.

Martin-Hilber, A., Hull, T. H., Preston-Whyte, E., Bagnol, B., Smit, J., Wacharasin, C., et al. (2009). A cross cultural study of vaginal practices and sexuality: Implications for sexual health. *Social Science & Medicine, 70,* 392–400.

Merli, C. (2008). Sunat for girls in southern Thailand: Its relation to traditional midwifery, male circumcision and other obstetrical practices. *Finnish Journal of Ethnicity and Migration, 3*(2), 32–41.

Minto, C. L., Liao, L-M., Woodhouse, C. R. J., Ransley, P. G., & Creighton, S. M. (2003). The effect of clitoral surgery on sexual outcome in individuals who have intersex conditions with ambiguous genitalia: a cross-sectional study. *Lancet, 361,* 1252–1257.

Murray, S. (2009). Within or beyond the binary/boundary? Intersex infants and parental decisions *Australian Feminist Studies, 24,* 265–274.

Muslim leaders ban female circumcision. (2010). *Sister Namibia, 22*(1), 33.

Newland, L. (2006). Female circumcision: Muslim identities and zero tolerance policies in rural west Java. *Women's Studies International Forum, 29,* 394–404.

Njambi, W. N. (2004a). A discourse in transition: Extending feminist dialogues on female circumcision. *Feminist Theory, 5,* 325–328.

Njambi, W. N. (2004b). Dualisms and female bodies in representations of African female circumcision: A feminist critique. *Feminist Theory, 5,* 281–303.

Nnaemeka, O. (Ed.). (2005). *Female circumcision and the politics of knowledge: African women in imperialist discourses.* Westport, CT: Praeger.

Obermeyer, C. M. (2005). The consequences of female circumcision for health and sexuality: An update on the evidence. *Culture, Health & Sexuality, 7,* 443–461.

OHCHR, UNAINDS, UNDP, UNECA, UNESCO, UNFPA, et al. (2008). *Eliminating female genital mutilation: An interagency statement.* Geneva: World Health Organization.

Ozar, D. T. (2006). Toward a more inclusive conception of gender-diversity for intersex advocacy and ethics. In S. E. Sytsma (Ed.), *Ethics and intersex* (pp. 17–46). Dordrecht, the Netherlands: Kluwer.

Pedwell, C. (2007). Theorizing "African" female genital cutting and "Western" body modifications: A critique of the continuum and analogue approaches. *Feminist Review, 86*(1), 45–66.

Pedwell, C. (2008). Weaving relational webs: Theorizing cultural difference and embodied practice. *Feminist Theory, 9*(1), 87–107.

Petchesky, R. P. (2000). Human rights, reproductive health, and economic justice: Why they are indivisible. *Reproductive Health Matters, 8*(15), 12–17.

Push for continent-wide ban on female genital mutilation. (2010). *Sister Namibia, 22*(2), 32.

Putranti, B. D. (2008). To Islamize: Becoming a real woman or commercialized practices? Questioning female genital cutting in Indonesia. *Finnish Journal of Ethnicity and Migration, 3*(2), 23–31.

Rahlenbeck, S. I., & Mekonnen, W. (2009). Growing rejection of female genital cutting among women of reproductive age in Amhara, Ethiopia. *Culture, Health, & Sexuality, 11,* 443–452.

Rahman, A., & Toubia, N. (2000). *Female genital mutilation: A guide to laws and policies worldwide.* London: Zed Books.

Ras-Work, B. (2006). *The impact of harmful traditional practices on the girl child*. New York: United Nations, Division for the Advancement of Women.

Reis, E. (2007). Divergence or disorder? The politics of naming intersex. *Perspectives in Biology and Medicine, 50*, 535–543.

Renganathan, A., Cartwright, R., & Cardozo, L. (2009). Gynecological cosmetic surgery. *Expert Review of Obstetrics & Gynecology, 4*(2), 101–104.

Robertson, C. C. (2002). Getting beyond the ew! factor: Rethinking U.S. approaches to African female genital cutting. In S. M. James & C. C. Robertson (Eds.), *Genital cutting and transnational sisterhood: Disputing U.S. polemics* (pp. 54–86). Urbana: University of Illinois Press.

Robotham, J. (2010, November 8). More women opt for genital plastic surgery. *Age*. Retrieved from http://www.theage.com.au/lifestyle/wellbeing/more-women-opt-for-genital-plastic-surgery-20101107–17j1f.html.

Roen, K. (2008). "But we have to do something": Surgical "correction" of atypical genitalia. *Body & Society, 14*(1), 47–66.

Rogers, J. (2009). A child is being mutilated: Fantasies of female genital mutilation law. *Australian Feminist Studies, 24*, 181–194.

Royal Australian and New Zealand College of Obstetricians and Gynaecologists. (2008). *Vaginal "rejuvenation" and cosmetic vaginal procedures* [New College Statement C-Gyn 24]. Melbourne, Victoria, Australia: Royal Australian and New Zealand College of Obstetricians and Gynaecologists.

Sax, L. (2002). How common is intersex? A response to Anne Fausto-Sterling. *Journal of Sex Research, 39*, 174–178.

Scorgie, F., Beksinska, M., Chersich, M., Kunene, B., Hilber, A. M., & Smit, J. (2010). "Cutting for love": Genital incisions to enhance sexual desirability and commitment in KwaZulu-Natal, South Africa. *Reproductive Health Matters, 18*(35), 64–73.

Serour, G. I. (2010). The issue of reinfibulation. *International Journal of Gynecology & Obstetrics, 109*, 93–96.

Serour, G. I., & Faúndes, A. (2006). Female genital cutting: FIGO Committee for the Ethical Aspects of Human Reproduction and Women's Health and FIGO Committee on Women's Sexual and Reproductive Rights. *International Journal of Gynecology & Obstetrics, 94*, 176–177.

Shell-Duncan, B. (2001). The medicalization of female "circumcision": Harm reduction or promotion of a dangerous practice? *Social Science & Medicine, 52*, 1013–1028.

Shell-Duncan, B. (2008). From health to human rights: Female genital cutting and the politics of intervention. *American Anthropologist, 110*, 225–236.

Shell-Duncan, B., & Johansen, R.E.B. (2010). *Dynamics of decision-making and change in the practice of female genital mutilation in the Gambia and Senegal*. Geneva: World Health Organization, Department of Reproductive Health and Research.

Silliman, J., Freid, M. G., Ross, L., & Gutierrez, E. R. (2004). *Undivided rights: Women of Color organize for reproductive justice*. Cambridge, MA: South End Press.

Small, R., Gagnon, A., Gissler, M., Zeitlin, J., Bennis, M., Glazier, R. H., et al. (2008). Somali women and their pregnancy outcomes postmigration: data from six receiving countries. *British Journal of Obstetrics and Gynaecology, 115*, 1630–1640.

Smith, C. (2008). Creating spaces: Challenging conventional discursive norms surrounding the marking of women's bodies. *Finnish Journal of Ethnicity and Migration, 3*(2), 54–63.

Snow, R. C., Slanger, T. E., Okonofua, F. E., Oronsaye, F., & Wacker, J. (2002). Female genital cutting in southern urban and peri-urban Nigeria: Self-reported validity, social determinants and secular decline. *Tropical Medicine & International Health, 7*(1), 91–100.

Sullivan, N. (2007). "The price to pay for our common good": Genital modification and the somatechnologies of cultural (in)difference. *Social Semiotics, 17,* 395–409.

Svoboda, J. S. (2010). *The limits of the law: Comparative analysis of legal and extralegal methods to control body mutilation practices.* New York: Kluwer.

Tag-Eldin, M. A., Gadallah, M. A., Ai-Tayeb, M. N., Abdel-Aty, M., Mansour, E., & Sallem, M. (2008). Prevalence of female genital cutting among Egyptian girls. *Bulletin of the World Health Organization, 86,* 269–274.

Tiefer, L. (2008). Female cosmetic genital surgery: freakish or inevitable? Analysis from medical marketing, bioethics, and feminist theory. *Feminism & Psychology, 18,* 466–479.

Tiefer, L. (2010). Activism on the medicalization of sex and female genital cosmetic surgery by the New View Campaign in the United States. *Reproductive Health Matters, 18*(35), 56–63.

Toubia, N. F., & Sharief, E. H. (2003). Female genital mutilation: have we made progress? *International Journal of Gynecology & Obstetrics, 82,* 251–261.

Triffin, M. (2010, July). WARNING: These doctors may be dangerous to your vagina. *Cosmopolitan,* 159–161.

Walley, C. J. (2002). Searching for "voices": Feminism, anthropology, and the global debate over female genital operations. In S. M. James & C. C. Robertson (Eds.), *Genital cutting and transnational sisterhood: Disputing U.S. polemics* (pp. 17–53). Urbana: University of Illinois Press.

Williams, B. G., Lloyd-Smith, J. O., Gouws, E., Hankins, C., Getz, W. M., Hargrove, J., et al. (2006). The potential impact of male circumcision on HIV in sub-Saharan Africa. *PLoS Medicine, 3,* e262.

Winkel, E. (1995). A Muslim perspective on female circumcision. *Women & Health, 23,* 1–7.

World Health Organization. (2000a). *Female genital mutilation: A handbook for front-line workers.* Geneva: Author.

World Health Organization. (2000b). *A systematic review of the health implications of female genital mutilation including sequelae in childbirth.* Geneva: Author, Department of Women's Health.

World Health Organization. (2010a). *Global strategy to stop health-care providers from performing female genital mutilation* Geneva: Author.

World Health Organization. (2010b). *Measuring sexual health: Conceptual and practical considerations and related indicators.* Geneva: Author.

World Health Organization, & UNAINDS. (2010). *Progress in male circumcision scale-up: country implementation and research update.* Geneva: Author.

World Health Organization, UNFPA, & UNICEF. (2009). *Technical consultation on medicalization of female genital mutilation.* Retrieved from http://www.unfpa.org/public/site/global/lang/en/pid/2942.

Yoder, P. S., & Khan, S. (2008). *Number of women circumcised in Africa: The production of a total.* Washington, DC: USAID.

Yount, K. M. (2004). Symbolic gender politics, religious group identity, and the decline in female genital cutting in Minya, Egypt. *Social Forces, 82,* 1063–1090.

Yount, K. M., & Abraham, B. K. (2007). Female genital cutting and HIV/AIDS among Kenyan women. *Studies in Family Planning, 38*(2), 73–88.

Chapter 3

Women's Power in Relationships: A Matter of Social Justice

Kathryn L. Norsworthy, Margaret A. McLaren, and Laura D. Waterfield

> Reproductive liberty must encompass more than the protection of an individual woman's choice to end her pregnancy. It must encompass the full range of procreative activities, including the ability to bear a child, and it must acknowledge that we make reproductive decisions within a social context, including inequalities of wealth and power. *Reproductive freedom is a matter of social justice, not individual choice.*
>
> (Roberts, 1997, p. 6).

The exploration of women's power in relationships within the context of global reproductive justice is complicated. As Roberts (1997) observed, often women's reproduction is reduced to a discussion of choice as if each woman is an individual divorced from familial, community, societal, cultural, and political forces that influence her level of empowerment or constraint in reproductive decision making.

Understanding women's power in relationships involves integrating the contributions of feminists from various regions of the Global South

and the Global North, as well as from diverse social groups within regions and countries. We deliberately use the terms *Global South* and *Global
North* to challenge the hierarchies implicit in references to these parts of
the world, such as *developed* and *developing* or *First World* and *Third World*.
As Chandra Mohanty (2003) explained,

> "North/South" is used to distinguish between affluent, privileged
> nations and communities, and economically and politically mar-
> ginalized nations and communities, as is "Western/non-Western."
> While these terms are meant to loosely distinguish the northern
> and southern hemispheres, affluent and marginal nations and com-
> munities obviously do not line up neatly within this geographical
> frame.... An example of this is Arif Dirlik's formulation of North/
> South as metaphorical rather than geographical distinction, where
> "North" refers to the pathways of transnational capital and "South"
> to the marginalized poor of the world regardless of geographical dis-
> tinction. (pp. 226–227)

Of particular interest are the contributions of transnational, postcolonial, socialist, radical, and liberal feminists as tools for understanding
the complexities of power, choice, agency, and rights within and across
countries, regions, and cultures. Transnational and postcolonial feminists
(Mohanty, 2003; Narayan, 2000; Tripp, 2006) explain that all women reside within societies, institutions, and communities constructed based on
systems of inequality and privilege that intersect and often profoundly
influence women's power and choice within their relationships. Further,
Mohanty (2003) observed that a decolonized feminist approach emphasizes that gender is not always the central or most important identity or
social location for women negotiating reproductive matters within their
relationships. Recognition that the interconnections and mutual influences of culture, race, ethnicity, sexual orientation, age, religion, and/or
gender intersect with women's economic, cultural, and sociopolitical context allows us to appreciate the realities of women's lives and their access
to power in their relationships.

Acknowledging the barriers, constraints, and differential levels of
power inherent in women's relationships and reproductive decision making also necessitates an appreciation for the role of justice. In 2005, the
U.S.-based Asian Communities for Reproductive Justice (2010, p. 242)
wisely noted:

> We believe reproductive justice is the complete physical, mental,
> spiritual, political, economic, and social well being of women and
> girls, and that it will be achieved when women and girls have the
> economic, social, and political power and resources to make healthy

decisions about our bodies, sexuality, and reproduction for ourselves, our families and our communities. For this to become a reality, we need to make change on the individual, community, institutional, and societal levels.

For example, although White U.S. feminists reside in a dominant culture that prizes individual freedom, rights, and responsibility, they encounter a multitude of social, political, economic, and cultural contexts and circumstances that influence their power in relationships, limit or facilitate their right to choose, and involve different forms of oppression, such as sexism, classism, and homophobia, that impinge on their social and relational power. Further, for women from cultural backgrounds where more communal worldviews and values of interdependence are present, the most important issues that influence their exercise of power in their relationships might involve interwoven cultural expectations regarding when and if to get married and to bear children and the socially prescribed expectation that women will take care of parents in their old age.

As we shall see, wealth, social class, and access to resources play important roles in determining the extent to which women have power in their intimate relationships and in making choices about reproductive issues. And, of course, one is never simply a woman located in a social class, but always a woman of a particular race, sexuality, culture, religious background, and ethnicity. This perspective recognizes that a network of systemic inequalities affect relationships between women and men, as well as relationships among women.

Often, dominant cultures follow a model that exemplifies hierarchical relationships and power-over approaches. These dominant cultures represent themselves as the norm, which results in the simultaneous subordination and *othering* of those who are different from "the norm." Griscom (1992, p. 391) stated that "White middle-class women have remained the norm, and women of color, poor women, lesbian women, and the like have been named 'different.' " It is this unbalanced distribution of power, rights, privilege, and access to resources that often keeps women from the Global North and Global South locked into distinctly polar positions. Thus, we are also interested in how women's lives are constructed within particular nations, societies, and cultures; the importance of local and national social movements; and dialogue across national boundaries that is aimed at building cross-border alliances (Mohanty, 2003).

In this chapter, we present a decolonized, social justice framework for analyzing women's power in their relationships and reproductive lives. To this end, we integrate perspectives from various feminisms into discussions of power and choice in the lives of women across the globe, and we show how power plays out in women's relationships and their reproductive lives given their intersecting identities, social locations, family, community, sociocultural, economic, and political contexts. We consider women's power both in their intimate relationships as well as in their relationships with one another, particularly across identities and social locations that are connected to privilege and oppression. As we are all interconnected, it is important to understand how systems of inequality and privilege play out among women situated differently in global and local power arrangements; for example, an economically advantaged woman's choice to utilize the surrogacy services of a poor woman can impact both women's power in their own relationships and reproductive decision making. Finally, we conclude the chapter by discussing a feminist vision in relation to women, power, and relationships, including ways that women can work in solidarity within and across borders to promote reproductive justice and rights and toward the empowerment of women across identities, social locations, and social contexts.

THE DYNAMICS OF POWER IN EVERYDAY LIFE

To illustrate the complexities involved in an exploration of women's power in relationships, consider the following dilemmas faced by women from different cultures and regions of the world.

Ying, a 27-year-old heterosexual woman from Shan State in Burma, lives in exile in Thailand due to the brutality perpetrated on her ethnic minority group by the military dictatorship in her home country. Ying lives without legal documentation; thus, she is constantly concerned about her safety and security because if the Thai government discovered her presence, she would be immediately deported and imprisoned in Burma. She is also vulnerable to sexual exploitation by the Thai men with whom she comes in contact while working as a cleaning woman in a local factory because she has no legal recourse should she be victimized. Her spouse, Wayan, is actively involved in an armed resistance movement by the Shan in their home state. They see one another every few months when he comes across the border to visit, and Ying depends on him for financial support for herself and her parents back in Burma. Wayan would very much like to have a child, particularly because he comes from a culture in which children signify the fulfillment of his masculinity, though caring for children is considered the responsibility of women. Ying, who feels the pressures of her culture because women are not considered complete until they are married and have children, is experiencing significant stress about this decision because her family is in Burma so she would have little support in her role as a mother. She also has reservations about bringing a child into her stress-filled life as a refugee without legal documentation and, thus, restricted access to adequate financial resources, health care, and educational opportunities. Finally, because she does not have access to medical care, she cannot utilize birth control methods such as the pill or IUD or access prenatal care should she become pregnant. In recent months, Wayan has become increasingly insistent that they not wait, and he has, at times, threatened to divorce Ying if she does not comply with his wishes.

Tara is a 28-year-old heterosexual, upper-middle-class, White-identified Australian woman of Italian descent who lives in Melbourne, Australia. She cohabitates with Josh, her partner of 8 years. Tara is currently enrolled in a doctoral program in engineering, and Josh is an architect. They have been discussing children, as Tara is nearing the end of her program and Josh would like to start a family as soon as possible. Tara's Roman Catholic parents, who are first-generation immigrants, have been waiting for grandchildren and have been vocal about it. Tara is in a dilemma; she wants children at some point but would like to have a couple of years to enjoy herself postgraduation before taking on that level of responsibility. She wants to get settled in her professional life first. She is proud of her Italian heritage, but she feels strongly that women should have the right to choose when and if they have children. Fortunately, she has a group of supportive friends who have been encouraging her to listen to herself and hold out for what she wants. After all, it is her life. Further, Josh, who is White, was raised by middle-class parents who worked hard to create a power-sharing relationship, and he has internalized these values himself. He doesn't want Tara to become pregnant until she is really ready to do so.

Lesbian couple, Nikki and May, ages 35 and 37, respectively, were born and raised in central Florida, in the United States, where they have continued to reside since they moved in together 8 years ago. Solidly working-class Nikki, who identifies as African American, is employed in the parts warehouse of one of the large county school boards, whereas May, a Vietnamese American, operates a small lawn service around the city of Orlando. They have been in discussions about having a baby or adopting a child for the last 4 years but have not yet agreed on whether and how to become parents due to the social, political, economic, religious, and other personal complexities connected to the decision. Both of these women grew up in family, community, and cultural climates of homophobia and heterosexism, and they admit that they each strongly internalized the cultural messages that lesbians are deviant and not fit to be parents. Until September 2010, Florida state law reinforced this perspective as Florida was the only U.S. state to ban lesbians and gay men from adopting children. Many Florida physicians still will not provide artificial insemination and other medical services for lesbians and bisexual women. Adoption and artificial insemination are both quite costly and would require the couple to borrow a very large sum of money, a thought that is particularly stressful for Nikki. Both members of the couple believe that they would be good parents individually and collectively and that they would enjoy the experience of raising one or more children, yet each of them has resisted at times when the other moves closer to readiness.

These couples' situations are each complex and point out how the intersections of culture, context, politics, identities, and social locations influence not only their choices about having children but also their perceptions of whether or not they actually have choices because each of them is in the midst of pressures and constraints based on community, institutional, systemic, and structural inequalities as well as individual relational variables.

Traditional psychological and sociological concepts of power define it as societal, for example, based on resources, wealth, influence, control, and physical strength (Miller & Cummins, 1992). This definition of power is associated with domination or *power over*. In a study (Harvey, Beckman, Browner, & Sherman, 2002, p. 284) of Mexican American couples' power in relationships, power was "perceived as control over one's partner and the ability to make decisions." This traditional conception of power can be measured, and the power relationship is a zero-sum game; as one person loses power, the other gains it. For example, Ying's relationship to her husband represents this type of power-over dynamic. If she capitulates to Wayan's demands for children at this time, as a functional single parent (other than during Wayan's infrequent visits), Ying loses her ability to earn an income, with which comes some autonomy and self-reliance; thus she becomes even more dependent on Wayan.

Feminists typically redefine power as *empowerment* or *power to* (Yoder & Kahn, 1992). From this view, power is the ability or capacity to do things, that is, to achieve goals, make choices, and be self-determining. Empowerment involves power sharing (Norwood & Zahau, in press); it is not based on the concept that when one person loses power, the other gains it, but instead is based on mutual enhancement (Miller & Cummins, 1992). The traditional notion of power is focused on interpersonal influence, whereas the feminist idea of empowerment also includes intrapersonal power. Intrapersonal power involves the ability to act, not merely react, and to make choices that are self-determined. Contrary to Ying's situation, Tara's relationship with Josh illustrates this type of power-to connection, as both partners are supportive and balanced in terms of power and decisions made within the unit. Further, despite familial pressure to have children right away and Josh's preference to do so, Tara seems able to postpone having children until they are both ready. We might speculate that Tara's White privilege, advanced education, and encouragement from her friendship circle support her sense of entitlement to assert her wishes within the relationship.

In any discussion of women's power in relationships, it is helpful to distinguish three levels at which women's choices are constrained: legally (laws vary across and within countries and communities), by social norms (differ from group to group within countries), and personally (i.e., who one is; e.g., personal history, beliefs, ethnic/racial/cultural/sexual identity, sense of personal empowerment). These different levels are layered and influence one another. The case of Nikki and May illustrates this point. Legally, the couple lives in a U.S. state that, for more than 40 years, had a law that banned LGB people from adopting children. Even though the ban has been declared unconstitutional, social justice issues (e.g., systemic barriers to equal access) remain. A new state government has been elected that is dominated by legislators, and a governor, who are explicitly in favor of reinstating the antigay adoption ban and are homophobic in a variety of other ways. This climate allows physicians to continue to feel entitled to refuse to provide medical services to lesbians who desire artificial insemination or present at the clinic pregnant. Further, the hostile social climate is an added barrier for Nikki and May as they think about raising a family in such a toxic environment.

Culturally, both Nikki and May come from families that do not support their daughters' sexual orientations and their relationship, much less a decision to have children. As they cycle through their own personal internalized homophobia and insecurities about being good parents, they each, in turn, block the other and themselves from actualizing their deep, shared desire to become parents together. Because they are financially interdependent, one does not seem to have more economic and social class power than the other to tip the scale toward going forward. An analysis of Nikki and May's dilemma illustrates how the forms of power they hold as individual players within their relationship are mediated by a complex set of interconnecting legal, social, political, cultural, and personal variables. Indeed, "the personal is political" in that the larger dynamics of homophobia and heterosexism play out in their relationship and serve as powerful backdrops to the ways that each of them inadvertently reinforce and are backed up by the oppression present in the larger social and political systems.

Equitable political and legal frameworks influenced by enlightened cultural norms and moral standards are necessary, but not sufficient, conditions for reproductive freedom. Without changes in social policy that make reproductive resources available to all women, regardless of ability to pay, poor and working-class women will still be disadvantaged with regard to reproductive choices and vulnerable to the assertion of pressure by male partners. As Ehrenreich (2008, p. 4) stated,

> [T]he government often contributes substantially to the limited choices women have. Governmental policies help create the conditions that shape women's options, so that even if the state doesn't directly interfere with women's reproductive choices, it can still have an important impact on their reproductive lives.

In Ying's challenging situation, it is clear that her power in her relationship with Wayan is diminished by the limits on her access to birth control as prescribed by current Thai policy restrictions on providing medical services to undocumented refugees. Each time he pressures her to have sex and she capitulates, she runs the risk of an unwanted pregnancy and increased dependence on Wayan and others for survival, safety, and security.

In relation to another policy issue, in nations without any type of social security or pension system, the choice to have children is imposed by a society where, not only is there an expectation that all women who are capable of having children will do so, but the reality is that those who do not have children will be without care or an income in their old age, which, of course, is also the case for Ying and Wayan, whether they are living at home in Burma or as refugees in Thailand. This fact further diminishes Ying's agency and authority in her relationship with Wayan because he has the full weight of the larger social and political systems behind him in his desire to produce children who can take care of them in their later years.

And, of course, having children in many societies and cultures actually elevates some elements of the power of a woman in her intimate and larger familial and social relationships. Therefore, Ying is caught in a dilemma: being a respectable woman, a woman of worth, means bearing children and becoming a mother. Her cultural norms instill that womanhood requires rearing children, yet to have a child without adequate resources places her life, and the life of her future child, in jeopardy. Without the social support of her family and community, particularly her partner, Ying is confined to a system that perpetuates gender inequality within her relationship even though she might gain some social and familial capital by acquiescing to Wayan's wishes.

China, a country with a history of strict governmental control over how many children a couple can have through its one-child policy, provides a different kind of example. Within this context, there are still reproductive choices to be made as the strong cultural preference for boys prompts some couples to abort female fetuses. Thus, a woman who finds herself pregnant with a girl may have diminished power to assert her wishes to carry the baby to term if her husband, backed by these strong cultural prescriptions, is not in agreement and wants her to have an abortion. Although producing a male offspring might heighten her status at home and in the community through the honor that she brings to the family and to herself, her male partner maintains the power to disproportionately influence most other aspects of her life (see chapter 11, "Female Feticide and Infanticide").

The issue of sex-selective abortion illustrates the ways that broadening reproductive choice is complicated (Moazam, 2004). On the one hand, easy access to abortions increases women's freedom of reproductive choice and supports women in avoiding decreased power within their intimate relationships with men. On the other hand, sex-selective abortion perpetuates gender inequality by reinforcing the devaluation of women, attitudes that clearly have an impact on women's influence, authority, and agency in their marriages and intimate partnerships.

Economic limitations and restricted access to resources affect women in intimate relationships worldwide (McLaren, 2008). Although women's control over their reproductive decision making has been found to improve significantly when they become better educated and have access to wage-earning jobs, many unwanted pregnancies and births still occur because women lack access to effective contraceptives or deliberate sterilization practices (McCarthy, 1995). Women are often forced to have more children than they would want as a result of cultural and societal conditions that render women as second-class citizens within the family and society:

> These factors constrict women's reproductive rights by keep[ing] women subservient to their husbands' wishes, prevent[ing] them from owning or inheriting property, bar[ring] them from well-paid jobs, deny[ing] them equal pay for equal work, and exclud[ing] them from participation in government and politics. (McCarthy, 1995, p. 630)

For example, the contrasting levels of power and influence reflected in Ying's and Tara's relationships with their husbands demonstrate how each of these women's levels of income generation, directly in relation to their social and political circumstances, contribute to the interpersonal relationship power they posses to assert themselves regarding when and if to have a child. Here we can see how social and political conditions may influence women's access to economic resources vis-à-vis employment, thus empowering or disempowering them in their relationships with their male partners.

Women are situated differently than one another depending on a variety of social, cultural, and political factors, but they are also situated differently from men because of the gender hierarchy:

> Gender, race, ethnicity, class, and sexuality are not merely personality and group differences; in our society they also function as large social-structural patterns of unequal power relations. As Unger and Crawford said, gender is a "system of dominance." (Griscom, 1992, p. 25)

Due to this system of gender dominance, women in relationships with men often report gender-based power imbalances. Moreover, these gender-based power imbalances can be culturally inflected.

In studies of power strategies within relationships, a gender difference in power in relationships was found to correlate to unequal social power. As Sagrestano (1992, p. 282) stated, "[Perhaps] because women typically find themselves in positions with less power (and may have less power simply because of their female status in patriarchal society), the types of strategies they choose reflect their social roles." Studies suggest that gender differences in power in relationships cannot be separated from differences in social power (Frieze & McHugh, 1992; Griscom, 1992; Harvey et al., 2002; Miller & Cummins, 1992; Sagrestano, 1992). For example, Sagrestano (1992) examined the ways gender and expertise impact strategies of negotiation in interpersonal relationships. Her findings reveal that expertise, which is correlated with greater social power, plays a larger role than gender in the strategies individuals choose for negotiating. Nonetheless, she concluded that, because women are all too often in less powerful social roles, they may resort to less powerful strategies of negotiation in their interpersonal relationships, such as indirect negotiation. How might this decision impact power in intimate relationships?

Miller and Cummins (1992) surveyed 125 women in the United States regarding when they felt the most powerful. Their analysis identified five significant areas in which women experience power, or lack of power: Self-enhancement, Reproductive Issues, Men/Work Issues, Relationships, and Control Over. It is interesting that women felt the least powerful with respect to reproductive issues; only 6.9 percent reported feeling powerful, whereas 62.7 percent reported never or almost never feeling powerful in terms of reproductive issues. Although the sample is small and specific to the United States, these results indicate that even women who are relatively privileged (88% of the sample was White, and 75% heterosexual; no socioeconomic information is available) feel a lack of power when it comes to reproductive issues.

Frieze and McHugh (1992) examined power and influence strategies in violent and nonviolent marriages, and they found that women married to violent men made fewer decisions than women in relationships with men who were nonviolent. Thus, it can be inferred that violence in intimate relationships plays a significant role in restricting women's choices about whether and when to have children. Moreover, violence or the threat of violence creates a power imbalance in any relationship, including same-sex relationships. For instance, if May were to abuse her partner Nikki, Nikki would be much less likely to assert her wishes regarding when and if to have children.

In a study about relationship power and decision making in U.S. couples of Mexican origin, Harvey et al. (2002) found that cultural ideologies, such as machismo, may exacerbate power differences between women and men. The Latin ideology of machismo emphasizes men's power and control over women, and it reinforces and exaggerates stereotypical gender roles. Asked to define power, one participant in that study said: "Power can be to order around. Since I recognize that he is the head and if he orders me to do something, I know that's the way it has to be. I subject myself to his rules because he has more power than I do" (p. 287).

This lack of power can be compounded if the woman is economically dependent on her husband, as is the case with Ying in her relationship with Wayan. Further, "[s]everal researchers have suggested women are likely to have difficulties in negotiating safer sex strategies with their male partners because of perceived imbalances in relationship power" (Harvey et al., 2002, p. 284).

Social conditions also support or constrain the power that women have in relationships with intimate partners. In the Indian state of Kerala, researchers have examined the lifestyles and reproductive environments of women in fishing communities. The lack of sanitary toilet facilities combined with "culturally embedded gender discrimination" impact the reproductive systems of poor women:

> Poverty and the absence of toilets affect both sexes. But women alone are condemned by the norms of modesty and shame to suffer bladder retention and postponed defecation ... the lack of sanitary pads and private places to use them during menstruation [lead to] unhygienic layers of soiled garments ... (Petchesky, 2002, p. 76).

These menstrual and toilet practices increase women's exposure to reproductive tract infections. In a culture in which a woman is expected to bear children and where she derives a certain degree of social power from doing so, her power to assert her will in her marriage is diminished when medical complications from these kinds of unsanitary conditions render her sterile or unable to get pregnant and safely carry a child to term. Here, again, we see that a woman's reproductive choice must be framed within a broader social context that is characterized by gender discrimination and unequal access to basic health resources, which in turn mediates her agency and authority within her intimate relationship.

THE INTERCONNECTION BETWEEN THE GLOBAL NORTH AND GLOBAL SOUTH

Despite all of our differences, the women of the world are interconnected, and economics and accessibility to resources can place a wedge between women of the Global North and Global South. Thai women interviewed by Norsworthy and Khuankaew (2008) reported that women from the South are often excluded from political and social decision making, do not have equal pay in relation to work output, and frequently are bound to rules and laws that require subservience to their husbands or partners. On the other hand, many privileged women of the Global North may be oblivious to the fact that their rights and choices, although constrained by their location in systems of interlocking oppressions and their own circumstances, are often far less constrained than the reproductive rights and choices of their sisters in the Global South as a result of economic, political, social, and cultural inequities. Here we show how women's reproductive choices affect their power in their relationships with other women and the interconnection of these choices with their power in intimate relationships.

Surrogacy

How do the choices one makes benefit, sustain, or hurt others? Take the reality of interconnection in the matter of globalized commercial surrogacy. Whereas birth control has been a form of negative eugenics (i.e., to prevent births), Roberts (2008) described the *new reproduction* (i.e., surrogacy) as a product of positive eugenics. Reproductive arrangements are presently made worldwide between individuals and/or couples from wealthy nations and those from socioeconomically underprivileged countries. Wealthy women and/or couples hire surrogate mothers for reproductive labor. (See also chapter 8, "Infertility and Assisted Reproductive Technologies.")

For example, India has recently seen a dramatic increase in its international surrogacy business (Chang, 2009). This business transaction is made possible as a result of affordability for those with financial resources, loose legal restrictions, and high rates of compensation, at least in the eyes of the poor, willing birth mothers.

For the surrogate mother, carrying another's child may have both drawbacks and benefits. She may suffer social stigma and discrimination for her choice, but the payment may enable her to have greater social and economic power, which, as we have already seen, can lead to more power within her intimate relationship and greater reproductive choice for herself because of increased access to resources through her income.

Despite her relative wealth, the woman who hires the surrogate may lose cultural capital and power within her intimate relationship because of her inability to fulfill the socially prescribed role of birth mother. Yet, despite these individual shifts in power, the institution of international surrogacy diverts money and resources away from those who need basic health care, and especially reproductive health care, in the countries that provide the service and toward those foreigners who can afford expensive fertility treatments or the option of surrogacy. In this case, economics serve as a driving force that perpetuates the cycles of inequality and imbalance among women from different regions of the world.

Childcare and Reproductive Justice

Some women rely on other women not only to carry their child to term, but also to care for the child once it is born. Here, again, we see how systemic inequalities of wealth, race, ethnicity, and nationality weave women together in relationships that are both constraining and enabling. Ehrenreich and Hochschild (2002) discussed the "care deficit" in the Global North; they noted that most caretaking of children in the United States is done by women of color from the Global South. Global economic inequality is the primary reason that women immigrate to find work. How does this impact reproductive choice and women's power in relationships with one another and with their intimate partners? Ehrenreich and Hochschild (2002, p. 11) noted:

> Increasingly often, as affluent and middle-class families in the First World come to depend on migrants from poorer regions to provide childcare, homemaking and sexual services, a global relationship arises that in some ways mirrors the traditional relationship between the sexes.

The inequalities between affluent women from the Global North and poor women from the Global South are analogous to gender inequalities within societies where those with less power and status (i.e., women) are expected to take primary responsibility for the domestic labor of cleaning and cooking as well as taking care of children and elders.

One significant aspect of reproductive decision making is childcare. Partners often negotiate about whether and when to have children, and they must also plan how to care for children after they are born. This decision may begin with the couple, but, like other reproductive decisions, the choice radiates outward: One woman's choice impacts other women's choices, as care work usually falls on the woman. Most migrant women childcare workers have children of their own whom they leave behind in their home countries:

> The average age of women migrants into the United States is twenty-nine, and most come from countries such as the Philippines or Sri Lanka, where female identity centers on motherhood, and where the birth rate is very high. Often migrants, especially the undocumented ones, cannot bring their children with them. Most mothers try to leave their children in the care of grandmothers, aunts, and fathers, roughly in that order. (Hochschild, 2002, p. 21)

So long as the work of caring for children remains primarily women's work, decisions about having and raising children will impact not only the relationships between women and men, but also the relationships among women. Reproductive rights include not only the right to give birth, but also the right to raise healthy children. Women from lower socioeconomic backgrounds are often denied that right as they leave their children in someone else's care to seek employment, ironically often caring for wealthier women's children. As we have shown, reproductive decisions made within the context of an intimate partnership may have far-reaching consequences for relationships among women across regions of the world in this age of interconnection and globalization.

FUTURE DIRECTIONS: WOMEN'S COLLECTIVE ACTION AND SOLIDARITY

Working together within and across national boundaries is imperative if women are to exercise power in making reproductive choices within the contexts of their relationships. For the majority of women, reproductive decisions are made within the context of a heterosexual relationship, thus women's relative lack of power in relation to men plays a significant role in circumscribing their ability to make choices about whether and when to have children. Although a number of factors contribute to women's lack of power relative to men, the gender dominance of men over women is linked to men's higher social status. Thus, women's power in intimate relationships can be increased through either a change in her individual status or a change in the status of women in general. Here we provide examples of women's collective actions that have changed the gendered power relations, removing some of the structural constraints that reinforce the subordination of women to men and limit women's decision-making power in intimate relationships.

Marketplace India

A nonprofit organization based in India provides one example of the connection between women's social status and the power exercised by individual women. The following discussion draws on research by McLaren (2011), who conducted interviews with members of Marketplace India in 2004. Marketplace India, founded in 1980 in Mumbai, is an umbrella organization for a group of 13 cooperatives that employ over 500 women; it provides job training, educational programs, and a centralized structure for marketing handmade clothing. A spirit of collaboration runs through every aspect of the organization, which combines gainful employment for marginalized women with social programs that educate and empower them. Marketplace India provides the structure and resources for each group to participate in workshops about health, parenting, social issues, global issues, and how to promote social change. Many Marketplace India artisans told McLaren about dramatic increases in their levels of self-confidence and in their ability to deal with problems in their personal lives and in the communities to which they belong.

Their increased self-confidence, combined with their newfound earning power, allowed them to change some of the conditions of their lives. For example, one woman in a cooperative was subject to domestic violence in her marriage. Her income from work as a cooperative member allowed her to move out of the house temporarily. Members of her cooperative visited her husband at home, confronted him about his violent behavior, and asked him to stop it. He agreed to curb his violent behavior if his wife returned home. She did return, but the terms of the relationship had changed. She now had the power to negotiate in the relationship because she had economic power based on her income and she had social power as a part of a collective that recognized the value of women, despite messages about women's inferiority from the larger culture (McLaren, 2011).

ReproSalud

For many women in the Global South, poverty and isolation are impediments to accessing health care in general, including reproductive health care. In Peru, a project called ReproSalud seeks to change the model of delivering reproductive services (i.e., the provider-patient model) and instead aims to empower women to take charge of their own reproductive health. ReproSalud follows a three step plan: First, they work with community-based organizations to identify the most pressing reproductive needs of the community; within each organization community leaders are identified to become *health promoters*. These leaders receive training and, subsequently, conduct the popular education identified as needed by the community. For instance, "where maternal mortality is a concern, Community-Based Organizations [CBO] promoters are being trained to identify women with high risk pregnancies, to educate them about their risk factors, and to refer them to the local health post" (Petchesky, 2003, p. 210).

Second, the CBOs form a coalition that works directly with government organizations and authorities to hold them accountable for helping to address women's reproductive needs. Third, ReproSalud includes income-generating projects in their quest for reproductive justice to enable the women to access reproductive services. One priority that emerged out of dialogues with the local women was including men as trainers and workshop participants. During the workshops with men, topics such as alcoholism, violence, and communication within families were discussed.

As noted earlier, violence in intimate relationships is a key factor in limiting women's power and decision making. Educating men about reproductive issues and addressing family dynamics is an important part of the process of shifting power relations within intimate relationships. ReproSalud works at two levels: (1) the intra-and interpersonal—to empower and educate women about their rights and their bodies and to enable them to communicate their desires to their husbands or partners; (2) the structural—to eliminate socioeconomic barriers to women's access to reproductive health care. "[I]n addition to cultivating women's sense of entitlement, ReproSalud also seeks to address the socioeconomic, cultural and gender-based barriers that prevent them from making decisions" (Petchesky, 2003, p. 209).

Feminist activist projects such as ReproSalud demonstrate the power of collective action by using a feminist model of power sharing and empowerment and challenging structural injustices of poverty, gender inequality, and cultural discrimination. As Petchesky (2003, p. 213) observed, "without the activities of Manuela Ramos through the ReproSalud project, it is highly doubtful whether feminist approaches to reproductive health would be available at all to impoverished and indigenous Peruvian women." ReproSalud exemplifies a decolonized feminist approach to reproductive justice; it addresses both intrapersonal and systemic issues, as both of these aspects, in turn, affect women's ability to exercise power with regard to reproductive decisions within their intimate relationships.

Sama-Resource Group for Women and Health

Sama-Resource Group for Women and Health (Sama), a women's health advocacy network in India, provides another example of a decolonized feminist approach to reproductive justice and to fostering and supporting women's empowerment within their relationships. *Sama,* which means "equality" in Sanskrit, was founded in 1999 by women with a history of feminist activism for women's health.

Sama's statement of purpose resonates with our multifaceted, decolonized, feminist approach:

> Sama believes that equality and empowerment can be ensured only when poverty, curtailment of capabilities, lack of livelihood rights, lack of health services and access to health care, illiteracy and multiple forms of discrimination based on caste, class, gender religion, ethnicity, sexual orientation and many other rubrics are structurally challenged. Our commitment is to integrate the gender, caste, class and rights analysis within the wider context of other social relations in order to emphasize the complexity of existing power relations that work towards exclusion and marginalization. (http://www.samawo menshealth.org)

Sama has been involved in a number of projects and studies in India concerning women's empowerment in reproductive decision making, including studies of the two-child norm, the effects of Depo Provera, and the rapidly growing use of assisted reproductive technologies (ARTs) in India (Sama-Resource Group for Women and Health, 2006). Their research addresses specific reproductive issues in India and their effects on women.

But their approach links the situation of the Global South together with that of the Global North, and it challenges the imperialistic relationship between the two as perpetuated through neoliberal globalization and the unbridled profit seeking of multinational corporations. For instance, in their study of Depo Provera, an injectable contraceptive long known to be linked to health problems, Sama members documented that it was marketed without all the required drug trials and that it was administered to women without informed consent, regardless of known health risks, such as diabetes. The work that Sama is doing provides an excellent opportunity for coalition building across national borders; women from the United States should be aware that dangerous contraceptives are being exported and promoted to the Global South, and they could put pressure on manufacturers at least to adhere to the same standards of testing and protocols of administering Depo Provera in India as in the United States.

Sama has trenchantly critiqued the ideology of choice that accompanies both the promotion of contraceptives and the expansion of ARTs. They questioned the promotion of Depo Provera, which they see, not as expanding women's reproductive choices, but rather as a form of population control and control of women in general. Women's groups (e.g., Sama-Resource Group for Women and Health, 2003, p. 7) involved in the campaign against new reproductive technologies have consistently raised their voices against the sudden concern of the establishment—which is otherwise intensely anti-women—for women's choice. Why a choice in contraception alone, they argue; why not give women choices in employment, food, education, access to health care, and civic amenities? At a more basic level, why not the choice to have the same rights as men in the family and society, or the right not to be killed in the womb?

Sama's (2003) insight that women's power in reproductive choice cannot be promoted in the absence of other choices for women is crucial; it frames reproductive decision making not as an individual issue, but as a matter of comprehensive social justice.

Projects such as Marketplace India, ReproSalud, and Sama illustrate the power of collective feminist organizing to elevate the power of women within their intimate relationships, within their communities and societies, and in their relationships with one another through social and political change, not as a liberal feminist matter of choice, but as an imperative of basic social justice. Women's power and empowerment within their relationships with intimate partners and with other women depends on it. Reproductive justice cannot exist without it.

REFERENCES

Asian Communities for Reproductive Justice. (2010). Reproductive justice: Vision, analysis, and action for a stronger movement. In G. Kirk & M. Okazawa-Rey

(Eds.), *Women's lives: Multicultural perspectives* (5th ed., pp. 242–246). Boston: McGraw-Hill.

Chang, M. (2009). Womb for rent: India's commercial surrogacy. *Harvard International Review, 31*, 11–12.

Ehrenreich, B., & Hochschild, A. R. (Eds.). (2002). *Global woman: Nannies, maids, and sex workers in the new economy.* New York: Metropolitan Books.

Ehrenreich, N. (2008). Introduction. In N. Ehrenreich (Ed.), *The reproductive rights reader: Law, medicine, and the construction of motherhood* (pp. 1–19). New York: New York University Press.

Frieze, I. H., & McHugh, M. C. (1992). Power and influence strategies in violent and nonviolent marriages. *Psychology of Women Quarterly, 16*, 449–465.

Griscom, J. L. (1992). Women and power: Definition, dualism, and difference. *Psychology of Women Quarterly, 16*, 389–414.

Harvey, S. M., Beckman, L., Browner, C., & Sherman, C. (2002). Relationship power, decision making, and sexual relations: An exploratory study with couples of Mexican origin. *Journal of Sex Research, 39*, 284–291.

Hochschild, A. R. (2002). Love and gold. In B. Ehrenreich & A. R. Hochschild (Eds.), *Global woman: Nannies, maids, and sex workers in the new economy* (pp. 15–30). New York: Metropolitan Books.

McCarthy, M. (1995). Women's lack of reproductive choice highlighted. *Lancet, 346*, 630–631.

McLaren, M. A. (2008, Spring). Gender equality and the economic empowerment of women. *Forum on Public Policy.* Retrieved from http://forumonpublicpolicy.com/archivespring08/mclaren.pdf.

McLaren, M. A. (2011). Women's rights and collective resistance: The success story of Marketplace India. In E. G. Polakoff & L. Lindio-McGovern (Eds.), *Gender & globalization: Patterns of women's resistance* (pp. 189–208). Whitby, Ontario, Cananda: de Sitter Publications.

Miller, C., & Cummins, A. G. (1992). An examination of women's perspectives on power. *Psychology of Women Quarterly, 16*, 415–428.

Moazam, F. (2004). Feminist discourse on sex screening and selective abortion of female foetuses. *Bioethics, 18*, 205–220.

Mohanty, C. (2003). *Feminism without borders: Decolonizing theory, practicing solidarity.* Durham, NC: Duke University Press.

Narayan, U. (2000). Essence of culture and a sense of history: A feminist critique of cultural essentialism. In U. Narayan & S. Harding (Eds.), *Decentering the center: Philosophy for a multicultural, postcolonial, and feminist world* (pp. 80–100). Bloomington: Indiana University Press.

Norsworthy, K. L., & Khuankaew, O. (2008). A new view from the women of Thailand about gender, sexuality, and HIV/AIDS. *Feminism & Psychology, 18*, 527–536.

Norwood, G. & Zahau, C. (2011). Fostering a grassroots women's movement through feminist leadership on the Burma-India border. *Women & Therapy, 34*(3), 223–241.

Petchesky, R. P. (2002). Human rights, reproductive health, and economic justice: Why they are indivisible. In N. Holstrom (Ed.), *The social feminist project: A contemporary reader in theory and politics* (pp. 74–82). New York: Monthly Review Press.

Petchesky, R. P. (2003). *Global prescriptions: Gendered health and human rights*. London: Zed.

Roberts, D. (1997). *Killing the black body: Race, reproduction, and the meaning of liberty*. New York: Pantheon.

Roberts, D. (2008). Race and the new reproduction. In N. Ehrenreich (Ed.), *The reproductive rights reader: Law, medicine, and the construction of motherhood* (pp. 308–319). New York: New York University Press.

Sagrestano, L. (1992). Power strategies in interpersonal relationships: The effect of expertise and gender. *Psychology of Women Quarterly, 16,* 481–495.

Sama-Resource Group for Women and Health. (2003). *Unveiled realities: A study on women's experiences with Depo-Provera, an injectable contraceptive*. New Delhi, India: Impulsive Creations.

Sama-Resource Group for Women and Health. (2006). *ARTs and women: Assistance in reproduction or subjugation?* New Delhi, India: Impulsive Creations.

Tripp, A. M. (2006). Challenges in transnational feminist mobilization. In M. M. Ferree & A. M. Tripp (Eds.), *Global feminism: Transnational women's activism, organizing and human rights* (pp. 296–312). New York: New York University Press.

Yoder, J. D., & Kahn, A. S. (1992). Toward a feminist understanding of women and power. *Psychology of Women Quarterly, 16,* 381–388.

Chapter 4

Sexual Assault: A Matter of Reproductive Justice

Thema Bryant-Davis, Shaquita Tillman, and Pamela A. Counts

Reproductive rights include access to sexual and reproductive health care as well as the right to be free from sexual violence. Sexual violence is a violation of both basic human rights and more specific reproductive rights (Kolbe & Hutson, 2006). Globally, women, men, girls, and boys of diverse nationalities are victimized by sexual violence every year, and that violence results in physical injuries, unwanted pregnancies, sexually transmitted infections (STIs), and psychological trauma for many of the victims (Herman, 1992).

Sexual assault is any nonconsensual sexual contact (Bryant-Davis, Tillman, Chung, & Belcourt, 2010), which can range from unwanted touching to bodily penetration (Ajuwon, Akin-Jimoh, Olley, & Akintola, 2001). Sexual assaults are often underreported, which results in many survivors not receiving the services they need and many offenders not facing legal consequences for their actions. Sexual violence has been documented by the UN as a war crime. It has also been used as a weapon against persons who speak up for social justice and even civilians of diverse backgrounds who are considered unworthy of protection (Totten, 2009). At its core, sexual violence is about power and control (Ullman, 2010). Sexual assault is an attempt to silence the violated and to objectify their humanity. It is critical for survivors, mental health professionals, policy makers, and the general public to understand the ways in which sexual violence destroys survivors' sense of safety, trust, and human dignity (Bryant-Davis, Ullman, Tsong, Tillman, & Smith, 2010).

Reproductive rights are the fundamental rights of individuals to ownership over their own bodies. Rape violates those rights on every level: mentally, physically, legally, and emotionally (Tavara, 2006). There are two primary reproductive rights that sexual violence encroaches upon: the right to safety from sexual violence and the right to appropriate care in the aftermath of sexual violence (Khanna, 2008). When a person or group of people forces sexual contact through threat, force, intimidation, substances, trickery, or manipulation, they deny the basic right that people have over their own bodies (Abbey, BeShears, Clinton-Sherrod, & McAuslan, 2004). This includes who has the right to touch or to enter one's body. Sexual violence disregards the barrier of consent and gives priority to the offender's rights over those of the victim (Tavara, 2006). It is important to note that a survivor might have given consent for one aspect of sexual touching without having given consent to another aspect of contact. For example, consent to kissing or sexual touching does not equal consent to intercourse. At all times, persons are to retain their rights in the form of consent. Sexual violence infringes upon these rights, forces unwanted sexual contact, and can result in bruises and other physical injuries, psychological distress, STIs, pregnancy, and, in some cases, death (Tavara, 2006).

Proponents of the reproductive justice framework argue that individuals should have ownership over their bodies, but there are others who disagree. Due to the patriarchal system and socialization processes, many people argue that women's bodies belong first to their family of origin and then, once married, to their husbands. Others, for example in Nigeria and other non-Western countries, argue that everyone's bodies belong to the community (Izugbara & Undie, 2008). Although in the best of circumstances, this collective perspective can lead the community to support and protect women, it can also lead to a denial of women's reproductive rights, as well as other basic human rights.

The end of the physical assault itself does not end the potential for reproductive rights violations of sexual assault survivors. Denial of appropriate health care options can, and often does, serve as an additional abuse of victims' rights (Ngwena, 2010). Health care needs following sexual violence can include, but are not limited to, mental health counseling, medical/forensic examination by a trained health professional, testing and treatment for STIs, pregnancy testing, pregnancy options including termination, and treatment of injuries by sensitive professionals (Ngwena, 2010). When religious, cultural, social, systemic, and economic barriers prevent access to these services, sexual violence survivors experience an additional violation (Sen, 2010). These violations can take multiple forms and have the potential to create lasting and severe consequences (Ajuwon et al., 2001).

THE GLOBAL SCOPE OF SEXUAL ASSAULT

Sexual assault is a form of violence that occurs at alarming rates worldwide. According to estimates by the UN Development Fund for Women (UNIFEM, 2005), 1 in 5 women across the globe will experience rape or attempted rape in her lifetime. In the United States, it is estimated that 1 in 5–7 women will experience rape (El-Mouelhy, 2004). Sexual violence is committed by intimate partners, other acquaintances, and strangers to reinforce sexual inequalities and to maintain unequal balances of power. In Peru, Samoa, and Tanzania, approximately 10–12 percent of women over the age of 15 years have experienced sexual violence by nonpartners (UNIFEM, 2005). In war-torn nations, the frequency of sexual violence by nonpartners increases, as it is often used as a tactic of war. This often results in forced pregnancy and, in some cases, the victim's entry into human trafficking (Hynes & Cardozzo, 2000; Renzetti, 2005). During the Bosnia War in 1992, for example, approximately 20,000–50,000 women were raped, and approximately 500,000 women were raped during the Rwanda Civil War in 1994 (Renzetti, 2005). Along with physical, verbal, and emotional abuse, sexual assault is a form of control sometimes used by perpetrators of intimate partner violence. In a study conducted in Zimbabwe, 26 percent of women who had been married reported having been forced to have sex with their husbands (Watts & Zimmerman, 2002). In China, higher lifetime prevalence of sexual violence is correlated with higher numbers of gynecological or obstetric visits; more women may seek medical help as a result of forced sex by intimate partners than by nonpartners (Tang & Lai, 2008). These numbers demonstrate that sexual violence is prevalent among developed and developing countries and is experienced in both intimate and nonintimate relationships.

TYPES OF SEXUAL ASSAULT

As noted above, sexual assault assailants can have different relationships to the survivors: intimate partners, acquaintances, or strangers. The victim-offender relationship is important given that it delineates an element of the diversity in sexual assault types and experiences. In the following sections, we describe the prevalence and correlates of different types of sexual assault perpetrated against women (i.e., stranger rape, marital rape, war-related rape, and sexually assaulted victims of human trafficking). All of these acts of sexual violence are similar in that they are representative of an egregious violation of the reproductive rights of female victims.

Stranger vs. Acquaintance Rape

Contrary to popular belief, perpetrators of rape are not typically strangers lurking in dark alleys or hiding behind bushes looking for their next victims; rather, the majority of sexual assaults involve a victim and an offender who had a relationship before the sexual assault occurred (Kirkwood & Cecil, 2001). In fact, it is estimated that acquaintance rapes make up more than 80 percent of all sexual assaults (Tjaden & Thoennes, 1999). Marital rape is an exemplary form of sexual assault in which the assailant is known to the victim, whereas war-related rape and sexually assaulted trafficking victims are indicative of the women most often sexually assaulted by a stranger.

Marital Rape

Sexual victimization in marriage has been occurring for centuries throughout the world (Russell, 1990), yet it is often ignored and, at one time, was legally sanctioned in most countries. Sir Matthew Hale (1736, as cited in Russell, 1990, p. 17), who was a chief justice in the United Kingdom, wrote the following: "But the husband cannot be guilty of a rape committed by himself upon his lawful wife, for by their mutual matrimonial consent and contract the wife hath given up herself in this kind unto her husband, which she cannot retract." His statement became known as the Lord Hale doctrine and represented a common-law marital rape exemption, under which husbands could not be accused of committing the crime of rape against their wives. That precedent was accepted for many years.

Unfortunately, today marital rape is often overlooked in clinical and research domains. This is shocking given that recent statistics suggest that husbands perpetrate 10–14 percent of sexual assaults against women in the United States (Bergen, 2006), where marital rape was not recognized as a crime in all 50 states until 1993. Yet, by May 2005, only 20 states had completely eliminated the marital rape exemptions from state laws; in the remaining 30 states, there were still some exemptions from sexual assault prosecution given to husbands (Bergen, 2006). Moreover, the signing of the Violence Against Women Act 2005 into law on January 5, 2006, resulted in changes in existing state rape laws, namely, that marital rape is to be treated as lesser crime than the rape of other victims (National Alliance to End Sexual Violence, 2007). Arguably, the legal recognition of marital rape as a criminal act, with punishment that fits the crime, is an important change that is long overdue. In many countries (e.g., Afghanistan, India, Malaysia, Pakistan), women are still not legally protected from marital rape (Ali, Israr, Ali, & Janjua, 2009; Coglan, 2009; Malkin & Thompson, 2005).

War-Related Sexual Assault

War-related sexual assaults are often perceived to be human rights violations (Amowitz et al., 2002). Observations indicate that a high percentage of women become victims of sexual assault in addition to abduction, beating, and killing in the event of an outbreak of political violence, civil unrest, or war. In Sierra Leone, the lifetime prevalence of non-war-related sexual assault committed against women by family members, friends, or civilians was 9 percent prior to the outbreak of the civil war; the prevalence rate increased to 17 percent with the addition of war-related sexual assaults (Sarkar & Sarkar, 2005). These findings suggest that, during times of war, women are at increased risk of being sexually violated and treated as spoils of war. They are thereby stripped of their human rights in general and their reproductive rights in particular.

Human Trafficking

Human trafficking, a form of modern-day slavery, is a global crisis in which sexual coercion and abuse are often inflicted upon enslaved victims (see chapter 5, "Reproductive Injustice"). As described by the UN, human trafficking involves "an act of recruiting, transporting, transferring, harboring or receiving a person through a use of force, coercion or other means, for the purpose of exploiting them" (United Nations Office on Drugs and Crime, 2009). Human traffickers tend to victimize the most vulnerable of the global community—women and children. Once trafficked, victims are typically forced into sex work in which they are required to work long hours performing sex acts with numerous customers. Furthermore, sexual coercion and abuse are often tactics used by traffickers to maintain control of trafficking victims. This exertion of control and forced sex work is a heinous infringement on the victims' human rights, and it ruins any chance many of these women might have had to choose their own partners and plan their own families.

NEGATIVE CONSEQUENCES OF SEXUAL ASSAULT

Health Issues

Sexual assault gravely impacts the survivors' mental and physical health, social life (e.g., intimate relationships), and overall quality of life. In the aftermath of sexual assault, the victims often contend with multiple health-related issues that include, but are not limited to, physical injury, STIs, and unplanned pregnancy.

Physical Injury

Injuries sustained during an assault range from minor to severe. Examples of minor injuries include bruising to arms or scrapes on knees. Moderate physical injures can be extensive bruising or cuts or a number of minor injuries. Severe injuries include a combination of internal and external extensive bruising, lacerations, or broken bones. Extant studies show few differences in physical injury by number of assailants; for example, Ullman (1999) found similar levels of physical injury for single-and multiple-offender rapes in samples of police-reported rapes in the United States. Most injuries following sexual assault do not warrant medical attention. However, police and rape crisis centers encourage victims to seek medical assistance (e.g., forensic examine) following victimization.

STIs

Epidemiological studies of STIs in sexual assault victims suggest that it is difficult to determine the rate of newly acquired STIs from sexual assault. However, prevalence rates of STIs in a sample of female sexual assault victims were 0–26.3 percent gonorrhea, 3.9–17 percent trachomatis, 0–5.6 percent treponema pallidum, 0–19 percent vaginalis, and 0.6–2.3 percent human papilloma virus (Reynolds, Peipert, & Collins, 2000). These rates are alarming given that the transmission of STIs during a sexual assault has dire consequences for the victims' physical health and reproductive justice (e.g., ability to conceive children in the future) if the infectious disease goes untreated or is inadequately treated (see chapter 6, "STI Prevention and Control for Women"). It should also be noted that the context of political conflict and forced migration increases the risk of contracting STIs (Dang, 2007). Research has demonstrated that women in developing and war-torn nations are at increased risk for the infection and transmission of HIV and other STIs as a result of poverty, limited access to education, and insufficient employment opportunities (Fang et al., 2008; Kim et al., 2009; Mills, Singh, Nelson, & Nachega, 2006; Okonkwo, Reich, Alabi, Umeike, & Nachman, 2007; Pitts, McMaster, Mangwiro, & Woolliscroft, 1999). For instance, Kim and associates (2009) found that women ages 15 to 49 years old in internally displaced persons (IDP) camps in the Democratic Republic of Congo were twice as likely as women in surrounding towns to be HIV+, which suggests that sexual violence against women in IDP camps contributes to higher prevalence rates of infection and transmission of HIV. Likewise, Fang and colleagues (2008) posited that women in developing countries, such as rural China, also have a high risk of contracting HIV and other STIs, as they are likely to be entered into sex work due to poverty and limited employment opportunities. Given that they do not have regular income, women in these areas generally do not have insurance, have limited financial resources to afford cost of treatment, and have limited or no access to quality health care; these factors reduce their likelihood of seeking treatment for HIV and other STIs (Okonkwo et al., 2007; Pitts et al., 1999).

Unplanned Pregnancy

The prevalence of unplanned pregnancies following sexual violence is difficult to assess. Multiple factors compound this issue; for example, the woman may have an abortion without disclosing/seeking treatment for sexual assault, and, in the context of marital rape, it may be impossible to determine retrospectively if conception occurred during sexual assault or consensual sexual activity. Nevertheless, the victim is faced with a health issue when she learns that she is pregnant by her perpetrator and must decide if she will carry the fetus to term or terminate the pregnancy. The option to terminate only exists for a limited number of women who actually have access to safe, affordable, and accessible services (see chapter 7, "Contraception and Abortion").

Mental Health Concerns

Psychological consequences of sexual assault can be devastating; these include posttraumatic stress disorder (PTSD), depression, anxiety, and sexual problems. A startling 17–65 percent of women with a lifetime history of sexual assault develop PTSD (Clum, Calhoun, & Kimerling, 2000), and approximately, 13–51 percent meet diagnostic criteria for depression (Acierno et al., 2002; Clum et al., 2000; Dickinson, deGruy, Dickinson, & Candib, 1999). An overwhelming majority of sexual assault victims develop fear and/or anxiety (73%–82%; Ullman & Seigal, 1993). Between 13 and 49 percent of survivors become dependent on alcohol, and 28–61 percent may use other illicit substances to cope with their emotional distress (Ullman & Najdowski, 2009a; Ullman & Brecklin, 2002). Given the emotional distress that arises in sexual assault victims, it is not surprising that 23–44 percent experience suicidal ideation (Petrak, Doyle, Williams, Buchan, & Forster, 1997), and 2–19 percent may attempt suicide (Davidson, Hughes, George, & Blazer, 1996).

PTSD

PTSD, which is characterized by reexperiencing the sexual assault (e.g., flashbacks, symptoms of increased arousal, avoidance of reminders of the assault), is one of the leading psychological consequences of victimization. Approximately one-third of female sexual assault victims are diagnosed with PTSD at some time following the assault (Kilpatrick, Edmunds, & Seymour, 1992). In a U.S. probability sample, 31 percent of female sexual assault survivors had developed PTSD at some time in their lives in contrast with only 5 percent of women who had never been victims of a crime (Kilpatrick et al., 1992); thus, PTSD is a common negative outcome of sexual assault, but it often goes untreated.

Substance Use

Substance abuse/alcohol problems and PTSD are highly correlated among trauma survivors, particularly female survivors (Stewart & Israeli, 2001). The self-medication hypothesis, which states that victims suffering from PTSD use alcohol to manage their symptoms, is often used to provide a rationale for this relationship (Epstein, Saunders, Kilpatrick, & Resnick, 1998). Although this form of coping may lessen trauma symptoms temporarily, it also may result in chronic PTSD. Additional factors have also been proposed to explain the relationship between PTSD and alcohol problems including trauma histories, social support, coping, self-blame, alcohol expectancies, and a history of drinking to cope with distress. Trauma histories and child sexual abuse (CSA) are related to greater risk of both PTSD and alcohol problems in women (Stewart & Israeli, 2001), and violent assaults with life threat and rape completion are related to more PTSD in women (Kilpatrick, Saunders, Amick-McMullan, & Best, 1989). Clinical samples in which women with PTSD only are compared to those with PTSD and alcohol abuse (Ouimette, Wolfe, & Chrestman, 1996) or women with PTSD and substance use disorders (Saladin, Brady, Dansky, & Kilpatrick, 1995) show greater CSA, sexual victimization, and trauma exposure in comorbid women.

Suicidal Ideation

The desire to live is sometimes compromised following victimization, and this manifests in suicidal ideation and/or suicide attempts among sexual assault survivors (Bryant-Davis, Tillman, et al., 2010). Risk of suicidal ideation/attempts is increased if the victim has a history of traumatic events. A prior history of CSA is particularly associated with more serious suicidal ideation among victims (Ullman, & Najdowski, 2009b). In addition, depression, coping by substance use, and coping by blaming oneself are highly correlated with more serious suicidal ideation (Stephenson, Pena-Shaff, & Quirk, 2006). Completed sexual assaults are associated with more reports of suicide attempts, and CSA and traumatic life events are related to greater likelihood of suicide attempts (Ullman & Najdowski,

2009a). These are important findings that reinforce the need to consider the role of cumulative trauma exposure (sexual and nonsexual) in suicidality.

Sexual Function

Intimacy, particularly sexual functioning, is irrevocably changed after an experience of sexual violence (Van Berlo & Ensink, 2000). Research has shown that the frequency of sexual contact decreases after sexual victimization (Öberg, Fugl-Meyer, & Fugl-Meyer, 2002). When women are sexually active, they report that satisfaction and pleasure during sexual intercourse seem to diminish for at least one year postassault (Öberg et al., 2002). Moreover, sexual assault victims often develop sexual problems (e.g., fear, dysfunction in arousal and desire) that could persist for many years after victimization (Leonard, Iverson, & Follette, 2008). Findings indicate that young age, a known assailant, and penetration during the assault were often associated with sexual problems (Leonard et al., 2008). Furthermore, the victim's emotional response, such as anger toward the self and shame or guilt felt during and immediately after the assault, might be predictive of later sexual problems (Van Berlo & Ensink, 2000).

PREVENTION OF REPRODUCTIVE RIGHTS VIOLATIONS

Considering Sexual Assault

Psychologists provide a unique contribution to the promotion of reproductive justice. Based on research and clinical practice, psychologists have identified a number of approaches to the prevention of sexual violence. It is important to note that, given the importance of avoiding victim blaming in actuality or in language, prevention of sexual violence is the responsibility of potential offenders and all community members. For potential victims of sexual violence, the aim is risk reduction. It is critical to reinforce the message that victims are not responsible for the behavior of perpetrators. They can engage in behaviors to reduce their vulnerability, but, if they are assaulted, they are not to blame.

With that awareness in mind, there are various types of sexual violence prevention programs that have primarily been documented and analyzed in the United States. The aims of the programs include awareness raising through psychoeducation, changing behavior, altering attitudes, and/ or teaching risk reduction strategies (Black, Weisz, Coats, & Patterson, 2000; Söchting, Fairbrother, & Koch, 2004). These programs have been conducted in community agencies, on university campuses, in schools, and on military bases (Kelley, Schwerin, Farrar, & Lane, 2005; Weisz & Black, 2001). Most prevention programs take the form of single events that last for less than one day, although it has been argued that prevention activities need to be repeated over time to maximize their impact (Anderson et al., 1998; Heppner, Humphrey, Hillenbrand-Gunn, & DeBord, 1995; Söchting et al., 2004).

The prevention program may include various components, such as didactic education, role play, live theater, film, bibliotherapy, and discussion groups (Söchting et al., 2004; Yeater, Naugle, O'Donohue, & Bradley, 2004). Some programs are coeducational, and some are for single-sex groups (Bradley, Yeater, & O'Donohue, 2009). The prevention message is usually presented by diverse speakers, such as survivors, community advocates, health professionals, peers, and criminal justice professionals (Milhausen, McBride, & Jun, 2006). The educational domains include definitions of various forms of sexual violence or one particular form of sexual violence, prevalence statistics, myths and facts, effects of violence, and prevention and risk-reduction strategies (Casey & Lindhorst, 2009). Risk-reduction education can include resistance training or self-defense, and these training programs can be single events or a series of classes over time. Campus-based prevention programs often focus on dating expectations, communication, and conceptualization of consent (Borges, Banyard, & Moynihan, 2008; Rothman & Silverman, 2007).

Much of the evaluation of these prevention programs is based on a pretest immediately before and a posttest immediately after the intervention. Prevention programs that use speakers and/or theater often produce a reduction in rape-supportive attitudes and reduced endorsement of rape myths (Foubert & Marriott, 1997; Heppner et al., 1995; Lonsway et al., 1998; Milhausen et al., 2006). These effects are more pronounced in female than in male attendees. There are a growing number of prevention programs for men that include developing empathy and perspective taking as a way to engage men as allies in the fight against sexual violence (Choate, 2003; Foubert & Newberry, 2006).

Policies that are informed by psychological science are critical in the creation of victim-sensitive systems and processes (Burgess, Lewis-O'Connor, Nugent-Borakove, & Fanflik, 2006). Psychologists have provided research to inform policy decisions at the local, national, and international level, including at the UN (Brubaker, 2009). Local policies can create a precedent for hospitals' use of sexual-assault response teams that consist of police officers, nurse examiners, and community advocates (Burgess et al., 2006). National policies have been developed in many countries (e.g., Australia, Germany, Nigeria, South Korea) to criminalize and concretize the response to sexual trafficking and slavery (Van Hook, Gjermeni, & Haxhiymeri, 2006). On an international level, the UN has created policies that define sexual violence as a war crime. The development of sexual violence policies is crucial for prevention, but, for optimal effect, these policies, once created, must be strictly enforced (Kolbe & Hutson, 2006). Enforcement requires actively combating corruption, sexism, and victim blaming by government officials and criminal justice professionals. This issue is truly brought to light when one considers the vulnerability of women who have been assaulted by a soldier, police officer, or high-status politician (Taback, Painter, & King, 2008).

One of the primary ways to promote the reproductive rights of those who are disenfranchised is through socioeconomic and political empowerment (Nicarthy, 1989). Economic, educational, vocational, and political marginalization increases the risk for both sexual violence and inadequate health care after a sexual violence (Niaz, 2003). To promote reproductive justice for all community members, it is necessary to create pathways for growth in all aspects of human potential, especially those that have been demonstrated to be protective factors (Sen, 2010). Although this area of prevention may seem to be outside of the scope of psychological practice, there are psychological factors that can serve as both barriers and promoters of empowerment (Ullman & Townsend, 2008). These factors are explored in a number of subfields of psychology such as community psychology, political psychology, social psychology, positive psychology, and feminist psychology. By attending to microlevel factors through prevention programs and macrolevel factors through policy development and enforcement, as well as to multidimensional empowerment, mental health professionals and social justice advocates can work to prevent the violation of reproductive rights in the form of sexual violence.

CONCLUSION

Reproductive justice requires more than nominal reproductive rights. According to the World Health Organization (2002), it necessitates the right to a healthy life, the rights to bodily integrity and security, the right to the benefits of quality treatment based on scientific progress, the right to accurate sex education, the right to equality in marriage and divorce, and the right to equality under the law. Sexual assault is a global crisis that denies reproductive justice to victims and violates their human rights. This violation is based on a dismissal of an individual's right to ownership of her body and her right to live without fear of sexual violence. Additional victims' rights are often denied by a lack of appropriate physical and mental health care in the aftermath of sexual violence, as well as pregnancies to which they did not consent. Sexual assault is manifested in a range of forms, but, regardless of the dynamics of the violation, there are often lasting physical and mental health consequences. To promote reproductive justice, prevention programs, public policies, and empowerment initiatives are needed, particularly for those who are most vulnerable to sexual violence. Safety from sexual violence is necessary to produce reproductive justice for the world's women. When women are denied the right to determine whether, when, and with whom to engage in sexual activity, these acts of injustice impede their ability to enjoy health, safety, and the right to family planning. The work of promoting reproductive justice in women's lives requires urgent, global, and sustained attention.

REFERENCES

Abbey, A., BeShears, R., Clinton-Sherrod, A., & McAuslan, P. (2004). Similarities and differences in women's sexual assault experiences based on tactics used by the perpetrator. *Psychology of Women Quarterly, 28,* 323–333.

Acierno, R., Brady, K., Gray, M., Kilpatrick, D. G., Resnick, H., & Best, C. L. (2002). Psychopathology following interpersonal violence: A comparison of risk factors in older and younger adults. *Journal of Clinical Geropsychology, 8,* 13–23.

Ajuwon, A. J., Akin-Jimoh, I., Olley, B. O., & Akintola, O. (2001). Perceptions of sexual coercion: Learning from young people in Ibadan, Nigeria. *Reproductive Health Matters, 9*(17), 128–136.

Ali, F. A., Israr, S. M., Ali, B. S., & Janjua, N. Z. (2009). Association of various reproductive rights, domestic violence and marital rape with depression among Pakistani women. *BMC Psychiatry, 9,* 1–13.

Amowitz, L., Reis, C., Lyons, K., Vann, B., Mansaray, B., Akinsulure-Smit, A., . . . Iacopino, V. (2002). Prevalence of war-related sexual violence and other human rights abuses among internally displaced persons in Sierra Leone. *Journal of the American Medical Association, 287,* 513–521.

Anderson, L., Stoelb, M. P., Duggan, P., Hieger, B., King, K. H., & Payne, J. P. (1998). The effectiveness of two types of rape-prevention programs in changing rape-supportive attitudes of college students. *Journal of College Student Development, 39,* 131–142.

Bergen, R. K. (2006). *Marital rape: New research and directions.* National Online Resource Center on Violence Against Women. Retrieved from http://new.vawnet.org/Assoc_Files_VAWnet/AR_MaritalRapeRevised.pdf.

Black, B., Weisz, A., Coats, S., & Patterson, D. (2000). Evaluating a psychoeducational sexual-assault prevention program incorporating theatrical presentation, peer education, and social work. *Research on Social Work Practice, 10,* 589–606.

Borges, A., Banyard, V., & Moynihan, M. (2008). Clarifying consent: Primary prevention of sexual assault on a college campus. *Journal of Prevention & Intervention in the Community, 36*(1–2), 75–88.

Bradley, A., Yeater, E., & O'Donohue, W. (2009). An evaluation of a mixed-gender sexual assault prevention program. *Journal of Primary Prevention, 30,* 697–715.

Brubaker, S. (2009). Sexual assault prevalence, reporting, and policies: Comparing college and university campuses and military service academies. *Security Journal, 22*(1), 56–72.

Bryant-Davis, T., Tillman, S., Chung, H., & Belcourt, A. (2010). From the margins to the center: Ethnic minority women and the mental health effects of sexual assault. *Trauma, Violence, & Abuse, 11,* 330–357.

Bryant-Davis, T., Ullman, S., Tsong, Y., Tillman, S., & Smith, K. (2010). Struggling to survive: Sexual assault, poverty, and mental health outcomes of African American women. *American Journal of Orthopsychiatry, 80,* 61–70.

Burgess, A., Lewis-O'Connor, A., Nugent-Borakove, M., & Fanflik, P. (2006). SANE/SART services for sexual assault victims: Policy implications. *Victims & Offenders, 1,* 205–212.

Casey, E., & Lindhorst, T. (2009). Toward a multi-level, ecological approach to the primary prevention of sexual assault: Prevention in peer and community contexts. *Trauma, Violence, & Abuse, 10,* 91–114.

Choate, L. (2003). Sexual assault prevention programs for college men: An exploratory evaluation of the men against violence model. *Journal of College Counseling, 6,* 166–176.

Clum, G. A., Calhoun, K. S., & Kimerling, R. (2000). Associations among symptoms of depression and posttraumatic stress disorder and self-reported heath in sexually assaulted women. *Journal of Nervous and Mental Disease, 188,* 671–678.

Coglan, T. (2009, April 16). Women protestors against "marital rape" law: Spat on and stoned in Kabul. *Sunday Times.* Retrieved from http://www.timeson line.co.uk/tol/news/world/asia/article6098614.ece.

Dang, S. (2007). HIV vulnerabilities and conflict dynamics. *Asia Pacific Journal of Public Health, 19,* 70–71.

Davidson, J., Hughes, D., George, L., & Blazer, D. (1996). The association of sexual assault and attempted suicide within the community. *Archives of General Psychiatry, 53,* 550–555.

Dickinson, L. M., deGruy, F. V., Dickinson, W. P., & Candib, L. M. (1999). Health-related quality of life and symptom profiles of female survivors of sexual abuse in primary care. *Archives of Family Medicine, 8,* 35–43.

El-Mouelhy, M. (2004). Violence against women: A public health problem. *Journal of Primary Prevention, 25,* 289–303.

Epstein, J., Saunders, B., Kilpatrick, D., & Resnick, H. (1998). PTSD as a mediator between childhood rape and alcohol use in adult women. *Child Abuse and Neglect 22,* 223–234.

Fang, X., Li, X., Yang, H., Hong, Y., Stanton, B., Zhao, R., . . . Liang, S. (2008). Can variation in HIV/STD-related risk be explained by individual SES? Findings from female sex workers in a rural Chinese county. *Health Care for Women International, 29,* 316–335.

Foubert, J., & Newberry, J. (2006). Effects of two versions of an empathy-based rape prevention program on fraternity men's survivor empathy, attitudes, and behavioral intent to commit rape or sexual assault. *Journal of College Student Development, 47,* 133–148.

Foubert, J. D., & Marriott, K. A. (1997). Effects of a sexual assault peer education program on men's belief in rape myths. *Sex Roles, 36,* 259–268.

Heppner, M. J., Humphrey, C. F., Hillenbrand-Gunn, T. L., & DeBord, K. A. (1995). The differential effects of rape prevention programming on attitudes, behavior, and knowledge. *Journal of Counseling Psychology, 42,* 508–518.

Herman, J. L. (1992). *Trauma and recovery: The aftermath of violence—from domestic abuse to political terror.* New York: Basic Books.

Hynes, M., & Cardozzo, B. L. (2000). Sexual violence against refugee women. *Journal of Women's Health & Gender-based Medicine, 9,* 819–823.

Izugbara, C., & Undie, C. (2008). Who owns the body: Indigenous African discourses of the body and contemporary sexual rights rhetoric. *Reproductive Health Matters, 16*(31), 159–167.

Kelley, M., Schwerin, M., Farrar, K., & Lane, M. (2005). An evaluation of a sexual assault prevention and advocacy program for U.S. Navy personnel. *Military Medicine, 170,* 320–326.

Khanna, R. (2008). Communal violence in Gujarat, India: Impact of sexual violence and responsibilities of the health care system. *Reproductive Health Matters, 16,* 142–152.

Kilpatrick, D., Edmunds, C., & Seymour, A. (1992). Rape in America: A report to the nation. *Interpersonal Violence, 8,* 223–255.

Kilpatrick, D. G., Saunders, B. E., Amick-McMullan, A., & Best, C. L. (1989). Victim and crime factors associated with the development of crime-related posttraumatic stress disorder. *Behavior Therapy, 20,* 199–214.

Kim, A. A., Malele, F., Kaiser, R., Mama, N., Kinkela, T., Mantshumba, J., . . . Diaz, T. (2009). HIV infection among internally displaced women and women residing in river populations along the Congo river, Democratic Republic of Congo. *AIDS and Behavior, 13,* 914–920.

Kirkwood, M., & Cecil, D. (2001). Marital rape: A student assessment of rape laws and the marital exemption. *Violence Against Women, 7,* 1235–1253.

Kolbe, A. R., & Hutson, R. A. (2006). Human rights abuse and other criminal violations in Port-au-Prince, Haiti: A random survey of households. *Lancet, 368,* 864–873.

Leonard, L. M., Iverson, K. M., & Follette, V. M. (2008). Sexual functioning and sexual satisfaction among women who report a history of childhood and/or adolescent sexual abuse. *Journal of Sex & Marital Therapy, 34,* 375–384.

Lonsway, K. A., Klaw, E. L., Berg, D. R., Waldo, C. R., Kothari, C., Mazurek, C. J., & Hegeman, K. E. (1998). Beyond "no means no": Outcomes of an intensive program to train peer facilitators for campus acquaintance rape education. *Journal of Interpersonal Violence, 13,* 73–92.

Malkin, E., & Thompson, G. (2005, November 17). Mexican court says sex attack by a husband still rape. *New York Times.* Retrieved from http://www.ncdsv.org/images/MexicanCourtSaysSexAttackbyHusband.pdf.

Milhausen, R., McBride, K., & Jun, M. (2006). Evaluating a peer-led, theatrical sexual assault prevention program: How do we measure success? *College Student Journal, 40,* 316–328.

Mills, E. J., Singh, S., Nelson, B. D., & Nachega, J. B. (2006). The impact of conflict on HIV/AIDS in Sub-Saharan Africa. *International Journal of STD & AIDS, 17,* 713–717.

National Alliance to End Sexual Violence. (2007). *Violence Against Women Act (VAWA) appropriations.* Retrieved from http://www.naesv.org.

Ngwena, C. G. (2010). Protocol to the African Charter on the Rights of Women: Implications for access to abortion at the regional level. *International Journal of Gynecology & Obstetrics, 110,* 163–166.

Niaz, U. (2003). Violence against women in South Asian countries. *Archives of Women's Mental Health, 6,* 173–84.

Nicarthy, G. (1989). From the sounds of silence to the roar of a global movement: Notes on the movement against violence against women. *Response to the Victimization of Women & Children, 12*(2), 3–10.

Öberg, K., Fugl-Meyer, K. S., & Fugl-Meyer, A. R. (2002). On sexual well-being in sexually abused Swedish women: Epidemiological aspects. *Sexual and Relationship Therapy, 17*, 329–342.

Okonkwo, K. C., Reich, K., Alabi, A. I., Umeike, N., & Nachman, S. A. (2007). An evaluation of awareness: Attitudes and beliefs of pregnant Nigerian women toward voluntary counseling and testing for HIV. *AIDS Patient Care and STDs, 21*, 252–260.

Ouimette, P., Wolfe, J., & Chrestman, K. (1996). Characteristics of PTSD-alcohol abuse comorbidity in women. *Journal of Substance Abuse, 8*, 335–346.

Petrak, J., Doyle, A., Williams, L., Buchan, L., & Forster, G. (1997). The psychological impact of sexual assault: A study of female attenders of a sexual health psychology service. *Sexual and Marital Therapy, 12*, 339–345.

Pitts, M., McMaster, J., Mangwiro, O., & Woolliscroft, J. (1999). Why do people delay obtaining treatment for an STD? Perspectives from a developing country. *Psychology, Health, & Medicine, 4*, 73–81.

Renzetti, C. M. (2005). Gender-based violence. *Lancet, 365*, 1009–1010.

Reynolds, M., Peipert, J., & Collins, B. (2000). Epidemiologic issues of sexually transmitted diseases in sexual assault victims. *Obstetrical and Gynecological Survey, 55*, 51–57.

Rothman, E., & Silverman, J. (2007). The effect of a college sexual assault prevention program on first-year students' victimization rates. *Journal of American College Health, 55*, 283–290.

Russell, D. (1990). *Rape in marriage* (expanded and rev. ed.). Bloomington: Indiana University Press.

Saladin, M., Brady, K., Dansky B., & Kilpatrick, D. (1995). Understanding comorbidity between PTSD and substance use disorder: Two preliminary investigations. *Addictive Behaviors, 20*, 643–655.

Sarkar, N., & Sarkar, R. (2005). Sexual assault on women: Its impact on her life and society. *Sexual and Relationship Therapy, 20*, 407–419.

Sen, G. (2010). Integrating family planning with sexual and reproductive health and rights: The past as prologue. *Studies in Family Planning, 41*(2), 143–146.

Söchting, I., Fairbrother, N., & Koch, W. (2004). Sexual assault of women: Prevention efforts and risk factors. *Violence Against Women, 10*(1), 73–93.

Stephenson, H., Pena-Shaff, J., & Quirk, P. (2006). Predictors of college student suicidal ideation: Gender differences. *College Student Journal, 40*(1), 109–117.

Stewart, S., & Israeli, A. (2001). Substance abuse and co-occurring psychiatric disorders in victims of intimate violence. In C. Wekerle & A. Hall (Eds.), *The violence and addiction equation* (pp. 98–122). New York: Hogrefe & Huber.

Taback, N., Painter, R., & King, B. (2008). Sexual violence in the Democratic Republic of the Congo. *Journal of the American Medical Association, 300*, 653–654.

Tang, C., & Lai, B. (2008). A review of empirical literature on the prevalence and risk markers of male-on-female intimate partner violence in contemporary China, 1987–2006. *Aggression and Violent Behavior, 13*, 10–28.

Tavara, L. (2006). Sexual violence. *Clinical Obstetrics & Gynecology, 20*, 395–408.

Tjaden, P., & Thoennes, N. (1999). *Violence and threats of violence against women and men, 1994–1996* (ICPSR version) [Computer file]. Denver, CO: Center for Policy Research [producer]. Ann Arbor, MI: Inter-university Consortium for Political and Social Research [distributor].

Totten, S. (2009). *Plight and fate of women during and following genocide.* Piscataway, NJ: Transaction.

Ullman, S. (1999). A comparison of gang and individual rape incidents. *Violence and Victims, 14,* 123–133.

Ullman, S. (2010). *Talking about sexual assault: Society's response to survivors.* Washington, DC: American Psychological Association.

Ullman, S., & Brecklin, L. (2002). Sexual assault history, PTSD, and mental health service seeking in a national sample of women. *Journal of Community Psychology, 30,* 261–279.

Ullman, S., & Seigal J. M. (1993). Victim-offender relationship and sexual assault. *Violence and Victims, 8,* 121–134.

Ullman, S., & Townsend, S. (2008). What is an empowerment approach to working with sexual assault survivors? *Journal of Community Psychology, 36,* 299–312.

Ullman, S. E., & Najdowski, C. J. (2009a). Correlates of serious suicidal ideation and attempts in female adult sexual assault survivors. *Suicide and Life-Threatening Behavior, 39*(1), 47–57.

Ullman, S. E., & Najdowski, C. J. (2009b). Revictimization as a moderator of psychosocial risk factors for problem drinking in female sexual-assault survivors. *Journal of Studies on Alcohol and Drugs, 70,* 41–49.

United Nations Development Fund for Women. (2005). *Violence against women — Facts and figures.* Retrieved from http://www.unifem.org/attachments/gender_issues/violence_against_women/facts_figures_violence_against_women_2007.pdf.

United Nations Office on Drugs and Crime. (2009). *Human trafficking.* Retrieved from http://www.unodc.org/unodc/en/human-trafficking/what-is-human-trafficking.html.

Van Berlo, W., & Ensink, B. (2000). Problems with sexuality after sexual assault. *Annual Review of Sex Research, 11,* 235–257.

Van Hook, M., Gjermeni, E., & Haxhiymeri, E. (2006). Sexual trafficking of women: Tragic proportions and attempted solutions in Albania. *International Social Work, 49*(1), 29–40.

Watts, C., & Zimmerman, C. (2002). Violence against women: Global scope and magnitude. *Lancet, 359,* 1232–1237.

Weisz, A., & Black, B. (2001). Evaluating a sexual assault and dating violence prevention program for urban youths. *Social Work Research, 25*(2), 89–102.

World Health Organization. (2002). *Defining sexual health* [Report of a technical consultation on sexual health]. Retrieved from http://www.who.int/reproductivehealth/topics/gender_rights/defining_sexual_health/en/index.html.

Yeater, E., Naugle, A., O'Donohue, W., & Bradley, A. (2004). Sexual assault prevention with college-aged women: A bibliotherapy approach. *Violence and Victims, 19,* 593–612.

Chapter 5

Reproductive Injustice: The Trafficking and Sexual Exploitation of Women and Girls

Nancy M. Sidun

If a woman cannot determine her own sexual partner or decide whether, when, or how to be sexual, she cannot experience reproductive justice. Sex is meant to be an expression of affectionate ties between individuals, but, for too many women and girls around the world, it is a form of torture and oppression. This chapter focuses on the exploding epidemic of the sexual trafficking of women and children and the intersection of trafficking with coerced prostitution. Specifically, the trafficking of women and girls and their forced entry into sexual exploitation and prostitution is explored: first, by delineating what constitutes trafficking, and, second, by situating sexual trafficking within the historical context of sexual exploitation and prostitution. Next, the social and individual factors that fuel one's vulnerability to trafficking and forced sexual exploitation and prostitution are explored. The chapter concludes with a discussion of the physical and psychological sequelae for those who have been trafficked and sexually exploited.

In our current global economy, women and girls performing sexual services for money, whether due to a lack of alternatives or to coercion, is an increasingly common form of work (Murray, 2008). At the extreme end of this spectrum is what is currently called *modern-day slavery,* or *human sexual trafficking,* the most common form of trafficking. Sex trafficking of women for the purposes of forced prostitution, sexual exploitation, and any other form of exploitation is violence against women and a denial of human rights. The Action Coalition on Human Trafficking Alberta (ACT Alberta, 2011) stated that 79 percent of those trafficked are sexually exploited; others have placed the percentage as high as 95 percent (Hynes & Raymond, 2002). Sex trafficking can be any kind of commercial sexual exploitation, including prostitution, pornography, stripping, military prostitution, and sex tourism. For the purpose of this chapter, all forms of sexual exploitation are subsumed under the heading of sexual exploitation.

WHAT IS TRAFFICKING OF HUMANS?

Although there has been some disagreement regarding the definition of human trafficking, in 2000 the U.S. Congress passed the Victims of Trafficking and Violence Protection Act that defined human trafficking as the illicit enslavement of individuals into labor or commercial sex through means of force, fraud, or coercion (Farrell & Fahy, 2009). All international and national laws stress that these three key elements (i.e., fraud, coercion, force) are essential to the definition of human trafficking (Jones, Engstrom, Hilliard, & Diaz, 2007). Human trafficking is defined by the United Nations' Office on Drugs and Crime (UNODC, 2005, para. 1) as

> the recruitment, transportation, transfer, harboring or receipt of persons, by means of the threat or use of force or other forms of coercion, of abduction, of fraud, of deception, of the abuse of power or of a position of vulnerability or of the giving or receiving of payments or benefits to achieve the consent of a person having control over another person, for the purpose of exploitation. Exploitation shall include, at a minimum, the exploitation of the prostitution of others or other forms of sexual exploitation, forced labor or services, slavery or practices similar to slavery, servitude or the removal of organs.

Although they are frequently confused, human smuggling or illegal immigration is distinct from human trafficking. There are four key differences between human trafficking and migrant smuggling: consent, exploitation, transnationality, and source of profits. Migrant smuggling involves consent of the migrants, regardless of the fact that they often undertake dangerous or degrading conditions to be smuggled. Trafficked persons, on the other hand, have either never consented or, if they initially consented, that consent was rendered meaningless by the coercive, deceptive, or abusive action of the traffickers. Migrant smuggling ends with the migrants' arrival at their destination, whereas those who are trafficked experience ongoing exploitation. Smuggling, in contrast to trafficking, is always transnational. For example, trafficking can and does occur when a person is trafficked to another country, between states and provinces in the same country, or within a state's or province's borders. Lastly, the source of profit differs. In smuggling cases, profits are derived from the facilitation of transportation for the illegal entry (or stay) of a person into another country, whereas for trafficked persons the profits are derived from their continued exploitation (UNODC, 2010). As defined by the Protocol Against the Smuggling of Migrants by Land, Sea, and Air (UN General Assembly, 2000, p. 2), smuggling is "the procurement, in order to obtain, directly or indirectly, a financial or other material benefit, of the illegal entry of a person into a State Party of which the person is not a national or a permanent resident." Trafficked and smuggled persons may leave a country of their own free will; however, an element of deception is involved in all cases of trafficking. Both smuggled and trafficked individuals may face similar threats and discomforts along their journeys; however, the essential component of human trafficking is exploitation, rather than transportation (ACT Alberta, 2011).

HUMAN TRAFFICKING IS NOT A NEW PHENOMENON

Despite legislation passed in the 19th century to outlaw it, human slavery is more widespread today than it was at the conclusion of the U.S. Civil War, and twice as many people are enslaved today as during the African slave trade, which lasted for centuries (King, 2004). Human trafficking has acquired grave dimensions worldwide in the context of globalization, and it is the most significant human rights violation in contemporary society. In an age of globalization of capital, information, and technology, organized trafficking operates as a transnational industry not restrained by national boundaries. It truly is a global problem as no country escapes involvement, whether as a destination, transit, or origin of trafficked persons. At least 120 nations are routinely plundered by traffickers for their human raw materials, and more than 130 nations are known destinations (Thompson, 2008). Destination countries for sexual trafficking tend to be wealthy, industrialized nations. However, as Monzini (2004) pointed out, because virtually all nations also function as points of origin, most countries serve as both destinations and origins. For instance, the United States is a top destination country (second only to Italy), but a significant number of children are trafficked from the United States to other industrialized nations with large sex industries, such as Germany, the Netherlands, and Japan (Estes & Weiner, 2001). All countries serve as transit countries through which women and children pass en route to their final destinations (Winterdyk & Reichel, 2010).

Human trafficking is the fastest growing area of organized crime; it has jumped in rank from third to second in illegal profit making, and it is currently ranked between the illegal drug and arms trades (Minnesota Office of Justice Programs, & Minnesota Statistical Analysis Center, 2010; Nam, 2007; Orhant, 2002). The recent European Commission Report (2010) stated that humans are the most trafficked commodities in Europe, more than illegal drugs or arms. Selling humans is a multibillion-dollar business; estimates range from 10 to 30 billion dollars annually (Nam, 2007; Thompson, 2008; United States Department of State [USDOS], 2005). Unlike drugs, humans can be sold over and over, which makes women and children very lucrative commodities (Hodge, 2008). Accurate data on how many people are trafficked is difficult to obtain given the illegal and clandestine nature of human trafficking; however, the estimates are staggering. According to U.S. State Department (USDOS, 2005) data, an estimated 600,000 to 800,000 men, women, and children are trafficked across international borders yearly, whereas the United Nations estimated that 2 to 4 million women are trafficked each year (Murray, 2008).

The International Labour Organization (ILO, 2011), a UN agency, estimated that, at any given time, there are 12.3 million people forced into different types of coerced labor worldwide, whereas antitrafficking campaigners frequently cite numbers as high as 27 million worldwide (Bales, 2000, 2010; Batstone, 2007). According to Olson (2010), 200,000 new slaves are introduced annually into the United States alone. These data do not capture the millions of victims around the world who are trafficked within their own countries. It is frequently assumed that trafficking implies people moving vast distances across continents; however, most exploitation takes place closer to one's home country.

HISTORY OF SEXUAL EXPLOITATION AND PROSTITUTION

Prostitution and sexual slavery have an equally long history, and, together, they lay the foundation for the exploitation of women's and girls' bodies for profit. The historical roots of the sexual servitude of women can be traced back to the beginnings of prostitution and the control of women's sexuality. "Sacred prostitution," according to Lerner (1986), was the earliest form of sexual servitude; this resulted from the ancient worship of fertility goddesses. The worship of goddesses in ancient Mesopotamia and during the Neo-Babylonian period set the groundwork for women to provide sexual favors as a benefit to the temples. When these women provided religious sexual intercourse in the name of the goddesses, men often made donations to the temple in return. Therefore, some priests promoted the use of slave women and lower-class female servants as prostitutes to benefit the temple, which led to the development of purely commercial prostitution (Lerner, 1986). This practice of dedicating young girls to temples where sexual servitude is expected continues to exist today (Power, 2000). In southern India, *davadasis* are girls from the lowest caste whose parents have given them to local temples as human offerings. These girls are married to god before puberty, and, after their first menstrual period, they become sexual servants to the villages' upper-caste men. Although this practice has been outlawed since 1982, human-rights activists have reported that as many as 15,000 girls still become *davadasis* annually (Power, 2000).

In addition to sacred prostitution, the enslavement of captured women was institutionalized by the military during the third millennium BC. During this same period, masters created brothels where their slaves were forced into prostitution. Kings who were admired for their wealth and power, which was determined by the numbers of servants and concubines they had, were imitated by the aristocrats and wealthy men with their attainment of large numbers of slaves and other women for sexual exploitation. Even today, poor families have found that they could sell their children to traffickers, which would allow them to pay off their debts (Lerner, 1986).

According to Parrot and Cummings (2008, p. 12), "the unifying elements that support sexual slavery and trafficking of girls and women . . . are generally the devaluation of females, patriarchal political systems and political instability." It is the most vulnerable women in society who are trapped into trafficking and forced into prostitution. Trafficking is driven by social, cultural, political, and economic factors. Education, cultural values, religion, socioeconomic status, family structure, geography, discrimination, employment status, patriarchal government policies, political unrest, criminal status, and natural disasters all have an impact on the extent of trafficking of girls and women (Parrot & Cummings, 2008). Dr. William Sanger, one of the foremost researchers on prostitution in the 19th century, found similar reasons why Victorian-era women became prostitutes. These women had limited options available to them due to poverty, social disgrace, and lack of education. Some had been expelled from their homes or had been deserted by their families; others were forced into prostitution in order for their families to survive, and still others who began as domestic servants were forced into sexual servitude after their masters seduced, and then abandoned, them, leaving them no other means of supporting themselves (Women's Issues Then and Now, 2002). Thus, in essence, "the reasons for trafficking are solely economic. Trafficking is a by-product of 'supply and demand' where devalued, marginalized women and girls are used for profit by men and for men" (Parrot & Cummings, 2008, p. 28).

WHO GETS TRAFFICKED?

The most vulnerable social groups—the poor, ethnic minority, indigenous, and disabled women and children—are the majority of those trafficked. The low economic status of women and children is closely associated with those most at risk of being trafficked (Murray, 2008). There are clearly gendered vulnerabilities; these vulnerabilities are the result of political, economic, and development processes that may leave women socially and economically dependent on men. If the support that men provide women is lessened, limited, or withdrawn, women become precariously susceptible to abuse. In many countries, women often have no individual protection or recognition under the law, inadequate access to health care and education, limited employment opportunities, little chance to own property, or high levels of social isolation. Research indicates that, in countries where women's economic status has improved, significantly fewer local women are trafficked into the commercial sex industry (USDOS, 2009). As Kristof and WuDunn (2009) pointed out, traffickers tend to prey on uneducated girls "precisely because they are the ones most likely to obey orders and resign themselves to their fate" (p. 47). Poverty, gendered inequality, global economic policies, ethnic conflicts, and economies in transition all contribute to and fuel trafficking (Farrell & Fahy, 2009). These same aspects are integrally linked to women's reproductive health, which is connected to and affected by conditions in women's lives that are shaped by socioeconomic status, human rights violations, race, sexuality, and nationality (Silliman, Fried, Ross, & Gutierrez, 2004).

It is the economic desperation created by globalization that provides the conditions for the current rapid growth in trafficking. Globalization has made it easier for women and girls to be smuggled across bounders or even across the globe. Technical innovations have served traffickers by providing ease of communication, which has enhanced traffickers' ability to transport trafficked women and girls.

Specific modes of recruitment, which can vary from geographic location to location, have been identified for women and girls who are trafficked internationally. The least known, yet most common, method is the use of false-front agencies, which attract women with promises of employment and assurances of a better life. Typically these women cannot afford their transportation costs, so they enter into an arrangement commonly referred to as *debt bondage*, where traffickers agree to pay transportation fees and then hold women captive until they repay the debt. Many women trafficked into prostitution report a never-ending cycle of debt. Initially they are charged excessive fees for the cost of transportation, but expenses for food, clothing, shelter, and condoms are added daily and mount up exponentially. Often the debt can never be repaid. In the event that trafficked women require medical treatment, such as an abortion or medication for a sexually transmitted infection (STI), this, too, is added to their debt (USDOS, 2007). The following stories of Maria and Seema illustrate the cyclical pattern in which many women find themselves.

Once Maria was over the Mexican border, she was kept at a safe house. From the safe house, she was transported to Florida. When she arrived in Florida, she was told by one of the ringleaders that she would be working at a brothel as a prostitute. Maria informed him that he was mistaken; she was told that she would be working in a restaurant not a brothel. The ringleader then ordered her to work in the brothel; he stated that she owed him a smuggling debt of approximately $220, and the sooner she paid it off, the sooner she could leave. Maria was 18 years old at the time, had never been far from home, and had no money or way to get back home.

Maria was given tight clothes to wear and was told what she must do. There were armed men selling tickets to customers in the trailer. Tickets were condoms. Each ticket would be sold each for $22 to $25. The client would then point at the girl he wanted, and the girl would take him to one of the bedrooms. At the end of the night, Maria had to turn in the condom wrappers. Each wrapper represented a supposed deduction to her smuggling fee. Maria and the other girls tried to keep their own records, but the bosses destroyed them. As a result Maria was never sure what she really owed.

Up to four girls were kept at each brothel; they were constantly guarded and abused. If anyone refused to go with a customer, she was beaten. If anyone adamantly refused, the bosses would brutally rape her to teach her a lesson. The girls were told that, if they refused again, the assault would be even worse the next time. Maria never knew where she was, as every 15 days, she was transported to another trailer in a nearby city.

Maria and the other girls worked 12-hour days, 6 days per week; they serviced 32–35 clients per day. Weekends, however, were the worst. At the end of the night when they were finished servicing customers, it would be the bosses' turn with the girls (Polaris Project—Maria, n.d., as cited in Parrot & Cummings, 2008, p. 29).

Seema was barely 12 years old when she left the poverty of her home village to work in Kathmandu. There a smooth-talking man approached her; he convinced her to go with him to Bombay with the promise of a better job. It was her hope that she would become a film star; instead she was sold into a brothel. Seema initially resisted by screaming, crying, and fighting off prospective customers, but the madam who ran the brothel quickly intervened and sent in a strong man to hold the Seema down while an old man raped her. The pain was so intense that Seema lost consciousness and had to be hospitalized for a week. After that, it was back to the brothel where the other child prostitutes told her that she could not win this battle. However, Seema's spirit was not broken. Nine months later, with the help of a woman, she escaped. They fled Bombay to Calcutta. Unfortunately in Calcutta, this woman sold Seema to another brothel. Now Seema is resigned to her fate. She hits the streets of central Calcutta as soon as it gets dark and stands near a lamppost soliciting customers. Her parents in Nepal have no idea where their daughter is. Seema does not have the courage to tell them, and she believes that it is probably best that they think she is dead (Polaris Project, n.d.-e).

Mail-order brides are another form of false-front agencies. *Mail-order bride* is a label applied to a woman who publishes her intent to marry someone from another, usually more developed, country. Women can publish their intent through an agency that provides potential spouse-seeking men with a written or online catalogue with the women's information. Over the past 25 years, such marriages were more common between Western men and Asian women, but, with the break up of the Soviet Union, the mail-order market has expanded into the former Soviet countries, especially Ukraine and Russia. It continues, however, to flourish around the globe.

Women have reported that they enter into these mail-order marriages because they believe that they will have a better life, and some do it because they have an aversion to the men in their home countries. Those women who seek a U.S. husband often have a Hollywoodized view of the American man; the typical age difference between these men and their foreign brides is 20–50 years (Glodava & Onizuka, 1994). Men have reported that they are seeking traditional marriages; often their main motivation is that they will have more control over their mate (Glodava & Onizudka, 1994), as these vulnerable women are typically more economically, psychologically, and linguistically dependent on their partners than other women are (Yakushko, 2009). Violence against women in such arranged marriages is significant and noteworthy, which has warranted an investigation of U.S. Congress (Immigration and Naturalization Services, 1999). For example, in September 2003, Alla Barney, a 26-year-old Ukrainian engineer and mail-order bride, bled to death on the floor of her car after her American husband, Lester Barney, age 58, had slashed her throat in front of the couple's 4-year-old son, Daniel (Yakushko, 2009).

If the women have no agency, cannot leave, cannot refuse, and are obligated to have sex on demand, clearly there is no reproductive justice for them. Although one might question the wisdom of these arranged marriages, there is little doubt that reproductive justice for mail order brides is compromised. Further, there is a subset of arranged marriages by fake husbands or marriage brokers that force women into commercial sexual exploitation. Many of these fake husbands are part of international trafficking rings (Parrot & Cummings, 2008).

Another mode of international trafficking involves women who are already engaged in the sex industry in their home countries. They are approached and promised higher earnings for doing similar work in wealthier nations. What is not disclosed to these women is the slave-like conditions in which they will be forced to work. Debt bondage is frequently employed in this situation, as is illustrated by Deng's and Gayla's stories.

Deng was in her late 20s when she was recruited in her native Thailand to travel voluntarily to Australia with the promise of making lots of money as a prostitute. However, once she arrived in Australia, she was met by traffickers, who locked her in a house and took away her passport. Deng was told that she would have to pay off a debt of over $30,000 by servicing 900 men. She was only allowed minimal food; regardless of her health, she was forced to work 7 days per week. Her traffickers told her that if she tried to escape, criminal allies of the trafficking ring would catch her. Deng's exploitation ended when Australian Immigration officials raided the brothel in which she was enslaved (Polaris Project, n.d.-b).

Gayla worked as a prostitute in Vanadzor, Armenia. A neighbor, who had just returned from a trip to Turkey, informed her that there were lucrative opportunities to do the same line of work there. The neighbor informed Gayla and her friends that she had contacts in Turkey, and she could arrange the travel and work details. Because they trusted her, they gave the neighbor their passports and money to make arrangements, and one week later the group traveled to Istanbul by bus. They were met by a man who informed them that Gayla's neighbor had arranged for him to meet them. He brought them to a building in a suburb of Istanbul that looked as though it could have been a house or a pub, and he informed the women that they would reside there. They were told that they were to meet men in the bar on the first floor and take them to the second floor. The man told the women that their clothes were inadequate. They needed to look more attractive, and he purchased clothing for them. Gayla and her friends agreed that 30 percent of their earnings would go to the man to cover food and lodging expenses. When they began to work, they received an unremitting flow of customers, and the women felt that it was impossible to accomplish what was being asked of them. They thought that the man was selling tickets for brief encounters with them, and, when they aired their concerns to him, he stated that it was the only way they would be able to earn a living after they reimbursed him for the expenses he had incurred for them (Polaris Project, n.d.-c).

A less frequent method is abduction, where the woman or child is kidnapped. The following stories demonstrate the gravity of this method of recruitment. They illustrate how vulnerable women and girls can be and how deception, fraud, and force are readily employed. Meena, from a poor family on the Nepal border, was kidnapped when she was eight or nine years old. She was sold to a Nutt clan (i.e., a low-caste tribe that controls the local sex trade), who took her to a house in a rural area. In this house a brothel owner kept prepubescent girls until they were mature enough to attract customers. When Meena was 12, she was taken to the brothel to begin her life as a prostitute. Meena stated that she resisted and fought her first client so much that the client's money was returned to him. As a result, Meena was mercilessly beaten with belts, sticks, and iron rods. Her captors showed her swords and threatened to kill her if she did not agree. Despite repeated beatings, Meena continued to refuse to give in. Finally her captors drugged her, and, while she was intoxicated, one of the brothel owners raped her. When she woke up and realized what had happened, she thought, "Now I am wasted"; she stopped fighting customers after that (Kristof & WuDunn, 2009).

Anita, a Nepali girl, was on an errand to buy vegetables when a Nepali man and woman seated beside her on a bus offered her a banana. Soon after eating it, Anita experienced a severe headache. The couple offered her a bottle of water and a pill for the headache. Immediately after taking the medicine and drinking the water, Anita became unfocused and fell into unconsciousness. When she awoke, Anita found herself in Gorakhpur, India. The man informed her not to draw attention to herself in any way because there was hashish tied to her waist, and, should she make a scene, she would be arrested for smuggling drugs across an international border. Anita did not know what to do, and she did not know how to get back to Nepal. The man informed Anita that she could trust him, and he told her to refer to him as her brother. They traveled by train for five days to Bombay. Once there, the man contacted a friend to meet them at the train station. He told Anita to go with his friend, and said that he would meet her at the friend's home later that afternoon. When evening fell and the man did not arrive, the friend informed Anita that her brother was not coming for her. Anita was very afraid and did not eat. When she realized that the house was a brothel, Anita screamed and cried; she said that she wanted to go. The woman told her that she had not come easily and she would not go easily. She informed Anita that she had been purchased and that Anita would have to work as a prostitute to repay the debt. Anita was never informed how much money had been paid for her (Polaris Project, n.d.-a).

> Gina's story: . . . a young child—only nine years old—living with her family in a small village in Nepal . . . Gina wasn't sold. She was stolen . . . Drugged with a "sweet drink" by a friend, Gina awoke on a train—never to see her family again. When Gina arrived in Bombay after a three-day journey, she remembers being grabbed by the hand, rushed down a crowded street through "a sea of legs" to a dingy brothel. They put makeup on her face and then the "seasoning" process began. She was repeatedly raped, beaten and starved until she was too afraid to leave her new "home." Because of Gina's young age, she was held out by her owners as a virgin—again and again. Sexual encounters numbered as many as 40 per day. Younger girls like Gina—especially virgins—command a higher price in the brothels.[1] (Polaris Project, n.d.-d).

Another method more frequently associated with poorer countries, or those that have recently experienced the displacement and upheaval of war, is the selling of children or young women to traffickers for altruistic reasons. Traffickers often approach families or guardians living in poverty and seek to purchase their girls and young women. The families accept with the belief that this money will allow them to care for their remaining family members and also with the trust, supplied to them by the traffickers, that their daughters will have a better life in another city (Raymond et al., 2002). Although untrue, many parents believe this because of the pervasiveness in Western media of the good, privileged life. The story of a brothel owner illustrates the desperation some economically distressed families face and the hard realities they choose to try to support their families.

> Brothel owner's story: For brothel owner Farzana Baig (not her real name), her two-storey house in a posh area of Lahore is the end of the road for desperate families wishing to sell their daughters into sex work. She said a number of girls were "sold by parents in rural areas, especially in the southern Punjab." Often the girls were told they were being sent to the city to work or attend classes. "These people are so poor, they have no choice. To feed their other children, they must sell one or maybe more," Baig said, adding that some of the girls "are so thin when they arrive I have to feed them for a week so they look healthier and more attractive. . .There is a big demand for young girls; we take in those as young as 10. Customers pay well for pre-pubescent children," she said.[2] (IRIN Humanitarian News and Analysis Service, 2010)

Unfortunately, there are a growing number of families, both within the United States and around the world, in which the parent(s) have drug addictions, which drive their actions (i.e., selling or prostituting their child for money to buy drugs). A resident of the Supportive Housing Program at the Minnesota Indian Women's Resource Center (MIWRC) shared her story. At the age of 12, her mother had prostituted her in order to support her crack addiction. By the time she was 14, she herself had begun to prostitute other young girls in order to feed her own drug habit (MIWRC, 2009).

This next story exemplifies how families can be deceived into believing that they are making a good decision for their child, when in truth they have unwittingly sold their child into slavery. Evelyn Chumbow was an outstanding student in her native country of Cameroon. In 1996, Theresa Mubang offered to take Evelyn to America; she assured her family that Evelyn would receive a top-rate education. With hopes of a bright future for their daughter, her parents allowed 11-year-old Evelyn to travel to suburban Maryland with Mubang. Once there, Evelyn did not receive an education. Instead, she was enslaved in Mubang's home and forced to work long hours with no monetary compensation (Thomas, Date, & Cook, 2007).

GLOBAL SEX TOURISM

Global sex tourism must be mentioned, as it is dramatically on the rise and is an extremely lucrative industry. The transnational sex industry generates an estimated 57 billion dollars per year (Hughes, 2000). In 1998, the ILO (as cited in Nair, 2010) reported its calculations that 2–14 percent of the gross domestic product of Indonesia, Malaysia, the Philippines, and Thailand derived from sex tourism. In Thailand alone, it is estimated that 66 percent of all men who arrive at the Bangkok airport came to Thailand for sex tourism (Olson, 2010). Although Asian countries, historically, have been the destinations of choice, sex tourism is increasing in Latin America, especially in Central America. Brazil has long been thought of as the region's leader in sex tourism, but recently Costa Rica, Guatemala, and Honduras have emerged as major destination countries (Hannum, 2002). Costa Rica stands out as a country where more than 30,000 Americans and several thousand Canadians have retired, not just for the climate, tax breaks, and other advantages, but also for the easy and cheap sexual access. These retired men are frequently referred to as *sex-pats* (as opposed to *ex-pats*; Hannum, 2002).

Children are considered an extremely valuable commodity, and the demand for them is growing at an alarming rate in the sex tourism industry. Within Cambodia alone, it is estimated that 20 million U.S. dollars per year are used to buy women and girls for sex; one-third of those purchased for sex are under 17 years old, and they service 7–10 men daily (Parrot & Cummings, 2008). The reasons for the growth of child sex tourism are many and similar to those in the adult sex tourism industry. Among the most significant factors in the boost in sex tourism are the availability of information on the Internet and the erroneous belief that younger girls are less likely to be infected with HIV (Hannum, 2002; Hughes, 2000; UNICEF, 2009).

DOMESTIC TRAFFICKING

Until recently, the United States considered human trafficking to be only an international issue. However, domestic trafficking is not a new or isolated problem; cases of domestic human trafficking have been reported in all 50 states, the District of Columbia, and some U.S. territories (Office of Safe and Drug-Free Schools [OSDFS], 2010). The Trafficking Victims Protection Reauthorization Act of 2005 cited the congressional finding that

100,000 to 300,000 children, predominately girls, are at risk for the commercial sex trade at any given time in the United States (Parrot & Cummings, 2008); 60 percent of these at-risk children are runaways or have been abandoned by their parents (Estes & Weiner, 2001). Domestic child sex trafficking is one of the largest forms of domestic sex trafficking in the United States. Domestic sex traffickers, commonly referred to as *pimps*, routinely target vulnerable children, particularly runaway and homeless youth, although this is not the only population that is manipulated by traffickers. Sex traffickers go after children because they are vulnerable and gullible and because of the market demand for young victims. The sexual exploitation of children is not limited to any particular racial, ethnic, or socioeconomic group, although children from lower-class families are at somewhat higher risk of being trafficked. Traffickers are only interested in the profit. Traffickers have reported targeting youth through telephone chat-lines, at clubs, on the street, through friends, and at malls, and they have girls recruit other girls at schools and after-school programs (OSDFS, 2010). Sexual exploiters consist mostly of men, but some women and juveniles, including older siblings, also recruit children (Estes & Weiner, 2001).

The average age of entry into the commercial sex industry is 11–12 years old (Frundt, 2010). Jill's story is an example of the vulnerability of young girls.

Jill's story: . . . I became a runaway teen, escaping sexual and physical abuse. . . . As a runaway teen, your old concerns quickly disappear and are replaced by new, life threatening ones . . . my concerns were more pragmatic, involving finding food, shelter, water. . . . As a runaway teen, I was viewed as something less than human. Still, it was safer than going home.

Into my hunger, loneliness and desperation came a man. . . . Attractive, well dressed and very charismatic, he approached me in a suburban mall and offered to "help" me. He could provide me with food, shelter, clothing, work. . . . When I questioned whether or not this "work" was prostitution, he retracted the offer and began to walk away. Desperate, I ran after him, pleading with him to give me another chance and to forgive my insult.

He brought me into his "office" . . . he explained that I had to audition for the job and should step on the stage and raise my hands. When I did so, I felt leather straps being put around my wrists but didn't understand what was going on. He pulled my pants down and my shirt up, leaving me virtually naked. When I tried to stop him . . . He shoved out the wooden box I was standing on . . . It was the beginning of my "training" for a position as a prostitute that catered to "clients," who wanted to act on their violent bondage/torture fantasies. While still hanging from my wrists, I was told that

unless I agreed then to sign a contract, I would never be let down . . .
I was . . . hit, punched, whipped and penetrated with a beer bottle . . .
I gave up and agreed to sign, at which point I was let down, bound
behind my back, gagged and blindfolded, thrown into a tiny closet
under the cellar stairs without food or water and left there. . . . What I
signed was what is known in these "rape and snuff" circles as a slave
contract. By doing so I was essentially agreeing that I was no longer
a human being, but rather, a slave, whose sole purpose in life was
the fulfillment of Bruce's desires and those of his "clients." The contract took away my right to feel, to speak without approval, to have
emotions. In it, I agreed to do anything that I was told and to accept
any punishment or training he determined necessary. . . . For three
years I was forced to let men rape me for Bruce's profit. During that
time, I'd nearly been killed several times . . . my captivity came to an
abrupt end. Bruce was arrested on unrelated charges, and I was able
to escape after he'd been handcuffed and taken away.[3] (J. Brememan,
personal communication, March 17, 2011)

Another disturbing area of U.S. domestic trafficking is within the American Indian (Native) community. In a three-year period, at least 345 American Indian women and girls in the state of Minnesota alone had been
sexually trafficked (MIWRC, 2009). In 2009, the MIWRC published a report that highlighted the gravity of Native women's and girls' experience
with sexual violence and as victims of trafficking: "sex trafficking of Native women and girls is neither a new problem nor a rare occurrence. It is,
however, a very complex problem in its origins, activities and solutions"
(MIWRC, 2009, p. 99). The report shows that Native women and girls experience sexual violence more frequently than other groups of women in
the United States and that there are many factors that contribute to Native
women's and girls' vulnerability to sex trafficking. An international report
on the commercial sexual exploitation of children described Canadian Ab-
original and American Indian youth as being at greater risk than any other
youth in Canada and the United States for sexual exploitation (Beyond
Borders, ECPAT-USA, & Shared Hope International, 2008).

HOW TRAFFICKING WORKS

Once the women and girls are trafficked, the traffickers and/or pimps
use a mixture of coercive techniques intended to destroy their physical
and psychological defenses, create dependency, and limit chances for escape (Rafferty, 2008). This is the beginning of the women's total loss of control and reproductive justice. These coercive techniques include physical,
sexual, and psychological violence; isolation; control of access to water,
food, and sleep; relocation to areas where the culture and language are

unknown to the victims; threats of harm to themselves and their families; forced dependence on drugs and/or alcohol; withholding money; confiscating and withholding passports, visas, and/or identification documents; and close supervision (Hossain, Zimmerman, Abas, Light, & Watts, 2010; Parrot & Cummings, 2008; Zimmerman et al., 2003). In order to survive, trafficked women and girls must become compliant with the traffickers' or pimps' demands (Zimmerman et al., 2003). According to Hossain et al. (2010) many of the same intimidating tactics used to control and dominate trafficked women and girls are described in the literature on torture. Like torture victims, trafficked women and girls have limited power to predict or control events that affect their health and safety. Yumi Li's story illuminates many of the characteristics of losing control.

Yumi Li was raised in northeastern China where she attended university and became an accountant. Yumi was ambitious and adventuresome, and she longed to travel overseas. A female employment agent offered her an opportunity to utilize her accounting skills in New York City at a salary of $5,000 per month. In order to pursue this opportunity, Yumi agreed to a $50,000 smuggling fee, and, to ensure that she would repay the fee from her earnings, her relatives pledged their homes as collateral. Upon her arrival in the United States, Yumi was told that she would work as a prostitute in a brothel. "When they first mentioned prostitution, I thought I would go crazy," said Yumi. "I was thinking, how can this happen to someone like me who is college educated? I wanted to die" (Kristof, 2010, para 6). Yumi was beaten, gang raped, and videotaped nude in unspeakable poses. They did not hurt her face, as that would impact her commercial worth. Her captors held a gun to her head for added intimidation. Yumi was told that, should she resist working as a prostitute, the video would be sent to her loved ones in China, and the relatives who had pledged their homes as collateral would become homeless. As she felt that she had no choice, Yumi worked as a prostitute for three years, playing her role mechanically. She was one of approximately 20 Asian women working at the brothel (Kristof, 2010).

When control of the trafficked women and girls has been attained, they are sexually exploited, and they have no control over when they will work or sleep, what they will eat, what type or how many clients they will service, or whether or not they can protect themselves with condom use (Hossain et al., 2010; Raymond, 2004). For example, in brothels in India the price of sex is negotiated between the customer and brothel owner. The customer can pay a few extra rupees for the right not to use a condom; the trafficked woman or girl has no say in the matter (Kristof & DuWunn, 2009). Thus, brothels become prisons (Farley, 2004) where some trafficked women and girls are reported to service 40–50 customers per night and to work 18-hour days (Zimmerman et al., 2003).

CONSEQUENCES OF BEING TRAFFICKED
AND FORCED INTO SEXUAL EXPLOITATION

The emotional, physical, and psychological consequences for trafficked women and children are multiple and long lasting. It is difficult to quantify the negative impact that trafficking and forced prostitution (sexual exploitation) has on people; not only has their physical body been violated and used and abused as an object, but they have been stripped of their freedom of self-determination and control. The impact can result in the devastating reality of having been deprived of their health and emotional well being for a lifetime.

Although there are only a limited number of studies that address the health consequences for women and girls who have been trafficked and forced into prostitution, one groundbreaking study (Farley et al., 2003, p. 34) of more than 850 people with current or former experience in prostitution showed "that prostitution was multi-traumatic: Seventy-one percent were physically assaulted in prostitution; 63% were raped; 89% of these respondents wanted to escape prostitution, but did not have other options for survival. A total of 75% had been homeless at some point in their lives; 68% met criteria for Posttraumatic Stress Disorder (PTSD)." These findings are consistent with those of other investigators, who found that 76–100 percent of survivors of sex trafficking have been physically assaulted, and 67–100 percent have been sexually assaulted (Raymond, Hughes, & Gomez, 2001; Zimmerman et al., 2003, 2006, 2008). Zimmerman et al.'s (2006) study showed that, of those who were injured while they were trafficked, 57 percent said that the injuries caused persistent problems or pain. Women and girls who have been prostituted have the highest rates of rape and homicide of any group of women. They are regularly verbally abused and physically assaulted, regardless of whether their working environment is the streets, massage parlors, hotels, or brothels (Farley, 2010).

The health consequences that result from the deplorable conditions to which the women and girls are subjected are profound. The physical price to women and girls who have been trafficked include drug and alcohol addiction, physical injuries, gastrointestinal problems, infectious diseases, dental or oral health problems, unhealthy weight loss due to food deprivation and poor nutrition, STIs, traumatic brain injuries, and reproductive health problems such as infertility, unwanted pregnancy, and other related diseases and dysfunctions (Rafferty, 2008; Raymond et al., 2002; Williamson, Dutch, & Clawson, 2010; Zimmerman et al., 2003, 2006). Zimmerman et al. (2008) studied 192 women and adolescent girls who were trafficked for sexual exploitation. The participants were asked about 26 physical symptoms that they might have experienced within the last two weeks, and the results indicated that they were bothered by a multitude of symptoms. These included headaches (82%), feeling easily tired (81%), dizzy spells (70%), back pain (69%), memory difficulty (62%), stomach pain (61%), pelvic pain (59%), and gynecological infections (58%).

The physical consequences of contracting HIV need additional attention, as it is a very problematic issue for trafficked women and girls. Women are about twice as likely as men to be infected during heterosexual sex with an HIV-positive partner (Kristof & WuDunn, 2009). The prevalence of HIV and STIs among trafficked women and girls varies greatly depending on the geographic location, but is significant regardless of site. It is estimated that 23–80 percent of those trafficked will contract HIV (Gupta, Raj, Decker, Reed, & Silverman, 2009; Silverman et al., 2006, 2008; Zimmerman et al., 2006), and ranges for STIs are equally varied (Grayman et al., 2005; Silverman et al., 2008; Zimmerman et al., 2006). Lack of autonomy appears to heighten trafficked women's and girls' vulnerability to HIV infection; for example, use of violent rape as a means of coercing initiation into sex work, inability to refuse sex, inability to demand condoms or negotiate their use, substance use as a coping strategy, and inadequate access to health care all are factors that increase the likelihood of contracting HIV (Gupta et al., 2009). Other research indicates that the duration of forced prostitution, and the number of locations where the women and girls are prostituted, positively correlate with HIV infection (Silverman et al., 2006, 2007); there is also increased risk among those trafficked prior to 15 years of age (Silverman et al., 2007). Furthermore, those who contract HIV while trafficked are also at a higher risk of contracting other STIs, especially syphilis and hepatitis B, than are those not infected with HIV (Silverman et al., 2008). A recent study (Decker, McCauley, Phuengsamran, Janyam, & Silverman, 2011) showed that trafficked sex workers were at greater risk of contracting HIV than nontrafficked sex workers; the HIV resulted in greater negative reproductive health outcomes and increased risk of ulcerative STIs.

Research on the health consequences of human trafficking is limited, and the majority of the studies have focused on the physical/medical consequences; however, recently some attention has been focused on the psychological consequences. As a result of the psychological trauma of trafficking, many women and girls experience anxiety, depression, sleep disorders, PTSD, disorientation, confusion, phobias, panic attacks, and suicidal ideation. Shame, grief, fear, distrust, hatred of men, self-blame, and self-hatred are frequently reported by survivors (U.S. Department of Health and Human Services, n.d.). Hossain et al.'s (2010) research indicates that psychological consequences are clustered around three mental health outcomes: 55 percent met criteria for high levels of depression symptoms, 48 percent met criteria for high levels of anxiety symptoms, and 77 percent had possible PTSD. Reported physical injuries during trafficking were significantly associated with all three mental health outcomes (i.e., depression, anxiety, PTSD), and physical violence (e.g., being hit or kicked) was positively associated with anxiety. Results further indicate that those trafficked for six months or longer had twice the likelihood of high levels of depression and anxiety of those trafficked less than six months. Other findings that shed light on how trafficked women and girls respond to their trafficked environment revealed that restricted freedom was linked with increased anxiety symptoms.

The costs to women and girls who are trafficked are clearly overwhelming and significant. In addition to the serious physical and psychological health costs, trafficking violates the basic and universal human rights to life, liberty, and the pursuit of happiness (USDOS, 2005), and it deprives individuals, communities, and countries the opportunity to reach their full potential.

CONCLUSION

Reproductive justice cannot exist for women and girls who are sexually exploited. Trafficking and forced prostitution will continue to increase unless there is a universal paradigm shift that addresses the gender inequities that justify and sustain sexual exploitation. Radhida Coomaraswamy, former UN Special Reporter on Violence Against Women, stated that "the root causes of migration and trafficking greatly overlap. The lack of rights afforded to women serves as the primary causative factor at the root of both women's migrations and trafficking in women. . . . By failure to protect and promote women's civil, political, economic and social rights, governments create situations in which trafficking flourishes" (as cited in USDOS, 2009, p. 6). Women cannot have full control over their reproductive lives unless issues such as socioeconomic disadvantage, race and sex discrimination, inequalities in wealth and power, and differential access to resources and services are addressed. Therefore, the reproductive justice framework that focuses on broader socioeconomic conditions to bring about structural change is invaluable in combating reproductive injustice; it also serves the fight against trafficking (Ross, 2006).

According to SisterSong (n.d.), a leading reproductive justice collective of women of color, reproductive justice can be achieved only when indigenous women and women of color have the power to (1) protect and advance their human rights, (2) determine the number and spacing of their children, (3) protect their bodily integrity, (4) protect their right to parent their children, (5) improve the quality of the environment in which they live, and (6) obtain the necessary social support to live healthy lives in healthy families and in safe and sustainable communities. These same aspirations are critical in supporting the efforts to eliminate sex trafficking as health and human rights violations. These are not new aspirations; 90 years ago, Margaret Sanger, founder of Planned Parenthood, wrote that "No woman can call herself free who does not own and control her body.

No woman can call herself free until she can choose consciously whether she will or will not be a mother" (Lewis, n.d.). It is past time for society to recognize and put an end to the denial of women's and girls' basic human rights—the freedom to control themselves, their bodies, and their reproductive lives. Only then will the sexual exploitation of women and girls cease. Only then can reproductive justice be achieved.

NOTES

1. Copyright by Shared Hope International. Reprinted with permission.
2. Copyright 2011 by IRIN Humanitarian News and Analysis service. Reprinted with permission.
3. Reprinted with permission.

REFERENCES

Action Coalition on Human Trafficking Alberta. (2011). *About human trafficking: What is human trafficking?* Retrieved from http://www.actalberta.org/about-human-trafficking.

Bales, K. (2000). *Disposable people: New slavery in the global economy.* Berkeley: University of California Press.

Bales, K. (2010). *Ending slavery: The book/the plan.* Retrieved from http://www.freetheslaves.net/Page.aspx?pid=332.

Batstone, D. (2007). *Not for sale.* New York: HarperCollins.

Beyond Borders, ECPAT-USA, & Shared Hope International. (2008). *Report of the Canada-United States consultation in preparation for World Congress III against Sexual Exploitation of Children and Adolescents.* Retrieved from http://www.ecpat.net/WorldCongressIII/PDF/RegionalMTGs/canada_us_consult_report_final.pdf.

Decker, M. R., McCauley, H. L., Phuengsamran, D., Jaynam, S., & Silverman, J. G. (2011). Sex trafficking, sexual risk, sexually transmitted infection, and reproductive health among female sex workers in Thailand. *Journal of Epidemiology and Community, 65,* 334–339.

Estes, R. J., & Weiner, N. A. (2001). *The commercial sexual exploitation of children in the U.S., Canada, and Mexico* [Executive Summary of the U.S. National Study]. Philadelphia: University of Pennsylvania. Retrieved from http://www.sp2.upenn.edu/restes/CSEC_Files/Exec_Sum_020220.pdf.

European Commission Report. (2010). *External relations: Trafficking in human beings (THB).* Retrieved from http://ec.europa.eu/external_relations/human_rights/traffic/index_en.htm.

Farley, M. (2004). "Bad for the body, bad for the heart": Prostitution harms women even if legalized or decriminalized. *Violence Against Women, 10,* 1087–1125.

Farley, M. (2010, October 18). *The real harms of prostitution.* Retrieved from http://www.mercatornet.com/articles/view/the_real_harms_of_prostitution/.

Farley, M., Cotton, M., Lynne, J., Zumbeck, S., Spiwak, F., Reyes, M. E., Alvarez, D., & Sezgin, U. (2003). Prostitution and trafficking in nine countries: An update on violence and posttraumatic stress disorder. *Journal of Trauma Practice, 2*(3/4), 33–74.

Farrell, A., & Fahy, S. (2009). The problem of human trafficking in the US: Public frames and policy responses. *Journal of Criminal Justice, 37,* 617–626.

Frundt, T. (2010). *Courtney's house: Giving child survivors the key to freedom.* Retrieved from http://www.courtneyshouse.org/About-Us.html.

Glodava, M., & Onizuka, R. (1994). *Mail order brides: Women for sale.* Fort Collins, CO: Alaken.

Grayman, J. H., Nhan, D. T., Huong, P. R., Jenkins, R. A., Carey, J. W., West, G. R., & Minh, T. T. (2005). Factors associated with HIV testing, condom use, and sexually transmitted infections among female sex workers in Nha Trang, Vietnam. *AIDS and Behavior, 9*(1), 41–51.

Gupta, J., Raj, A., Decker, M. R., Reed, E., & Silverman, J. G. (2009). HIV vulnerabilities of sex-trafficked Indian women and girls. *International Journal of Gynecology and Obstetrics, 107,* 30–34.

Hannum, A. B. (2002, Winter). *ReVista: Tourism in the Americas—Development, culture, and identity.* David Rockefeller Center for Latin American Students. Retrieved from http://www.drclas.harvard.edu/revista/articles/view/53.

Hodge, D. R. (2008). Sexual trafficking in the United States: A domestic problem with transnational dimensions. *Social Work, 53,* 143–152.

Hossain, M., Zimmerman, C., Abas, M., Light, M., & Watts, C. (2010). The relationship of trauma to mental disorders among trafficked and sexually exploited girls and women. *American Journal of Public Health, 100,* 2442–2449.

Hughes, D. (2000). "Welcome to the rape camp": Sexual exploitation and the internet in Cambodia. *Journal of Sexual Aggression, 6,* 1–3.

Hynes, P. H., & Raymond, J. (2002). Put in harm's way: The neglected health consequences of sex trafficking in the United States. In J. Sillimand & A. Bhattacharjee (Eds.), *Policing the national body: Sex, race, and criminalization* (pp. 197–229). Cambridge, MA: South End Press.

Immigration and Naturalization Services. (1999). *International matchmaking organizations: A report to Congress.* Washington, DC: Author. Retrieved from http://www.uscis.gov/files/article/Mobrept_full.pdf.

International Labour Organization. (2011) *Forced labour.* Retrieved from http://www.ilo.org/global/topics/forced-labour/lang—en/index.htm.

IRIN Humanitarian News and Analysis Service. (2010, April 25). *Pakistan: Sold into sex work.* Retrieved from http://www.irinnews.org/Report. aspx?ReportId=88921.

Jones, L., Engstrom, D. W., Hilliard, T., & Diaz, M. (2007). Globalization and human trafficking. *Journal of Sociology & Social Welfare, 34,* 107–122.

King, G. (2004). *Woman, child for sale: The new slave trade in the 21st century.* New York: Penguin.

Kristof, N. D. (2010, November 27). A woman. A prostitute. A slave. *New York Times.* Retrieved from http://www.nytimes.com/2010/11/28/opinion/28Kristof. html?_r=1&emc=eta1.

Kristof, N. D., & WuDunn, S. (2009). *Half the sky: Turning oppression into opportunity for women worldwide.* New York: Random House.

Lerner, G. (1986). The origin of prostitution in ancient Mesopotamia. *Signs, 11,* 236–254.

Lewis, J. J. (n.d.). *Margaret Sanger quotes: Margaret Sanger (1884–1965)*. Retrieved from http://womenshistory.about.com/od/quotes/a/margaret_sanger.htm.

Minnesota Indian Women's Resource Center. (2009). *Shattered hearts: The commercial sexual exploitation of American Indian women and girls in Minnesota*. Retrieved from http://www.miwrc.org/shattered_hearts_full_report-web_version.pdf.

Minnesota Office of Justice Programs, & Minnesota Statistical Analysis Center. (2010). *Human trafficking in Minnesota: A report to the Minnesota Legislature*. Retrieved from http://www.ojp.state.mn.us/cj/publications/Reports/2010_Human_Trafficking_Report.pdf.

Monzini, R. (2004). Trafficking in women and girls and the involvement of organized crime in western and central Europe. *International Review of Victimology, 11*, 73–88.

Murray, A. F. (2008). *From outrage to courage: Women taking action for health and justice*. Monroe, ME: Common Courage Press.

Nair, S. (2010). *Child sex tourism*. U.S. Department of Justice, Child Exploitation and Obscenity Section. Retrieved from http://www.justice.gov/criminal/ceos/sextour.html.

Nam, J. S. (2007). The case of the missing case: Examining the civil rights of action for human trafficking victims. *Columbia Law Review, 107*, 1655–1703.

Office of Safe and Drug-Free Schools. (2010). *Human trafficking of children in the United States: A fact sheet for schools*. Retrieved from http://www2.ed.gov/about/offices/list/osdfs/factsheet.html.

Olson, L. (2010, May 22). *Human trafficking stats*. Retrieved on November 14, 2010, from http://lizolson.theworldrace.org/?filenam=human=trafficking=stats.

Orhant, M. (2002). Human trafficking exposed. *Population Today, 30*, 1–4.

Parrot, A., & Cummings, N. (2008). *Sexual enslavement of girls and women worldwide*. Westport, CT: Praeger.

Polaris Project. (n.d.-a). *Anita, trafficked in India, originally from Nepal*. Retrieved from http://actioncenter.polarisproject.org/the-frontlines/survivor-testimonies/38-testimonies/56-testimony-of-anita.

Polaris Project. (n.d.-b). *Deng, trafficked in Australia, originally from Thailand*. Retrieved from http://actioncenter.polarisproject.org/the-frontlines/survivor-testimonies/38-testimonies/60-testimony-of-deng.

Polaris Project. (n.d.-c). *Galya, trafficked in Turkey, originally from Armenia*. Retrieved from http://actioncenter.polarisproject.org/the-frontlines/survivor-testimonies/38-testimonies/71-testimony-of-galya.

Polaris Project. (n.d.-d). *Gina, trafficked in India, originally from Nepal*. Retrieved from http://actioncenter.polarisproject.org/the-frontlines/survisior-testimonies/38-testimonies/72-testimony-of-gina.

Polaris Project. (n.d.-e). *Seema, trafficked in India, originally from Nepal*. Retrieved from http://actioncenter.polarisproject.org/the-frontlines/survivor-testimonies/38-testimonies/121-testimony-of-seema.

Power, C. (2000, June 25). Becoming a "servant of god." Devadasis are Dalit women sold into sexual slavery. Is this the end of a cruel tradition? *Newsweek*. Retrieved from http://www.hartford-hwp.com/archives/52a/013.html.

Rafferty, Y. (2008). The impact of trafficking on children: Psychological and social policy perspectives. *Child Development Perspectives, 2*(1), 13–18.

Raymond, J. G. (2004). Prostitution on demand. *Violence Against Women, 10,* 1156–1186.

Raymond, J. G., D'Cunha, J., Dzuhayatin, S. R., Hynes, H. P., Rodriguez, Z. R., & Santos, A. (2002). *A comparative study of women trafficked in the migration process: Patterns, profiles, and health consequences of sexual exploitation in five countries (Indonesia, the Philippines, Thailand, Venezuela, and the United States).* Amherst, MA: Coalition Against Trafficking in Women. Retrieved from http://www.oas.org/atip/Migration/Comparative%20study%20of%20 women%20trafficked%20in%20migration%20process.pdf.

Raymond, J. G., Hughes, D. N., & Gomez, C. J. (2001). *Sex trafficking of women in the United States: International and domestic trends.* Amherst, MA: Coalition Against Trafficking in Women. Retrieved from http://www.uri.edu/artsci/ wms/hughes/sex_traff_us.pdf.

Ross, L. J. (2006, May). *Understanding reproductive justice.* SisterSong, Women of Color Reproductive Health Collective. Retrieved from http://www.sister song.net/publications_and_articles/Understanding_RJ.pdf.

Silliman, J., Fried, M. G., Ross, L., & Gutierrez, E. R. (2004). *Undivided rights: Women of color organize for reproductive justice.* Cambridge, MA: South End Press.

Silverman, J. G., Decker, M. R., Gupta, J., Dharmadhikari, A., Seage III, G. R., & Antia, R. (2008). Syphilis and hepatitis B, co-infection among HIV-infected, sex trafficked women and girls, Nepal. *Emerging Infectious Diseases, 14,* 932–934.

Silverman, J. G., Decker, M. R., Gupta, J., Maheshwari, A., Patel, V., & Raj, A. (2006). HIV prevalence and predictors among rescued sex-trafficked women and girls in Mumbai, India. *Journal of Acquired Immune Deficiency Syndromes, 43,* 588–593.

Silverman, J. G., Decker, M. R., Gupta, J., Maheshwari, A., Willis, B. M., & Raj, A. (2007). HIV prevalence and predictors of infection in sex-trafficked Nepalese girls and women. *Journal of the American Medical Association, 298,* 536–542.

SisterSong. (n.d.). *Herstory.* SisterSong, Women of Color Reproductive Health Collective. Retrieved from http://www.sistersong.net/herstory.html.

Thomas, P., Date, J., & Cook, T., (2007, May 21). *Beatings, isolation, and fear: The life of a slave in the U.S.* ABC News: Retrieved from http://abcnews,go.com/WN/ story?id=3190006&page=1.

Thompson, E. (2008). Slavery in our times. *Newsweek, 151*(11). Retrieved from http://www.newsweek.com/2008/03/08/slavery-in-our-times.html.

UN General Assembly. (2000). *Protocol against the smuggling of migrants by land, sea, and air, supplementing the United Nations Convention against transnational organized crime.* Retrieved from http://www.unhcr.org/refworld/ docid/479dee062.html.

UNICEF. (2009). *Child protection from violence, exploitation, and abuse: Child trafficking.* Retrieved from http://www.unicef.org/protection/index_exploitation. html.

United Nations Office on Drugs and Crime. (2005). *What is human trafficking?* Retrieved from http://www.unodc.org/unodc/en/human-trafficking/what-is-human-trafficking.html#What_is_Human_Trafficking.

United Nations Office on Drugs and Crime. (2010). *World drug report 2010: Human trafficking FAQs*. Retrieved from http://www.unodc.org/unodc/en/human-trafficking/fags.html#How_widespread_is_human_trafficking.

United States Department of Health and Human Services. (n.d.). *Fact sheet: Sex trafficking*. Retrieved from http://www.acf.hhs.gov/trafficking/about/fact_sex.pdf.

United States Department of State. (2005). *Trafficking in persons report, 2005*. Retrieved from http://www.state.gov/g/tip/rls/tiprpt/2005/.

United States Department of State. (2007). *Trafficking in persons report: Topics of special interest*. Retrieved from http://www.state.gov/g/tip/rls/tiprpt/2007/82808.htm.

United States Department of State. (2009). *Trafficking in persons report 2009: Topics of special interest*. Retrieved from http://www.state.gov/g/tip/rls/tiprpt/2009/123128.htm.

Williamson, E., Dutch, N. M., & Clawson, H. J. (2010, April). *Medical treatment of victims of sexual assault and domestic violence and its applicability to victims of human trafficking*. Retrieved from http://aspe.hhs.gov/hsp/07/humantrafficking/SA-DV/index.shtml#medical.

Winterdyk, J., & Reichel, P. (2010). Human trafficking: Issues and perspectives. *European Journal of Criminology, 7*(1), 5–10.

Women's Issues Then & Now. (2002). *Prostitution: Then and now*. Retrieved from http://www.cwrl.utexas.edu/'ulrich/feminist/sex-work.shtml.

Yakushko, O. (2009, June). *Buying and selling love online: "Mail order brides."* Paper presented at the Interamerican Congress of Psychology, Guatemala City, Guatemala.

Zimmerman, C., Hossain, M., Yun, K., Gajdadziev, V, Guzun, N., Tchomarova, M., ... Watts, C. (2008). The health of trafficked women: A survey of women entering post-trafficking services in Europe. *American Journal of Public Health, 98,* 55–59.

Zimmerman, C., Hossain, M., Yun, K., Roche., B., Morrison, L., & Watts, C. (2006). *Stolen smiles: The physical and psychological health consequences of women and adolescents trafficked in Europe*. London: London School of Hygiene and Tropical Medicine.

Zimmerman, C., Yun, B. R., Adams, B., Shvab, I., Trappolin, L., Treppete, M., et al. (2003). *The health risks and consequences of trafficking in women and adolescents: Findings from a European study*. London: London School of Hygiene and Tropical Medicine.

Chapter 6

STI Prevention and Control for Women: A Reproductive Justice Approach to Understanding Global Women's Experiences

Dionne P. Stephens, Vrushali Patil, and Tami L. Thomas

Global rates of sexually transmitted infections (STIs) among women have increased significantly over the past decade despite major improvements in prevention and treatment. According to estimates from the World Health Organization (WHO), 340 million new adult cases of curable STIs occur annually throughout the world, including gonorrhea (62 million), chlamydia (92 million), syphilis (12 million), and trichomoniasis (174) (WHO, 2001). Transmission rates of other STIs-including the human immunodeficiency virus (HIV), syphilis, genital herpes, and human papillomavirus (HPV)—continue to rise despite the increased availability of testing centers and effective treatment. The rates of infection are particularly high among women, who continue to outnumber infected men by a 2:1 ratio (UNAIDS & WHO, 1998). In fact, STIs rank in the top five disease categories for which women in developing countries seek health care services, and they are among the most common causes of illness in the world (Gerbase, Rowley, Heymann, Berkley, & Piot, 1998; WHO, 2008). For these reasons, governments and global health organizations now view the prevention of STIs among women as a primary public health issue.

Women are particularly vulnerable to STIs and experience complications more severe than men's (Gerbase et al., 1998). Women infected with STIs experience acute symptoms, chronic infection, and serious delayed consequences such as infertility, ectopic pregnancy, cervical cancer, and the potential death of both themselves and their infants. The rates of these occurrences are highest among women living in sub-Saharan Africa, Latin America, and the Caribbean (Bernstein & Hansen, 2006). Many researchers have pointed to inadequate health care, lack of access to prevention tools, low education, poverty, and various forms of oppression as contributors to these developing nations' higher incidences of infection among women (e.g., Aral, Over, Manhart, & Holmes, 2006; Bunkle, 2003; Csete, 2005; Hanlon, Carlisle, Reilly, Lyon, & Hannah, 2010; Rankin, Lindgren, Kools, & Schell, 2008). Yet, the STI-related health disparities experienced by women living in wealthy nations illustrate that no country is immune from these phenomena. In the United States, for example, women of color have higher rates of STI infection than non-Hispanic White women do (Einwalter, Ritchie, Ault, & Smith, 2005; Ford, Jaccard, Millstein, Bardsley, & William, 2004; Sipkin, Gillam, & Grady, 2003). Similarly, immigrant women living in Australia report lower rates of STI knowledge and higher rates of infection than nonimmigrants (Dawson & Gifford, 2001).

The shared burdens of STI health disparities across diverse groups of women provide evidence that researchers must move beyond focusing solely on incidence rates to include examinations of social, cultural, political, and economic factors that shape women's vulnerability to infection. This is necessary as women's physical experiences with STI infection are interwoven within the cultural, social, economic, and political fabrics of women's multiple identities. Whenever we consider women's experiences, we should be particularly interested in the ways that these fabrics inform gender's intersections with race, culture, religion, and the international political economy. As such, we cannot simply consider women's STI decision-making processes and outcomes as isolated individual acts but rather acknowledge them as an extension of women's interactions with others and their environments. The use of a reproductive justice framework is especially appropriate here. This perspective provides a means through which we can more easily make connections between STI rates of infection disparities and engendered sociopolitical complexities that impact women's sexual health globally. By identifying familial, community, societal, generational, political, and (global) economic levels of gendered influence, we can enrich health care providers' education, increase access to health care for marginalized populations, and enhance the quality of life and reproductive justice for the greatest number of women.

To address the need to examine the multiple engendered levels of influence on women's STI experiences, we begin with a brief overview of STI prevalence among women around the world. We then introduce the reproductive justice framework as it pertains to the study of sexual health disparity research. Next, we present key issues that inform women's STI acquisition experiences. Finally, we suggest possible practical applications of this approach for researchers and health care providers working on STI issues that affect women around the world.

GLOBAL PREVALENCE OF STIs AMONG WOMEN

It is estimated that more than 1 billion STIs are contracted each year, which equals approximately one infection per three adults (Glasier, Gülmezoglu, Schmid, Moreno, & Van Look, 2006; WHO, 2008). Of the more than 30 different bacteria, parasites, and viruses that cause STIs-including genital herpes, genital warts, HPV, HIV, and hepatitis B, only 4 STIs (chlamydia, gonorrhea, syphilis, and trichomoniasis) are responsible for an estimated 340 million infections that occur annually (Glasier et al., 2006; WHO, 2001). These infections are usually passed from person to person through vaginal intercourse, but they can also be passed through anal sex, oral sex, skin-to-skin contact, or from mother to child during pregnancy or childbirth.

Although both women and men are infected and affected by STIs, research shows that women are biologically more susceptible to STIs, endure more STI-related complications, and are more apt to suffer from asymptomatic infections. Further, women are more likely to have untreated STIs and less likely to seek treatment, even for symptomatic infections. These delays in STI responses are problematic given that many symptoms can be disruptive to a woman's daily functioning and long-term well-being. For example, about one-half of women with trichomoniasis experience inflammation of the vagina, with red spotting and noxious, abnormal discharge; coinfections of gonorrhea or bacterial vaginosis are also common with trichomoniasis (Heymann, 2008; WHO, 2001). Similarly, women infected with genital herpes and untreated syphilis can develop genital ulcers and lesions that increase their risk of HIV transmission three-fold (Low et al., 2006). Women with untreated syphilis also are at an increased risk for possible blindness, mental disorders, and heart problems.

Morbidity is a key area of inquiry among researchers studying STIs in female populations. In women between 15 and 44 years of age, the morbidity and mortality due to STIs, excluding HIV, are second only to childbirth-related deaths (WHO, 2008). Research on HPV has received increased attention in the United States and abroad since its links to cervical cancer—the leading cause of cancer death in women—were made clear (WHO, 2001). This death rate is alarming given the fact that HPV is one of the most common STIs in the world, and it results in the global loss of 3.3 million disability-adjusted life years (Centers for Disease Control [CDC], 2008a; Low et al., 2006). In the United States, HPV is the most common STI; at least one-half of all sexually active American women become infected at some time in their lives (CDC, 2008b). However, the rates are higher in poorer nations; 80 percent of cervical cancer cases and 85 percent of cervical cancer–related deaths occur in the developing world. Each year HPV-related cervical cancer causes 274,000 deaths worldwide; the majority occur in developing countries, particularly in Ethiopia, India, Malawi, and Uganda (Low et al., 2006; Okonofua, 2007).

Similarly, women are disproportionately affected by HIV and AIDS; an estimated 50 percent of the 33.3 million infected adults worldwide are women (UNAIDS, 2010). Researchers have asserted that 98 percent of these women live in developing countries (UNAIDS/ UNFPA/ UNIFEM, 2004). However, rates are increasing among women across both developing and industrialized nations primarily as a result of unprotected heterosexual intercourse. For example, the number of women living with HIV in India (UNAIDS, 2010) and Canada (Health Canada, 2004) nearly doubled in the last 15 years, and intercourse with infected men remained the primary mode of transmission in both nations. Like HPV, the AIDS epidemic has had a unique impact on women, exacerbated by their role within society and their biological vulnerability to HIV infection. Unfortunately, women diagnosed with HIV tend to have a lower survival rate than men do, in part, because of gendered experiences including delays in treatment, higher rates of poverty, and lack of access to adequate health care. In fact, WHO concluded that AIDS was the leading cause of death and disease among women ages 15 to 44 in 2009 (UNAIDS, 2010).

Finally, STI-related complications can lead to serious problems for women of reproductive age, especially for those who are pregnant. STIs are the main preventable cause of infertility in women; both chlamydia and gonorrhea can cause inflammation of the fallopian tubes; infected women are at a significantly increased risk for infertility, and they are 6 to 10 times more likely to develop an ectopic (tubal) pregnancy (Edgardh et al., 2009; Risser & Risser, 2007; Welch, 2010). More than 50 percent of involuntary infertility cases in the United Kingdom have been attributed to chlamydial infection (Bevan, Johal, Mumtaz, Ridgway, & Siddle, 1995). Among pregnant women with untreated early syphilis, 25 percent have stillbirths and 14 percent experience neonatal death (Heymann, 2008); undetected syphilis causes an estimated 492,000 stillbirths and infant deaths globally each year (Low et al., 2006). Also, gonorrhea-caused conjunctivitis (i.e., pink eye) can develop into blindness or, more commonly, corneal injury without immediate treatment in newborns (WHO, 2001). WHO (2001) estimated that between 1,000 and 4,000 newborn babies become blind every year because of this condition. Further, children of STI-infected mothers are at risk for STI acquisition, as viruses such as herpes and HIV are easily spread through blood and other bodily fluids during pregnancy and childbirth if early preventative measures are not taken.

Given the serious consequences of STI infection for women, it comes as no surprise that billions of funding dollars, pages of governmental reports, and hours of research interventions have been put forth to address this public health issue. Those in the field strongly agree that the most effective means to avoid becoming infected with or transmitting STIs is to abstain from sexual intercourse or to have sexual intercourse only within a long-term, mutually monogamous relationship with an uninfected partner. Further, thousands of dollars have been poured into efforts to distribute latex condoms, which, when used consistently and correctly, are highly effective in reducing the transmission of HIV and other STIs, including gonorrhea, chlamydia, and trichomoniasis. A focus on these individual level behaviors, however, is not enough. Although the epidemiological data and various prevention guidelines appear to provide a clear picture of appropriate approaches to STI management, a focus only on a goal of absence of infection fails to acknowledge the contexts that increase STI risks and ultimately lead to the high rates of infection among women. To address this requires a multilevel and multidimensional approach.

A REPRODUCTIVE JUSTICE FRAMEWORK

The reproductive justice framework is particularly relevant for providing a multilevel framework from which to examine women's STI experiences globally. This approach provides a starting point from which researchers, educators, and health care providers can develop an integrated analysis, holistic vision, and comprehensive strategies for the improvement of structural and societal conditions that inform women's STI experiences. This framework emerged from the advocacy work of American women of color's grassroots health organizations in the 1990s to create links between reproductive health and social justice (Luna, 2009). A foundational assertion of this framework is that reproductive oppression is a result of the intersections of multiple oppressions that have to do with race, class, culture, and so on, and that it is inherently connected to the struggle for social justice and human rights (Asian Communities for Reproductive Justice [ACRJ], 2005; Luna, 2009).

> The central theme of the reproductive justice framework is a focus on the control and exploitation of women's bodies, sexuality and reproduction as an effective strategy of controlling women and communities, particularly those of color. Controlling a woman's body controls her life, her options and her potential. Historically and currently, a woman's lack of power and self-determination is mediated through the multiple oppressions of race, class, gender, sexuality, ability, age, and immigration status. Thus, controlling individual

women becomes a strategic pathway to regulating entire communities. (ACRJ, 2005, p. 3)

Although this framework emerged from an American racialized political context, we believe it is particularly appropriate for examining the complexity of women's experiences globally. Indeed, its emphasis on multiple oppressions readily recognizes the myriad racial/ethnic, cultural, nationality, class, and other oppressions that shape women's varied reproductive health experiences around the world. For example, studies that assess race, culture, socioeconomic status, sexual orientation, immigrant status, religion, and age discrimination have shown that these individual level experiences contribute to poor STI infection outcomes and threaten a woman's decision making regarding her body, her family, and her community. For example, Miller, McDermott, McCulloch, Fairley, and Muller (2003) found that, among Australian indigenous populations, younger age, being female, lower socioeconomic status, and the structure of community health services were independently associated with a higher prevalence of bacterial STI. In a study of Brazilian women's HIV risk, it was also found that the context of gender and socioeconomic conditions create and recreate greater disadvantages for Black women and their exposure to HIV risk than is the case for women who are not Black (Lopes, Buchalla, de Carvalho, & Ayres, 2007).

In addition, the focus on institutions and structures beyond the individual underscores the significance of context in women's ability to negotiate and determine their sexual health outcomes and choices. For example, the economic strife, growth of the sex industry, and deterioration of health systems during the 1990s in the Soviet Union and Baltic regions correlated with increased rates of syphilis and gonorrhea among women there (Heymann, 2008; WHO, 2001). After a prolonged war and periods of intense civil strife, Afghanistan also saw an increase in HIV risk-related behaviors and subsequent higher rates of infections among women (Bergenström, 2003).

Thus, women's shared gendered experiences with varied degrees of economic insecurity, oppression, discrimination, and lack of resources contribute to a common vulnerability to STI infection. This is reinforced by the reproductive justice approach, which is integrative of existing theories to allow for the development of an overarching framework that acknowledges that individuals' perceptions and realities do not develop in a vacuum but are products of external influences and experiences. STI-related decision making and outcomes, as such, result from the interplay between the psychological characteristics of the person and the specific environments in which she interacts (Best et al., 2003; Hanlon et al., 2010; Thomas & Stephens, 2009). One cannot be defined without reference to the other. This is not to say that specific decision-making processes do not occur as isolated individual acts; rather this framework seeks to acknowledge that there are some common experiences shared by women that inform their decision-making processes and options. Through the use of the reproductive justice framework, researchers and practitioners seek to identify and consider all relevant information on a person's life, thus encouraging an examination of interactions with others and the environment rather than focusing solely on individual behaviors.

With regard to STI infection, this paradigm seeks to illustrate what Gilliam, Neustadt, and Gordon (2009) suggested are real-life connections between infection and all other aspects of individual sexual health concerns (e.g., gender-role expectations, social status, interpersonal identities, beliefs about sexuality) and interrelated social and environmental issues (e.g., poverty, access to health care services, interpersonal violence, community resources, infection stigma). Further, it does not simply stop at complex links between direct and indirect determinants of health and between the individual and the environment; reproductive justice approaches further advocate for raising awareness of an entitlement to a healthy quality of life—including the provision of appropriate services— as part of reproductive health.

The ultimate goal of reproductive justice advocates is to build self-determination for individuals and communities. Thus, for reproductive justice to be applicable and effective, change needs to be made at all levels of society. Activists who embrace this tradition believe that translating their vision of this agenda into action will bring about change on the individual, community, institutional, and societal levels that will lead to worldwide transformations (ACRJ, 2005).

Three Dimensions of STI Prevention and Control

To illustrate the multilevel factors that inform women's experiences with STI infection, we provide specific examples of where reproductive justice frameworks can be successfully integrated into STI prevention and control efforts to bring about change. By systemically reviewing the prior research that identifies individual, interpersonal, and broader contextual factors that influence STI risks and outcomes among women worldwide, we can strengthen our multidimensional understandings of these infection trends and their broader social impacts. This is particularly important as the high and increasing vulnerability of women to STI has been attributed to social, economic, and political inequalities between women and men, which result in sexual violence and unequal access to prevention, education, training, and health care (Bandyopadhyay & Thomas, 2002; Glasier et al., 2006; Jagger, 2002; Katz & Tirone, 2010).

WHO has distinguished three dimensions of reproductive health that guided our categorization of the factors that influence STI prevention and control among women: (1) human condition, (2) services, and (3) approach (Sadana, 2002). The identification of these dimensions allows the complex links between direct and indirect determinants of health and between the individual and the environment to be systemically explored.

Human Condition

This dimension refers to issues related to general health and well-being. The human condition encompasses the contexts and situations that individuals face daily. Although typically this is discussed in terms of negative life events such as suffering, war, oppression, poverty, or disappointment, it also includes positive life events such as economic security and improved quality of life. For example, research shows that human conditions that promote positive health outcomes provide both a sense of belonging and intimacy and help people to be more competent and self-efficacious. Acknowledging that positive sexual health outcomes rest on the shoulders not only of individuals but also of their families and communities means that we must examine the values and resources that shape women's STI outcomes. Below we specifically examine the influence of gender-role expectations, partner influences, and sex work as an economic option as human conditions that affect women's STI experiences.

Diversity in Cultural Expectations

Women's gender roles provide us with an important framework for identifying individual level factors that inform sexual health decision-making processes. Understanding how a woman views herself as a sexual being is also important, as sexual behaviors tell us more about an individual's view and feeling about the self as a sexual being than about the sex act itself (Stephens & Phillips, 2005). In turn, how an individual gives meaning to her gender has been shown to be instrumental in overriding the effects of external gendered messages about sexuality (Stephens & Phillips, 2005). There is a need to recognize, however, that, although researchers often use gender as the primary framework that shapes sexual identity development for women, several other identity factors also influence experiences across and within groups of women. An individual's sexual identity and gender-role understandings are multidimensional and dynamic concepts. Explicit and implicit rules imposed by society, as defined by one's gender, age, economic status, ethnicity, and other factors, influence an individual's gender-role socialization. More specifically, researchers have found that women's understandings of appropriate STI risk-reduction behaviors are processed through gender role socialization and vary by identity traits including social class, race/ethnicity, nationality, sexual orientation, ability, and religion (Chewning, 2001; Kouta & Tolma,

2008; Lopes et al., 2007; Sadana, 1998; Skandrani, Baubet, Taïeb, Rezzoug, & Moro, 2010; Stephens, Phillips, & Few, 2009). Studies of the extent to which the combined effect of these identities buffer and promote women's risk for STI infection have shown that cultural cues, such as race and nationality norms, are often more influential than gender. For example, researchers have identified racial and ethnic identity as one of the most important and salient domains of African American and Hispanic young adult women's sexual identity development (Faulkner, 2003; Stephens & Phillips, 2005). These researchers noted that knowledge about sexual risks did not translate into behavior changes; instead, meanings about behaviors shaped by African American and Hispanic cultural values emerged as significant predictors of sexually risky behavior outcomes. For example, studies have shown that the influence of religiosity has led some African American and Hispanic adolescent girls to engage in anal or oral sex as a means of protecting their virginity (Gorbach et al., 2009; Haglund, 2003; Halpern-Felsher, Cornell, Kropp, & Tschann, 2005; Roye, Krausse, & Silverman, 2010). It has also been asserted by researchers that Chinese young adult women are less likely than their U.S. and U.K. counterparts to date at an early age, to date frequently, and to have sex with their dates due to more conservative attitudes about female sexuality in China (Higgins, Zheng, Liu, & Sun, 2002; Li, Cottrell, Wagner, & Ban, 2004; Sharpe, 2003). Collectively, these messages regarding gender-appropriate sexual behaviors indicate that women from different countries, religions, social classes, ability levels, and racial/ethnic groups may need distinctly different tools for negotiating their sexuality.

Engendered Messages about Abstinence, Virginity, and Intercourse

Gender roles can serve as a central organizing identity framework into which cultural issues of class, race, nationality, ability, sexual orientation, and religion are integrated. The cultural context within which women have been defined across most cultures in the world is embedded in a patriarchal system. Women's gender roles are defined by the dominant social group (i.e., men) through a socialization process mediated by family, community, schools, religious institutions, and the media. In practice, in most places in the world, this has come to mean male dominance/female subordination. Women's subordination is further complicated by culturally specific politics of submissiveness, respectability, and silence about sexuality that often characterizes women's gender-role standards. In many societies, good women are expected to be ignorant about sex and passive in sexual interactions. This makes it difficult for women to be informed about risk reduction or, even when informed, difficult for them to be proactive in negotiating safer sex. For example, many Latin American (e.g., Bernasconi, 2010; Giordano, Thumme, & Sierra, 2009; López, 2004),

Asian (e.g., Castro-Vázquez & Kishi, 2007; Pyke & Johnson, 2003; Santillán, Schuler, Anh, Minh, & Mai, 2002), North American (Katz & Tirone, 2010; Sharma, 2008; Stephens et al., 2009), and Mediterranean (e.g., Kouta & Tolma, 2008; Ozyegin, 2009; Skandrani et al., 2010) cultures both subtly and overtly pressure women to remain virgins or to abstain from sexuality unless they are within a martial relationship, a standard to which men are not held. In cases where women's virginity is promoted without the provision of sexual health information or skills building, women are at a greater risk for negative health outcomes. Sexual coercion that stems from a belief among men that sex with a virgin is safe or can cleanse a man of infection is common in some parts of Africa (Bajaj, 2008; Kis, 2010; Molleman & Franse, 2009). Further, because it restricts their ability to ask for information about sex out of fear that they will be thought to be sexually active, women in these cultural contexts are more likely to let their male partner dictate their interactions (Carpenter, 2002; Katz & Tirone, 2010; Kawai et al., 2008). Finally, some women make the decision to remain virgins solely out of fear, or they practice alternative sexual behaviors that place them at significant risk for STI acquisition, such as unprotected anal sex or oral sex because they believe that these practices preserve their virginity (Baumeister & Vohs, 2004; Bersamin, Fisher, Walker, Hill, & Grube, 2007; Weiss, Whelan, & Gupta, 2000). In other cases, various gendered sexual expectations and standards are maintained through actions that directly increase a woman's STI risks, such as female genital cutting (Anuforo, Oyedele, & Pacquiao, 2004; Molleman & Franse, 2009).

Being too knowledgeable about sexual health or one's own sexuality is often seen as problematic for women. Although the degree to which women are held to these gendered standards differs across countries, there remain inequalities between men's and women's gender-role expectations, access to sexual health resources, and decision-making authority. For example, despite the promotion of positive sexuality among women in Denmark, women there still face the possibility of being negatively labeled as sexually promiscuous if they are considered too sexually experienced (Staunæs, 2005). Vietnamese young men report increased ambivalence toward gendered morality and the significance of women's virginity, yet continue to believe that women should not become too sexually knowledgeable or gain too much sexual power (Martin, 2010). Similarly, educated, upper-class Turkish young women report that they continue to maintain virginal facades to meet traditional sexual identity expectations for unmarried women, despite having gained greater sexual freedom and liberty (Ozyegin, 2009).

Inequalities in gender-role standards of sexuality for women and men are referred to as the sexual double standard. The stricter standards applied to women lead to increased stigmatization, suppression, and subservience in regards to STI control and prevention. Gender role expectations that reinforce silence, passivity, and submissiveness directly affect women's STI knowledge and outcomes. For example, in their study of immigrant Salvadorean women, Dawson and Gifford (2001) found that the taboo nature of sex for women in their culture created a silence within the family, especially between mothers and daughters. The women reported having little knowledge about sexual health matters, sexual intercourse, and STIs. Shock, fear, and trauma characterized their memories of first intercourse; these were accompanied by reports of strong feelings of inadequacy, which reinforced their low levels of STI protective skills and knowledge. Further, although Swedish women have levels of sexual activity comparable to those reported in the United States, women in Sweden report much lower rates of STIs than American women do (Panchaud, Singh, Feivelson, & Darroch, 2000). This may be because messages about female sexuality in Sweden tend to be more pragmatic and open as manifested in familial communications, mass media portrayals, school-based sex education, and public discussion about sexual health (Edgardh, 2002). In contrast, the United States places more restrictions—both physical and psychological—on women's sexual health knowledge (i.e., access to education) and reproductive freedom (i.e., access to birth control and abortions), which directly contribute to the high rates of STI transmission (Panchaud et al., 2000). Essentially, without a strong sense of their sexual identity, women are less prepared psychologically and in terms of prevention to engage in healthy or empowered sexual interactions within the gender-role contexts in which they live.

One proven approach to addressing gender-role barriers to women's ability to negotiate safer sex and protect themselves against STI transmission is through the promotion of empowering sexuality messages. Empowering women with knowledge and skills to protect their health and successfully claim their reproductive and sexual rights increases women's self-esteem, subjectivity, and sense of sexual self. This then translates into a greater sense of sexual empowerment for women, as they have been given the space to discuss, explore, and identify their beliefs regarding healthy and safe sexuality. Even in formalized sexual health programming, the provision of empowering messaging and skills has improved STI outcomes across diverse groups of women. For example, sex workers in China received an intervention that sought not only to promote condom use and sexual health care, but also to raise the women's self-esteem and sexual subjectivity through empowerment-focused activities (Rou et al., 2007). Results indicate that the awareness-raising portions of the intervention directly affected increased condom use and reduced STIs among the sex workers.

Clearly, a focus on gender-role expectations as a starting point for empowering women can directly improve STI outcomes. Use of this gendered concept as the starting point for an examination of individual level identities allows us to move forward to identify how these factors shape women's STI decision-making options and outcomes.

ECONOMIC OPTIONS AND SURVIVAL STRATEGIES

Contemporary globalization comprises neoliberal economic reforms including the free flow of goods and capital; reduced government regulation; governmental refusal of responsibility for social welfare; and increased privatization of public sectors, services, and resources. These processes are exacerbated in poorer countries with large debt burdens. Reducing government safety nets and simultaneously increasing economic vulnerability for those at the bottom is especially problematic for the world's poor and marginalized people, among whom women are always overrepresented. Thus, as scholars who have examined globalization and gender have long argued, contemporary globalization has particularly complex and problematic implications for women (Bunkle 2003; Ehrenreich & Hoschild, 2003; Harcourt 2001; Hawkesworth 2006). It is within this shifting economic landscape and narrowing of traditional options that poor women engage in a number of specific survival strategies today, including labor migration and the selling of sex (Ehrenreich & Hoschild, 2003; Jagger, 2002). Both activities have important implications for reproductive justice.

Regarding labor migration, millions of women have migrated either domestically or internationally in search of employment in factories, private households, and the sex industry. Their increasing numbers have led some to name this trend the "feminization of migration" (e.g., Ehrenreich & Hoschild, 2003). Female migrant workers are especially vulnerable to STIs such as HIV due to the intersection of their low bargaining power, their susceptibility to sexual violence, and their low status as women and migrants. For example, Bandyopadhyay and Thomas (2002) found that 54 percent of migrant women in Hong Kong reported feelings of vulnerability due to their female status. In fact, in a review of the experiences of women migrants from Asia to the Arab states, the United Nations Development Program (2008) reported several problems faced by women migrants. First, limited preparedness and poor access to information and services render migrant women vulnerable to STIs. Second, excessive recruitment fees and poor wages push them into debt traps that often lead to sexual exploitation. Third, abusive and exploitative working conditions and lack of redress mechanisms also trap women in a vicious cycle of poverty and STI vulnerability. Fourth, deportation of women with sexual health issues, particularly HIV-positive women, by host countries and the absence of reintegration programs in their countries of origin exacerbate their misery.

Whether within or outside of the context of migration, women's participation in the sex industry occurs in a broader neoliberal climate. For example, governments seeking economic development and growth today are increasingly turning to tourism, which now constitutes one of the world's largest industries (Apostolopoulos & Sönmez, 2001). Although tourism comprises a variety of products and services, many scholars have noted that the sexualized marketing of tourist destinations, as well tourists' own expectations of the kinds of services that will be available in exotic destinations, has led to the growth of sex tourism across the globe (Hall, 1996; Ryan & Kinder, 1996; Yukota, 2006). Race is significant within sex tourism, as images of black and brown bodies are considered by Westerners to be more erotic and sexual, and this has fed the growth of sex tourism in Asia, Africa, the Americas, and the Caribbean (Kempadoo, 2004). Hence, the ongoing development of the tourism sector and women's participation within the sexual services dimension of that sector are associated with greater risk of STIs (Csete, 2005; Jagger, 2002).

Services

The provision of health care services, access to them, and utilization of those services fall under the category of the WHO's second dimension of reproductive health. The successful management or treatment of any health problem is achieved through the availability of infrastructures that adequately address women's physical, psychological, and emotional well-being. The importance of service provision can be seen in the improvement of overall reproductive health outcomes. Women benefit from STI-related services that not only address specific control and prevention tools, but also assist women in overcoming broader life issues that serve as barriers to empowerment. We next examine the importance of access to health care services as it informs women's STI outcomes under this dimension.

Health Care Services

There is a general consensus among researchers and clinicians that the use of health care services reduces STI transmission and mortality and improves the reproductive health of women. Specifically, early diagnosis and treatment of STIs is considered central to comprehensive STI-management and, thus, STI prevention. Unfortunately, universal access to comprehensive reproductive health services integrated into a well-functioning health system remains an unfulfilled objective in the majority of countries. The considerable variation in STI rates among women and men is believed to be due partly to differences in the availability of and access to health services. Clearly, access to health care is a global concern that does not discriminate by nationality. Even in wealthier nations where services are more numerous, economic barriers make it difficult for poor and other marginalized groups of women to access STI-related health services. In the United States, many women at elevated risk for STIs do not have insurance to access medical care; thus, they do not routinely access clinical services where regular STI screening tests and counseling can occur (Ethier, Kershaw, Niccolai, Lewis, & Ickovics, 2003). Although the amount and quality of the services may differ, these same reasons have been found to increase the rates of STIs acquisition among women in Afghanistan (Bergenström, 2003), Greece (Kouta & Tolma, 2008), sub-Saharan Africa (Gant, Heath, & Ejikeme, 2009), China (Rou et al., 2007), Latin America, and the Caribbean (Zacarias, Martin, & Cuche, 2000). Thus, we cannot ignore the fact that, even with variations in costs, outcomes, and cultural beliefs about women's health, access to health care clearly has a significant impact on STI management across various groups of women.

A key barrier to increasing women's access to health care services is economics. At a macrolevel, the cost of STI diagnostics alone can exceed the per capita national health care budgets of many low-income countries (Dallabetta, Field, Laga, & Islam, 1997). As a result, decisions about women's reproductive health care are based upon cost-benefit analyses whereby evaluations place a monetary value on benefits and outcomes tied to services (Paavonen, 1997). Unfortunately, women's reproductive health issues are typically not considered a national funding priority; thus fewer resources and services and less funding are directed to these specific health care initiatives. This is particularly true for STI-related issues, as there is a tendency to frame STIs as individual-level concerns. As a result, the estimated 250 million STI infections that occur in the developing world are considered to be a by-product of the lack of access to quality basic health services, and women are among the least-served populations (Best et al., 2003).

The repercussions of the inaccessibility to health care for women are serious. Women diagnosed with AIDS in Italy and England, for example, were found to have lower survival rates than men with AIDS due, in part, to later diagnosis or delay of treatment because of misdiagnosis of early symptoms and lack of access to adequate health care (Chadborn, Delpech, Sabin, Sinka, & Evans, 2006; Girardi, Sampaolesi, Gentile, Nurra, & Ippolito, 2000). Similarly, although invasive HPV-related cervical cancer can be prevented by regular screening, testing remains relatively low among U.S. minority populations such as Hispanic and Black women; morbidity rates are highest among these groups of women due to later diagnosis and barriers in access to services (CDC, 2008b). Clearly, timely access to diagnostic STI test results improves health outcomes. Yet, even if women at risk for STIs are aware of the importance of, and need for, early treatment and the potential risks due to delayed treatment, nothing can be done if they are unable to access health services readily.

Even when health services are provided, the quality and types of services differ greatly in their impact on women's STI experiences. Cultural restrictions can have a particularly significant impact on a woman's personal freedom by dramatically limiting her access to health care. At the Fourth World Congress on Women in Beijing, it was acknowledged that, in many cultures, men and community elders are given the responsibility for making health care decisions about seeking health services (Maran, 1996). The patriarchal structures of many societies, then, remove women's ability to seek knowledge and services that can empower them to engage in better STI prevention and treatment. In many countries, fewer women than men are treated in hospitals, receive prescriptions for medication and timely treatment from qualified practitioners, and survive common diseases (Seufert-Barr, 2008). Globally, women often place their own health care at a lower priority than the care of their children and partners. Meyer-Weitz, Reddy, Van den Borne, Kok, and Pietersen (2000) found, for example, that only when the severity of the STI symptoms affected their male partner or his attitudes toward them did urban South African women feel motivated to seek out health services. Otherwise, women routinely suffer silently through STI and other reproductive-related ill health (Bang et al., 1989).

Women's culturally defined gender relations and their sociocultural understanding of STIs also influence to whom they turn when they need health services. For example, many women rely on individuals who do not have specific reproductive health disease management skills to address their STI needs. Research on STI management in Latin America, the Caribbean, and Africa has shown that a significant number of women turn to drugstore clerks, traditional healers, and street vendors for their STI concerns (Mayhew, Nzambi, Pépin, & Adjei, 2001; Peltzer, Mngqundaniso, & Petros, 2006; Zacarias et al., 2000). These sources of support are ideal because they provide client-centered and personalized health care that is tailored to meet the needs and expectations of their patients, and they pay special respect to social and spiritual matters. However, they also lack accurate or up-to-date STI prevention information (Peltzer et al., 2006). Further, these providers can also reinforce patriarchal beliefs that do not empower women to manage or negotiate their reproductive, specifically their STI, health care needs.

It is the responsibility of the entire international community to facilitate access to health care. This engagement must include efforts that empower women not only to access services but also to utilize them, as there is a great deal of diversity in how much, when, and in what ways women can and will be able to utilize services in ways that benefit them due to cultural gender norms. Success, and reproductive justice, depends on women's consistent ability to access culturally appropriate health care services for the treatment and prevention of STIs.

Approach

The third and final dimension of the WHO's reproductive health framework concerns policies, legislation, and governmental attitudes. It is important to examine decisions at these levels as they also set the stage for the funding, planning, and delivery of sexual health services and sex education. Here we explore STI control and prevention-related governmental funding experiences to illustrate this category of reproduction health action.

The Politics and Priorities of Governmental Funding

In this time of neoliberal economic reforms, the reduction of aid and public expenditures due to adjustment packages and subsequent debt servicing have not only exacerbated women's poverty, but also led to deteriorating health services, equipment, and facilities, which have negatively impacted women's health (Harcourt, 2001; Jagger, 2002). Particularly affected are STI and HIV/AIDS prevention and treatment programs. In some places, this has resulted in the narrowing of family planning programs and services (Subramaniam, 1999). This dire economic climate is further complicated by the politics and priorities of U.S. policy and funding. For example, prior to the U.S. approach termed PEPFAR (President's Emergency Plan for AIDS Relief), the United States was a principal global supplier of condoms for HIV prevention programs (Csete, 2005), albeit limited during President Reagan's administration by a restriction on funding for any organization that provided or promoted abortions. This restriction was subsequently repealed by President Clinton, but reinstalled by President George W. Bush in 2001. Although PEPFAR was technically not to be subjected to this restriction, in practice it was (Dietrich, 2007). Csete (2005) argued further that PEPFAR actually became a vehicle for the institutionalization of the values of President Bush's fundamentalist Christian supporters. For example, President Bush's administration lessened U.S. support for delivery of services to men who have sex with men and sex workers, as well as research on their health problems. The Republican-controlled Congress, reflecting the wishes of the president, passed a bill in June 2003 that required one-third of U.S. assistance to HIV prevention programs to support abstinence-only (until marriage) approaches. Csete (2005) suggested that, beyond merely teaching sexual abstinence as part of a range of choices in HIV prevention, this version of abstinence only also entailed sending messages that condoms are ineffective for HIV prevention. By 2005, any organization seeking to use PEPFAR funds was required to spend two-thirds of all money designated for prevention on "Abstinence and Be Faithful initiatives" (Parsitau, 2009). Regarding condom distribution, moreover, PEPFAR targeted only specific high-risk populations, and it prohibited the use of funds to discuss condom use with in-school youth under age 14, the distribution of condoms in school settings, and the establishment of marketing campaigns that target youth and encourage condom use as a primary preventive strategy (Dietrich, 2007).

Such an approach, especially the focus on abstinence and faithfulness, fits well with the teachings of many Christian churches and other faith-based organizations (FBOs). Based on an examination of one such church in Kenya, however, Parsitau (2009) argued that a predominant focus on abstinence and faithfulness ignores the social, political, and economic situations that actually fuel the spread of HIV. For example, FBOs' insistence on abstinence and faithfulness leaves women with less power within sexual relationships and fewer options to protect themselves (Rankin et al., 2008). The restriction against condom distribution to high-risk populations is as problematic for married women whose partners have other sexual partners as it is for single youth (Dietrich, 2007). Recent work in Guinea also underscores cultural context; the research showed that, although a focus on faithfulness may seem to resonate, local conceptions of fidelity differed from those generally understood in other contexts, including engagement in short-term marriages (Kis, 2010). Finally, work in sub-Saharan Africa suggests that initiatives that improve overall health and living conditions in the at-risk populations are necessary before traditional intervention programs can effectively combat the spread of STIs such as HIV/AIDS. This is because continued engagement in risky sexual behavior, in many circumstances associated with deplorable living conditions and high mortality, is the only viable option for avoiding what many consider complete reproductive failure: dying without leaving surviving descendents (Gant et al., 2009).

INTEGRATING A REPRODUCTIVE JUSTICE FRAMEWORK IN OUR PRACTICE, EDUCATION, AND RESEARCH

Although the scope of the problem may seem overwhelming, there are day-to-day actions we can take to contribute to reproductive justice for the world's women. If we embrace the feminist assertion that the personal is political, as researchers, educators, and practitioners we have the opportunity to engage the WHO's three dimensions of STI prevention and control through our own work. We are in the unique position of having access to information, resources, and individuals that directly affect STI outcomes globally. From our daily interactions with clients and patients, or our development of research ideas and/ or teaching approaches, we can practice reproductive justice approaches that can contribute to positive global changes in STI rates for women at the human condition, services, and approach levels. As physical and mental health care providers, we can promote clinical practices grounded in the reproductive justice framework to ensure that our patients have the necessary medical, social, and educational resources to have healthy families. Thus, we are able to contribute to efforts to ensure that women live in cultures that support healthy and safe communities. Examples of actions toward this goal include the following:

- Engage in efforts that seek to reduce cultural barriers to women's STI prevention and care. This could include increasing our own understandings of social cues, religious values, gender-role expectations, linguistic cues, and sexual mores among others. Expanding our affiliations with local and national services and educational and advocacy organizations concerned with the needs of women from diverse backgrounds can informally open doors to awareness. At the organizational level, we can review our clinic's accessibility to marginalized women and ability to assess the experiences of underserved women; we can work in coalition with women of color-led organizations to evaluate our organizational mission's inclusion of cultural competence (i.e., ask them how well we are doing). Cross-cultural knowledge, which enhances personal insight and empathy with people from diverse cultures, will enable individuals and organizations to treat and communicate with their clients/patients more effectively.

- Address the significant influence of STI stigma and shame through improved education about compassionate and culturally competent approaches. Stigmas about STIs can influence how women perceive reactions to the disclosure of their sexual behavior to health care providers and, in turn, can influence women's decision to seek STI-related care. Health care providers need to ensure that clients/patients are given the necessary information about STIs that is at their level and not judgmental. Research on diverse populations, for example, has shown that, by increasing education about and raising awareness of the prevalence of certain STIs women's level of shame can be reduced (Cunningham, Tschann, Gurvey, Fortenberry, & Ellen, 2002; Fortenberry et al., 2002; Waller, Marlow, & Wardle, 2007). By taking this approach we can better meet the needs of women who are already infected and provide prevention information to those who are not.

- Provide and maintain connections to services and support systems that facilitate women's ability to avoid STI risks and contexts. As poorer health status among women has been associated with lower levels of knowledge, information, skills, purchasing power, income-earning capacity, and access to essential health services, it is important that clinicians appreciate that their role exists within a larger circle of care (Bernstein & Hansen, 2006; Gazmararian et al.,

2000). For example, by empowering women with income-generating life skills, along with improved health sexual knowledge, the collaborative Kawempe Community Health and Development Project (KCHDP) in Uganda has successfully reduced negative STI-related outcomes and increased options for economic independence among sex workers. This integrative approach led to a reduction in STIs from 15 percent to 9 percent, a reduction in unwanted pregnancies from 17.7 percent to 10.1 percent, and an increase in employment outside of the sex trade by 73 percent; more than 70 percent of the women quit the sex trade altogether in the two-year period of this project (KCHDP, 2008).

In our roles as educators we have direct access to the populations we seek to educate, to emerging generations of scholars, and to educational tools often inaccessible to others. Through our teaching, we can introduce the reproductive justice framework and incorporate reproductive justice into our STI education curricula. Some ways we can do this include the following:

- Promote increased investment in reproductive and sex education that empowers women by providing culturally competent skills that embrace relationship, familial, and community values. For example, research shows that Native American adolescent girls who lived on a reservation and spoke a tribal language had sex for the first time at an older age than their peers did and were more likely than their peers to use condoms (Aguilera, 2005; Chewning, 2001; Steenbeek, 2004). Thus, educators cannot ignore the importance of cultural values, traditions, and tools of education/communication in our sexual health efforts. By using a culturally appropriate approach, educators working with Native American women—and other women of color or other marginalized populations—are better able to encourage positive sexual health behaviors and to address contextual issues that may put theses populations at risk for STIs (Aguilera, 2005; Steenbeek, 2004). A broad but integrated perspective on the cultural and sexual health issues provides women a space to feel empowered without alienating their cultural beliefs.

- Design cross-cultural curricula and educational materials to prepare students to be effective practitioners, scholars, and researchers in an increasingly diverse global community. Such tools can increase students' understanding and appreciation of cultural differences and similarities within, among, and between groups. The U.S. Health Resources and Services Administration (2001), for example, has recommended that academic programs, research fellowships, and medical training include some form of diversity training and cross-cultural exposure as part of a multilevel strategy to reduce racial and ethnic disparities in health care. Educators must encourage the integration of international perspectives and skills in core curricula to ensure that students are able to meet the needs of the global community.

- Maintain communications, networks, and collaborations with educators who serve diverse populations. As with other health issues, many STI educators must seek out resources and expertise from other educators and organizations to stay current. Given that STI information changes quickly, educators must continually educate themselves. Professional organizations, women's health advocacy groups, and/or online community networks can provide a space for the dissemination and discussion of news, views, events, and other happenings of interest to members in different parts of the world. For example, the Sexual and Reproductive Health Listserv's purpose is to increase access to state-of-the-art information and to encourage networking, mobilization, and sharing of lessons learned among those who work in the area of reproductive health in various countries (http://groups.google.com/group/care-srh-listserv).

Researchers are directly involved in the construction and legitimization of new forms of knowledge, including those that inform ideas about gender, race, ethnicity, and nationality in health contexts. In this role, we have the capability to add to the existing body of scientific knowledge about gendered health outcomes, to create tools of measurement, and to influence policy makers responsible for allocating funding for STI research as described below.

- Develop tools and research designs that accurately capture the scope of STI outcomes among women globally. The interpretation and usefulness of multidimensional measures of STI outcomes will be strengthened by testing, in advance, hypothesized relationships with different illness and disease groups, socioeconomic and demographic groups (including vulnerable or marginalized subpopulations), or other external criteria. Furthermore, the interests of those being assessed must be considered as indicators are being constructed and tested in different sites. Development of appropriate and reliable research approaches is critical for the implementation and evaluation of STI intervention strategies that target diverse female populations.

- Engage in research that acknowledges the diversity of women's identities and make connections across shared gendered experiences. Researchers across disciplines emphatically agree that interventions designed to achieve changes in attitudes toward and beliefs about racial-/ethnic-minority sexuality that fail to recognize the unique cultural messages that influence these processes are likely to fail (Aguilera, 2005; Bajaj, 2008; Kis, 2010; Thomas & Stephens, 2009). Further, it is important to understand how research contributions expected to improve STI health and wellness outcomes are practiced in real-world settings. For example, whether or not local populations prefer different ways of collecting data, or describe and value health states differently, shapes the interpretation and legitimacy of the indicators developed (Sadana, 1998).

- Ensure that academic institutions, professional organizations, and funding agencies prioritize the need for research to identify the underlying reasons for disparities in STI outcomes among the world's women. This includes the continued support of scholarships, awards, research clusters, and grants for scholars to address STI issues. Although a wide range of research topics related to STI health prevention could be included, studies focused on gender-appropriate interventions and on the conditions for which they are most frequently used should be particularly encouraged.

- Advocate for funding mechanisms that support interdisciplinary, cross-cultural, and international research projects. When informed by a reproductive justice framework, collaborators can pool their knowledge to produce reliable and powerful results that come to publication faster than they would if the research were done independently. Collaborative research funding is particularly important now given the global recession threats to the renewal and maintenance of current support at existing levels. For example, in 2009 the United States and the European Commission decreased their international funding of preventive HIV vaccination by 25 percent and 5 percent, respectively (UNAIDS, 2010). The continued funding of collaborative STI research is critical to ensure that researchers have sufficient resources to advance important, international prevention efforts for women's health and reproductive justice.

CONCLUSION

Given that the global disease burden of STIs among women is a major public health concern, we sought to provide an overview of key areas through a reproductive justice lens. This perspective provides valuable insights into the intersectionality of women's national, racial, gender, and sexual identities with STI experiences at the global level. Further, the categories that we explored through this approach serve to contextualize the current research on women's STI experiences through both a woman-centered point of view and an environmental framework. That is, both the shared experiences of women and their unique identities must be central concerns whenever we are analyzing their behaviors within contexts that influence their potential experiences with STI. It's hoped that by doing this, we will be better able to identify the varied covert and overt sexual health messages being disseminated across diverse cultural contexts and to assess the impact of these messages on STI-related behavioral and psychological outcomes among women. This can be used for the next step of identifying innovative, alternative STI interventions that are reflective of the unique experiences of women in their individual contexts and across global communities. In conclusion, it is hoped that the reproductive justice framework used in this chapter can contribute toward closing the gap between research and practice and toward the development of an overarching framework through which to envision comprehensive STI health promotion strategy approaches. However, there is a critical need for further theory and research in the area of STI infection among women globally. Although the emerging research continues to provide evidence that rates are increasing, our level of knowledge about the linkages that have led to a shared experience with STI infections among women around the world have not kept pace. As the contexts that are shaped by gender, race/ethnicity, nationality, and sexuality frameworks continue to inform STI outcomes, greater attention must be paid to these. By bringing together women and connecting their unique identities and issues of concern, we will be able achieve the necessary momentum with which women and communities can truly transform their lives.

REFERENCES

Aguilera, S. (2005). Culturally appropriate HIV/AIDS and substance abuse prevention programs for urban native youth. *Journal of Psychoactive Drugs, 37,* 299–304.

Anuforo, P., Oyedele, L., & Pacquiao, D. (2004). Comparative study of meanings, beliefs, and practices of female circumcision among three Nigerian tribes in the United States and Nigeria. *Journal of Transcultural Nursing, 15,* 103–113.

Apostolopoulos, Y., & Sönmez, S. (2001). Working producers, leisured consumers: Women's experiences in developing regions. In Y. Apostolopoulos, S. Sevil, & T. Dallen (Eds.), *Women as producers and consumers of tourism in developing regions* (pp. 3–18). Westport, CT: Praeger.

Aral, S.O., Over, M. Manhart, L., & Holmes, K. K. (2006). Sexually transmitted infections. In D. T. Jamison, J. G. Breman, A. R. Measham, G. Alleyn, M. Claeson, D. B. Evans, . . . P. Mangrove (Eds.), *Disease control priorities in developing countries* (pp. 311–330). Washington, DC: World Bank.

Asian Communities for Reproductive Justice. (2005). *A new vision for advancing our movement for reproductive health, reproductive rights and reproductive justice.* Oakland, CA: Author.

Bajaj, M. (2008). Schooling in the shadow of death: Youth agency and HIV/AIDS in Zambia. *Journal of Asian and African Studies, 43,* 307–329.

Bandyopadhyay, M., & Thomas, J. (2002). Women migrant workers' vulnerability to HIV infection in Hong Kong. *AIDS Care, 1,* 509–521.

Bang, R. A., Bang, A. T., Baitule, M., Choudhary, Y., Sarmukaddam, S., & Tale, O. (1989). High prevalence of gynecological diseases in rural Indian women. *Lancet, 333,* 85–88.

Baumeister, R. F., & Vohs, K. D. (2004). Sexual economics: Sex as female resource for social exchange in heterosexual interactions. *Personality and Social Psychology Review, 8,* 339–363.

Bergenström, A. (2003). Afghanistan: HIV/AIDS vulnerability and prevention. *Journal of Health Management, 5,* 215–226.

Bernasconi, O. (2010). Being decent, being authentic: The moral self in shifting discourses of sexuality across three generations of Chilean women. *Sociology, 44,* 860–875.

Bernstein, S., & Hansen, C. J. (2006). *Public choices, private decisions: Sexual and reproductive health and the millennium development goals.* New York: UN Millennium Project.

Bersamin, M. M., Fisher, D. A., Walker, S., Hill, D. L., & Grube, J. W. (2007). Defining virginity and abstinence: Adolescents' interpretations of sexual behaviors. *Journal of Adolescent Health, 41,* 182–188.

Best, A., Stokols, D., Green, L. W., Leischow, S., Holmes, B., & Buchholz, K. (2003). An integrative framework for community partnering to translate theory into effective health promotion strategy. *American Journal of Health Promotion, 18,* 168–176.

Bevan, C. D., Johal, B. J., Mumtaz, G., Ridgway, G. L., & Siddle, N. C. (1995). Clinical, laparoscopic, and microbiological findings in acute salpingitis: Report on a United Kingdom cohort. *British Journal of Obstetrics and Gynecology 102,* 407–414.

Bunkle, P. (2003). The limits to sexual and reproductive health rights in a corporatized competitive global economy. *Development, 46*(2), 27–32.

Carpenter, L. M. (2002). Gender and the meaning and experience of virginity loss in the contemporary United States. *Gender & Society, 16,* 345–365.

Castro-Vázquez, G., & Kishi, I. (2007). Silence, condoms, and masculinity: Heterosexual Japanese males negotiating contraception. *Men & Masculinities, 10,* 153–177.

Centers for Disease Control and Prevention. (2008a). *Fact sheet: Genital HPV infection.* Atlanta, GA: Author.

Centers for Disease Control and Prevention. (2008b). *HPV vaccine information for clinicians: Sexually transmitted diseases treatment guidelines.* Retrieved from http://www.cdc.gov/std/hpv/STDFact-HPV-vaccine-hcp.htm.

Chadborn, T., Delpech, V. C., Sabin, C. A., Sinka, K., & Evans, B. G. (2006). The late diagnosis and consequent short-term mortality of HIV-infected heterosexuals (England and Wales, 2000–2004). *AIDS, 20,* 2371–2379.

Chewning, B. (2001). Protective factors associated with American Indian adolescents' safer sexual patterns. *Maternal and Child Health Journal, 5,* 273–280.

Csete, J. (2005). A comfortable home: Globalization and changing gender roles in the fight against HIV/AIDS. In I. Kickbusch, K. A. Hartwig, & J. M. List

(Eds.), *Globalization, women, and health in the 21st century* (pp. 167–182). New York: Palgrave Macmillan.

Cunningham, S. D., Tschann, J., Gurvey, J. E., Fortenberry, J. D., & Ellen, J. M. (2002). Attitudes about sexual disclosure and perceptions of stigma and shame. *Sexually Transmitted Infections 78*, 334–338.

Dallabetta, G. A., Field, M. L., Laga, M., & Islam, Q. M. (1997). Global burden and challenges for control. In G. A. Dallabetta, M. Laga, & P. R. Lamptey (Eds.), *Control of sexually transmitted diseases: A handbook for the design and management of programs* (pp. 1–21). Arlington, VA: AIDSCAP and Family Health International.

Dawson, M. T., & Gifford, S. M. (2001). Narratives, culture, and sexual health: Personal life experiences of Salvadorean and Chilean women living in Melbourne, Australia. *Health, 5,* 403–425.

Dietrich, J. W. (2007). The politics of PEPFAR: The president's emergency plan for AIDS relief. *Ethics & International Affairs, 21,* 277–292.

Edgardh, K. (2002). Adolescent sexual health in Sweden. *Sexually Transmitted Infections, 78,* 352–356.

Edgardh, K., Kühlmann-Berenzon, S., Grünewald, M., Rotzen-Östlund, M., Qvarnström, I., & Everljung, J. (2009). Repeat infection with chlamydia trachomatis: A prospective cohort study from an STI-clinic in Stockholm. *BMC Public Health, 9,* 198–204.

Ehrenreich, B., & Hoschild, A. (2003). *Global woman: Nannies, maids, and sex workers in the new economy.* New York: Metropolitan Books.

Einwalter, L. A., Ritchie, J. M., Ault, K. A., & Smith, E. M. (2005). Gonorrhea and chlamydia infection among women visiting family planning clinics: Racial variation in prevalence and predictors. *Perspectives on Sexual Reproductive Health, 37,* 135–140.

Ethier, K. A., Kershaw, T., Niccolai, T., Lewis, J. B., & Ickovics, J. R. (2003). Adolescent women underestimate their susceptibility to sexually transmitted infections. *Sexually Transmitted Infections, 79,* 408–411.

Faulkner, S. (2003). Good girl or flirt girl: Latinas' definitions of sex and sexual relationships. *Hispanic Journal of Behavioral Sciences, 25,* 174–200.

Ford, C. A., Jaccard, J., Millstein, S. G., Bardsley, P. E., & William, W. C. (2004). Perceived risk of chlamydial and gonococcal infection among sexually experienced young adults in the United States. *Perspectives on Sexual and Reproductive Health, 36,* 258–264.

Fortenberry, J. D., McFarlane, M., Bleakley, A., Bulls, S., Grimley, D., Malotte, K., & Stoner, B. (2002). Relationships of stigma and shame to gonorrhea and HIV screening. *American Journal of Public Health, 92,* 378–381.

Gant, L., Heath, K. & Ejikeme, G.C. (2009). Early motherhood, high mortality, and HIV/AIDS rates in sub-Saharan Africa. *Social Work in Public Health, 24,* 39–46.

Gazmararian, J. A., Petersen, R., Spitz, A. M., Goodwin, M. M., Saltzman, L. E., & Marks, J. S. (2000). Violence and reproductive health: Current knowledge and future research directions. *Maternal Child Health Journal, 4,* 79–84.

Gerbase, A. C., Rowley, J. T., Heymann, D. H., Berkley, S. F., & Piot, P. (1998). Global prevalence and incidence estimates of selected curable STDs. *Sexually Transmitted Infections, 74,* S12–16.

Gilliam, M. L., Neustadt, A., & Gordon, R. (2009). A call to incorporate a reproductive justice agenda into reproductive health clinical practice and policy.
Contraception, 79, 243–246.

Giordano, F. G., Thumme, B., & Sierra, G. P. (2009). The hopes and dreams of Hon-
duran women regarding their daughters' sexuality. *Qualitative Health Research, 19,* 996–1009.

Girardi, E., Sampaolesi, A., Gentile, M., Nurra, G., & Ippolito, G. (2000). Increasing
proportion of late diagnosis of HIV infection among patients with AIDS in
Italy following introduction of combination antiretroviral therapy. *Journal
of Acquired Immune Deficiency Syndromes, 25,* 71–76.

Glasier, A., Gülmezoglu, A., Schmid, G., Moreno, C., & Van Look, P. (2006). Sexual
and reproductive health: A matter of life and death. *Lancet, 368,* 1595–1607.

Gorbach, P. M., Manhart, L. E., Hess, K. L., Stoner, B. P., Martin, D. H., & Holmes,
K. K. (2009). Anal intercourse among young heterosexuals in three sexu-
ally transmitted disease clinics in the United States. *Sexually Transmitted
Diseases, 36,* 193–198.

Haglund, K. (2003). Sexually abstinent African American adolescent females' descriptions of abstinence. *Journal of Nursing Scholarship, 35,* 231–236.

Hall, M. C. (1996). Gender and economic interests in tourism prostitution: The na-
ture, development, and implications of sex tourism in southeast Asia. In Y.
Apostolopoulos, S. Leivadi, & A. Yiannakis (Eds.), *The sociology of tourism:
Theoretical and empirical investigations* (pp. 265–280). New York: Routledge.

Halpern-Felsher, B. L., Cornell, J. L., Kropp, R. Y., & Tschann, J. (2005). Oral versus
vaginal sex among adolescents: Perceptions, attitudes, and behavior. *Pediatrics, 115,* 845–851.

Hanlon, P., Carlisle, S., Reilly, D., Lyon, A., & Hannah, M. (2010). Enabling well-
being in a time of radical change: Integrative public health for the 21st century. *Public Health, 124,* 305–312.

Harcourt, W. (2001). Women's health, poverty, and globalization. *Development, 44,*
1, 85–90.

Hawkesworth, M. E. (2006). *Globalization and feminist activism.* Lanham, MD:
Rowan & Littlefield.

Health Canada. (2004). *HIV and AIDS in Canada: Surveillance report to June 30, 2003.*
Ottawa, Ontario, Canada: Centre for Infectious Disease Prevention and
Control–Health Canada.

Heymann, D. L. (2008). *Control of communicable diseases manual.* Washington, DC:
American Public Health Association.

Higgins, L. T., Zheng, M., Liu, Y., & Sun, C. H. (2002). Attitudes toward marriage
and sexual behaviors: A survey of gender and culture differences in China
and United Kingdom. *Sex Roles, 46,* 75–89.

Jagger, A. (2002). Vulnerable women and neo-liberal globalization: Debt burdens
undermine women's health in the global south. *Theoretical Medicine and Bioethics, 23,* 425–440.

Katz, J., & Tirone, V. (2010). Going along with it: Sexually coercive partner behavior predicts dating women's compliance with unwanted sex. *Violence
Against Women, 16,* 730–742.

Kawai, K., Kaaya, S. F., Kajula, L., Mbwambo, J., Kilonzo, G. P., & Fawzi, W. W.
(2008). Parents' and teachers' communication about HIV and sex in relation

to the timing of sexual initiation among young adolescents in Tanzania. *Scandinavian Journal of Public Health, 36,* 879–888.

Kawempe Community Health and Development Project. (2008). *Kawempe Community Health and Development Project annual project report.* Kampala, Uganda: African Medical and Research Foundation.

Kempadoo, K. (2004). *Sexing the Caribbean: Gender, race, and sexual labor.* New York: Routledge.

Kis, A. D. (2010). ABC for AIDS prevention in Guinea: Migrant gold mining communities address their risks. *AIDS Care, 22,* 520–525.

Kouta, C., & Tolma, E. L. (2008). Sexuality, sexual and reproductive health: An exploration of the knowledge, attitudes and beliefs of the Greek-Cypriot adolescents. *Global Health Promotion, 15,* 24–31.

Li, Y., Cottrell, R. R., Wagner D., & Ban, M. (2004). Needs and preferences regarding sex education among Chinese college students: A preliminary study. *International Family Planning Perspectives, 30,* 128–133.

Lopes, F., Buchalla, C. M., de Carvalho, J. R., & Ayres, M. (2007). Black and non-black women and vulnerability to HIV/AIDS in São Paulo, Brazil. *Revista de Saúde Pública, 41,* 1–7.

López, N. (2004). Gender in Latin America. *Contemporary Sociology, 33,* 294–296.

Low, N., Broutet, N., Adu-Sarkodie, Y., Barton, P., Hossain, M., & Hawkes, S. (2006). Global control of sexually transmitted infections. *Lancet, 368,* 2001–2016.

Luna, Z. (2009). From rights to justice: Women of color changing the face of U.S. reproductive rights organizing. *Societies without Borders, 4,* 343–365.

Maran, R. (1996). After the Beijing women's conference: What will be done? *Social Justice, 23,* 1–2.

Martin, P. (2010). "These days virginity is just a feeling": Heterosexuality and change in young urban Vietnamese men. *Culture, Health, & Sexuality, 12,* 5–18.

Mayhew, S., Nzambi, K., Pépin, J., & Adjei, S. (2001). Pharmacists' role in managing sexually transmitted infections: Policy issues and options for Ghana. *Health Policy and Planning, 16,* 152–160.

Meyer-Weitz, A., Reddy, P., Van den Borne, H. W., Kok, G., & Pietersen, J. (2000). Health care–seeking behaviour of patients with sexually transmitted diseases: Determinants of delay behavior. *Patient Education and Counseling, 41,* 263–274.

Miller, G. C., McDermott, R., McCulloch, B., Fairley, C. K., & Muller, R. (2003). Predictors of the prevalence of bacterial STI among young disadvantaged indigenous people in north Queensland, Australia. *Sexually Transmitted Infections, 79,* 332–335.

Molleman, G., & Franse, L. (2009). The struggle for abandonment of female genital mutilation/cutting (FGM/C) in Egypt. *Global Health Promotion, 16,* 57–60.

Okonofua, F. (2007). HPV vaccine and prevention of cervical cancer in Africa. *African Journal of Reproductive Health, 11,* 7–9.

Ozyegin, G. (2009). Virginal facades: Sexual freedom and guilt among young Turkish women. *European Journal of Women's Studies, 16,* 103–123.

Paavonen, J. (1997). Is screening for chlamydia trachomatis infection cost effective? *Genitourinary Medicine, 73,* 103–104.

Panchaud, C., Singh, S., Feivelson, D., & Darroch, J. E. (2000). Sexually transmitted diseases among adolescents in developed countries. *Family Planning Perspectives, 32,* 24–32.

Parsitau, S. D. (2009). Keep holy distance and abstain till he comes: Interrogating a Pentecostal church's engagements with HIV/AIDS and the youth in Kenya. *Africa Today, 56*, 45–64.

Peltzer, K., Mngqundaniso, N., & Petros, G. (2006). A controlled study of an HIV/AIDS/STI/TB intervention with traditional healers in KwaZulu-Natal, South Africa. *AIDS & Behavior, 10*, 683–690.

Pyke, K. D., & Johnson, D. L. (2003). Asian American women and racialized femininities: "Doing" gender across cultural worlds. *Gender & Society, 17*, 33–53.

Rankin, S., Lindgren, T., Kools, S. M., & Schell, E. (2008). The condom divide: Disenfranchisement of Malawi women by church and state. *Journal of Obstetric, Gynecologic, & Neonatal Nursing, 37*, 596–606.

Risser, W. L., & Risser, J.M.H. (2007). The incidence of pelvic inflammatory disease in untreated women infected with chlamydia tracomatis: A structured review. *International Journal of STDs & AIDS, 18*, 727–731.

Rou, K., Wu, Z., Sullivan, S. G., Li, F., Guan, J., Xu, C., . . . Yin, Y. (2007). A five-city trial of a behavioural intervention to reduce sexually transmitted disease/HIV risk among sex workers in China. *AIDS, 21*, S95–101.

Roye, C. F., Krausse, B., & Silverman, C. L. (2010). Prevalence and correlates of heterosexual anal intercourse among Black and Latina female adolescents. *Journal of the Association of Nurses in AIDS Care, 21*, 291–301.

Ryan, C., & Kinder, R. (1996). Sex, tourism, and sex tourism: Fulfilling similar needs? *Tourism Management, 17*, 507–518.

Sadana, R. (1998, April). *A closer look at the WHO/World Bank Global Burden of Disease Study's methodologies: How do poor women's values in a developing country compare with international public health experts?* Paper presented at the Public Health Forum, London.

Sadana, R. (2002). Definition and measurement of reproductive health. *Bulletin of the World Health Organization, 80*, 407–409.

Santillán, D., Schuler, S., Anh, H. T., Minh, T. H., & Mai, B. T. (2002). Limited equality: Contradictory ideas about gender and the implications for reproductive health in rural Vietnam. *Journal of Health Management, 4*, 251–267.

Seufert-Barr, N. (2008). Empowering women: More education, better health care, less poverty. *United Nations Chronicle*. Retrieved from http://findarticles.com/p/articles/mi_m1309/is_n2_v32/ai_17369704/.

Sharma, S. (2008). Young women, sexuality, and Protestant church community: Oppression or empowerment? *European Journal of Women's Studies, 15*, 345–359.

Sharpe, T. H. (2003). Adult sexuality. *Family Journal, 11*, 420–426.

Sipkin, D. L., Gillam, A., & Grady, L. B. (2003). Risk factors for chlamydia trachomatis infection in California collegiate population. *Journal of American College Health 52*, 65–72.

Skandrani, S., Baubet, T., Taïeb, O., Rezzoug, D., & Moro, M. R. (2010). The rule of virginity among young women of Maghrebine origin in France. *Transcultural Psychiatry, 47*, 301–313.

Staunæs, D. (2005). From culturally avant-garde to sexually promiscuous: Troubling subjectivities and intersections in the social transition from childhood into youth. *Feminism & Psychology, 15*, 149–167.

Steenbeek, A. (2004). A holistic approach in preventing sexually transmitted infections among First Nation and Inuit adolescents in Canada. *Journal of Holistic Nursing, 22*, 254–266.

Stephens, D. P., & Phillips, L. D. (2005). Integrating Black feminist thought into conceptual frameworks of African American adolescent women's sexual scripting processes. *Sexualities, Evolution, & Gender, 7,* 37–55.

Stephens, D. P., Phillips, L. D., & Few, A. L. (2009). Examining African American female adolescent sexuality within mainstream hip hop culture using a womanist-ecological model of human development. In S. Loyd, A. L. Few, & K. Allen (Eds.), *Handbook of feminist theory, methods and praxis in family studies* (pp. 160–174). Newbury Park, CA: Sage.

Subramaniam, V. (1999). The impact of globalization on women's reproductive health and rights: A regional perspective. *Development, 42,* 145–149.

Thomas, T. L., & Stephens, D. P. (2009). Young women speak: Why we seek health care and what we need from our providers. *Journal of the Florida Medical Association, 108,* 18–26.

UNAIDS. (2010). *UNAIDS report on the global AIDS epidemic.* Retrieved 2010 from http://www.unaids.org/globalreport/Global_report.htm.

UNAIDS/ UNFPA/ UNIFEM. (2004). *Women and HIV/AIDS: Confronting the crisis* [joint report from UNAIDS/UNFPA/UNIFEM]. Retrieved from http://www.unfpa.org/hiv/women/docs/women_aids.pdf.

UNAIDS & World Health Organization. (1998). *Report on the Global HIV/AIDS Epidemic: December 1998.* Retrieved from http://data.unaids.org/pub/Report/1998/19981125_global_epidemic_report_en.pdf.

United Nations Development Program. (2008). *HIV vulnerabilities faced by women migrants: from Asia to the Arab states.* Colombo, Sri Lanka: Author.

U.S. Health Resources and Services Administration. (2001). *Key ingredient of the national prevention agenda: Workforce development companion document to healthy people 2010.* Washington, DC: HRSA Bureau of Health Professions.

Waller, J., Marlow, L.A.V., & Wardle, J. (2007). The association between knowledge of HPV and feelings of stigma, shame, and anxiety. *Sexually Transmitted Infections, 83,* 155–159.

Weiss, E., Whelan, D., & Gupta, G. R. (2000). Gender, sexuality, and HIV: Making a difference in the lives of young women in developing countries. *Sexual and Relationship Therapy, 15,* 233–245.

Welch, J. (2010). STIs in women: Symptoms and examination. *Medicine, 38,* 226–230.

World Health Organization. (2001). *Global prevalence and incidence of selected curable sexually transmitted infections.* Retrieved from www.who.int/hiv/pub/sti/who_hiv_aids_2001.02.pdf.

World Health Organization. (2008). *Sexually transmitted infections fact sheet no. 110.2007* Retrieved from www.who.int/mediacentre/factsheets/fs110/en/index.html.

Yukota, F. (2006). Sex behavior of male Japanese tourists in Bangkok, Thailand. *Culture, Health, and Sexuality, 8,* 115–131.

Zacarias, F., Martin, D., & Cuche, P. (2000, July). *From policy to action: Syndromic STD management in Latin America and the Caribbean (LAC).* Paper presented at the International Conference on AIDS, Durban, South Africa (National Library of Medicine No. ThPeC5455).

Chapter 7

Contraception and Abortion: Critical Tools for Achieving Reproductive Justice

Nancy Felipe Russo and Julia R. Steinberg

Because women's ability to time, space, and limit childbearing is a necessary condition for full participation in social, economic, and political life, reproductive rights have profound implications for the health, social, economic, and political status of women. In particular, the interconnections between women's ability to control reproduction and their ability to take advantage of educational and employment opportunities means that reproductive rights provide a basis to attain the related rights of health, equality, and nondiscrimination, among others (Erdman & Cook, 2008).

As Chrisler and Garrett (2010) pointed out, reproductive rights provide a necessary but not sufficient condition for achieving reproductive justice, which requires access to the reproductive health services needed to exercise such rights without sanction or discrimination. This fundamental fact means that access to birth control (i.e., contraception and abortion) is essential for reproductive justice. The interconnecting web of reproductive rights with other human rights means that disparities in reproductive justice can undermine efforts to achieve social and economic equality for women, particularly for poor women.

Indeed, achieving reproductive justice is a necessary condition for meeting the eight Millennium Development Goals (MDGs) of the United Nations' (UN) campaign to eliminate worldwide poverty (UN, 2011a). As Cates and his colleagues (2010, p. 1603) pointed out, family planning is a "cost-effective cross-cutting intervention" for achieving MDGs such as eliminating poverty and hunger, improving child health, achieving gender equality through education and empowerment, combating HIV/AIDS, ensuring environmental sustainability, and fostering global partnerships across diverse ideologies. The MDGs are important because many countries use them to set funding priorities. Given its fundamental cross-cutting importance, universal reproductive health care should have been specifically named as a targeted MDG, but social conservatives were successful keeping it off the initial list (Greene & Merrick, 2005). It was only after the five-year program review that universal access to reproductive health became separately mentioned as a target under the goal of improving maternal health (Singh, Darroch, Ashford, & Vlassoff, 2009). Today, the UN website recognizes inadequate funding for family planning as a "major failure in fulfilling commitments to improving women's reproductive health" (UN, 2011a).

OBSTACLES TO ACHIEVING REPRODUCTIVE JUSTICE

The power of social conservatives is but one of a multitude of factors, such as religion, custom, culture, and poverty, that converge to impede access to effective contraception and safe abortion (Amnesty International, 2011). Women who seek reproductive health services must negotiate what they have described as an obstacle course that includes inadequate or misleading information; social and financial barriers; restrictive laws and bureaucratic procedures that lead to delay or denial of care; financial malfeasance and corruption; lack of standards and guidelines; substandard or absent health care facilities; poor referral practices; lack of continuity of care; mistreatment, discrimination, abuse, and cultural insensitivity on the part of health care providers; and no mechanisms to ensure accountability (Human Rights Watch, 2010, p. 2).

A instructive example of how multiple influences can converge to undermine reproductive justice comes from northern Nigeria: Wall (1998, p. 341) has vividly described the plight of "dead mothers and injured wives" that results from the convergence of "an Islamic culture that undervalues women; a perceived social need for women's reproductive capacities to be under strict male control; the practice of *purdah* (wife seclusion), which restricts women's access to medical care; almost universal female illiteracy; marriage at an early age and pregnancy often occurring before maternal pelvic growth is complete; a high rate of obstructed labor; directly harmful traditional medical beliefs and practices; inadequate facilities to deal with obstetric emergencies; a deteriorating economy; and a political culture marked by rampant corruption and inefficiency." Examples can also be found across Latin America, where a complex mix of social, political, economic, legal, and religious forces shape women's ability to exercise their reproductive rights. This mix differs across the region and leads to variation in the outcomes associated with denial of reproductive justice in different countries (Padilla, Pingel, Reyes, & Fiereck, 2010).

Women's reproductive rights are often controversial, particularly insofar as a woman's control over her sexuality and reproduction is seen as threatening to moral values, family integrity, and gendered power relationships (Erdman & Cook, 2008). Moreover, because women's sexual and reproductive autonomy may be seen as threatening to the patriarchal social order, efforts to attain reproductive justice may be suppressed, sometimes in coercive and violent ways (Amnesty International, 2011).

In this chapter, we focus on contraception and abortion and refer readers to other works for a more detailed discussion of sexuality (Castaneda & Ulibarri, 2010; see also chapter 3, "Women's Power in Relationships"; chapter 4, "Sexual Assault"; and chapter 5, "Reproductive Injustice"). We recognize that exercising one's reproductive rights requires the means to prevent, as well as terminate, unintended pregnancy; thus we focus on disparities indicative of reproductive justice denied that are related to (1) unintended pregnancy and childbearing, (2) the unmet need for contraception, and (3) unsafe abortion. The disparities that emerge make the case that addressing women's unmet need for contraception and increasing the safety of abortion, particularly for poor women, is a necessary foundation for achieving reproductive justice internationally.

UNINTENDED PREGNANCY AND CHILDBEARING

In 2008, an estimated 41 percent of pregnancies around the world were unintended (Singh, Wulf, Hussain, Bankole, & Sedgh, 2009). Reducing unintended pregnancy becomes a priority reproductive rights concern because of the host of negative outcomes that result from unintended childbearing (see Gipson, Koenig, & Hindin, 2008) and unsafe abortion (Singh, Wulf, et al., 2009). Thus, variations in rates and percentages of unintended pregnancy, birth, and abortion can be used as indicators of disparities in reproductive justice. Such variations also signal potential threats to other human rights. Below, we provide information on these indicators at global and regional levels; we use individual country information only to illustrate a particular point. For additional country-specific information, see the recent wall charts that are readily available on the UN's website (UN, 2011b, 2011c).

Relationships between unintended pregnancy and its consequences for women and their families reflect a complex mix of personal, social, and contextual factors that vary within and across countries, regions, and stages in a woman's life cycle. This complexity means that research on unintended pregnancy and its outcomes is fraught with definitional, measurement, and analytical challenges over and above those typically found in international research (Gipson et al., 2008, discuss these challenges in more detail).

Methodological Issues

In general, researchers have defined an unintended pregnancy as one that a woman reports as either unwanted (i.e., occurring when no children, or no more children, are desired) or mistimed (i.e., occurring earlier than desired; Santelli et al., 2003). The proportion of pregnancies that are unwanted and mistimed varies across studies due to sampling differences, as well as a host of religious, cultural, and contextual differences cross-nationally that change the mix of reasons why women seek to avoid pregnancy. This variation can contribute to inconsistency in the picture within and across countries because women's characteristics and outcomes may differ for subcategories of unintended pregnancy (D'Angelo, Gilbert, Rochat, Santelli, & Herold, 2004).

Challenges to data gathering in demographic and health surveys also vary across country and region (Singh, Wulf, et al., 2009). Further, such surveys typically rely on cross-sectional designs involving retrospective reports of pregnancy intention, and thus are likely to underestimate unintended pregnancy rates. For example, panel studies in India and Morocco have shown that women are more likely to reclassify their intentions from "unwanted" to "wanted" when intentions are requested by retrospective report (Bankole & Westoff, 1998; Koenig, Acharya, Singh, & Tarun, 2006).

Some studies of reproductive outcomes that focus on abortion or denial of abortion do not directly assess pregnancy intention or wantedness (Gipson et al., 2008). Instead researchers assume that pregnancies terminated by abortion are, by definition, unwanted. Unwanted fertility rates provide another indicator of unwanted births. The unwanted fertility rate is calculated by determining the difference between wanted fertility and actual total fertility. In keeping with conventional practice, unless otherwise noted we use the term *unintended pregnancy* when discussing research based on samples of women who reported both mistimed and unwanted pregnancies and the term *unintended birth* when discussing births that are the result of unintended pregnancy. We use the term *unwanted pregnancy* when the pregnancies are reported by the woman as unwanted or are terminated by abortion and the term *unwanted birth* for births that result from unwanted pregnancies or reflect calculations of unwanted fertility rates based on the gap between desired and actual family size.

In summary, methodological and definitional issues in research on unintended pregnancy compound the usual difficulties found in international research. Nonetheless, by focusing on patterns that emerge from the data, it is possible to identify disparities in reproductive justice around the world.

Rates of Unintended Pregnancy and Birth

Rates of unintended pregnancy have declined as contraceptive use has increased. In 2008, the global unintended pregnancy rate per 1,000 women aged 15–44[1] was 55, down from 69 in 1995. Rates were higher in less developed countries, where 89 percent of the world's pregnancies occurred. When China was included in the analyses, the unintended pregnancy rate for less developed countries was one-third higher than that for developed countries (57 vs. 42). When China was excluded, the rate was 60 percent higher than that for developed countries—67 vs. 42 (Singh, Wulf, et al., 2009).

The African and Latin American/Caribbean regions had the highest rates of unintended pregnancy (86 and 72 per 1,000 women, respectively), followed by Asia (49), North America (48), Oceania (44), and Europe (38). Regional averages mask wide variability in rates within subregions. For example, in eastern Africa, where the highest rates of unintended pregnancy in the world are found, unintended pregnancy rates ranged from a high of 118 in eastern Africa to a low of 56 in northern Africa. In Oceania, rates ranged from 51 in Australia and New Zealand to 26 for the rest of Oceania (Singh, Wulf, et al., 2009).

In interpreting the meaning of these numbers, keep in mind that the rates are calculated with a denominator of 1,000 women of reproductive age (15–44 years), regardless of whether or not the women are married or sexually active. Both the proportions of sexually active unmarried women and the overall proportions of unmarried women vary across cultures, which makes comparisons across cultures problematic when marital status and sexual activity are not controlled. A common approach is to report rates separately by marital status. When research resources are scarce, studies focus on married women, who are assumed to be sexually active if they are of reproductive age.

In 2008, an estimated 39 percent of unintended pregnancies worldwide ended in unintended birth; 49 percent and 12 percent ended in abortion and miscarriage, respectively (Singh, Wulf, et al., 2009). When miscarriages are excluded from the analyses, 44 percent of all unintended pregnancies worldwide ended in birth and 56 percent ended in abortion; developing countries had a lower proportion of unintended births than developing countries did. Among the less developed countries, the range of unintended births was substantial: Swaziland had the highest proportion of unintended births (67%), and Turkmenistan the lowest (3%; Singh, Wulf, et al., 2009).

Factors Associated with Unintended Pregnancy and Childbearing

Poverty, youth, and gender-based violence are all implicated in high rates of unintended pregnancy and childbearing. Unintended pregnancy is associated with socioeconomic status within countries, even in more developed nations. In the United States, rates of unintended pregnancy are highest for women with few economic resources, that is, women who are poor, lack a high school degree, unmarried (particularly if cohabitating), or Black or Hispanic (Finer & Henshaw, 2006). In developing nations, women of lower socioeconomic status also are more likely than women with more economic resources to have unintended pregnancies (Greene & Merrick, 2005). In addition, younger women, who usually have fewer economic resources than older women, are at higher risk of unintended pregnancy than other women regardless of level of national development (Finer, 2010; Finer & Henshaw, 2006; Lakha & Glasier, 2006).

Gender-based violence has major implications for reproductive justice. Around the world, women with violence in their lives are at higher risk for unintended pregnancy than other women are (Amnesty International, 2011; Pallitto, Campbell, & O'Campo, 2005; Sarkar, 2008). In diverse contexts, including Azerbaijan, Bangladesh, Colombia, India, Moldova, Peru, Ukraine, and the United States, women who experienced physical or sexual intimate partner violence were more likely than women who did not to have an unintended pregnancy (Cripe et al., 2008; Dietz et al., 2000; Ismayilova, 2010; Martin et al., 1999; Pallitto & O'Campo, 2004; Silverman, Gupta, Decker, Kapur, & Raj, 2007). Kishor and Johnson (2004, p. 85) found that in eight of the nine developing countries studied,[2] among women who had ever given birth, those who had experienced intimate partner violence had a greater likelihood than those who had not of having had a pregnancy end in nonlive birth (i.e., miscarriage, abortion, stillbirth). Further, in the seven countries where information was available, women who had experienced violence in the past year had a higher unmet need for contraception than did women who had never experienced violence.

Kishor and Johnson (2004) also found that a partner's controlling behaviors were associated with intimate partner violence, which in turn was associated with an unwanted birth. Pregnancy coercive behaviors (i.e., behaviors that increase pregnancy risk) and birth control sabotage (i.e., interfering with contraceptive use or effectiveness) have been linked to unintended pregnancy among women who experience violence (Miller et al. 2007, 2010; Moore, Frohwirth, & Miller, 2010). More needs to be known about how such behaviors contribute to unintended and unwanted pregnancy around the world (Russo, 2006).

Rape has been officially recognized by the UN as a weapon of war (UN, 2008), and genocidal rape aimed at destroying cultures and cleansing bloodlines by impregnating women is a severe example of violence as a form of social control (Human Rights Watch, 2011). Rape related to armed conflict has occurred on a massive scale in numerous countries historically, and it continues today (Amnesty International, 2004). In the Congo, more than 15,000 cases of sexual violence were reported in 2009, where more than one-half of the victims were under 18 years of age. In Liberia, where rape also occurs at alarming rates, the majority of victims are under age 16 (Human Rights Watch, 2011; see chapter 4, "Sexual Assault," for more information).

Consequences of Unintended Pregnancy and Childbearing

A wide range of negative health, psychological, social, and economic consequences are associated with unintended pregnancy and childbearing (see Gipson et al., 2008, for a review). Unintended pregnancy and childbearing outcomes are interrelated and depend on the life stage and status of the woman. They also differ for mistimed and unwanted births; adverse outcomes generally are more common for unwanted births (D'Angelo et al., 2004). We highlight five aspects of unintended pregnancy that reflect reproductive justice denied and are of particular concern because of their interrelationships with other negative consequences for women, their families, and society: maternal and child mortality, adolescent fertility, closely spaced births, large family size, and unwanted childbearing.

Maternal and Child Health

Unplanned pregnancies account for an estimated 30 percent of the global burden of disease associated with maternal conditions and 90 percent of the burden from unsafe abortions (World Health Organization [WHO], 2009). Maternal mortality has improved but continues to be unacceptably high, particularly for women in developing countries, which account for 99 percent of maternal deaths (WHO, 2010) and 95 percent of the world's orphans (UNICEF, 2001). Effects of losing a mother in the developing world are compounded by larger family sizes, lack of economic resources, and inadequate health and social service systems. In sub-Saharan Africa, it is estimated that fulfilling women's unmet need for contraception would lower the number of children who would otherwise become orphans by 59 percent (Singh, Darroch, et al., 2009).

Disparities in risk for dying during pregnancy and childbirth around the world are appalling. Lifetime risk of maternal death in 2008 was 1 in 31 in sub-Saharan Africa, 1 in 110 in Oceania, 1 in 120 in south Asia, and 1 in 4,300 in developed countries (WHO, 2010). The most common causes of maternal death include complications during labor and childbirth (e.g., obstructed labor, hemorrhage, hypertensive complications), in the immediate postpartum period (e.g., sepsis, hemorrhage), and unsafe abortion. Women also die from diseases (e.g., malaria) that are exacerbated by pregnancy. Lack of access to skilled health personnel, inadequate services for emergency obstetric care, inability to deal with complications of unsafe abortion, and ineffective referral systems further contribute to the high rates of maternal mortality and morbidity found in developing countries (Singh, Wulf, et al., 2009). According to WHO, in developing countries, five women die every hour due to complications from unsafe abortions (WHO, 2011a). This is the context in which pro-life social conservatives in the United States and Canada have succeeded in prohibiting funding for legal abortion in international aid packages (Greene & Merrick, 2005; Russo & Denious, 2005; Zangeneh, 2010). (See also chapter 9, "Pregnancy and Prenatal Care"; chapter 11, "Female Feticide and Infanticide"; and chapter 12, "Reproductive Justice for Women and Infants," for information on maternal mortality.)

Family planning plays a critical role in reducing infant and child mortality and morbidity, particularly among poor women (Potts & Thapa, 1991). Disparities between developed and developing countries are found in child health indicators: 99 percent of deaths during the first month of life occur in developing nations (Singh, Darroch, et al., 2009). Infants are more likely to die in poor households than rich ones in every region of the world. In Indonesia and Nicaragua, infants of the poorest women (bottom 20% of income distribution) are more than three times as likely to die as the infants of the wealthiest women (top 20%) (UN, 2010).

Adolescent Fertility

In 2009, 88 percent of the 1.2 billion adolescents in the world lived in developing countries. Child marriage is common in many countries, particularly the poorest countries; in the least developed countries, 48 percent of women 15–49 years of age were married or in a union before age 18 (UNICEF, 2011). The ability to delay first births is critically important for women who become sexually active at an early age. Adolescents are at higher risk for complications of pregnancy and maternal death, which are among the leading causes of death globally for girls 15–19 years of age. Maternal mortality in adolescence is five times higher than in later years, partially because of reproductive immaturity (Rowbottom, 2007). In addition, women who are more likely to have unintended pregnancies (i.e., young, uneducated, poor) are also more likely to report high-risk behaviors (e.g., smoking) and high-risk conditions (e.g., violence) that compound health risks to both mother and child (Gilbert, Johnson, Morrow,

Gaffield, & Ahluwalia, 1999). The consequences of having a child during adolescence can be so grave that adolescent fertility is one of the two indicators used for the reproductive health component of the UN's Gender Inequality Index; the other is maternal mortality (UN, 2010).

Adolescent fertility rates vary widely around the globe. They reflect a country's level of human development as assessed by the UN's four-part index of human development (very high, high, medium, low), which is based on a composite measure that combines information on life expectancy, education, and income. Adolescent fertility ranged from 19 births per 1,000 women aged 15–19 in countries with very high human development to 109 births for countries with low human development. There is substantial variation in developing countries by region; rates range from 18 in east Asia and the Pacific to 122 in sub-Saharan Africa (UN, 2010).

Within countries, adolescent fertility rates vary by wealth. A study (Greene & Merrick, 2005) based on data from 55 countries showed that rates varied from 63 for the richest 20 percent of women to 149 for the poorest 20 percent. The largest differential was found in the Latin America/Caribbean region where rates were 37 and 173 for richest and poorest women, respectively. A large proportion of adolescents experience unsafe abortion: 13 percent of an estimated 19 million women having unsafe abortions each year in developing countries are 15–19 years of age (Singh, Wulf, et al., 2009).

Closely Spaced Births

The ability to space births is more than simply a matter of convenience; it has implications for the health for both mothers and children. Closely spaced pregnancies (less than 2 years apart), along with inadequate prenatal, birthing, and postpartum care, can result in both acute and chronic disability and illness of mothers due to infection, hemorrhage, hypertension, anemia, and obstetric fistula (WHO, 2005).

Infants with close birth intervals have a higher risk of dying their first year than do those with wider birth intervals in both developed and developing countries. Analyses of data from Hungary, Sweden, and the United States show that spacing births more than two years apart would reduce the risk of low birth weight and neonatal death by an estimated 5–10 percent (Miller, 1991). Infants are more likely to die if the interval between a mother's previous birth and her next pregnancy is under 15 months than they are if the interval is at least 36 months (Rutstein, 2008). Rutstein (2008) argued that, in developing nations, if the interval from birth to the next conception were spaced at least three years apart, mortality rates of infants and children under five years old would be reduced by 11 percent and 25 percent, respectively.

Direct benefits of longer birth intervals also include improved health and nutrition for all children in the family (Dewey & Cohen, 2007; Rutstein, 2005, 2008). The full effects of close birth intervals have yet to be investigated, but close birth intervals have been implicated in risk for autism as well. A study (Cheslack-Postava, 2011) of 662,730 second-born children showed that those with short birth intervals (under three years) had a higher risk for autism than did those children with longer birth intervals. Children with the shortest birth intervals (less than 1 year) were three times as likely to develop autism as those with longer birth intervals; children with two-year intervals were twice as likely to develop autism.

In recognition of the adverse outcomes associated with close childbirth intervals, WHO (2005) recommended a two-year waiting period after a birth before the next pregnancy. The U.S. Agency for International Development recommended a three-to four-year interval between birth and the next pregnancy for the lowest risk of neonatal, infant, and under-five mortality (Rutstein, 2005).

Large Family Size

Large family sizes place substantial psychological, social, and economic burdens on families. For example, research from the Philippines has shown that an increase in number of children is linked to a decline in family savings, reduced maternal employment rates and income, and a lower proportion of children attending school (Orberta, 2005). When additional children are not desired and an unwanted pregnancy occurs, the health outcomes of that pregnancy to both mother and child depend on the childbearing context, including number of existing children and access to needed psychological, social, and economic resources. Each additional mouth to feed calls on family resources, and when families have scarce resources, malnutrition can result. For example being born unwanted has been linked to stunted growth in early childhood in Indonesia (Hardee, Eggleston, Wong, Irwanto, & Hull, 2004) and Bolivia (Shapiro-Mendoza, Selwyn, Smith, & Sanderson, 2005).

Family size preferences vary across countries and have long been understood to decline with increased modernization and higher education of women (e.g., Bulatao & Lee, 1983). Whereas in some cultures a larger desired family size could be considered a choice, in others it could be seen as reflecting a "motherhood mandate" (Russo, 1976) and as an indicator of the oppression and stigmatization of women who seek to have roles outside the home. In keeping with the view of reproductive rights as rooted in respect for the inherent dignity of the individual, we focus on variations in births defined as unwanted from the point of view of the woman as a key indicator of disparities in reproductive justice.

Unwanted Childbearing

The destructive impact of denying women reproductive justice is manifested in the problems experienced by their children, beginning prenatally with higher risk for premature birth, low birth weight, and fetal malformation, among other negative outcomes (Blomberg, 1980; Shah, Balkhair, Ohlsson, Beyene, & Frick, 2011). Being unwanted during pregnancy does not necessarily mean a child will always be unwanted. Nonetheless, if a pregnant woman identifies a pregnancy as unwanted, her subsequent child will be at risk for a wide range of negative outcomes, including deficits in cognitive, emotional, and social processes that may become apparent at different stages over the life cycle and transmitted intergenerationally (Barber, Axinn, & Thornton, 1999; David, 2006, 2011; Forssman & Thuwe, 1988; Hőők, 1963; Joukamma et al., 2003).

The existence of population-wide health registry data in Scandinavian countries makes it possible to conduct large longitudinal studies to investigate uncommon but severe effects (e.g., fetal malformation, schizophrenia) that require a large sample size for sufficient power to detect them. The studies show that effects of being unwanted during pregnancy can begin prenatally, emerge at different stages over the life cycle, and occur even in developed countries where the disadvantages of unwantedness are not compounded by extreme poverty, experiences of war, pervasive violence, famine, and other conditions of severe privation.

For example, research in Sweden based on children born to women who applied for, but were denied, a legal abortion showed them to have a higher incidence of malformation than paired matched controls (2.2% vs. 0.3%). Significant interactions were found between being unwanted, social class, and maternal age: In the unwanted group, malformations were higher in the lower social classes and for older mothers; this pattern was not found for controls (Blomberg, 1980).

Other research in Scandinavia has also shown that being unwanted during pregnancy, *even when abortion is legal and accessible,* can be associated with negative long-term outcomes in adulthood. As adults, individuals who were born to women who had unwanted pregnancies but did not seek abortion have been found to be at higher risk for a variety of mental health problems, some of them severe, including schizophrenia (Myhrman, Rantakallio, Isohanni, Jones, & Partanen, 1996) and alexithymia[3] (Joukamma et al., 2003).

In Finland, risk for schizophrenia was found to be higher for unwanted individuals (1.5% vs. 0.7%, respectively) even when potentially confounding pregnancy, prenatal, and sociodemographic variables were controlled (Myhrman et al., 1996). The proportion of alexithymia was found to be nearly twice as high for unwanted individuals as for others (11.6% vs. 6.9%). Increased risk was associated with larger family sizes as well.

A mother who had more than four children nearly doubled a child's risk of alexithymia over that of a child whose mother had fewer children (10.0% vs. 6.4%) (Joukamma et al., 2003).

The most in-depth longitudinal study of the disadvantages of being born unwanted on developing children comes from the former Czechoslovakia, in which children born to women who applied for and were twice denied abortion were compared to matched controls. As a child, being unwanted was linked to being less likely to have a secure family life, more likely to perform poorly in school, and more likely to be rejected by peers. As an adult, being unwanted meant being more likely to have an unstable marriage, engage in criminal behavior, be on welfare, and receive psychiatric services. In a follow-up study that compared the unwanted group with their wanted siblings, the unwanted group had higher rates of psychiatric problems on nine indicators of poor mental health that ranged from psychiatric inpatient treatment to unsatisfactory sexual relations (David, 2006, 2011).

David's (2006, 2011) research was conducted in a country where the disadvantage of being unwanted was not compounded by social and economic deprivation and lack of access to health care. His findings, particularly when combined with the longitudinal findings from Scandinavia and elsewhere, provide compelling evidence that children born to women denied abortion can experience negative cognitive, emotional, and social outcomes, outcomes that, in turn, can be transmitted to their own children. Further, the finding that unwanted children were underrepresented on every indicator of excellence (e.g., academic achievement, job satisfaction, parenting) underscores the important role that the mother's affirmative desire for a child plays in developing that child's full potential.

In summary, there are a host of adverse outcomes associated with unintended pregnancy and unwanted childbearing, particularly for women who are poor, young, and in violent circumstances, but such circumstances are not necessary for a negative impact of unwantedness. Fortunately, the high rates and adverse consequences associated with unintended pregnancy and unwanted childbearing are largely preventable by the effective use of modern contraception and access to safe abortion.

CONTRACEPTION

Providing sexually active women the means to prevent pregnancy is a critical step in enabling them to achieve their childbearing goals. Further, lack of access to contraception has profound implications for women's health: In 2004, unsafe sex and lack of contraception together were the second leading contributor to the female global burden of disease, accounting for 39,954 and 11,501 disability-adjusted life years (WHO, 2009). Although unsafe sex constitutes the majority of cases for women when both indicators are combined, it seems inappropriate to separate them here, given that access to barrier methods of contraception is critical in efforts to prevent the spread of HIV/AIDS and other sexually transmitted infections.

As the desire for smaller family sizes has spread around the world, contraceptive use has risen. The global decline in unintended pregnancy rates witnessed over the last decade is clearly associated with the increased use of contraceptives (Singh, Darroch, et al., 2009). In the developing world, approximately two-thirds of unintended pregnancies occur among women who do not use contraceptives; an additional 16 percent occur among women who use traditional methods (e.g., periodic abstinence, withdrawal), and 17 percent among women who do not use modern contraceptive methods consistently or correctly (Singh, Darroch, et al., 2009).

Readers should consider that the situation will change as new reproductive technologies are developed, disseminated, and made more accessible via the Internet (e.g., women aged 17 and over can purchase the emergency contraception Plan B online without a prescription at http://www.drugstore.com, among other places). Research is needed on the impact of new contraceptive methods and modes of distribution, but the situation is changing rapidly and thus is difficult to assess cross-nationally. Contraceptive developments provide opportunities to decrease disparities in reproductive justice, but have the potential to increase disparities as well (e.g., by privileging women with access to the Internet and overnight delivery). For now, however, it is important to keep in mind that the findings are based on the technologies that existed at the time that the research was conducted. Fortunately, WHO, which is responsible for providing evidence-based family planning guidance around the world, has established a partnership with others to ensure that newly published studies are systematically identified and reviewed. The system that has been established ensures that WHO guidelines are regularly updated with the best available evidence (Mohllajee et al., 2005).

Rates of Contraception

Approximately 63 percent of married women of reproductive age use some form of family planning, although a higher percentage do in more developed than in less developed countries (72% vs. 61%); when China is excluded, the figure for less developed countries is 53 percent. The percent of women who use any form of contraception ranges from a high of 88 percent in Norway to a low of 3 percent in Chad. In the United States, the figure is 78 percent (Singh, Wulf, et al., 2009).

Type of contraceptive used also differs between more developed and less developed countries. Married women in developed countries are more likely to use modern methods of contraception (61.3%); the highest proportion use oral contraceptives (18.4%), followed by male condoms (17.8%), IUDs (9.2%), and female sterilization (8.2%).[4] In less developed countries, 55.2 percent use modern methods of contraception, but methods that are less likely to require ongoing negotiation with a partner have higher usage: Female sterilization (20.6%) has the highest usage, followed by IUDs (15.1%), oral contraceptives (7.3%), male condoms (5.9%), and injectable contraception (4.0%; UN, 2011c). See Hatcher, Trussell, and Nelson (2008) for more information on methods of contraception.

When subregions are taken into account, the highest rates for using any contraception/using modern contraception are found in eastern Asia (83/81), led by China (84/84) and South Korea (80/70), and in northern Europe (80/77). The lowest rates are found in Africa, where the overall percentages are 29/22 for using any/using modern contraception, respectively; percentages are lowest for western Africa (14/9). In four countries (i.e., China, Norway, Portugal, and the United Kingdom), 80 percent or more married women are using a modern method of contraception (UN, 2011c).

Even within richer countries, economic resources play a critical role in enabling women to control their childbearing (which, in turn, allows them to enhance their socioeconomic status by enabling pursuit of education and employment opportunities). Around the world, women who are poor are less likely than other women to use modern means of contraception (Population Reference Bureau, 2008). Among low-and middle-income countries, the wealthiest individuals (top 20%) are nearly twice as likely as the poorest individuals (bottom 20%) to use contraceptives (Gwatkin et al., 2007). Strong efforts to ensure universal accessibility of family planning in all communities, including poor or rural areas, can overcome the income disparity in contraceptive use (Population Reference Bureau, 2008).

The Unmet Need for Contraception

Women with a low rate of contraceptive use may want to have a child, so they would not have an unmet need for contraception. However, the persistence of high unintended-pregnancy rates, particularly in developing countries, suggests a persistent and substantial unmet need for contraception. Women are considered to have an unmet need when they are married/in a union or sexually active, able to conceive a pregnancy, do not want to have a child (or another child) in the next two years or at all, and are not using a method of contraception (modern or traditional). The concept of unmet need was an important development, as it has been a bridge between the interests of those who focus on population growth and those who focus on women's health and rights (Sinding, Ross, & Rosenfield, 1994).

The high rates of unmet need for contraception, particularly in developing countries, where resources are lacking and a large proportion of the population is poor, are disturbing. According to the UN (2011c), in 2009 an estimated 11 percent of women had an unmet need for family planning. Need varied within and across regions, and was highest in sub-Saharan Africa and Sudan, where, despite larger desired family sizes, 25 percent of married women had unmet need. This figure was substantially higher than the rates of unmet need found for each of the regions of Asia, which ranged from 2 percent to 15 percent. Fourteen of the 36 countries in Europe were identified as having unmet need; percentages ranged from 2 percent in France to 30 percent in Bulgaria. In Latin America and the Caribbean region (overall rate 10%), percentages ranged from 8 percent in South America to 20 percent in the Caribbean. The Caribbean had the widest range in the region, from a low of 4 percent in Puerto Rico to a high of 38 percent in Haiti.

Within countries, the poorest women (bottom 20% in income) are at higher risk for unmet need than are the wealthiest women (top 20%). For example, in a study of 53 developing countries, in 43 of them married women who were poor had a greater unmet need for contraception than other women did (Sedgh, Hussein, Bankole, & Singh, 2007). The reverse pattern was only found in eight sub-Saharan African countries,[5] where the percentages of women with unmet need were higher among nonpoor women, possibly because higher income women desired a smaller family size than lower-income women did. In two countries the level of unmet need did not vary by wealth category.

In summary, there is a large variation in contraceptive prevalence, but in general, it is higher in the more developed regions of the world, and, within countries, poor women have a greater unmet need for contraception. In many countries there are substantial numbers of women who use contraception but rely on traditional (less effective) methods. The demand for contraceptives is expected to continue to grow as the desire for smaller families increases and as the larger cohorts of young people enter their reproductive years (ages 15–49). Unless access to modern methods of effective contraception keeps pace with the increased demand that is concomitant with decreases in desired family size, reproductive justice, particularly for poor women, will be increasingly difficult to achieve.

ABORTION

Women's reasons for terminating unwanted pregnancies reflect the economic, social, and cultural forces that shape their lives. A woman may be in adolescence, unmarried, divorced, widowed, or at the end of her reproductive years. She may already have one or more young children. A pregnancy may threaten a women's life or health, involve fetal impairment, or result from rape or incest. She may have HIV/AIDS, malaria, cancer, cardiovascular disease, or some other condition worsened by pregnancy. Her living conditions may involve famine, armed conflict, or natural disaster. She may live in poverty, with an abusive or violent partner, or in a refugee/displaced persons' camp. She may have relationship problems or be unable to meet responsibilities to existing children or other family members. She may be the sole support of the family and fear that having a baby would compromise her educational goals or ability to work to earn the income needed for family survival (Broen, 2005; Finer, Frohwirth, Dauphinee, Singh, & Moore, 2005).

In patriarchal societies, a married woman may not be allowed to refuse sex or to use contraception, and she may not have control over an abortion decision. For example in Tamil Nadu, India, nearly 1 of 10 women who had an abortion reported having been compelled to do so by her husband or in-laws (Ravindran & Balasubramanian, 2004). Even in highly developed countries, however, such as Australia, Norway, and Sweden, some women identify their partner's wishes as the most important reason for seeking an abortion (Broen, 2005). The mix of reasons for abortion varies across countries and cultures and reflects women's age, health, marital and socioeconomic status, and existing number of children, among other factors.

Readers should keep in mind that new reproductive technologies are influencing access to and outcomes of abortion and that research findings reflect the technologies in existence at the time the research was conducted. For example, misoprostol requires less medical training than other techniques to administer, has a home self-administration option, and can be safely used in low-resource settings (Harper, Blanchard, Grossman, Henderson, & Darney, 2007). It also has a lower risk of complications than many traditional methods of unsafe abortion and is considered to have contributed to a reduction in rates of harmful outcomes associated with unsafe abortion in countries that have restrictive abortion laws (Singh, Wulf, et al., 2009). For example, in Uruguay, where abortion is illegal but misoprostol is available for treating peptic ulcer, a risk-reduction strategy of inviting women who want an abortion to take advantage of before and after counseling sessions was found to reduce abortion complications to a minimal level (Briozzo et al., 2006).

Legalization

Reproductive justice requires abortion to be safe and accessible. When abortion is legally performed by a competent provider and meets medical standards, the death ratio is less than 1 in 100,000 abortions (Pazol et al., 2007). In comparison, the maternal mortality ratio is 17 per 100,000 live births for developed countries, 290 for developing countries, and 590 in the least developed countries. In the four countries with the highest maternal mortality ratio (i.e., Afghanistan, Chad, Guinea-Bissau, Somalia), the rates range from 1,000 to 1,400 per 100,000 births (UN, 2011b).

Although legal status is a major factor in accessibility to abortion and often reflects the cultural attitude toward abortion, it does not fully account for the wide variation in abortion rates across countries. For example, abortion is generally legal across Europe, but European abortion rates vary widely, from a high of 44 per 1,000 women in eastern Europe to a low of 12 per 1,000 women in western Europe. Despite severe restrictions on access to abortion, Latin America/Caribbean countries have substantially higher rates of abortion than western European countries do, at 31 vs. 12, respectively (Singh, Wulf, et al., 2009). In Chile, one of the few countries that prohibits abortion in all circumstances, an estimated 20–40 percent of pregnancies are terminated by clandestine abortions (Human Rights Watch, 2011). This variation underscores the determination of women to avoid having unwanted children despite substantial legal and social sanctions. As long as nothing is done to reduce the reasons why women have abortions, restrictions on abortion will fail to deter women from seeking them.

The legal status and grounds for permitting abortion have varied across and within countries and over time. In general, the trend over the past two decades has been toward liberalization, but progress is slow and uneven. Of the 22 countries or areas within countries that changed their abortion laws between 1996 and 2009, 19 were changed in a more liberal direction, and 12 became more restrictive (Singh, Wulf, et al., 2009).

In 2009, 29 percent of countries permitted abortion on request (although there were often regulations with regard to gestational and other limits); 97 percent of countries permitted abortion to save a woman's life, 67 percent to preserve physical health, and 63 percent to preserve mental health. Rape or incest and fetal impairment were slightly less common at 49 percent and 47 percent, respectively. Thirty-four percent permitted abortion for economic or social reasons (UN, 2011b). The majority of countries with highly restrictive laws were in the developing world, particularly in Africa and Latin America, where 92–97 percent of women live under restrictive abortion laws (Singh, Wulf, et al., 2009). Country-specific information can be found in the UN *World Abortion Policies* wall chart (UN, 2011b).

Legalization plays an important role in increasing the safety and accessibility of abortion. Nonetheless, in many places abortion may be legal but rarely practiced because there are no government-assisted services that allow eligible women to obtain safe abortions (Singh, Wulf, et al., 2009). Procedural requirements take time and may undermine abortion safety by increasing the gestational age of the fetus including mandatory waiting periods, parental or spousal consent, and type of health provider permitted to perform an abortion. In some places a judge must approve a legal abortion. In addition to the difficulties in negotiating bureaucracy, women may want to avoid engaging with judicial systems that they viewed as corrupt or frightening. Consequently, many women may seek abortion from unauthorized providers or attempt to induce abortion on their own. In any case, poor women may be more likely to attempt self-abortion or seek abortion from someone not medically trained (Grossman et al., 2010). Even when abortion is illegal, affluent women may be able to afford services from qualified physicians who perform safe illegal abortions.

Unsafe Abortion

The safety of abortion is a major public health concern in many countries (Faúndes, 2010; WHO, 2011a, 2011b). As defined by WHO (2011a, p. 2), *unsafe abortion* is a "procedure for terminating an unwanted pregnancy carried out either by persons lacking the necessary skills or in an environment lacking the minimal medical standards or both." Note that this definition encompasses circumstances that occur before, during, and after an abortion, and require more than simple access to an abortion procedure.

Rates of Unsafe Abortion

According to WHO (2011b), an estimated 21.6 million unsafe abortions took place in 2008, accounting for approximately 13 percent of maternal deaths. Although rates of safe abortion were higher in more (24 per 1,000 women) than in less (13) developed countries, the reverse pattern was found for unsafe abortion (2 vs. 16, respectively). Rates of unsafe abortion are highest in the African and Latin American/Caribbean regions (29), followed by Asia (11), and Europe and Oceania (3). Rates in North America are negligible (below 0.5).

Although there is variation across countries, a larger proportion of abortions are unsafe in countries with restrictive laws: More than 95 percent of abortions in Africa and Latin America are unsafe, and, when east Asia is excluded, 55 percent of abortions in Asia are unsafe. In countries with less-restrictive laws (e.g., countries in North America, Australia/New Zealand, eastern Asia, northern and western Europe), only a tiny proportion of abortions are unsafe (Singh, Wulf, et al., 2009; WHO, 2011b).

Outcomes of Unsafe Abortion

As Hessini (2005, p. 89) observed, differentials in deaths and injuries from unsafe abortion "constitute one of the greatest disparities in reproductive health between the developed and developing worlds." Unsafe abortion results in a wide variety of adverse outcomes. Direct outcomes include heightened risk for illness, disability, death, and lost years of productivity. Women who survive unsafe abortion may suffer serious complications, including anemia, weakness, chronic pain, pelvic inflammatory disease, inflammation of the reproductive tract, and other conditions that compromise their health. Other costs include what can be a substantial financial expense for treatment of health complications. In developing countries, where nearly all unsafe abortion takes place, maternal mortality and morbidity place a substantial burden on already inadequate health and social service systems (Singh, Wulf, et al., 2009).Whatever the context, how abortion is practiced has profound health, social, and economic implications for women, their families, and society.

Natural experiments that occur when the legality of, and access to, abortion changes illustrate what happens when abortion is restricted and becomes unsafe. A stark example of the effects of restriction and liberalization is found in Romania. After a decade of living under the most liberal abortion law in Europe, in 1966 the repressive pronatalist regime of Nicolae Ceausescu abruptly reversed the law without warning. Legal and political machinery were put in place to ensure that the repressive policies were enforced, including mandatory reproductive health examinations for women workers by factory physicians who monitored women's pregnancies[6] for the state (the physicians received full salary only if plant workers met their birth quota).

Consequences for Romanian women's health were severe: To put it most simply, when abortion is restricted, women die. In 1 year, maternal mortality went from 85.9 in 1966 to 96.8 in 1967 and continued upward as the pronatalist policies were ever more stringently enforced until it reached a high of 169.6 in 1989. This reflects changes in maternal deaths due to abortion that more than doubled the first year (from 64 in 1966 to 173 in 1967) and reached a high of 545 in 1989 (Baban, 1999).

When Ceausescu was overthrown in December of 1989, the new government immediately reversed the restrictive legislation. In 1 year, maternal mortality dropped from 169.6 in 1989 to 83.6 in 1990 and continued to decline until it reached 41.4 in 1997. Maternal deaths directly related to abortion dropped from 545 in 1989 to 181 in 1990 and declined to 50 in 1997 (see Baban, 1999, for a more in-depth discussion of these events).

In the case of Romania, the legal restriction was immediate and without warning, and the government went to extreme and punitive lengths to enforce its pronatalist policies. But the case is not unique in demonstrating that maternal mortality rates are linked to women's ability to avoid unwanted births. A recent example is Nicaragua, where maternal deaths were witnessed after abortion was criminalized (Arie, 2006). The law imposed prison terms on health professionals who caused harm to a fetus, regardless of intent, which further compounded women's health risks insofar as medical interventions (e.g., certain medications, cancer treatments) were delayed or avoided because of possible risk to the fetus (Amnesty International, 2011).

When abortion laws are liberalized, maternal death rates go down. For example, after abortion was legalized in South Africa in 1996, deaths from unsafe abortion declined by 91 percent between 1994 and 1998–2001 (Jewkes & Rees, 2005). In 1970, after legalization in New York State, there was nearly a 50 percent reduction in abortion deaths in New York City (Tietze, Pakter, & Berger, 1973). Similarly, in 1967, illegal abortion was the leading cause of maternal death in the United Kingdom; 15 years later, after the law was liberalized, death from illegal abortion was nil (Drife, 2010).

These cases provide real life demonstrations of the impact of abortion policies on women's health and show why reproductive justice is a necessary condition for the human right to health. Although abortion debates are multidimensional and involve feminist, social, political, economic, and religious stakeholders (among others), the unequal impact of unsafe abortion on poor women around the globe should not be forgotten. Recent events in the United States in which conservative members of Congress attempted to hold the federal budget as hostage unless all funding to Planned Parenthood was prohibited, even though those funds were not used for abortions, remind us all that access to affordable reproductive health care of any form should not be taken for granted, even in the developed world.

Although concerns for women's physical safety are the primary focus of health agendas in countries where abortion remains illegal and thus unsafe, arguments against abortion on grounds of physical health have become less relevant in developed countries where abortion is legal and safe and the effects of unsafe abortion are all too often forgotten. In the United States, a new tactic has emerged: Opponents utilize women-protective arguments and express concern about the effects of abortion on mental health. The focus on mental health initially reflected a strategy to overturn *Roe v. Wade,* the Supreme Court decision that legalized abortion, by arguing that the Court failed to balance its concern for the negative effects of unwanted pregnancy and childbearing with the harm that abortion does to women's mental health. That claim, which is based on anecdotal reports and deeply flawed studies (for critical reviews, see Charles, Polis, Sridhara, & Blum, 2008; Major et al., 2009; Robinson, Stotland, Russo, Lang, & Occhiogrosso, 2009). The argument is increasingly raised in other areas of the world as well, and has been found in areas as diverse as New Zealand and central and eastern Europe (David, 1999).

In summary, abortion laws have been liberalized in numerous countries, contraceptive use has increased, and new and safer technologies of contraception and abortion are becoming more widely available. Nonetheless, the need for access to safe abortion persists. In addition to the fact that all contraceptives have some probability of failure, not all women have equal access to effective methods, let alone the information or support they need to use those methods effectively. Further, even if a pregnancy is planned, circumstances can change: A woman may discover she has cancer, or she may contract malaria, lose her husband through death or divorce, lose her home through war or natural disaster, or experience some other personal crisis. There is also sexual violence and coercion, by partners but also in wartime, that can result in unwanted pregnancies and births, which in turn have a host of negative outcomes for women, children, and society. Thus, even if effective modern contraceptive methods were available and widely used around the world, abortion would continue to serve as an essential tool for women to exercise their reproductive rights.

CONCLUSION

In the final analysis, reproductive rights are inextricably and synergistically linked to women's rights of equality and empowerment. As social conservatives and religious fundamentalists become increasingly aggressive in their opposition to reproductive rights and to safe abortion and full access to family planning, reproductive justice can be expected to erode; in turn, disparities will widen, adverse consequences will increase, and the status of women around the world will decline. Unintended pregnancies, unwanted births, and unsafe abortions will increase and reproductive justice will be further denied, particularly for women who are poor or young, unless a woman's right to decide whether and when to have a child is valued and respected and her decision making is free of violence and coercion. Meanwhile, access to effective contraception and safe abortion remain necessary, but underused, tools for exercising reproductive rights and achieving reproductive justice around the world.

NOTES

1. All rates reported in this chapter are based on the rate per 1,000 women aged 15–44 unless otherwise specified.

2. Cambodia, Colombia, Dominican Republic, Egypt, Haiti, India, Nicaragua, Peru, and Zambia.

3. Alexithymia is a personality construct with features that reflect deficits in cognitive processing and regulation of emotions (Bagby & Taylor, 1997).

4. Modern methods encompass hormonal methods (including the pill, injectable, and patch), the IUD (including those that release hormones), male and female sterilization, and the condom.

5. Benin, Central African Republic, Chad, Guinea, Mali, Mozambique, Niger, and Nigeria.

6. Space precludes a full discussion of coercive pronatalist policies such as mandatory pregnancy testing around the world, but it is notable that General Motors did not end the practice of mandatory testing in its Mexican factories until 1997 (Human Rights Watch, 1998).

REFERENCES

Amnesty International. (2004). *Lives blown apart: Crimes against women in times of conflict.* London: Author.

Amnesty International. (2011). *The gender trap: Women, violence and poverty.* London: Author.

Arie, S. (2006). Woman dies after doctors fail to intervene because of new abortion law in Nicaragua. *British Medical Journal, 333,* 1037.

Baban, A. (1999). Romania. In H. P. David (Ed.), *From abortion to contraception: A resource to public policies and reproductive behavior in central and eastern Europe from 1917 to the present* (pp. 191–221). Westport, CT: Greenwood Press.

Bagby, R. M., & Taylor, G. J. (1997). Affect dysregulation and alexithymia. In G. J. Taylor, R. M. Bagby, & J.D.A. Parker (Eds.), *Disorders of affect regulation: Alexithymia in medical and psychiatric illness* (pp. 26–45). Cambridge: Cambridge University Press.

Bankole, A., & Westoff, C. (1998). The consistency and validity of reproductive attitudes: Evidence from Morocco. *Journal of Biosocial Sciences, 30,* 439–455.

Barber, J. S., Axinn, W. G., & Thornton, A. (1999). Unwanted childbearing, health, and mother-child relationships. *Journal of Health and Social Behavior, 40,* 231–257.

Blomberg, S. (1980). Influence of maternal distress during pregnancy and fetal malformations. *Acta Psychiatrica Scandinavica, 62,* 315–330.

Briozzo, L., Vidiella, G., Rodriquez, F., Gorgoroso, M., Faúndes, A., & Pons, J. E. (2006). A risk reduction strategy to prevent maternal deaths associated with unsafe abortion. *International Journal of Gynecology and Obstetrics, 95,* 221–226.

Broen, A. N. (2005). Reasons for induced abortion and their relation to women's emotional distress: A prospective, two-year follow-up study. *General Hospital Psychiatry, 27,* 36–43.

Bulatao, R. A., & Lee, R. (1983). *Determinants of fertility in developing countries* (Vol. II). New York: Academic Press.

Castaneda, D., & Ulibarri, M. (2010). Women and sexuality: An international perspective. In M. A. Paludi (Ed.), *Feminism and women's rights worldwide* (Vol. 3, pp. 81–100). Santa Barbara, CA: Praeger.

Cates, W., Karim, Q. A., El-Sadr, W., Haffner, D. W., Kalema-Zikusoka, G., Rogo, K., . . . Averill, E.M.D. (2010). Family planning and the millennium development goals. *Science, 329,* 1603.

Charles, V. E., Polis, C. B., Sridhara, S. K., & Blum, R. W. (2008). Abortion and long-term mental health outcomes: a systematic review of the evidence. *Contraception, 78,* 436–50.

Cheslack-Postava, K. (2011). Closely spaced pregnancies are associated with increased odds of autism in California sibling births. *Pediatrics, 127,* 246–253.

Chrisler, J. C., & Garrett, C. (2010). Women's reproductive rights: An international perspective. In M. A. Paludi (Ed.), *Feminism and women's rights worldwide* (Vol. 3, pp. 129–146). Santa Barbara, CA: Praeger.

Cripe, S. M., Sanchez, S. E., Perales, M. T., Lam, N., Garcia, P., & Williams, M. A. (2008). Association of intimate partner physical and sexual violence with unintended pregnancy among pregnant women in Peru. *International Journal of Gynecology and Obstetrics, 100,* 104–108.

D'Angelo, D. V., Gilbert, B. C., Rochat, R. W., Santelli, J. S., & Herold, J. M. (2004). Differences between mistimed and unwanted pregnancies among women who have live births. *Perspectives on Sexual and Reproductive Health, 36*(5), 192–197.

David, H. P. (1999). Overview. In H. P. David (Ed.), *From abortion to contraception: A resource to public policies and reproductive behavior in Central and Eastern Europe from 1917 to the present* (p. 322). Westport, CT: Greenwood Press.

David, H. P. (2006). Born unwanted: 35 years later — The Prague study. *Reproductive Health Matters, 14*(27), 181–190.

David, H. P. (2011). Born unwanted: Mental health costs and consequences. *American Journal of Orthopsychiatry, 81,* 184–192.

Dewey, K. G., & Cohen, R. J. (2007). Does birth spacing affect maternal or child nutritional status? A systematic literature review. *Maternal and Child Nutrition, 3,* 151–173.

Dietz, P., Spitz, A. M., Anda, R. F., Williamson, D. G., McMahon, P. M., Santelli, J. S., & Kendrick, J. S. (2000). Unintended pregnancy among adult women exposed to abuse or household dysfunction during their childhood. *Journal of the American Medical Association, 282,* 1359–1364.

Drife, J. O. (2010). Historical perspective on induced abortion through the ages and its links with maternal mortality. *Best Practices and Research in Clinical Obstetrics and Gynecology, 24,* 431–441.

Erdman, J. A., & Cook, R. J. (2008). Reproductive rights. In H. K. Heggenhougen & S. Quah (Eds.), *International encyclopedia of public health* (pp. 532–538). Amsterdam: Elsevier.

Faúndes, A. (2010). Unsafe abortion — the current global scenario. *Best Practices and Research in Clinical Obstetrics and Gynaecology, 24,* 467–477.

Finer, L. B. (2010). Unintended pregnancy among U.S. adolescents: Accounting for sexual activity. *Journal of Adolescent Health, 47,* 312–314.

Finer, L. B., Frohwirth, L. F., Dauphinee, L. A., Singh, S., & Moore, A. M. (2005). Reasons U.S. women have abortions: Quantitative and qualitative perspectives. *Perspectives on Sexual and Reproductive Health, 37*(3), 110–118.

Finer, L. B., & Henshaw, S. K. (2006). Disparities in rates of unintended pregnancy in the United States, 1994 and 2001. *Perspectives on Sexual and Reproductive Health, 38*(2), 90–96.

Forssman, H., & Thuwe, I. (1988). The Göteberg cohort, 1939–1977. In H. P. David, Z. Dytrych, Z. Matejcek, & V. Schüller (Eds.), *Born unwanted: Developmental effects of denied abortion* (pp. 37–45). New York: Springer.

Gilbert, B.J.C., Johnson, C. H., Morrow, B., Gaffield, M. E., & Ahluwalia, I. (1999). Prevalence of selected maternal and infant characteristics, Pregnancy Risk Assessment Monitoring System (PRAMS), 1997. *MMWR CDC Surveillance Summaries 48*(5), 1–37.

Gipson, J. D., Koenig, M. A., & Hindin, M. J. (2008). The effects of unintended pregnancy on infant, child, and parental health: A review of the literature. *Studies in Family Planning, 39*(1), 18–38.

Greene, M. E., & Merrick, T. (2005). *Poverty reduction: Does reproductive health matter?* Washington, DC: World Bank.

Grossman, D., Holt, K., Peña, M., Lara, D., Veatch, M., Córdova, D., . . . Blanchard K. (2010). Self-induction of abortion among women in the United States. *Reproductive Health Matters, 18,* 136–146.

Gwatkin, D. R., Rutstein, S., Johnson, K., Suliman, E., Wagstaff, A., & Amouzou, A. (2007). *Socio-economic differences in health, nutrition, and population within developing countries: An overview.* Washington, DC: World Bank.

Hardee, K., Eggleston, E., Wong, E. L., Irwanto, & Hull, T. H. (2004). Unintended pregnancy and women's psychological well-being in Indonesia. *Journal of Biosocial Science, 26,* 617–626.

Harper, C. C., Blanchard, K., Grossman, D., Henderson, J. T., & Darney, P. D. (2007). Reducing maternal mortality due to elective abortion: Potential impact of misoprostol in low-resource settings. *International Journal of Gynecology and Obstetrics, 98,* 66–69.

Hessini, L. (2005). Global progress in abortion advocacy and policy: An assessment of the decade since ICPD. *Reproductive Health Matters, 13*(25), 88–100.

Höök, K. (1963). Refused abortion: A follow-up study of 249 women whose applications were refused by the National Board of Health in Sweden. *Acta Psychiatrica Scandinavica, 39*(Suppl. 168), 1–156.

Human Rights Watch. (1997). *No guarantees: Sex discrimination in Mexico's maquiladora sector.* New York: Author.

Human Rights Watch. (1998). Mexico: A job or your rights—Continued sex discrimination in Mexico's macquiladora sector. Retrieved from http://www. bhrd.org/pdfs/164_Ajob%20or%20yourRights.pdf.

Human Rights Watch. (2010). *Unaccountable: Addressing reproductive health care gaps.* New York: Author.

Human Rights Watch. (2011). *World report, 2011: Events of 2010.* New York: Author.

Ismayilova, L. (2010). *Intimate partner violence and unintended pregnancy in Azerbaijan, Moldova, and Ukraine* [DHS Working Papers No. 79]. Calverton, MD: ICF Macro.

Jewkes, R., & Rees, H. (2005). Dramatic decline in abortion mortality due to the Choice on Termination of Pregnancy Act. *South African Medical Journal, 95*(4), 250.

Joukamaa, M., Kokkonen, P., Vejola, J., Läksy, K., Karvonen, J. T., Jokelainen, J., & Järvelin, M. (2003). Social situation of expectant mothers and alexithymia 31 years later in their offspring: A prospective study. *Psychosomatic Medicine, 65,* 307–312.

Kishor, S., & Johnson, K. (2004). *Profiling domestic violence: A multi–country study.* Calverton, MD: ORC Macro.

Koenig, M. A., Acharya, R., Singh, S., & Tarun, K. R. (2006). Do current measurement approaches underestimate levels of unwanted childbearing? Evidence from rural India. *Population Studies, 60,* 243–256.

Lakha, F., & Glasier, A. (2006). Unintended pregnancy and use of emergency contraception among a large cohort of women attending for antenatal care or abortion in Scotland. *Lancet, 368,* 1782–1787.

Major, B., Applebaum, M., Beckman, L., Dutton, M. A., Russo, N. F., & West, C. (2009). Abortion and mental health: Evaluating the evidence. *American Psychologist, 64,* 863–890.

Martin, S. I., Kilgallen, B., Tsui, A. O., Maitra, K., Singh, K. K., & Kupper, L. L. (1999). Sexual behaviors and reproductive health outcomes: Associations with wife abuse in India. *Journal of the American Medical Association, 282,* 1967–1972.

Miller, E., Decker, M. R., McCauley, H. L., Tancredi, D. J., Levenson, R. R., Waldman, J., & Silverman, J. G. (2010). Pregnancy coercion, intimate partner violence, and unintended pregnancy. *Contraception, 81,* 316–322.

Miller, E., Decker, M. R., Reed, E., Raj, A., Hathaway, J. E., & Silverman, J. G. (2007). Male pregnancy promoting behaviors and adolescent partner violence: Findings from a qualitative study with adolescent females. *Ambulatory Pediatrics, 7,* 360–366.

Miller, J. E. (1991). Birth intervals and perinatal health: An investigation of three hypotheses. *Family Planning Perspectives, 23*(2), 62–70.

Mohllajee, A. P., Curtis, K. M., Flanagan, R. G., Rinehart, W., Gaffield, M. L., & Peterson, H. B. (2005). Keeping up with evidence: A new system for WHO's evidence-based family planning guidance. *American Journal of Preventive Medicine, 28,* 483–90.

Moore, A. M., Frohwirth, L., & Miller, E. (2010). Male reproductive control of women who have experienced intimate partner violence in the United States. *Social Science & Medicine, 70,* 1737–1744.

Myhrman, A., Rantakallio, P., Isohanni, M., Jones, P., & Partanen, U. (1996). Unwantedness of a pregnancy and schizophrenia in the child. *British Journal of Psychiatry, 169,* 637–640.

Orberta, A. C. (2005). *Poverty, vulnerability, and family size: Evidence from the Philippines* [ADB Institute Discussion Paper No. 29]. Retrieved from http://www.adbi.org/discussion-paper/2005/07/27/1289.poverty.vulnerability.family/.

Padilla, M. B., Pingel, E., Reyes, A. M., & Fiereck, K. (2010). Gender, sexuality, health and human rights in Latin America and the Caribbean. *Global Public Health, 5,* 213–220.

Pallitto, C. C., Campbell, J. C., & O'Campo, P. (2005). Is intimate partner violence associated with unintended pregnancy? A review of the literature. *Trauma, Violence, & Abuse, 6,* 217–235.

Pallitto, C. C., & O'Campo, P. (2004). The relationship between intimate partner violence and unintended pregnancy: Analysis of a national sample from Colombia. *International Family Planning Perspectives, 30*(4), 165–173.

Pazol, K., Zane, S. B., Hall, L. R., Gamble, S. B., Berg, C., & Cook, D. A. (2011, February 25). Abortion surveillance 3—United States, 2007. *MMWR Surveillance Summaries, 60*(1), 1–40.

Population Reference Bureau. (2008). *Family planning worldwide: 2008 datasheet.* Washington, DC: Author.

Potts, M. & Thapa, S. (1991). *Child survival: The role of family planning.* Research Triangle Park, NC: Family Health International.

Ravindran, T.K.S. & Balasubramanian, P. (2004). "Yes" to abortion but "no" to sexual rights: The paradoxical reality of married women in rural Tamil Nadu, India. *Reproductive Health Matters, 12*(23), 88–99.

Robinson, G. E., Stotland, N. S., Russo, N. F., Lang, J. A., & Occhiogrosso, M. (2009). Is there an "Abortion Trauma Syndrome"? A critical review. *Harvard Review of Psychiatry, 17,* 268–290.

Rowbottom, S. (2007). *Giving girls today and tomorrow: Breaking the cycle of adolescent pregnancy.* New York: United Nations Population Fund.

Russo, N. F. (1976). The motherhood mandate. *Journal of Social Issues, 32,* 143–154.

Russo, N. F. (2006). Violence against women: A global health issue. In Q. Jing, M. R. Rosenzweig, G. d'Ydewalle, H. Zhang, H. Chen, & K. Zhang (Eds.), *Progress in Psychological Science Around the World* (Vol. 2, pp. 181–198). New York: Psychology Press.

Russo, N. F., & Denious, J. (2005). Controlling birth: Science, politics, and public policy. *Journal of Social Issues, 61,* 181–191.

Rutstein, S. O. (2005). Effects of preceding birth intervals on neonatal, infant, and under-5 years mortality and nutritional status in developing countries: Evidence from the demographic and health surveys. *International Journal of Gynecology and Obstetrics, 89,* S7–S24.

Rutstein, S. O. (2008). *Further evidence of the effects of preceding birth intervals on neonatal, infant, and under-five-years mortality and nutritional status in developing countries: Evidence from the demographic and health surveys* [DHS Working Paper Series]. Calverton, MD: United States Agency for International Development.

Santelli, J., Rochat, R., Hatfield-Timajchy, K., Gilbert, B. C., Curtis, K., Cabral, R., & Schieve, L. (2003). The measurement and meaning of unintended pregnancy. *Perspectives on Sexual and Reproductive Health, 35*(2), 94–101.

Sarkar, N. N. (2008). The impact of intimate partner violence on women's reproductive health and pregnancy outcomes. *Journal of Obstetrics and Gynaecology, 28,* 266–271.

Sedgh, G., Hussein, R., Bankole, A., & Singh, S. (2007). *Women with an unmet need for contraception in developing countries and their reasons for not using a method.* New York: Guttmacher Institute.

Shah, P. S., Balkhair, T., Ohlsson, A., Beyene, J., & Frick, C. (2011). Intention to become pregnant and low birth weight and preterm birth: A systematic review. *Maternal and Child Health Journal, 15,* 205–216.

Shapiro-Mendoza, C. Selwyn, B. J., Smith, D. P., & Sanderson, M. (2005). Parental pregnancy intention and early childhood stunting: Findings from Bolivia. *International Journal of Epidemiology, 34,* 387–396.

Silverman, J. G., Gupta, J., Decker, M. R., Kapur, N., & Raj, A. (2007). Intimate partner violence and unwanted pregnancy, miscarriage, induced abortion, and stillbirth among a national sample of Bangladeshi women. *British Journal of Obstetrics and Gynecology, 114,* 1246–1252.

Sinding, S. W., Ross, J. A., & Rosenfield, A. G. (1994). Seeking common ground: Unmet need and demographic goals. *International Family Planning Perspectives, 20*(1), 23–27, 32.

Singh, S., Darroch, J., Ashford, L. S., & Vlassoff, M. (2009). *Adding it up: The costs and benefits of investing in family planning and maternal and newborn health.* New York: Guttmacher Institute.

Singh, S., Wulf, D., Hussein, R., Bankole, A., & Sedgh, G. (2009). *Abortion worldwide: A decade of uneven progress.* New York: Guttmacher Institute.

Tietze, C., Pakter, J., & Berger, G. S. (1973). Mortality with legal abortion in New York City, 1970–1972. *Journal of the American Medical Association, 225,* 507–509.

UNICEF. (2011). *The state of the world's children, 2011.* New York: Author.

United Nations. (2008). *UN Security Council resolution 1820 on women and peace and security.* Retrieved from http://www.ohchr.org/en/newsevents/pages/rapeweaponwar.aspx.

United Nations. (2010). *The real wealth of nations: Pathways to human development.* New York: United Nations Development Programme. Retrieved from http://hdr.undp.org/en/reports/ebooks/.

United Nations. (2011a). Millennium development goals. Retrieved from http://www.un.org/millenniumgoals.

United Nations. (2011b). *World abortion policies: 2011* (Wall chart). New York: Author. Retrieved from http://www.un.org/esa/population/publications/2011abortion/2011wallchart.pdf.

United Nations. (2011c). *World contraceptive use: 2011* (Wall chart). New York: Author. Retrieved from http://www.un.org/esa/population/publications/contraceptive2011/wallchart_front.pdf.

Wall, L. L. (1998). Dead mothers and injured wives: The social context of maternal morbidity and mortality among the Hausa of northern Nigeria. *Studies in Family Planning, 29*(4), 341–359.

World Health Organization. (2005). *Trends in maternal mortality: 1990–2008.* Geneva: Author.

World Health Organization. (2009). *Global health risks: Mortality and burden of disease attributable to selected major risks.* Geneva: Author.

World Health Organization. (2010). *Trends in maternal mortality: 1990 to 2008.* Geneva: Author.

World Health Organization. (2011a). *Preventing unsafe abortion.* Retrieved from http://www.who.int/reproductivehealth/topics/unsafe_abortion/en/index.html.

World Health Organization. (2011b). *Unsafe abortion: global and regional estimates of incidence of unsafe abortion and associated mortality in 2008* (6th ed.). Geneva: Author.

Zangeneh, M. (2010). Maternal health, social conservatism, and hypocrisy: Canadian edition. *International Journal of Mental Health Addiction, 8,* 421–422.

Chapter 8

Infertility and Assisted Reproductive Technologies: Matters of Reproductive Justice

Lisa R. Rubin and Aliza Phillips

Infertility is estimated to affect 80 million people worldwide (Vayena, Rowe, & Griffin, 2002). Approximately 1 in 10 couples experience infertility, but rates vary across countries, from less than 5 percent to more than 30 percent. Most of the those who experience infertility live in the developing world, and they face infertility as a result of, for example, untreated sexually transmitted infections (STIs) or illegal (and, therefore, often unsafe) abortions. Although the global burden of infertility may not be considered a public health priority and generally receives considerably less attention as a component of family planning, it is a central concern in the lives of those who experience it, and it can lead to social and psychological suffering for both women and men.

The past 30 years—since the birth in England in 1978 of Louise Brown, the first baby born via in vitro fertilization (IVF)[1]—have been marked by significant advances in the development of assisted reproductive technologies (ARTs) to treat individuals and couples with infertility. Much of the recent attention devoted to infertility in Western and developed nations has been focused on these technologies and their tendency to press the limits of nature and transform definitions of family. ARTs have enabled countless individuals and couples—including infertile heterosexual couples, single women and men, and LGBT couples—to have biologically related children. However, although ARTs represent promising technologies, they also raise a host of new challenges and important social, psychological, legal, and ethical considerations. These concerns include (but are not limited to): differential access to ARTs and related technologies, the impact of ARTs and repro-genetic technologies on the lives of people with disabilities, health risks to women and children, and potential commercialization and commodification associated with their use (Darnovsky, 2009; van Balen & Inhorn, 2002). In this chapter, we provide an overview of the global burden of infertility and its social and psychological consequences, followed by consideration of the reproductive justice concerns that are raised, or exacerbated, by ARTs.

REPRESENTATIONS AND REALITIES
OF INFERTILITY AND ARTS

In the West, stereotypical representations of infertility are usually of middle-or upper-class couples or single women who have put their careers ahead of childbearing, and are now willing and able to spare any expense to have a genetically related child. A caricature on all accounts, at best these images represent those who most have *access* to infertility treatments, rather than those most likely to be affected by infertility. In fact, the casting of involuntary childlessness (a dilemma that cross cuts history and societies) as *infertility*[2] (a medical condition) is relatively recent and connected to the development of new technologies to assist reproduction, such as IVF (Sandelowski & de Lacey, 2002; van Balen & Inhorn, 2002). The implicit pairing of infertility with reproductive technologies, particularly in the West, may conceal the ways in which involuntary childlessness is experienced, and managed, throughout the world. Some practitioners argue that viewing infertility as a medical condition rather than a socially constructed need is important for insurance coverage for infertility treatments (e.g., Katz, Nachtigall, & Showstack, 2002); however, we contend that this either/or framing constructs a false dichotomy. In contrast, Rothman (2000) suggested that we think about infertility as disability, as such a framing opens both medical and social solutions, ideally without privileging one over another. This is a particularly important point, given that approximately 50 percent of those who initiate IVF will not conceive (Stolwijk, Wetzels, & Braat, 2000).

Feminism and New Reproductive Technologies

Reproductive technologies are embedded in, and have the potential to reproduce or radically destabilize, extant gender relations and identities. Perhaps for this reason, feminist scholars and activists, as a whole, have been ambivalent about the development and proliferation of new reproductive technologies (NRTs), including prenatal screening and ARTs. Although a comprehensive review of feminist responses to reproductive technologies is beyond the scope of this chapter, a general overview of these feminist tensions is central to an understanding of reproductive justice as it relates to infertility and ARTs. Several years before the birth of the first IVF baby, radical feminist Shulamith Firestone (1970) embraced the possibility of NRTs as a way to overcome gender inequity rooted in biological difference. However, many more feminists were critical of the role of NRTs in the medicalization and pathologization of pregnancy and childbirth and as furthering patriarchal control of women's bodies through medicine (see Thompson, 2002, for a review). Organizations such as the Feminist International Network of Resistance to Reproductive and Genetic Engineering were deeply critical of the relationship between reproductive and genetic engineering and the socioeconomically stratified use of NRTs; they integrated a transnational perspective on these issues (Mahjouri, 2004). Feminist debates have engendered some "strange bedfellows" (Sandelowski & de Lacey, 2002, p. 33) as feminists have found themselves aligned with conservative, and often anti-choice, activists in denouncing ARTs as bad for women and against nature.

ARTs have been viewed as furthering the "motherhood mandate" (Russo, 1976, p. 143), privileging biological aspects of motherhood, and delimiting alternative discourses of parenting. This normalization of biological motherhood, in conjunction with the technological imperative (i.e., the notion that, if something *can* be done, then it *ought* to be done) supports a "never-enough" quality of reproductive interventions (Sandelowski, 1991) that results in subjecting women's bodies, in particular, to intensive medical surveillance, intervention, and risks (e.g., ovarian hyperstimulation), as well as financial consequences, sometimes with limited chances of success. This never-enough quality has particular resonance within the U.S. health care context, which is characterized by its generally for-profit approach to medicine and a neoliberal philosophy that situates patients as enterprising individuals who are responsible for their health outcomes (Novas & Rose, 2000). Indeed, Mamo (2010, p. 173) dubbed the field of reproductive medicine "Fertility, Inc."

A tension within feminist scholarship is the extent to which NRTs increase women's and couples' reproductive choices, options, and autonomy and whether they further attach women to the motherhood role, depoliticize reproduction, and offer specific kinds of (market-oriented) solutions to women's problems, whether as consumers of reproductive medicine or as producers who sell their gametes or "rent" their wombs. More recent feminist scholarship cautions against binary thinking (i.e., the tendency to label NRT as *either* oppressive *or* liberatory); as Sawicki (1991, p. 88) succinctly noted: "although new reproductive technologies certainly threaten to reproduce and enhance existing power relations, they also introduce new possibilities for disruption and resistance." ARTs do not restructure the androcentric workplace to match women's reproductive realities, but, for individual women or couples who have delayed childbearing for whatever reason(s), ARTs do create more possible paths to parenthood when that is a desired option. ARTs do not eliminate homophobia or discrimination against single mothers, but they do have the potential to destabilize the hegemony of the nuclear family form. We follow Inhorn and Birenbaum-Carmeli's (2008, p. 178) assessment that ARTs are "sociotechnical products," which means that they are shaped both by their technical features and also by the economic, political, cultural, psychological, and moral contexts in which they are utilized. Thus, rather than characterize ARTs as inherently enabling or hindering reproductive justice, we attempt to examine the contexts in which infertility and ARTs are, or are not, experienced and accessed.

Psychological Approaches to Infertility

Infertility and infecundity can be among the most significant losses faced by couples and individuals (Horowitz, Galst, & Elster, 2010). Despite the aforementioned tensions within feminism, many feminist psychologists have been at the forefront in calling for infertility to be taken seriously as a feminist issue, even while simultaneously challenging mainstream psychological theorizing that reinforces dominant social beliefs about motherhood as an essential component of womanhood and necessary for psychological completeness (e.g., Pfeffer & Woolett, 1983; Spector, 2004; Ulrich & Weatherall, 2000). Historically, infertility was constructed as a women's issue, and psychogenic models focused on the role of women's emotional well-being (Pasch & Dunkel-Schetter, 1997). However, rigorously designed studies have by and large failed to support a psychogenic model of infertility (Wischmann, 2003); furthermore, results suggest that the biological origin of infertility is as likely to be male as female (Lefièvre et al., 2007). Thus, most contemporary psychological research is focused on infertility (and infertility treatment) as a stressor rather than as a consequence of psychological conflict or distress (Greil, Slauson-Blevins, & McQuillan, 2010; Stanton, Lobel, Sears, & DeLuca, 2002; Verhaak et al., 2007). Although some researchers continue to investigate the link between psychological variables and women's difficulties conceiving or carrying a pregnancy to term, their emphasis is now on a complex interaction among biological, psychological, and environmental stressors, rather than a psychological conflict model (e.g., Nakamura, Sheps, & Arck, 2008). As yet, there is little research available on psychological influences on, and consequences of, infertility in men.

Research on psychosocial aspects of infertility and infertility treatment is generally characterized by significant methodological limitations, such as the reliance on treatment-seeking samples that are likely to have different psychological and demographic characteristics than comparison samples who do not seek medical treatment. Nonetheless, results of these studies suggest that the experience of infertility can have a serious psychological impact. One study (Freeman, Boxer, Rickels, Tureck, & Mastroianni, 1985) showed that 49 percent of women and 15 percent of men described infertility as the most upsetting event of their lives. Studies of psychological symptoms and syndromes associated with infertility have been equivocal; some show that infertile individuals and couples grapple with increased levels of anxiety and depression, and others show little difference between couples who present to IVF clinics (before undergoing treatment) and the general population (Verhaak et al., 2007). Quantitative researchers have frequently measured the distress caused by infertility in clinical samples using self-report measures (Griel, 1997). However relying on those measures to gauge the emotional pain caused by infertility may exclude women and men who suffer emotional distress that is profound, but outside of the parameters of what a questionnaire is designed to measure. For example, qualitative research has illuminated the ways in which infertility affects the everyday social and emotional welfare of individuals. The experience of infertility can force a person to confront the limits of the body; challenge social identity in terms of the ability to parent, be a spouse, or be a sexual partner; and can threaten the sense of having control over one's own life and future (e.g., Clarke, Martin-Matthews, & Matthews, 2006).

Moreover, research from the West suggests that the process of IVF is stressful both for the woman undergoing the treatment and for her partner and that the period spent waiting for the pregnancy test results is particularly anxiety provoking (Eugster & Vingerhoets, 1999; Verhaak et al., 2007). When IVF does not lead to pregnancy, men's and women's negative feelings may endure beyond the treatment cycle. This signals not just the stress of the treatment but the added burden of having to deal anew with involuntary childlessness (Eugster & Vingerhoets, 1999). However, most researchers agree that the woman undergoing the treatment suffers a greater psychological burden. In a review of the research on emotional adjustment to IVF, Verhaak et al. (2007) demonstrated that, in addition to the stress that mounts over the course of a treatment cycle, 10–25 percent of women experience levels of clinical depression after one or more unsuccessful IVF attempts.

Although, after some time, most women ultimately adjust well to failed IVF (Eugster & Vingerhoets, 1999), the psychological weight of the process falls on women's shoulders for at least two reasons. First, although the percentage of male factor infertility is on the rise (Mundy, 2007), women continue to be the locus of the medical treatment. In any attempt to become pregnant through IVF, a woman receives injections during the first half of her menstrual cycle, which aim to stimulate her ovaries. During this time, the woman repeatedly visits her doctor's office for blood tests that monitor her hormone levels and ultrasounds that monitor her follicle growth. When the woman is ready to ovulate, she is given a final injection to make sure the oocytes mature. She then goes to the clinic for oocyte retrieval. In this phase of IVF treatment, the woman is put under general anesthesia and her oocytes are aspirated; then they are transferred to a laboratory to be combined with sperm. If the oocytes fertilize, then, a few days later, one or more embryos are transferred to the woman's uterus. The woman or couple then waits for a blood test 9 to 11 days after the transfer to see if the woman has indeed become pregnant. This is the standard IVF procedure regardless of whether the infertility arises from a male factor or a female factor.

Women also endure more of the psychological burden of IVF treatment. Although, at least in the West, women have an increasing array of choices other than motherhood as a path through adulthood, the "mandate" for motherhood, or the idea that motherhood is key to fulfilling a woman's adult identity, remains strong (Phoenix, Woollett, & Lloyd, 1991). Contemporary research shows that a woman's sense of well-being, is bound up with becoming a parent (e.g., Spector, 2004) more often than a man's is (e.g., Hardy & Makuch, 2002). There is some evidence that this may be more true of younger, less-educated women, who are more likely to stake the majority of their adult identity on conceiving and raising children (Fekkes et al., 2003), than of older, professional women who delay childbearing and then seek infertility treatment.

Because of lingering questions about the relationship of stress to pregnancy rates and the distress caused both by infertility and IVF treatment, psychosocial interventions have been developed to alleviate the distress of infertility and the stress of treatment, and some interventions were used to increase rates of pregnancy. As with the attempts to investigate the relationship between anxiety/depression and infertility, the attempts to gauge the effects of psychosocial interventions have yielded varied results. A review (Boivin, 2003) showed that psychosocial interventions were unlikely to effect pregnancy rates and that interventions were more successful at reducing anxiety than at changing interpersonal functioning. The review also indicated that therapies that are educational, including interventions that emphasize coping skills or relaxation training, were more helpful than those that emphasize emotional expression. In contrast, Hämmerli, Znoj, and Barth (2009) found that psychological interventions aided conception rates, though only for couples who did *not* utilize ARTs. As some psychological interventions increased the frequency of sexual intercourse, it may be that the increase in conception rates following psychological interventions simply follow from greater opportunity to conceive (Häm-merli et al., 2009).

The majority of the research on the psychology of infertility is derived from the experiences of couples presenting for treatment at fertility clinics in the West. However, the psychological ramifications of infertility and the need for the development of more effective psychological interventions may be even greater in the developing world, where women have few opportunities other than motherhood for identity development and so-cioemotional and financial security (van Balen & Inhorn, 2002). As social context is increasingly understood to shape the experience of infertility (Greil et al., 2010), large-scale research projects in the West may not ac-curately capture the experience of infertility for women and men in other parts of the world.

In addition, the underrepresentation of ethnic minority women in the infertility research is indicative of the lack of access to infertility treat-ment by women in the developing world and by poor and ethnic minority women in the United States. Despite the widely held perception that infer-tility distress is the province of upper-middle class, older, White women, rates of infertility are higher among women of color and women with fewer financial means, and U.S. government health plans do not cover the cost of treatment (Nsiah-Jefferson & Hall, 1989). The emphasis on expen-sive means to treat infertility, rather than a focus on prevention (e.g., im-proved access to and use of basic reproductive health care, research into environmental causes of infertility), means that many of the women in most need of the treatment are unable to make use of it (Ombelet, Cooke, Dyer, Serour, & Devroey, 2008). In addition to the lack of available tech-nology, cultural barriers, including local attitudes toward assisted repro-duction and infertility, may also stand in the way of access to infertility treatment (Beckman & Harvey, 2005).

Therefore, researchers are increasingly arguing that there is a repro-ductive justice imperative to learn more about the experience of infertility in developing nations in an effort to increase the quality of service for infertile women in their local contexts. Recent years have seen a growth in both quantitative and qualitative studies designed to gauge the effects of infertility and its treatment on women in the developing world. In particu-lar, that research has been focused in two regions (i.e., sub-Saharan Africa, the Middle East) that have become of interest to medical anthropologists and, increasingly, to psychologists.

Sub-Saharan/Central Africa has been termed the "infertility belt" be-cause of an unusually high rate of involuntary childlessness in the region, due in large part to infection (Collet et al., 1988; Ombelet et al., 2008). Women suffering from infertility in this region experience levels of so-cial and psychological distress that may be unimaginable to their Western peers. For feminists theorizing about the psychological and social experience of infertility (Thompson, 2002), involuntary childlessness in developing nations raises complicated issues that sometimes are strikingly different from the concerns infertility raises in the West. For example, women who do not bear a sufficient number of children for their husbands may be economically disadvantaged, divorced by their husbands, and not considered to be fully adult members of the community (e.g., Ombelet et al., 2008; van Balen & Inhorn, 2002; Vayena et al., 2002). An example from the Ijo community in southern Nigeria illustrates the way that infertility and the lack of treatment options present a complicated matrix. Ijo women do not attain full womanhood until they undergo clitoridectomy, which is generally performed in a woman's seventh month of pregnancy. Uncircumcised women have marginal status, may be divorced from their husband, and cannot be buried in town with the community (Hollos, 2003). Hollos (2003) documented how infertile women in this community sometimes feign pregnancy or miscarriage in order to be circumcised. Thus, the case of Ijo women illustrates how infertility intersects with other complex reproductive justice concerns. The complicated ways in which ARTs interact with culture (Inhorn & Birenbaum-Carmeli, 2008) should be taken into account as women in search of greater fertility increasingly avail themselves of the few infertility treatment resources that exist in this region. To date, no studies have been conducted on what women in this region want from treatment or the psychological ramifications of treatment (Gerrits & Shaw, 2010).

In parts of the Middle East, where treatment options are more accessible than in sub-Saharan Africa, a growing body of research illustrates the ways in which women and men experience IVF and attendant technologies and the ways in which these technologies destabilize the traditional gender structures of the region (Inhorn & Birenbaum-Carmeli, 2008). Here the results echo some of the findings from the West. Higher levels of negative affect are found in samples of women and men undergoing infertility treatment than in the general population (Ashkani, Akbari, & Heydari, 2006; Yassini, Khalili, & Hashemian, 2005). Symptoms of depression seem to increase with length of treatment (Ashkani et al., 2006), and women undergoing treatment show more anxiety (Yassini et al., 2005) and report a lesser quality of life (Rashidi et al., 2008) than men do. Furthermore, as in the West, infertility is largely still considered to be a women's problem (Inhorn, 2002). Research has illustrated the distress caused by living with infertility beyond symptoms of anxiety and depression, and researchers have described new psychosocial issues raised by treatment advances and opportunities. In many ways the advancement of IVF and attendant technologies in the Middle East increase fertility options for women, thereby decreasing psychological distress. For example, some women described IVF as a "marriage saviour" (Inhorn, 2006, p. 46) because their relationships improved once they were able to bear children. On the other hand, the advent of intracytoplasmic sperm injection, a technology that injects sperm directly into an oocyte, means that infertile husbands who stayed in marriages despite their inability to conceive with their wives may now leave their wives, no longer of reproductive age, for younger wives, with whom they can reproduce with the help of technology. Furthermore, IVF treatments may not be accessible to women of few financial means, which presents a justice imperative, as women of lower socioeconomic status may experience the social and emotional impacts of infertility more severely than wealthier women do (Abbasi-Shavazi, Inhorn, Razeghi-Nasrabad, & Toloo, 2008).

As in the West, research from the Middle East indicates that couples ultimately learn to cope with infertility (Ramazanzadeh, Noorbala, Abedinia, & Naghizadeh, 2009), yet a need for emotional support remains (Omu & Omu, 2010). As culture shapes the experience of infertility and its treatment, psychosocial interventions tested on women and men in Western cultures can not necessarily be expected to apply to infertile individuals and couples in other parts of the world. There has been some progress in designing culturally appropriate interventions to help with the stress of infertility. For example, in Hong Kong, a body-mind-spirit therapy based on traditional Chinese medicine has been reported (Chan, Chan, Ng, Ng, & Ho, 2005), but much work remains to be done.

Access to ARTs

The World Health Organization (WHO) defined reproductive rights as "the basic rights of all couples and individuals to decide freely and responsibly the number, spacing, and timing of their children and to have the information and means to do so" (International Conference on Population and Development [ICPD] Programme of Action-Principles, n.d., Principle 8). Thus, for couples and individuals affected by infertility, this should include the right to access ARTs among those who are interested. However, in the United States, and throughout many parts of the developing world, access to ARTs is limited both by high cost and by policies and practices set by legal authorities, religious authorities, insurance providers, and/or fertility clinics. In countries with few resources for providing basic health care, rights to ARTs are further complicated by a limited availability of medical resources, including few trained medical professionals and lower prioritization of infertility relative to other health concerns. In many of these countries, an emphasis on fertility control (sometimes desired but inaccessible, other times naively and/or coercively imposed; e.g., Maternowska, 2006) has overshadowed the importance of infertility both within public health and reproductive rights' frameworks. As noted in our review of psychosocial concerns, the lived experience of infertility may be significantly more devastating to the individuals and community than is perceived by public health experts, as was noted in the WHO's Global Burden of Disease estimates, in which nonprofessionals in Zimbabwe and Cambodia rated infertility as substantially more burdensome than did the WHO experts (Snow, 2008). Colen (1995, p. 78) coined the term "stratified reproduction" to describe the structural and power relations that encourage and empower some categories of people to reproduce, yet deny and devalue the reproductive goals of others.

Financial and Structural Barriers

One of the greatest barriers to treatment is the exceedingly high costs of ARTs, such as IVF. In the United States, the estimated cost of a standard IVF cycle is $12,513 (Chambers, Sullivan, Ishihara, Chapman, & Adamson, 2009); success rates average 24.7 percent per cycle across all procedures and age groups (Katz et al., 2002). Thus, many individuals/couples who choose IVF will undergo multiple cycles, with a median cost of $56,419 per live birth (Katz et al., 2002). The actual cost of IVF per live birth varies significantly across countries, perhaps as a result of different health care delivery systems and IVF-specific practices across countries. Chambers et al.'s (2009) comparison of six developed countries (i.e., Australia, Canada, Japan, Scandinavia, United Kingdom, United States) showed that the mean health care cost of ARTs per live birth was highest in the United States ($41,132) and lowest in Japan ($24,485). Infertility treatment is included in national health policies in most developed countries, although not in the United States, where patient out-of-pocket costs are highest. These out-of-pocket expenses account for 44 percent of the disposable income of an average worker *after* insurance coverage is factored in, compared with 6 percent of an average worker's disposable income in Australia. In the United States, only 14 states have laws that require infertility coverage. Most of those mandate quite limited coverage, and several limit coverage to married, heterosexual couples; only four states require coverage for at least one cycle of IVF (American Society for Reproductive Medicine [ASRM], 2011). Moreover, federal law allows states to refuse coverage of fertility drugs, and most states do not provide such coverage, even though federal law *mandates* coverage for erectile dysfunction drugs, such as Viagra (Connolly, 2001). Thus, unmet demand for infertility treatment in the United States and Canada is high; just 24 percent of estimated demand for treatment has been met (Chambers et al., 2009).

When patients themselves pay for their infertility services, market forces may contribute to health risks for women and children, as both patients and clinicians face considerable pressure to maximize pregnancy rates, such as by transferring multiple embryos to a woman's uterus at once. Multiple births are a significant factor in the overall economic and physical costs attributable to IVF due to antenatal, obstetrical, and neonatal complications (Katz et al., 2002). Studies in the United States suggest that insurance coverage for IVF decreases the risk of multiple births associated with transfer of three or more embryos (Reynolds, Schieve, Jeng, & Peterson, 2003). This is also supported by evidence from many European countries that provide coverage for infertility services, which demonstrate lower multiple birth rates relative to initiated ART cycles (Katz et al., 2002).

Considering the financial barriers to infertility services within the developed world, it is not surprising that access to infertility services, and particularly advanced reproductive technologies, is quite limited within the developing world. In Latin America, by and large, ARTs are not provided in public hospitals (Luna, 2002). Thus, as in the United States, the poor generally cannot access these technologies, although, as Roberts' (2009) ethnographic research on IVF in Ecuador indicates, many working-class and poor patients do make their way to private clinics, often by assuming substantial debt. Roberts reported that, at the time of her research, the cost of an IVF cycle in Ecuador ranged from $3,000 to $5,000. Although substantially less expensive than in the United States (due in part to differences in labor costs), it is nonetheless a huge expense in a nation where the average middle-class person's annual salary in 2007 was approximately $7,040 (Population Reference Bureau, 2008).

Gerrits and Shaw (2010) conducted a systematic review of research on biomedical infertility care within sub-Saharan Africa, including research on infertility service delivery. They noted that, whereas some kind of infertility care is provided throughout localities in sub-Saharan Africa in both the public health care system and private clinics, ARTs are generally provided only within private clinics; the exception was South Africa, where treatment may be somewhat more accessible. Across studies, infertility care within the public health care system, including the diagnosis of infertility, treatment of STIs associated with infertility, hormonal treatments, and sperm testing, was described as haphazard and not up to WHO standards. Private clinics, most based in capital cities, provide ARTs for patients who can afford their services, although the success rates, estimated at 5–15 percent (Owagie, 2002, as cited in Gerrits & Shaw, 2010), are substantially lower than those in the developed world. Moreover, the cost of ARTs, which ranges from $1,200 to $4,000 (United States) across sub-Saharan countries, makes them prohibitively expensive for the average citizen. One study (Donkor & Sandall, 2007) indicated that the cost for one IVF cycle in Ghana is equivalent to 18 months of a nurse's salary.

Religious Practice and Policy Barriers

Access to infertility treatment, particularly ARTs, may be limited by formal legislation, as well as by less formal practice guidelines that vary across the globe. Thus, individuals who require ARTs for reproduction are often subject to greater scrutiny regarding their suitability for parent-hood than are those who are able to become pregnant without interven-tion. These guidelines are generally driven by religious and sociopolitical values, and they often pertain to a woman's marital status or sexual ori-entation. A survey conducted by the International Federation of Fertility Societies (IFFS, 2007) designed to assess the guidelines and regulations regarding ARTs internationally showed that 4 of the 57 countries surveyed had enacted laws to limit access to ARTs exclusively to married couples (i.e., Hong Kong, Taiwan, Tunisia, Turkey), and 10 others had laws that require individuals to be married *or* in stable relationships (i.e., Austria, Czech Republic, Denmark, France, Germany, Italy, Norway, Slovenia, Sweden, Switzerland). Although other countries did not have explicit laws, some have guidelines that similarly limit access to individuals who are married and/or in stable relationships (i.e., Argentina, China, Colom-bia, Croatia, Ecuador, Egypt, Ireland, Japan, Jordan, Lithuania, Malaysia, Morocco, the Philippines, Portugal, Singapore, Uruguay). In several coun-tries, ARTs were available (i.e., not restricted) to either single women (i.e., Greece, Hungary, India, Latvia, Russia, Spain, Vietnam) or to both single women and lesbian couples (i.e., Australia, Belgium, Brazil, Canada, Israel, the Netherlands, New Zealand, South Africa, United Kingdom, United States), although the absence of restrictions does not guarantee access. For example, a survey (Stern, Cramer, Garrod, & Green, 2001) of ART clinics in the United States showed that, among those who responded, 79 percent reported a willingness to treat single women, and 74 percent reported that they treat lesbian couples. These numbers may overestimate access, as it is likely that clinics that did not respond have more discriminatory policies. Only 40 percent of centers reported that they have a written set of policies, which may increase the risk for discrimination. Moreover, single women and lesbian couples may face discrimination in more specialized domains of ARTs that require more intensive psychological screening, such as in oocyte donation. Notably, both oocyte donors and recipients may face discrimination based on sexual orientation. A survey (Kingsberg, Apple-garth, & Janata, 2000) of embryo donation programs in the United States showed a much lower willingness to treat single women or lesbian cou-ples (55% and 59% of couples, respectively), despite the extensive psycho-logical research that demonstrates equivalent, if not better, socioemotional development among children raised by lesbian mothers (e.g., Golombok, Tasker, & Murray, 1997; Stacey & Biblarz, 2001). Moreover, insurance laws or policies that restrict access to those with proven infertility may make it more difficult for single women and lesbian couples to obtain insurance coverage.

Access to care may also be affected by screening practices that limit access based on factors such as the prospective parents' age and health (psychological and physical) status. A reproductive justice framework includes considerations of the health and well-being of children conceived through ARTs, and it balances these considerations with principles of reproductive autonomy (see Horowitz et al., 2010). Psychologists who work in reproductive medicine often occupy a gatekeeping role, and they must be mindful of how biases in psychiatric diagnosis based on race, class, and sexual orientation (Ali, 2004; Bullock, 2004), including diagnosis of severe mental illness, may further hinder access to infertility services. Stern et al.'s (2001) survey indicated a lack of consistency across clinics in their use of substance abuse history and mental illness to screen patients, but only 27 percent of clinics reported that they would treat patients with a history of schizophrenia.

Religion and religious values may influence both individuals' decisions to pursue ARTs, as well as government policies regarding ARTs availability. The Catholic Church, which holds that life begins at conception, has not only opposed ARTs, but the Vatican has explicitly condemned their use (Raspberry, 2009). Some societies influenced by the Catholic Church have imposed formal or informal restrictions on ARTs to accommodate Catholic doctrine. For example, Italy restricts cryopreservation of excess embryos and obligates implantation of all produced embryos, yet sets a mandatory limit of three embryos for transfer, which creates a very difficult set of conditions to meet and increases the number and complexity of treatments that a woman must undergo (Benagiano & Gianaroli, 2004). Costa Rican law is the most restrictive, as the country banned all forms of ART through a constitutional amendment (Luna, 2002). IVF is acceptable within Islamic practice, but can be performed only for a husband and wife (Schenker, 2005). Generally, third-party reproduction is unacceptable, although Shia religious decrees (*fatwas*) have opened the door to third-party reproduction in Iran and Lebanon (Inhorn & Birenbaum-Carmeli, 2008). Within Jewish law, there is an emphasis on the commandment "to be fruitful and multiply," and rabbinic law generally is considered to be quite accommodating toward ARTs. Israel, in fact, has among the most generous state funding for infertility treatment, which is available to women of all marital statuses and sexual orientations up to age 45 (or older with donor oocytes) until they have two children (Birenbaum-Carmeli, 2009). In Germany, it is a cultural history of scientific/medical human rights' abuses, rather than religion, that contributed to its development of some of the West's most restrictive policies toward ARTs, preimplantation genetic diagnosis (PGD), and embryo research.

Disease, Disability, and ARTs

Among the most deep-seated anxieties concerning ARTs are their "brave-new-world" associations with genetic engineering. PGD, often (albeit somewhat inaccurately) referred to as the "designer-baby" method, is one of the most recent of the NRTs to inspire anxiety about the appropriate limits of human intervention in the arena of reproduction. As a technology that unites ARTs with medical genetics, PGD involves analysis of the chromosomal make up of an in vitro embryo. Specifically, as with standard IVF, PGD involves ovarian stimulation, oocyte retrieval, and creation of in vitro embryos, but with an additional testing phase that involves removal and genetic testing of one to two cells from a (typically) eight-cell stage embryo, and transfer of selected embryos to the uterus with the hope of establishing a pregnancy (Baruch, Kaufman, & Hudson, 2006). PGD, first successfully used in humans in the United Kingdom in 1989, was initially developed as an alternative to prenatal diagnosis for known carriers of serious hereditary conditions who wish to have a genetically related child without that particular condition (Franklin & Roberts, 2006). Whereas the "designer-baby" rhetoric conjures up notions of eugenics, with images of elite parents selecting physically and intellectually superior children, Franklin and Roberts's (2006, p. 18) ethnography of PGD in the United Kingdom illustrates a significantly more tempered reality:

> Far from seeking perfection, many couples who opt for PGD are enacting a profound sense of obligation, drawn from the experience of watching a child of theirs die after a life of suffering (often at only a few months of age), to do everything in their power to prevent imposing that burden again . . . far from seeking desired traits . . . they would be happy to have any kind of child at all, as long as it does not have to be born with its own inbuilt genetic guarantee of a painful and premature death.

Their conclusions are particularly noteworthy, given that the United Kingdom is considered to be the most liberal in regulation among countries that regulate repro-genetic technologies.

PGD not only unites the features, but also the costs, associated with ARTs and medical genetics, as it adds an estimated cost of at least $3,500 (Spar, 2006) to the price of IVF in the United States and other countries where it is not covered by national health care policies. According to the PGD International Society, by 2002 approximately 1,000 babies had been born through PGD (Preimplantation Genetic Diagnosis International Society, 2008); the number of babies born each year has increased with improved technology and more widespread use. In addition to the use of PGD to avoid heritable, single gene disorders (e.g., cystic fibrosis, sickle cell anemia, Tay-Sachs disease, spinal muscular atrophy) or (albeit less commonly) for immunologically compatible (i.e., Human Leukocyte Antigen [HLA] matched) sibling donors (i.e., "savior siblings"), PGD increasingly is being used for late-onset disorders with a genetic predisposition, such as hereditary breast/ovarian cancer (BRCA) or colon cancer (HNPCC) risk (Offit et al., 2006), and as an accompaniment to IVF to screen for an-euploidy conditions (caused by an extra or missing chromosome, such Trisomy 21, Turners syndrome). PGD for sex selection for nonmedical rea-sons is prohibited in 36 countries throughout the world, including India and China (Darnovsky, 2009). In the United States, the ASRM discourages (but does prohibit) the use of PGD for sex selection (Ethics Committee of the ASRM, 1999), except for purposes of family balancing (Ethics Com-mittee of the ASRM, 2001), for which PGD is offered and even marketed. Even when prohibited, there is nonetheless concern about the use of PGD for sex selection in many parts of the developing world, where many mil-lions of girls are already "missing" as a result of sex selection through selective abortion or infanticide (George, 2006; Lai-wan, Blyth & Hoi-yan, 2006; see also chapter 11, "Female Feticide and Infanticide"). Although the currently high expense of PGD means few couples in the developing world are likely to choose this route in the near future, it has nonethe-less already been used for this purpose. One clinic in Mumbai claimed to have treated 36 couples seeking sex selection, until their advertising was removed from their website following intervention by the Indian Su-preme Court (George, 2006). Practitioners at the Farah Hospital in Jordan contend that ASRM's position should not be generalized to other cultural contexts (Kilani & Hassan, 2002, p. 68):

> In our cultural context, which is situated within a predominantly Muslim environment, there is a high premium placed on couples having at least one male offspring. As clinicians, we are faced with *reasonable* requests by couples to assist them in their desire and need to end their suffering in not being able to have a child of the desired gender [emphasis added].

We contend that a cultural logic that deems social sex selection a reason-able request is incongruent with a reproductive justice framework, but it does highlight the subjective, and often culturally embedded, task of drawing lines around acceptable uses of reproductive technologies.

Whereas the use of PGD for sex selection raises clear concerns from a reproductive justice framework, the use of PGD to screen for disease and disability also raises important considerations. The term *stratified reproduc-tion* not only captures social hierarchies that structure access to ARTs, but also how ARTs, and particularly repro-genetic technologies, may contrib-ute to the stratification of disease and disability. Adopting a framework of reproductive justice toward ARTs requires consideration of their social impact, particularly on the lives of marginalized groups in a society, such as those living with chronic disease and disability. For disability rights ad-vocates, technologies such as PGD, as well as earlier technologies such as prenatal diagnosis, have the potential to devalue the lives of individuals with genetic differences (Galpern, 2007). Disability rights activists have highlighted the socially constructed nature of disability and the often ambiguous line between disability and disease, and they continue to raise important concerns about whether the current focus on eliminating disability through expensive repro-genetic technologies impacts investment in resources for those living with chronic disease and disability, both now and in the future (e.g., Shakespeare, 1999). This is especially important, given the impact of socioeconomically stratified access to repro-genetic technologies. In regard to prenatal diagnosis, Rapp (1999, p. 50) summed up the reproductive concerns of those who work at the intersection of the feminist reproductive rights and disability rights movements: "How is it possible to contest the eugenic and stigmatizing definition of disabilities which seem to underlie prenatal [and preimplantation] diagnosis, while still upholding the rights of individual women to determine what kind of medical care, and what sorts of pregnancy decisions, are in their best interests?" Fortunately, some models exist, such as the British Council on Disabled People, which supports a women's right to choose, "but opposes research which only seeks to increase pre-natal screening, not therapy" (Shakespeare, 1999, p. 683).

Krahn and Wong (2009) argued for a contextualized perspective on reproductive autonomy in relation to PGD by drawing on feminist relational theories of self. They supported a model of reproductive autonomy and control, defined as "the ability to positively act in ways that conform to one's reproductive desires or goals and not being prevented from acting in this way" (p. 35), but also questioned whether the normalization of certain aspects of PGD actually increases choice, or whether it actually makes it more difficult for prospective PGD clients to refuse these technologies. When PGD is framed as a parental responsibility (Rubin, 2011), as doing everything that can be done to benefit their prospective children (Zeiler, 2004), parents may feel obliged to choose this option, particularly in a context where social services for persons with disabilities and their caretakers are limited. Rather than restricting access to PGD, reproductive autonomy may be best accomplished by ensuring that the availability of PGD is accompanied by increased attention to educational concerns and social supports for people with disabilities and their caretakers (Krahn & Wong, 2009).

Commodification and Exploitation

One of the most important concerns in relation to the development and proliferation of reproductive technologies is their impact on the objectification and commodification of the body. These concerns have been raised in relation to the use of all ARTs, but they are particularly salient in the context of third-party reproduction, which refers to the use of oocytes, sperm, or embryos that have been donated by another person to enable an infertile individual or couple to become parents, as well as the use of traditional surrogacy and gestational carrier arrangements (ASRM, 2006).

Oocytes for Sale

The common use of the term *donation,* which suggests generosity and gift giving, illustrates the ways in which language regarding *third-party reproduction* is euphemized to avoid discomfort with a marketplace model of reproduction, despite the fact that the majority of gamete transfers involve monetary exchange (Shanley, 2002). Moreover, this discomfort appears to be gendered, as oocyte donors, who are paid more than sperm donors (due to the greater time and associated health risks), are expected to report that financial compensation is less important than the opportunity to help others (Almeling, 2006; Ragoné, 1999). Psychological research suggests that oocyte and sperm donors report a mix of altruistic and financial motivations, but women are more likely than men to mention altruistic donation (Schover, Collins, Quigley, Blankstein, & Kanoti, 1991; Schover, Rothman, & Collins, 1992). However, the reality is that countries that restrict payment for oocytes face a dearth of donations relative to demand (Spar, 2007).

That technological reproduction is commodified, to varied degrees, throughout the globe is difficult to dispute (Spar, 2006). The social and reproductive justice question often debated by feminists and bioethicists is whether payment for reproductive services (i.e., sperm and oocyte donation, traditional or gestational surrogacy) is exploitative. The question of exploitation is connected to feminist and ethical debates and tensions about women's autonomy, choice, and agency (Nahman, 2008). For example, Papadimos and Papadimos (2004, p. 56), in their consideration of one common context for recruiting ooycte sellers, contended that "a female university student in need of financial resources to pay for her education cannot make an autonomous choice to trade her genes for tuition." But denying these women *any* agency is also problematic.

These bioethical questions must include a feminist and global frame as, in the absence of international regulation, the consequences of barring compensation in one country to guard against exploitation of its female citizens, as has been done, for example, in Germany, Israel, and the United Kingdom, can promote *reproductive tourism,* as individuals and couples travel overseas for reproductive services that are less expensive and less regulated than they are at home. The potential for exploitation is arguably greater for women in developing countries whose life choices may be particularly constrained by extant poverty and gender hierarchies. Nahman (2008) acknowledged this reality for Romanian oocyte sellers; nonetheless she cautioned against seeing the women she interviewed as "passive objects" of the global ova trade. She noted that "both agency and choice, we know, operate within a neoliberal epistemology rather than outside it" (p. 67). In other words, although Romanian women who sell their oocytes may do so as a result of dismal financial circumstances and limited choices, their actions may also be a way to gain a sense of dignity (as defined within global capitalism, even as they also perpetuate that system) and a way to experience reproductive autonomy (however circumscribed it may be) in a region where abortions had for years been strictly banned.

As the market for oocytes is driven by the desire and preferences of the predominantly White recipients seeking ooctyes from racially similar women, a further dilemma is that, whereas White women in the United States and in eastern Europe have the choice to sell their oocytes for what could be construed as relatively substantial compensation, women of color in both developed and developing countries generally do not. However, increasingly, women throughout the world are considered sources for oocytes for the purposes of stem cell research, an area of biomedical research that has developed alongside advances in ARTs. Whereas in the United States, the national debate on stem cell research has been informed by abortion politics, particularly questions about the moral status of the embryo, concerns regarding the commodification and exploitation of women have received considerably less public attention. But this potential has already been realized through a scandal in South Korea. Woo Suk Hwang was found to have fabricated claims to have created the world's first cloned embryo, and he was also accused of using inappropriate practices to acquire an enormous number of human oocytes (2,221 oocytes from 121 women) from both paid and unpaid donors, including through possible coerced "donation" from female members of his research team, and by misrepresenting the purpose of donation, which unpaid donors believed to be for therapeutic purposes rather than for basic research (Leem & Park, 2008).

Surrogacy

In traditional surrogacy, a woman is inseminated with sperm for the purpose of conceiving a child for an intended recipient. In this arrangement, the surrogate has a genetic and biological link to the pregnancy she might carry. The advent of IVF has enabled gestational surrogacy, in which embryos created through IVF by intended parents either with their own, or donor gametes, are transferred into the surrogate's uterus, which has been prepared hormonally to carry a pregnancy. Thus, in gestational surrogacy, the "carrier" has no genetic link to the fetus (ASRM, 2006). Surrogacy is a complicated issue from emotional, medical, legal, and ethical perspectives. For some, surrogacy is problematic because it has the potential to disturb traditional concepts of family, motherhood, and gender roles. In contrast, feminists' difficulties with surrogacy have concerned the commodification and control of women's bodies. Whether surrogacy represents a more extreme form commodification of women's bodies, as compared, for example, with ova selling, or simply a more visible one, it has been viewed by many as especially troubling. For Rothman (2000), what is of greatest concern about surrogacy is the disconnection and compartmentalization of pregnancy and motherhood and the necessary disavowal of the relationship between a pregnant woman and the fetus she carries/the baby she births. Nonetheless, for some feminists, any attempt to restrict surrogacy is paternalistic and represents a threat to reproductive autonomy. Despite extensive controversy regarding surrogacy, there is relatively limited psychosocial research on this topic (Ciccarelli & Beckman, 2005). However, Ciccarelli and Beckman's (2005) review showed that, across studies, acceptability of commercial (paid) surrogacy was lower than acceptability of NRTs. Despite these general prevailing attitudes, there is little evidence of concerns about whether contractual parenting is emotionally damaging or exploitive for mothers, children, or intended parents.

Most surrogates are not poor, but working class (Ciccarelli & Beckman, 2005) and White, which some advocates for surrogacy mention, along with their often reported altruistic motivations, to dispel concerns about possible exploitation (e.g., Lev, 2006). Nonetheless, within the United States, the financial cost of surrogacy to intended parents is high, and intended parents are generally much better educated and have higher socioeconomic status than surrogates (Horowitz et al., 2010). As surrogacy "goes global" (Spar, 2006), and more individuals and couples opt for international surrogacy, either due to the lower price tag or fewer restrictions (e.g., such as the availability for gay intended fathers), these socioeconomic differences are likely to widen. Thus, just as more research is needed on the psychosocial aspects of surrogacy within domestic contexts, there is considerable need for research on the psychological, social, and familial consequences of international surrogacy.

CONCLUSION

Despite popular representations, infertility is a health concern for women and men throughout the world; it is not restricted to the developed West. Although considerable attention is devoted to ARTs, which are costly and inaccessible to the vast majority of the global population affected by infertility, a great deal of suffering related to infertility can be alleviated with improved access to basic reproductive health care. It is unlikely that costly ARTs will be integrated into health care priorities of developing nations in the near future; however, infertility and its treatment can still be considered and dealt with as an important public health concern, with a focus on preventable infertility. There is nothing contradictory in assuring access to both infertility *and* contraceptive and abortion services for all women who choose them (Rothman, 2000). In fact, these services often go hand in hand, as access to appropriate contraception and safe abortions at one stage of life potentially protects women's fertility in another.

ARTs are technical and cultural products, and the way they are taken up within a cultural context often reflects its prevailing values. Problems of inequities in access to care, commodification of bodies, and marginalization of persons with disabilities are not created by ARTs, but their use in certain contexts can heighten these concerns. Although the availability of ARTs provides individuals and couples who can access them with more options, and more decisions, regarding childbearing, more options and decisions are not necessarily the same as increased reproductive choice and autonomy. Moreover, the availability of third-party reproduction, and the globalization of ARTs, means that reproductive choices are increasingly intertwined with the lives of others and have implications for their reproductive autonomy as well as that of the infertility patients themselves. By and large, ARTs in their current practice offer solutions to individual dilemmas, whether those arise from biology, society, or their intersection, without radically transforming power inequities. Nonetheless, the controversies that surround ARTs could help to identify key priorities for those who work to provide reproductive justice for the world's women.

NOTES

1. With IVF, oocytes are obtained from a woman after her ovaries have been stimulated with fertility drugs. Oocytes are obtained through an ultrasound-guided needle inserted into the ovaries through the vaginal wall. These oocytes are then fertilized in a laboratory (in vitro) with sperm, and the developing embryos are cultured for 3 to 6 days. Embryos are then transferred back to the woman's uterus. Approximately 10–12 days after embryo transfer, a blood sample can be taken to determine if they have implanted and are developing into a pregnancy.

2. The American Society for Reproductive Medicine defined *infertility* as a condition marked by "the failure to achieve a successful pregnancy after 12 months or more of regular unprotected intercourse" (Practice Committee of the American Society for Reproductive Medicine, 2008, p. S60) but justified earlier evaluation and treatment among women over age 35 or based on medical history.

REFERENCES

Abbasi-Shavazi, M. J., Inhorn, M. C., Razeghi-Nasrabad, H. B., & Toloo, G. (2008). The "Iranian ART Revolution": Infertility, assisted reproductive technology, and third-party donation in the Islamic Republic of Iran. *Journal of Middle East Women's Studies, 4,* 1–28.

Ali, A. (2004). The intersection of racism and sexism in psychiatric diagnosis. In P. J. Caplan & L. Cosgrove (Eds.), *Bias in psychiatric diagnosis* (pp. 71–75). Lanham, MD: Rowan & Littlefield.

Almeling, R. (2006). "Why do you want to be a donor?" Gender and the production of altruism in egg and sperm donation. *New Genetics and Society, 25,* 143–157.

American Society for Reproductive Medicine. (2006). *Third party reproduction (sperm, egg, and embryo donation and surrogacy): A guide for patients.* Retrieved from http://www.asrm.org/uploadedFiles/ASRM_Content/Resources/ Patient_Resources/Fact_Sheets_and_Info_Booklets/thirdparty.pdf.

American Society for Reproductive Medicine. (2008). Definitions of infertility and recurrent pregnancy loss. *Fertility and Sterility, 90*(S3), S60.

American Society for Reproductive Medicine. (2011). State infertility insurance laws. Retrieved from http://asrm.org/insurance.aspx.

Ashkani, H., Akbari, A., & Heydari, S. T. (2006). Epidemiology of depression among infertile and fertile couples in Shiraz, southern Iran. *Indian Journal of Medical Sciences, 60,* 399–406.

Baruch, S., Kaufman, D., & Hudson, K. L. (2006). Genetic testing of embryos: Practices and perspectives of U.S. IVF clinics. *Fertility and Sterility, 83,* 1708–1716.

Beckman, L. J., & Harvey, S. M. (2005). Current reproductive technologies: Increased access and choice? *Journal of Social Issues, 61,* 1–20.

Benagiano, G., & Gianaroli, L. (2004). The new Italian IVF legislation. *Reproductive BioMedicine Online, 9,* 117–125.

Birenbaum-Carmeli, D. (2009). The politics of "the natural family" in Israel: State policy and kinship ideologies. *Social Science & Medicine, 69,* 1018–1024.

Boivin, J. (2003). A review of psychosocial interventions in infertility. *Social Science & Medicine, 57,* 2325–2341.

Bullock, H. E. (2004). Diagnosis of low-income women. In P. J. Caplan & L. Cosgrove (Eds.), *Bias in psychiatric diagnosis* (pp. 115–120). Lanhman, MD: Rowan & Littlefield.

Chambers, G. M., Sullivan, E. A., Ishihara, O., Chapman, M. G., & Adamson, G. D. (2009). The economic impact of assisted reproductive technology: A review of selected developed countries. *Fertility and Sterility, 91*(6), 2281–2294.

Chan, C.H.Y., Chan, C.L.W., Ng, S. M., Ng, E.H.Y., & Ho, P. C. (2005). Body-mind-spirit intervention for IVF women. *Journal of Assisted Reproduction and Genetics, 22,* 419–427.

Ciccarelli, J., & Beckman, L. J. (2005). Navigating rough waters: An overview of psychological aspects of surrogacy. *Journal of Social Issues, 61,* 21–43.

Clarke, L. H., Martin-Matthews, A., & Matthews, R. (2006). The continuity and discontinuity of the embodied self in infertility. *Canadian Review of Sociology/ Revue Canadienne de Sociologie, 43,* 95–113.

Colen, S. (1995). "Like a mother to them": Stratified reproduction and West Indian childcare workers and employers in New York. In F. D. Ginsburg & R. Rapp (Eds.), *Conceiving the new world order: The global politics of reproduction* (pp. 78–102). Berkeley: University of California Press.

Collet, M., Reniers, J., Frost, E., Gass, R., Yvert, F., Leclerc, A., et al. (1988). Infertility in central Africa: Infection is the cause. *International Journal of Gynecology & Obstetrics, 26,* 423–428.

Connolly, E. L. (2001). Constitutional issues raised by states' exclusion of fertility drugs from Medicaid coverage in light of mandated coverage of Viagra. *Vanderbilt Law Review, 54,* 451–480.

Darnovsky, M. (2009). *Countries with laws or policies on sex selection* [A memo prepared for the April 2009 New York City sex selection meeting]. Retrieved from http://www.geneticsandsociety.org/downloads/200904_sex_selection_memo.pdf.

Donkor, E., & Sandall, J. (2007). The impact of perceived stigma and mediating social factors on infertility-related stress among women seeking infertility treatment in southern Ghana. *Social Science & Medicine, 65,* 1683–1694.

Ethics Committee of the American Society of Reproductive Medicine. (1999). Sex selection and preimplantation genetic diagnosis. *Fertility and Sterility, 72,* 595–598.

Ethics Committee of the American Society of Reproductive Medicine. (2001). Preconception gender selection for nonmedical reasons. *Fertility and Sterility, 75,* 861–864.

Eugster, A. & Vingerhoets, A.J.J.M. (1999). Psychological aspects of in vitro fertilization: A review. *Social Science & Medicine, 48,* 575–589.

Fekkes, M., Buitendijk, S. E., Verrips, G.H.W., Braat, D.D.M., Brewaeys, A.M.A, Dolfing, J. G., et al. (2003). Health-related quality of life in relation to gender and age in couples planning IVF treatment. *Human Reproduction, 18,* 1536–1543.

Firestone, S. (1970). *The dialectic of sex: The case for feminist revolution.* New York: Morrow.

Franklin, S., & Roberts, C. (2006). *Born and made: An ethnography of preimplantation genetic diagnosis.* Princeton, NJ: Princeton University Press.

Freeman, E. W., Boxer, A. S., Rickels, K., Tureck, R., & Mastroianni, L. (1985). Psychological evaluation and support in a program of in vitro fertilization and embryo transfer. *Fertility and Sterility, 43,* 48–53.

Galpern, E. (2007). *Assisted reproductive technologies: Overview and perspective using a reproductive justice framework.* Retrieved from http://www.geneticsandsociety.org/downloads/ART.pdf.

George, S. (2006). Millions of missing girls: From fetal sexing to high technology sex selection. *Prenatal Diagnosis, 26,* 604–609.

Gerrits, T., & Shaw, M. (2010). Biomedical infertility care in sub-Saharan Africa: A social science review of current practices, experiences, and view points. *Facts, Views, & Vision in OBGYN, 2,* 194–207.

Golombok, S., Tasker, F., & Murray, C. (1997). Children raised in fatherless families from infancy: Family relationships and the socioemotional development of children of lesbian and single heterosexual mothers. *Journal of Child Psychology and Psychiatry, 38,* 783–791.

Greil, A. L. (1997). Infertility and psychological distress: A critical review of the literature. *Social Science & Medicine, 45,* 1679–1704.

Greil, A. L., Slauson-Blevins, K., & McQuillan, J. (2010). The experience of infertility: A review of recent literature. *Sociology of Health and Illness, 32,* 140–162.

Hämmerli, K., Znoj, H., & Barth, J. (2009). The efficacy of psychological interventions for infertile patients: A meta-analysis examining mental health and pregnancy rate. *Human Reproduction Update, 15,* 1–17.

Hardy, E., & Makuch, M. Y. (2002). Gender, infertility, and ART. In E. Vayena, P. J. Rowe, & P. D. Griffin (Eds.), *Current practices and controversies in assisted reproduction* (pp. 272–280). Report of a meeting on "Medical, Ethical, Social, Aspects of Assisted Reproduction" held at WHO headquarters in Geneva, Switzerland, September 17–21, 2001. Retrieved from http://whqlibdoc.who.int/hq/2002/9241590300.pdf.

Hollos, M. (2003). Infertility in southern Nigeria: Women's vices from Amakiri. *African Journal of Reproductive Health/La Revue Africaine de la Santé Reproductive, 7,* 46–56.

Horowitz, J. E., Galst, J. P., & Elster, N. (2010). *Ethical dilemmas in fertility counseling.* Washington, DC: American Psychological Association.

Inhorn, M. C. (2002). The "local" confronts the "global": Infertile bodies and new reproductive technologies in Egypt. In M. Inhorn & F. van Balen (Eds.), *Infertility around the globe: New thinking on childlessness, gender, and reproductive technologies* (pp. 263–282). Berkeley: University of California Press.

Inhorn, M. C. (2006). Islam, IVF, and everyday life in the Middle East. *Anthropology of the Middle East, 1,* 42–50.

Inhorn, M. C., & Birenbaum-Carmeli, D. (2008). Assisted reproductive technologies and culture change. *Annual Review of Anthropology, 37,* 177–196.

International Federation of Fertility Societies. (2007). IFFS Surveillance 07. *Fertility and Sterility, 87*(Suppl.), S1–S67.

International Conference on Population and Development Programme of Action-Principles. (n.d.). Retrieved from http://web.unfpa.org/intercenter/advocating/icpd-poa.htm.

Katz, P., Nachtigall, R., & Showstack, J. (2002). The economic impact of the assisted reproductive technologies. *Nature Medicine, 8,* 29–32.

Kilani, Z., & Hassan, H. (2002). Sex selection and preimplantation genetic diagnosis at the Farah Hospital. *Reproductive BioMedicine Online, 4*(1), 60–70.

Kingsberg, S. A., Applegarth, L. D., & Janata, J. W. (2000). Embryo donation programs and policies in North America: Survey results and implications for health and mental health professionals. *Fertility and Sterility, 73,* 215–220.

Krahn, T., & Wong, S. I. (2009). Preimplantation genetic diagnosis and reproductive autonomy. *Reproductive BioMedicine Online, 19*(S2), 34–42.

Lai-wan, C. C., Blyth, E., & Hoi-yan, C. C. (2006). Attitudes toward and practices regarding sex selection in China. *Prenatal Diagnosis, 26,* 610–613.

Leem, S. Y., & Park, J. H. (2008). Rethinking women and their bodies in the age of biotechnology: Feminist commentaries on the Hwang affair. *East Asian Science, Technology, and Society, 2,* 9–26.

Lefièvre, L., Bedu-Addo, K., Conner, S. J., Machado-Oliveira, G. S., Chen, Y., Kirkman-Brown, J. C., et al. (2007). Counting sperm does not add up any more: Time for a new equation? *Reproduction, 133,* 675–684.

Lev, A. I. (2006). Gay dads: Choosing surrogacy. *Lesbian & Gay Psychology Review, 7,* 73–77.

Luna, F. (2002). Assisted reproductive technology in Latina America: Some ethical and sociocultural issues. In E. Vayena, P. J. Rowe, & P. D. Griffin (Eds.),

Current Practices and Controversies in Assisted Reproduction (pp. 31–40). Report of a meeting on "Medical, Ethical, and Social Aspects of Assisted Reproduction" held at WHO headquarters in Geneva, Switzerland, September 17–21, 2001. Retrieved from http://whqlibdoc.who.int/hq/2002/9241590300.pdf.

Mahjouri, N. (2004). Techno-maternity: Rethinking the possibilities of reproductive technologies. *Thirdspace, 4*(1). Retrieved from http://www.thirdspace.ca/journal/article/view/mahjouri/157.

Mamo, L. (2010). Fertility, Inc.: Consumption and subjectification in U.S. lesbian reproductive practices. In A. E. Clarke, L. Mamo, J. R. Fosket, J. R. Fishman, & J. K. Shim (Eds.), *Biomedicalization: Technoscience, health, and illness in the U.S.* (pp. 173–196). Durham, NC: Duke University Press.

Maternowska, M. C. (2006). *Reproducing inequalities: Poverty and the politics of population in Haiti.* New Brunswick, NJ: Rutgers University Press.

Mundy, L. (2007). *Everything conceivable: How the science of reproduction is changing our world.* New York: Knopf.

Nahman, M. (2008). Nodes of desire: Romanian egg sellers, "dignity," and feminist alliances in transnational ova exchanges. *European Journal of Women's Studies, 15*(2), 65–82.

Nakamura, K., Sheps, S., & Arck, P. C. (2008). Stress and reproductive failure: Past notions, present insights, and future directions. *Journal of Assisted Reproduction and Genetics, 25*, 47–62.

Novas, C., & Rose, N. (2000). Genetic risk and the birth of the somatic individual. *Economy and Society, 29*, 485–513.

Nsiah-Jefferson, L., & Hall, E. J. (1989). Reproductive technology: Perspectives and implications for low-income women and women of color. In K. S. Ratcliff (Ed.), *Healing Technology: Feminist Perspectives* (pp. 93–114). Ann Arbor: University of Michigan Press.

Offit, K., Kohut, K., Clagett, B., Wadsworth, E. A., Lafaro, K. J., Cummings, S., et al. (2006). Cancer genetic testing and assisted reproduction. *Journal of Clinical Oncology, 24*, 4775–4782.

Ombelet, W., Cooke, I., Dyer, S., Serour, G., & Devroey, P. (2008). Infertility and the provision of infertility medical services in developing countries. *Human Reproduction Update, 14*, 605–621.

Omu, F. E., & Omu, A. E. (2010). Emotional reaction to diagnosis of infertility in Kuwait and successful clients' perception of nurses' role during treatment. *BioMed Central Nursing, 9*(article 5).

Papadimos, T. J., & Papadimos, A. T. (2004). The student and the ovum: The lack of autonomy and informed consent in trading genes for tuition. *Reproductive Biology and Endocrinology, 2*(article 56).

Pasch, L. A. & Dunkel-Schetter, C. (1997). Fertility problems: Complex issues faced by women and couples. In S. J. Gallant, G. P. Keita, & R. Royak-Schaler (Eds.), *Health care for women: Psychological, social, and behavioral influences* (pp. 187–201). Washington, DC: American Psychological Association.

Pfeffer, N., & Woolett, A. (Eds.). (1983). *Women's experiences of infertility.* London: Virago.

Phoenix, A., Woollett, A., & Lloyd, E. (1991). *Motherhood.* London: Sage.

Population Reference Bureau. (2008). *2008 world population data sheet.* Retrieved from http://www.prb.org/pdf08/08WPDS_Eng.pdf.

Practice Committee of the American Society for Reproductive Medicine. (2008). Definitions of infertility and recurrent pregnancy loss. *Fertility and Sterility, 90,* S60.

Preimplantation Genetic Diagnosis International Society. (2008). *History of pre-implantation genetic diagnosis (PGD).* Retrieved from http://www.pgdis.org/history.html.

Ragoné H. (1999). The gift of life: Surrogate motherhood, gamete donation, and the constructions of altruism. In L. L. Layne (Ed.), *Transformative motherhood: On giving and getting in a consumer culture* (pp. 65–88). New York: New York University Press.

Ramazanzadeh, F., Noorbala, A. A., Abedinia, N., & Naghizadeh, M. M. (2009). Emotional adjustment in infertile couples. *Iranian Journal of Reproductive Medicine, 7,* 97–103.

Rapp, R. (1999). *Testing women, testing the fetus: The social impact of amniocentesis in America.* New York: Routledge.

Rashidi, B., Montazeri, A., Ramezanzadeh, F., Shariat, M., Abedinia, N., & Ashrafi, M. (2008). Health-related quality of life in infertile couples receiving IVF or ICSI treatment. *BMC Health Services Research, 8,* 186. Retrieved from http://www.biomedcentral.com/1472–6963/8/186/.

Raspberry, K. (2009). The genesis of embryos and ethics in vitro: Practicing pre-implantation genetic diagnosis in Argentina. In D. Birenbaum-Carmeli & M. C. Inhorn (Eds.), *Assisted reproduction, testing genes: Global encounters with new biotechnologies* (pp. 213–238). New York: Berghahn.

Reynolds, M. A., Schieve, L. A., Jeng, G., & Peterson, H. B. (2003). Does insurance coverage decrease the risk for multiple births associated with assisted re-productive technology? *Fertility and Sterility, 80,* 16–23.

Roberts, E. R. (2009). The traffic between women: Female alliance and familial egg donation in Ecuador. In D. Birenbaum-Carmeli & M. C. Inhorn (Eds.), *Assisted reproduction, testing genes: Global encounters with new biotechnologies* (pp. 113–143). New York: Berghahn.

Rothman, B. K. (2000). *Recreating motherhood.* New Brunswick, NJ: Rutgers University Press.

Rubin, L. (2011, March). *Family risk and parental responsibility: Repro-genetic testing for inherited breast/ovarian risk among BR(east)CA(ncer) mutation carriers.* Invited presentation to the Doctoral Program in Social Personality Psychology, the Graduate Center, City University of New York.

Russo, N. F. (1976). The motherhood mandate. *Journal of Social Issues, 32,* 143–153.

Sandelowski, M. (1991). Compelled to try: The never-enough quality of conceptive technology. *Medical Anthropology Quarterly, 5,* 29–47.

Sandelowski, M., & de Lacey, S. (2002). The uses of a "disease": Infertility as a rhetorical vehicle. In M. C. Inhorn, & F. van Balen (Eds.), *Infertility around the globe: New thinking on childlessness, gender, and reproductive technologies* (pp. 33–51). Berkeley: University of California Press.

Sawicki, J. (1991). *Disciplining Foucault: Feminism, power, and the body.* New York: Routledge.

Schenker, J. G. (2005). Assisted reproduction practice: Religious perspectives. *Reproductive BioMedicine Online, 10*(3), 310–319.

Schover, L. R., Collins, R. L., Quigley, M. M., Blankstein, J., & Kanoti, G. (1991). Psychological follow-up of women evaluated as oocyte donors. *Human Reproduction, 6*, 1487–1491.

Schover, L. R., Rothmann, S. A., & Collins, R. L. (1992). The personality and motivation of semen donors: A comparison with oocyte donors. *Human Reproduction, 7*(4), 575–579.

Shakespeare, T. (1999). "Losing the plot"? Medical and activist discourses of contemporary genetics and disability. *Sociology of Health & Illness, 21*, 669–688.

Shanley, M. L. (2002). Collaboration and commodification in assisted procreation: Reflections on an open market and anonymous donation in human sperm and eggs. *Law & Society Review, 36*, 257–284.

Snow, R. C. (2008). Sex, gender, and vulnerability. *Global Public Health, 3*(S1), 58–74.

Spar, D. (2006). *The baby business: How money, science, and politics drive the commerce of conception.* Boston: Harvard Business School Press.

Spar, D. (2007). The egg trade: Making sense of the market for human oocytes. *New England Journal of Medicine, 356*, 1289–1291.

Spector, A. R. (2004). *Psychological issues and interventions with infertile patients.* In J. C. Chrisler (Ed.), *From menarche to menopause: The female body in feminist therapy* (pp. 91–105). New York: Haworth Press.

Stacey, J., & Biblarz, T. (2001). (How) does the sexual orientation of parents matter? *American Sociological Review, 66*, 159–183.

Stanton, A. L., Lobel, M., Sears, S., & DeLuca, R. (2002). Psychosocial aspects of selected issues in women's reproductive health: Current status and future directions. *Journal of Consulting and Clinical Psychology, 70*, 751–770.

Stern, J. E., Cramer, C. P., Garrod, A., & Green, R. M. (2001). Access to services at assisted reproductive technology clinics: A survey of policies and practices. *American Journal of Obstetrics and Gynecology, 184*, 591–597.

Stolwijk, A. M., Wetzels, A. M., & Braat, D. D. (2000). Cumulative probability of achieving an ongoing pregnancy after in-vitro fertilization and intracytoplasmic sperm injection according to a woman's age, subfertility diagnosis and primary or secondary subfertility. *Human Reproduction, 15*, 203–220.

Thompson, C. M. (2002). Fertile ground: Feminists theorize infertility. In M. C. Inhorn & F. van Balen (Eds.), *Infertility around the globe: New thinking on childlessness, gender, and reproductive technologies* (pp. 52–78). Berkeley: University of California Press.

Ulrich, M., & Weatherall, A. (2000). Motherhood and infertility: Viewing motherhood through the lens of infertility. *Feminism & Psychology, 10*, 323–336.

van Balen, F., & Inhorn, M. C. (2002). Interpreting infertility: A view from the social sciences. In M. C. Inhorn & F. van Balen (Eds.), *Infertility around the globe: New thinking on childlessness, gender, and reproductive technologies* (pp. 3–32). Berkeley: University of California Press.

Vayena, E., Rowe, P. J., & Griffin, P. D. (Eds.). (2002). *Current practices and controversies in assisted reproduction.* Geneva: World Health Organization. Retrieved from http://citeseerx.ist.psu.edu/viewdoc/download?doi=10.1.1.122.5172&rep=rep1&type=pdf.

Verhaak, C. M., Smeenk, J.M.J., Evers, A.W.M., Kremer, J.A.M., Kraaimaat, F. W., & Braat, D.D.M. (2007). Women's emotional adjustment to IVF: A systematic review of 25 years of research. *Human Reproduction Update, 13,* 27–36.

Wischmann, T. H. (2003). Psychogenic infertility—Myths and facts. *Journal of Assisted Reproduction and Genetics, 20,* 485–494.

Yassini, M., Khalili, M. A., & Hashemian, Z. (2005). The level of anxiety and depression among Iranian infertile couples undergoing in vitro fertilization or intra cytoplasmic sperm injection cycles. *Journal of Research in Medical Sciences, 10,* 358–362.

Zeiler, K. (2004). Reproductive autonomous choice—A cherished illusion? Reproductive autonomy examined in the context of preimplantation genetic diagnosis. *Medicine, Heath Care, and Philosophy, 7,* 175–183.

Chapter 9

Pregnancy and Prenatal Care: A Reproductive Justice Perspective

Lynda M. Sagrestano and Ruthbeth Finerman

Every pregnancy is unique, and the global lived experience of pregnancy is rich and diverse. Reproduction's multiple trajectories are shaped only in part by biology. Pregnancy is also situated in a context of environmental pressures; psychosocial forces; and individual, community, and state worldviews and practices. A reproductive justice perspective recognizes that the institutional and often patriarchal forces that dominate women's social and economic status, agency, and barriers to quality care differentially influence pregnancy and reproductive outcomes for women and their families around the world.

In this chapter we explore two orienting themes related to reproductive justice that are based on psychological and anthropological theory and research: (1) medicalization and the devaluing of authoritative knowledge, and (2) poverty and structural disparities that constrain agency and access to reproductive services. These themes are introduced and used to illuminate three topics: preconception health, pregnancy, and prenatal care.

THE MEDICALIZATION OF PREGNANCY AND
DEVALUATION OF AUTHORITATIVE KNOWLEDGE

Western and industrialized nations tend to adopt the medical model in place of culturally contextualized alternative healing systems. This community of practice gained legitimacy by downgrading, dismissing, and supplanting traditional yet nonauthoritative models of reproductive care (Cahill, 2001). Authoritative knowledge "is persuasive because it seems natural, reasonable, and consensually constructed" to be "in the best interest of all parties" (Jordan, 1997, p. 57). The medical model frames health as a physical state, and disease is attributed to the presence of some pathogen, biochemical imbalance, or neurophysiological abnormality. This model assumes that psychological and behavioral processes are independent of disease processes, a dualistic approach that separates mind and body (Engel, 1977).

The medicalization of pregnancy has its roots in the rise of modern medicine, which channeled science as a means to tame nature and transformed life cycle events (e.g., birth, menstruation, menopause, aging, death) into disease states that require medical management (Lock & Nguyen, 2010; Stone, 2009; Unnithan-Kumar, 2004). This yielded a biomedical interpretation of pregnancy as pathological or physically defective and in need of medical intervention (Barker, 1998; Cahill, 2001). Indeed, current medical conceptions frame pregnancy as a physical stressor to the body (Dunkel-Schetter, Gurung, Lobel, & Wadhwa, 2001). The introduction of new medical technologies and treatments in the context of medical facilities is justified by the medical establishment in the name of safety (Cahill, 2001). For example, in the United States, 44 percent of births took place out of hospitals in 1940, but only 1 percent did in 1969. Rates have remained steady at less than 1 percent over the last several decades (Centers for Disease Control and Prevention [CDC], 2010). Not coincidentally, the medicalization of pregnancy and childbirth in Western cultures coincided with the devaluation of midwifery, which effectively shifted the locus of control of women's bodies from women's sphere to the professional sphere of medicine, which, at the time, was men's sphere (Cahill, 2001; McCool & Simeone, 2002; Stone, 2009).

The United States is witnessing a movement toward a biopsychosocial perspective, which recognizes that physiological processes take place in the context of psychological and social systems (Engel, 1977, 1980; Taylor, 1990). Specifically, the biopsychosocial model recognizes that disease and illness arise from a complex interaction of factors, including biological (e.g., genetic predisposition), psychological (e.g., the experience of stress, lifestyle, personality, cognitions, emotions, motivations), and social (e.g., social support from family, friends, and community; societal hierarchies; cultural values) influences. From the biopsychosocial perspective, pregnancy can be regarded as a "normative developmental transition involving changes of many kinds" that takes place in the context of biological, psychological, and social processes (Dunkel-Schetter et al., 2001, p. 496). A biopsychosocial approach to understanding pregnancy and prenatal care is advantageous as it allows for a more humanistic, holistic approach that emphasizes health rather than illness and gives women more control and increased understanding of their role in self-care.

Although Western nations have largely relegated complementary and alternative reproductive care systems to the fringes of medical practice and subjected them to censure and state control, there has been some debate about the value of technological intervention in a healthy pregnancy (Davis-Floyd & Sargent, 1997). Since the 1930s the natural childbirth movement has sought to demedicalize low-risk pregnancy (Dick-Read, 1933), advocated for minimal intervention, and encouraged the inclusion of kin and more traditional attendants such as midwives and doulas (Davis-Floyd & Sargent, 1997). Systematic cross-cultural research on midwifery in Guatemala, Sweden, and the Netherlands further reinforced the value of traditional pregnancy care (Jordan, 1993). However, the movement's impact remains modest, and its influence varies between countries, communities, health care providers, and households, whereas the medical model's legitimacy and authoritative knowledge continues to expand and supplant traditional pregnancy care in both developed and developing nations (Cahill, 2001; Selin & Stone, 2009).

POVERTY, STRUCTURAL DISPARITIES, AND CONSTRAINED AGENCY

Agency here refers to the ability to exercise autonomous choice in selecting among health care models and providers. In the context of pregnancy and prenatal care, reproductive agency includes "ideas, actions, thinking and planning in the domain of human reproduction" in relation to health care seeking and decisions to decline care (Unnithan-Kumar, 2004, p. 6). Social variables (e.g., gender, ethnicity, class, age, education, religion) may influence health care preferences; however, larger structural forces (e.g., poverty, racism, patriarchy) often exert more powerful barriers to the effective exercise of agency (Dudgeon & Inhorn, 2009; Farmer, 1996).

In the United States, women and people of color are disproportionately represented among the poor, and women of color are more than twice as likely as White women to be living in poverty (U.S. Census Bureau, 2008). It is estimated that 30 percent of pregnant women are living in poverty, and another 20 percent are near poor (Braveman et al., 2010). Compared to all women of childbearing age, women who actually bear children have lower incomes (Braveman et al., 2010), which probably reflects insufficient access to birth control methods and abortion. Poverty during pregnancy is associated with a high incidence of serious hardship, such as inability to pay bills, homelessness, joblessness, and divorce (Braveman et al., 2010). These hardships inevitably lead to stress, which has been associated with adverse birth outcomes such as low birth weight and preterm birth (Dominguez, Dunkel-Schetter, Mancuso, Rini, & Hobel, 2005; Giscombe & Lobel, 2005).

The role of poverty in reproductive health is broad. Low income women have less access to informational and material resources that are instrumental in maintaining a healthy pregnancy, including adequate nutrition, safe housing, health care, transportation, and insurance. Recent estimates in the United States suggest that approximately 36 percent of Hispanics, 33 percent of Native Americans, 22 percent of African Americans, and 13 percent of European Americans are without health insurance (U.S. Census Bureau, 2008); although racial and ethnic minorities account for approximately one-third of the population, they account for approximately one-half of the uninsured (Kaiser Commission on Medicaid and the Uninsured, 2007). Indeed, among women of childbearing age in the United States, more than 20 percent are uninsured, and another 13.2 percent are insured through Medicaid (Sonfield, 2010). Although low-income pregnant women who are at 200 percent of poverty (e.g., those who make twice the federal poverty level) qualify for Medicaid (in most states), many who qualify never seek coverage due to lack of information about eligibility and other barriers to enrollment, or they enroll too late to receive adequate prenatal care (Sonfield, 2007, 2010). Lack of insurance is associated with later entry into prenatal care. Women uninsured throughout their entire pregnancy are the most likely to have untimely prenatal care, followed by those who become insured after the first trimester (Egerter, Braveman, & Marchi, 2002). Outside of the United States, few countries have an insurance-based system of health care. Most industrialized countries and many developing counties have universal access to health care (Uberti, 2011), although the health care infrastructure itself may limit access, especially among the poor.

It is difficult to quantify poverty, as the definition is relative within and between societies. The World Bank estimates that almost one-half the world's population lives on a daily income of less than US$2.50, and one-quarter live on US$1.25–1.45 per day (Shah, 2010). Women are disproportionately represented among the poor; some estimate that 70 percent of the world's poor are women (UNIFEM, 2010). Poverty can be a death sentence for pregnant women in the developing world. More than 500,000 women die each year due to reproductive complications, yet "not all women are at increased risk of adverse outcomes in pregnancy" (Farmer, 1996, p. 261). Pregnant women in the poorest countries currently face 300 times the risk of death faced by women in developed nations. Between 1990 and 2005 global maternal mortality declined only slightly, from 430 to 400 deaths per 100,000 live births. Yet, maternal death in the West averaged just 8 per 100,000 births (UNICEF, 2009). For example, health spending represents just 1 percent of Bangladesh's GDP, and more than 85 percent of pregnancies and births are managed at home, despite generations of colonial and postcolonial denigration and marginalization of midwifery care (Afsana & Rashid, 2009). Even so, the country recently invested in midwife training, and between 1997 and 2005 maternal mortality declined from 440 to 380 deaths per 100,000 live births (World Health Organization [WHO], 2006a).

Authoritative knowledge and constrained reproductive agency redefine reproductive justice in relation to women's experiences of preconception health, pregnancy, and prenatal care.

PRECONCEPTION HEALTH

Preconception health refers to a woman's health before conception, whether before a first or a subsequent pregnancy (Johnson et al., 2006). In an effort to optimize pregnancy outcomes, there has been increased focus on the preconception period as an opportunity for intervention. The American Academy of Pediatrics, the American College of Obstetricians and Gynecologists, and the U.S. CDC have each developed guidelines and recommendations for preconception care that include identifying and modifying biomedical, behavioral, and social risks and classifying care into the categories of physical assessment, risk screening, vaccinations, and counseling (Johnson et al., 2006; Lu, 2007). The specific CDC (2006) recommendations include (1) individual responsibility across the life span, (2) consumer awareness, (3) preventive visits, (4) interventions for identified risks, (5) interconception care, (6) prepregnancy checkup, (7) health insurance coverage for women with low incomes, (8) public health programs and strategies, (9) research, and (10) monitoring improvements. The strategic plan recommends that all individuals and couples have a reproductive life plan (i.e., a set of personal goals about having or not having children, a plan to achieve those goals), from menarche to menopause, even if they do not plan to have children. Initiatives should include addressing chronic disease, evaluating hereditary and environmental risk factors, modifying lifestyle (e.g., diet, exercise, drug and alcohol use, medication use), and preventing unintended pregnancy.

There are several health promotion measures that women of reproductive age can take to optimize pregnancy outcomes. For example, both overnutrition and chronic undernutrition can negatively impact pregnancy (Black et al., 2008; Chisholm & Coall, 2008; Núñez-de la Mora & Bentley, 2008; Pollard & Unwin, 2008). Balanced nutrition and exercise prevent hypertension and obesity-related complications. In the United States, rates of obesity among women of childbearing age are steadily increasing; almost one-quarter of women ages 18–44 were classified as obese in 2009 (March of Dimes, 2010), and prevalence was highest among the poor (Ogden, 2009). The World Health Organization projects that by 2015, more than 2 billion adults worldwide will be overweight and more than 700 million will be obese. Although rates are highest in the wealthiest nations, urban centers in low-income countries are also witnessing increased rates of obesity, or even the "double burden" of chronic undernutrition and obesity "existing side-by-side within the same country, the same community, and even within the same household" where the hunger and overindulgence are present in different people in the same household (WHO 2006b, Double Burden: A Serious Risk, para. 3). Although obesity is a growing concern, this issue masks more pervasive problems of hunger, malnutrition, and food insecurity (Food and Agriculture Organization [FAO] of the United Nations, 2010). For instance, more than 1 billion people were reported as undernourished in 2009 (FAO of the United Nations, 2009), and 60 percent of the world's chronically hungry are women (Food, Agriculture, and Natural Resources Policy Analysis Network, 2010).

A balance of specific micronutrients, both before and during pregnancy, protects women and their children. For example, adequate folic acid intake prevents neural tube defects (e.g., spina bifida). In the United States, it is estimated that, although high percentages of women know about folic acid and its impact on birth outcomes, only 11 percent know that it should be taken before a woman becomes pregnant. It is estimated that only 27 percent of women ages 18–24 take folic acid daily (including as a component of a multivitamin), as compared to 41 percent of women aged 25–34. These rates are fairly stable across racial and ethnic groups; however, those with no college education and those with lower household incomes are less likely than their peers to take folic acid (March of Dimes, 2008). Similarly, a diet rich in iron prevents anemia and lowers risks of preterm birth and low birth weight. Yet, the global prevalence of anemia is highest among nonpregnant women of reproductive age; nearly 470 million cases were reported in 2008. Rates are highest in low-income countries in Africa and southeast Asia (WHO & CDC, 2008).

Moreover, adequate iodine intake before and during pregnancy promotes fetal cognitive development (Glinoer, 2001). Although the risk for iodine deficiency disorders is low in the United States and decreasing worldwide, women and children remain at risk in low-income countries (WHO, 2004). Traditional diets tend to offer a balance of macro-and micronutrients including folic acid, iron, and iodine (Turner, Maes, Sweeney, & Armelagos, 2008), yet "women very often suffer hunger and famine more severely than men because of their socioeconomic and political subordination in many countries" (Counihan & Kaplan, 2004, p. 2). The risk for nutritional deprivation increases in low income households, especially in populations that face acculturation pressures and dietary change, including the promotion of processed foods and cheaper and calorie-dense, but less nutritious, fast foods (Kuhnlein & Receveur, 1996; Pollan, 2006).

The use of tobacco or exposure to tobacco smoke before and during pregnancy also increases the potential for perinatal complications (e.g., ectopic pregnancy, intrauterine growth retardation, low birth weight, prematurity; CDC, 2007b; da Veiga & Wilder, 2008; Dietz et al., 2010; Nordentoft et al., 1996; Roelands, Jamison, Lyerly, & James, 2009) that increase the risk for childhood intellectual, learning, behavioral, and attention disorders (Button, Thapar, & McGuffin, 2005; Wakschlag, Pickett, Cook, Benowitz, & Leventhal, 2002). Although smoking prevalence during pregnancy varies among subcategories of women in the United States, 10–40 percent of women smoke during pregnancy; the highest prevalence is found among low-income women and those with lower levels of education (Bailey, 2006; CDC, 2007b; Kahn, Certain, & Whitaker, 2002; Martin et al., 2008). Depending on demographic characteristics, 20–40 percent of female smokers are able to quit smoking during pregnancy, although most relapse within one year after birthing (McBride & Pirie, 1990; Mullen, Quinn, & Ershoff, 1990). Variables that predict smoking cessation during pregnancy include maternal age, education, marital status, prepregnancy level of nicotine addiction, alcohol use, partner smoking, and social support (Martin et al., 2008). There is limited global data on women's exposure to tobacco during pregnancy, but it is considered to be a leading risk, and smoking rates continue to grow in low-and middle-income countries (Nichter et al., 2010). For example, tobacco advertising campaigns are pervasive in Indonesia, and, although few women there use tobacco, 62 percent of men do so; thus women are exposed to others' second-hand smoke (Nichter et al., 2007).

Although many of these best practices have the potential to improve reproductive outcomes (e.g., taking folic acid to prevent neural tube defects; smoking cessation to reduce risk of low birth weight), the strategy is highly medicalized, and, from a biopsychosocial perspective, we question whether this one-size-fits-all model of preconception health has resonance with the experiences of women in industrialized nations. Goals such as creating a reproductive plan at menarche make limited sense in light of the fact that the average age of onset of puberty has decreased (Biro et al., 2010; Christensen et al., 2010). Similarly, modifying preconception health behavior, and eliminating exposure to environmental risk, may be unrealistic even for women who possess knowledge and access to key resources that would allow them to achieve such goals. Behavioral changes, for example, may require a level of support that is not available to all.

This medical model may have even less relevance in lesser developed countries. Understandings of preconception health often encompass culturally based values and opinions about issues such as family size, appropriate parentage, the timing and spacing of pregnancies, and traditional beliefs about health and the body. For example, low-income agrarian societies with less mechanized production systems tend to value large families, view children as a vital economic resource, and encourage shorter pregnancy intervals (Schultz, 1997). A number of cultures maintain the custom of arranged marriage, which reduces a woman's agency in mate selection. (See chapter 1, "The Choice before the Choice.") Similarly, China's "One Child Per Family" policy mandates age at marriage, contraception, and pregnancy timing, and there are rare opportunities for pregnancy spacing (Greenhalgh, 2008). Many traditional healing systems base preconception health on a humoral theory of the body's metabolic balance, which shapes nutrition and other preventive behaviors (de Boer & Lamxay, 2009). For example, in Sri Lanka a humorally balanced diet is thought to increase blood potency which, in turn, enhances fertility and reproductive success (McGilvray, 1994). Culturally based models of preconception health promotion may also be constrained by social-justice considerations (e.g., status of women, household wealth and resources, access to services; Farmer, 1996).

PREGNANCY

Although pregnancy is a physical state, there are diverse worldviews and responses to it. These views can be shaped by whether a pregnancy is planned and/or welcomed, or whether it is unplanned and/or unwanted. In the United States, almost one-half of all pregnancies (47%) are unplanned. Among women under the age of 20, more than 80 percent are unplanned. This tapers off with age, but is higher among unmarried women (72% among unmarried women aged 15–44). Among women living at less than 200 percent of poverty (e.g., twice the federal poverty level), more than one-half of pregnancies are unplanned. There is also racial/ethnic variability in unplanned pregnancy in the United States; non-Hispanic Blacks report the highest rate of unplanned pregnancy (69%), followed by Hispanics (54%), and non-Hispanic Whites (40%; Finer & Henshaw, 2006). In countries with low access to birth control, virtually all pregnancies are unplanned. The very language of pregnancy planning reflects a Western, medicalized view that focuses on population control and ignores sexual health, maternal well-being, and reproductive rights (Petchesky, 2000).

In the United States, research on attitudes toward pregnancy has focused on positive responses (e.g., feeling confident, lucky, excited, happy, special, pleased, healthy), distress (e.g., feeling upset or in conflict), fear (e.g., afraid, panicky), and concern. The research indicates that women with positive attitudes initiate prenatal care earlier (Daniels, Noe, & Mayberry, 2006) and report less stress, more support from the baby's father, and better health behaviors (e.g., less substance use; Blake, Kiely, Gard, El-Mohandes, & El-Khorazaty, 2007; Hellerstedt et al., 1998). By contrast, negative attitudes are associated with higher rates of emotional problems during pregnancy, stress, perinatal death, and postpartum complications (Sable & Wilkinson, 2000).

Traditional cultures uniformly regard pregnancy as a natural experience and a significant rite of passage (Davis-Floyd & Sargent, 1997). Beliefs about conception vary. For instance, women in Andean Ecuador at one time held both ovist and homunculist views: girls were thought to be produced by the mother, and boys implanted into a womb by the father. The womb protected and nurtured the fetus until birth (Belote & Belote, 1984). Famed early ethnographer Bronislaw Malinowski (1916) reported Trobriand Island claims that babies are reincarnated maternal ancestors whose spirits entered the womb in dreams or as women bathe. Although such explanatory models may lack scientific merit, they are not obsolete; rather, they validate conception as both normal and meaningful, and they grant women biological and psychosocial ownership of their pregnancy.

Although traditional models treat pregnancy as normal, though not without risk, the biomedical worldview treats it as an inherently dangerous medical condition, occasionally characterized as parasitic in nature (e.g., Fiorini, 1969; Meilaender, 1998). The biomedical model is also distinct in that it partitions pregnancy into three separate stages or trimesters. Moreover, each phase features unique risks, which mandate intensive technological intervention under the care of certified providers (Davis-Floyd & Sargent, 1997; Jordan, 1997). Although the biomedical model predominates in much of the industrialized world, other countries are adopting this perspective, along with deference to sanctioned communities of practice. For instance, Harvey and Buckley (2009) reported that control over pregnancy in China's post-Mao period was wrested from the home and reassigned to the state's hospitals as part of the Mandate for Modernity. Women, particularly in lower income rural areas, now wait for hours and often all day for prenatal visits, which are promoted as more scientific and modern, and receive little or no information about their treatment. In India, hospitalization and elective cesareans have become the "delivery of choice" for many young women because, seen through a Western lens, the practice appears to be "modern" and progressive (Donner, 2004, p. 125).

Most women associate pregnancy with indicators such as the delay or loss of menses, breast tenderness, and morning sickness; however, symptoms are highly variable (Gadsby, Barnie-Adshead, & Jagger, 1993). Research shows that women who are trying to get pregnant tend to recognize these signs sooner than do women who do not intend to become pregnant. Early detection allows women to begin sooner to modify behaviors that can optimize outcomes, such as smoking cessation, avoiding alcohol, and initiating prenatal care (Daniels et al., 2006). Decisions regarding unintended pregnancies can also be addressed earlier.

Traditional cultures use a variety of techniques to detect pregnancy (e.g., signs in body secretions). For instance, Quichua women in Ecuador study a woman's urine and spittle for evidence of cloudiness, discoloration, and solids that denote pregnancy (Finerman, 1982). Pregnancy and fetal gender were detected in Pharaonic Egypt if grain germinated after exposure to a woman's urine; sprouted wheat indicated a boy, and spouted spelt indicated a girl (Ghalioungui, Khalil, & Ammar, 1963). Reliable or not, such customs empower women and give them confidence to initiate self-care and prenatal planning.

Home pregnancy tests are an increasingly popular tool to enhance women's agency; the kits have even been characterized as a "feminist technology" (Layne, 2009, p. 61). However, home tests pose reliability dilemmas: Accuracy averages 65–87 percent, and it can be as low as 8 percent for some brands (Tomlinson & Ellis, 2008). False negatives result if tests are attempted before levels of human chorionic gonadotropin (hCG) hormone are sufficient to detect; this can take up to three weeks after fertilization. Women taking fertility drugs often experience false positive test results. Uncertainty about test results constrains agency, as women must turn to biomedical testing to confirm a diagnosis, thus normalizing reproductive intervention (Browner & Press, 1995).

For women in rural areas, low-income populations, and less industrialized nations, access to home testing poses a greater concern. Potential barriers include limited retailers, transportation to vendors, and functional literacy to read and follow directions. Expense is an additional burden; prices range from $8.00 to $20.00 in the United States, but relative costs are higher in other countries. For example, the only home test currently available in India (Pregcolor) costs roughly 45 rupees or INR (approx. US$1). India has, by some measures, significantly reduced poverty in recent decades, but more than 40 percent of its citizens still fall below the international poverty line, and more than 77 percent live on INR 20 per day, which makes test kits unaffordable for many women (Dugal, 2004; Greenhalgh, 1987). Ironically, Kenya provides free pregnancy tests through its National School Health Policy 2009, but its Ministry of Education uses the results to expel pregnant students, and schools face no penalty if they refuse readmission post pregnancy (http://ipsnews.net/africa/nota.asp?idnews=34137).

Although most pregnancies are healthy, there is the potential for complications, which are shaped by psychosocial forces as well as individual risk factors such as age and family history. Some health threats are specific to pregnancy, such as gestational diabetes mellitus (GDM) and pregnancy-induced hypertension (i.e., toxemia, preeclampsia, eclampsia), both of which strongly correlate with stress and socioeconomic disparity (Beard et al., 2009; Hayman, 2009; Hunsberger, 2010; Zwart et al., 2011). Rates of GDM have increased 8–20 percent in the last two decades, and are highest in developing countries and among U.S. ethnic minorities (Dabelea et al., 2005; Ferrara, 2007; Sahin, 2003). Similarly, high blood pressure affects 6–8 percent of all US pregnancies, and it is especially prevalent in impoverished nations. The prevalence of maternal risk peaks in countries where women have low social value and experience nutrition deficits, high stress, early marriage, and short pregnancy intervals (Conde-Agudelo, Rosas-Bermúdez, & Kafury-Goeta, 2007; Fantahun, Berhane, Wall, Byass, & Högberg, 2007; Mohamed, Kishk, Shokeir, & Kassem, 2006; Norton, 2005).

An increasing body of evidence indicates that psychosocial factors, such as prenatal maternal stress, anxiety, depression, and social support, have an impact on birth outcomes (Dunkel-Schetter et al., 2001). Prenatal maternal stress, in particular, has shown a consistent pattern of association with low birthweight, and a less consistent association with gestational age and preterm delivery (Hobel, Dunkel-Schetter, Roesch, Castro, & Arora, 1999; Rondo et al., 2003; Wadhwa, Sandman, Porto, Dunkel-Schetter, & Garite, 1993). The timing and chronicity of stressors are also important considerations in the effects of stress on pregnancy outcomes. The first and third trimesters are often regarded as the most physically and psychologically stressful (Beck et al., 1980). The question of whether there is a particular time frame when prenatal stress increases the risk of adverse birth outcomes has therefore been a topic of speculation; recent evidence suggests that chronic stress may be more detrimental than specific episodes of high stress at critical periods (Glynn, Wadhwa, Dunkel-Schetter, Chicz-DeMet, & Sandman, 2001).

Another consideration is the interaction of stress with demographic variables. For example, single pregnant women tend to experience more stressful life events during pregnancy than married women do (MacDonald, Peacock, & Anderson, 1992). And younger, poor, and ethnic minority women tend to experience more stress during pregnancy than others do (DaCosta, Larouche, Dritsa, & Brender, 1999). Specifically, women with fewer resources report more stress during pregnancy, which is associated with shorter gestation (Rini, Dunkel-Schetter, Wadhwa, & Sandman, 1999). Higher levels of stress are associated with lower birth weight and shorter gestation in African American and Latina women in the United States (Giscombe & Lobel, 2005).

Prenatal maternal depression has not been researched as extensively as stress as a factor in birth outcomes (Chung, Lao, Yip, Chiu, & Lee, 2001), as the study of depression and pregnancy has typically focused on postpartum rather than prepartum depression. However, evidence suggests that nearly one-half of postpartum depressed women were also depressed during pregnancy, and onset of depression at each of these times may in fact be associated with different psychosocial variables (Gotlib, Whiffen, Mount, Miline, & Cordy, 1989). Maternal depression has been associated with decreased social support, adverse health behaviors, poor maternal weight gain, and obstetric complications, each of which has been linked to negative birth outcomes (Chung et al., 2001; Marcus, Flynn, Blow, & Barry, 2003). Demographic factors (e.g., low socioeconomic status, being single, having young children) may place women at higher risk for developing prepartum depression (Cunningham & Zayas, 2002; Marcus et al., 2003; Ritter, Hobfoll, Lavin, Cameron, & Hulsizer, 2000). For example, rates of depression among low-income women may be twice as high as among middle-income women (Hobfoll, Ritter, Lavin, Hulsizer, & Cameron, 1995).

In general, prenatal maternal social support appears to have a positive effect on birth outcomes, and it has been found to mediate the effects of high levels of stress, anxiety, and depression. Evidence suggests that social support serves not only as a buffer, but also has a direct or main positive effect on birth outcomes (Feldman, Dunkel-Schetter, Sandman, & Wadhwa, 2000).

The relation between stress and social support, however, is complex. Women with high chronic stress tend to receive less social support (Dunkel-Schetter, 1998). The type and amount of available social support may be influenced by a woman's marital status, ethnicity, and whether she is a first-generation immigrant; there also may be cultural differences in the role of support during pregnancy from different members of the social network (Dunkel-Schetter, Sagrestano, Feldman, & Killingsworth, 1996; Sagrestano, Feldman, Rini, Woo, & Dunkel-Schetter, 1999). In addition, enmeshed family relationships and negative interactions with one's spouse or partner may be a source of stress for some pregnant women (Arizmendi & Affonso, 1987; Norbeck & Anderson, 1989; Ramsey, Abell, & Baker, 1986); therefore, not all relationships provide positive support.

One of the clearest examples of stress is domestic violence during pregnancy. Recent studies have documented that 4–37 percent of women in the United States experience acts of violence during the perinatal period (Martin, Mackie, Kupper, Buescher, & Moracco, 2001; Torres et al., 2000). Some researchers have noted that a significant number of women report that partners who had not previously used violence against them began to use violence during pregnancy or soon after (Gielen, O'Campo, Faden, Kass, & Xue, 1994; Jasinski & Kantor, 2001), whereas others have noted that pregnancy can be a respite from violence for some women (Campbell, Oliver, & Bullock, 1998). Physical assault during pregnancy is cause for special concern because it poses a threat to the health of both the pregnant woman and the fetus. For the woman, violence during pregnancy may be related to both physical and mental health outcomes (Cokkinides & Coker, 1998; Parker, McFarlane, & Soeken, 1994). In addition, there is preliminary evidence that women abused during pregnancy are more at risk than nonpregnant abused women for being murdered by their partner (Campbell, Soeken, McFarlane, & Parker, 1998). Results regarding the fetus have been mixed, but indicate that violence and stress during pregnancy may be associated with lower birth weight (Campbell et al., 1999; Lipsky, Holt, Easterling, & Critchlow, 2003).

Sexually transmitted infections pose a further risk during pregnancy. More than 25 diseases are transmitted through sexual contact, and approximately 15 million cases are reported annually in the United States; approximately one-half occur among young people ages 15–24. Several STIs can be passed to an infant before, during, and after pregnancy, and some STIs can cause pregnancy complications (CDC, 2009). For example, with treatment, the risk for transmission of HIV from mother to infant can be reduced from 25 percent to 2 percent (Cooper et al., 2002), yet the CDC (2007a) estimated that 25 percent of women infected with HIV are not aware of their status, which puts them at high risk of transmitting HIV to their infants if they become pregnant. Of course, many women, especially those living in poor and less developed nations that lack adequate health care infrastructure, do not receive HIV treatment during pregnancy. In 2005 only about 15 percent of HIV+ pregnant women worldwide received care for the prevention of mother-to-child transmission, but by 2009 global services reached more than one-half of all cases, despite treatment supply bottlenecks and insufficient funding, infrastructure, and trained staff. Even so, just 26 percent of pregnant women in low-and middle-income countries were actually tested for HIV in 2009, and more than 1,000 infants per day continue to contract HIV during pregnancy, at delivery, or through breastmilk (WHO & UNICEF, 2010).

Preventive care and medical intervention offer a crucial advantage for high risk pregnancy, and there have been major advances in the treatment of many complications. For example, the U.S. maternal mortality rate (MMR) declined by 74 percent in the last century, from 800 deaths per 100,000 live births in 1920 to 100 deaths per 100,000 live births by 1950, as a result of public health initiatives (e.g., sanitation campaigns) and the introduction of antibiotics to prevent and treat infections during pregnancy (Loudon, 1991; Omran, 1977). Even so, a 2010 global report revealed that U.S. MMR increased by 28 percent in the last decade, 45th in world maternal survival. Less developed nations fare far worse. For example, the MMR for Malawi and Mozambique is 1,100 per 100,000 live births; lifetime risk of maternal death in Sierra Leone is 1 in 8 (Hogan et al., 2010). Moreover, primary prevention has not kept pace with treatment. For instance, toxemia's precise cause remains a mystery, there is no effective prevention (Maynard & Thadhani, 2009; Sahin, 2003), and treatment cannot substitute for effective primary prevention. For instance, neural tube defects, such as spina bifida and anencephaly, can be prevented with adequate prenatal intake of folic acid, but the complications themselves cannot be reversed.

Moreover, services to manage complications are not universally accessible, and, when available in low income countries, the quality of care is often inferior (Burgard, 2004; Obermeyer, 2003; Wheatley, Kelley, Peacock, &

Peacock, 2008). Sesia (1997) reported that, in Oaxaca, which had double Mexico's national MMR at the time of the study, interventions failed to increase referrals for complications. And, if women were directed to treatment, Oaxaca's rural regions had extremely limited and poorly prepared facilities to handle high-risk pregnancies. Globally, MMR remains high despite decades of intervention (http://www.whiteribbonalliance.org/ Resources/Documents/WRA%20Global%20Maternal%20Mortality%20 Fact%20Sheet%2020092.pdf). Maternal-care access and quality are inversely correlated with women's social status; huge disparities exist between the highest and lowest wealth quintiles (Amery, 2009), and global inequality in maternal care is "ubiquitous" (Victora et al., 2010, p. 253).

At least some indicators of risk suffer from faulty data. Even so, authoritative knowledge has influenced the public discourse and spurred recrimination and even legal action. For example, research in the United States pointed to a crack baby epidemic in the 1980s, which triggered the prosecution of hundreds of mothers—mostly poor and ethnic minorities—on charges of child abuse and neglect. Although cocaine has negative impacts on growth and development (Espy, Francis, & Riese, 2000; Espy, Kauffman, & Glisky, 1999), this syndrome is no longer recognized as evidence based (Chavkin, 2001). Yet it stigmatized women, and it retains credence as conventional wisdom. Similarly, sociopolitical agendas shaped the dialogue on prenatal drug use to target low-income and minority users (Gregory, 2010).

Tradition can also negatively impact health care seeking. For instance, women in Mozambique delay prenatal care, even in the face of complications, in order to hide their condition from harmful supernatural human and spirit forces. Instead, they mobilize limited prenatal care resources outside the formal clinic setting (Chapman, 2003). Similarly, researchers (e.g., Donner, 2004) have cautioned against excessive nostalgia for pregnancy customs, and noted that poor young women in India increasingly prefer hospital care as safer and more effective than traditional practices.

PRENATAL CARE

Biomedical and traditional healing systems manage pregnancy in different ways and with the participation of different types of caregivers. Women's choice of provider is guided by which prenatal care model (or models) they, their partners, their families, and the state recognize as legitimate. Of course, each model also features an idealized and often unrealistic vision of pregnancy (Johnson, 2010; Rogers, 1992).

Traditional Prenatal Care

Nearly all societies rely on autonomous kin-based networks for prenatal care and, if greater expertise is needed, traditional birth attendants such as midwives. In some (but not all) societies, fathers play an active part in prenatal care, and may even experience culturally contextualized sympathetic pregnancy or "couvade," which validates their paternal role (Han, 2009; Ivry, 2010 Munroe, Munroe, & Whiting, 1973; Reed, 2005).

The cultural view of pregnancy as normal informs a restrained approach to care. Practices center on diet, exercise, and spiritual support. To a large extent, traditional prenatal care emphasizes women's entitlement to choices that promote a healthy pregnancy: women can eat better, rest and relax more, and receive greater social and spiritual support when they are pregnant.

In most societies, women enjoy larger than normal meals and higher quality foods once they become pregnant (e.g., Donner, 2004). An array of traditional food supplements and taboos are recommended to protect the mother and fetus (Dove, 2010; Ivry, 2010 Nichter & Nichter, 1983; Thornton, Kieffer, & Salbarria-Pena, 2006), and women are usually encouraged to satisfy cravings (Ayres, 1967; Meyer-Rochow, 2009; Obeyesekere, 1963). Pica, a craving for nonfoods, may also be accepted as normative. For example, several African populations advise geophagy: eating dirt or clay (Henry & Kwong, 2003; Hunter, 1993). This custom endures among some African Americans, who may also crave laundry starch (Corbett, Ryan, & Weinrich, 2003; Vermeer & Frate, 1975). Although the practice causes consternation among biomedical providers, research indicates that it generally poses no medical risk and may provide relief from morning sickness and increased calcium intake (Callahan, 2003; Corbett et al., 2003; Wiley & Katz, 1998). Often, diet is moderated to promote humoral balance (Chang, 1974; Finerman, 1984, 1987; Liamputtong, 2009; Martin, 2001). Some dietary conventions are symbolic, such as shunning twinned or clustered fruits to forestall multiple pregnancy, declining strawberries to avoid birthmarks, refusing monkey meat so the baby will not be hairy, and eschewing monkfish to preclude ugly babies (Ayres, 1967; Henderson & Henderson, 1982; Morsy, 1982). A richer diet clearly improves prenatal health, especially in societies where women suffer extreme neglect and chronic nutritional deprivation. Other food customs encourage women's engagement in their pregnancy and grant a greater sense of control over the outcome.

Most traditional societies release pregnant women from heavy workloads and carrying large burdens (Liamputtong, 2009), which allows them to conserve energy and promotes social support. Still, there are exceptions to this trend. For instance, pregnant women in Sierra Leone continue to perform chores as a show of strength (Kyomuhendo, 2009), a practice that could be interpreted as both empowering and repressive. Some customs have symbolic associations, such as avoiding proximity to knives or sharp tools thought to injure the fetus (Lefèber &Voorhoeve, 1998; Martin, 2001). Pregnant women in Andean Ecuador limit use of sewing machines so that the motion does not waken a gestating baby too soon, and they protect the body's humoral balance from heat (e.g., no standing in the sun without a hat) and cold (e.g., no bathing in streams; Finerman, 1984). Most cultures allow women to refuse their partner's sexual demands as this, too, may injure the fetus (Kyomuhendo, 2009). Traditional populations also claim to impose severe censure on men who subject a pregnant woman to emotional or physical abuse that risks miscarriage (Mattson & Rodriguez, 1999; Morsy, 1982; Stenson, Sidenvall, & Heimer, 2005). Such socially constructed and shared conventions may grant women greater legitimacy to demand respectful treatment.

Spiritual traditions vary even more than does advice on diet and comportment, but generally center on encouraging emotional well-being and protecting the mother and fetus from harmful supernatural forces (e.g., Donner, 2004). For instance, pregnant Navajo women attend a Blessingway Ceremony to promote harmony; some compare the ritual to a prenatal checkup (Begay, 2009). Thai women avoid funerals, but receive amulets that protect them and permit freedom of movement. Both Navajo and Thai women wait to purchase material items, such as baby clothes, to avoid "tempting fate" (Begay, 2009, p. 247; Liamputtong, 2009), but receive social and spiritual support from their kin and community. The prevalence and richness of sacred customs highlights both the life-changing nature of reproduction and concern for the recognized risk of morbidity and mortality.

Adverse symptoms, such as nausea and pain, receive judicious care (e.g., herbal teas, poultices, aromatic baths; de Boer & Lamxay, 2009; Finerman, 1984; Henderson & Henderson, 1982), massage (Burk, Wieser, & Keegan, 1995; Sesia, 1997), rest, repositioning (Beim, Fullerton, Palinkas, & Anders, 1995; Donner, 2004), and emotional encouragement (Davis-Floyd & Sargent, 1997; Jordan, 1993). All of these practices have been shown to be beneficial by research, even for cases of breech position (Field, Diego, Hernandez-Reif, Deeds, & Figereido, 2009; Lefèber & Voorhoeve, 1997). However, it is crucial not to idealize traditional prenatal care practices; none are sufficient to manage severe complications such as hemorrhage, placenta previa, or pregnancy-induced toxemia.

Western Prenatal Care

The biomedical model stresses risk and impending complications across each trimester. As a result, prenatal care, particularly in the United States, includes more frequent, invasive, and technologically driven interventions, which are supervised by a community of practice that controls authoritative knowledge and legitimacy of treatment (Browner & Press, 1995; Jordan, 1997). Moreover, the transition from tradition to biomedicine shifts from expanded agency with everything pregnant women *can* do to confounded agency with all the things they *should* do (e.g., listen to their doctor, take prenatal vitamins) and especially what they should *not* do (e.g., no gardening, pets, dental work, spa treatments, hot tubs, allergy or other medications, caffeine, fish, lunch meat, alcohol, tobacco, excessive exercise).

Prenatal appointments feature a battery of tests to detect abnormalities, which promotes a "culture of fear" (Selin & Stone, 2009, p. xiv). Care is also costly and contributes to a system of "stratified reproduction" (Rapp, 2001). A blood test screens for Rh incompatibility, sexually transmitted infections, anemia, toxoplasmosis, vulnerability to rubella, and hereditary risks (e.g., cystic fibrosis, sickle-cell anemia, thalassemia, Tay-Sachs). A urine sample screens for bladder or kidney infection, diabetes, and preeclampsia. One of seven types of ultrasound may indicate ectopic pregnancy, congenital or structural abnormalities, multiple pregnancy, or amniotic fluid problems. Women also undergo a comprehensive medical history, breast and cervical examination, and biometric measures (e.g., weight, blood pressure). Finally, the patient may be cautioned about behavior, diet, exercise, and weight control. Results from undisclosed prenatal drug screenings have been used in the United States to prosecute mothers, nearly all of them low-income and minority. States continue to criminalize prenatal drug use, but may refer women to treatment rather than prison. Even so, few addiction programs treat pregnant patients (Gregory, 2010; Steverson & Rieckmann, 2009).

In the first trimester, pregnant women in the United States—and increasingly in other countries—may undergo chorionic villus sampling and a first trimester screen to identify risk for chromosomal abnormalities. Results have high false positive rates, but may guide decisions to abort a pregnancy in the early stages (Rapp, 2001).

The second trimester features even more routine and elective procedures, including the maternal serum alpha-fetoprotein, amniocentesis, cordocentesis or percutaneous umbilical cord sampling (PUBS), quad screening, and triple screen tests. All concentrate on exposing possible genetic disorders and structural abnormalities, though one PUBS can also detect infections that may or may not be treatable. Most tests were originally intended only for women at elevated risk (e.g., family history, age 40 or older), but are increasingly recommended to younger mothers and anyone worried about birth defects. All can be stressful, some are painful, and, although the results are reified, many have false positive or false negative errors, which, again, reduce women's agency (Rapp, 2001).

Routine tests in the third trimester check for gestational diabetes (the glucose challenge, possibly followed by a glucose tolerance test) and for an infection that may transmit from mother to infant during birthing (Group B Strep). Further measures, such as a biophysical profile and/or fetal non-stress test, are administered if there are questions about fetal health.

The transformation of prenatal care from a focus on wellness to an obsession with genetic imperfection and diseased futures has been dubbed "genomania" (Hubbard, 1995, p. 20; Woliver, 2002, p. 48). As few genetic conditions can be treated or reversed, women's agency is reduced to the choice to continue or terminate pregnancy (Rapp, 1999). Genetic testing has redefined normality (Wolbring, 2001; Woliver, 2002), including gender: Ultrasound has been embraced as the weapon of choice for female infanticide via sex-selective abortion, especially in south and southeast Asia, but also in the United States and elsewhere in the world (Bechtold & Graves, 2010, Heyd, 2009; Miller, 1993; see also chapter 11, "Female Feticide and Infanticide"). Moreover, such resources are available only to a limited few who live in industrialized nations and possess insurance to cover these costly services. These diverse models of pregnancy and prenatal care, and the disparities that have engendered stratified reproduction, can only be reconciled through a social justice framework.

CONCLUSION

Two key themes shape the experience of pregnancy and prenatal care globally. Medicalized authoritative knowledge has displaced traditional customs and practices in industrialized and many developing nations, and left women with few alternatives but to surrender agency to patriarchal and hegemonic systems of practice. At the same time, structural forces have placed poor and underserved women at greater risk for complications and decreased access to effective and culturally appropriate services. Such risks are virtually insurmountable for the world's most vulnerable populations, such as lower caste, uninsured, incarcerated, homeless, and undocumented women.

These challenges are evident at all phases of reproduction, and they cut across time and space, defying conventional distinctions of class and ethnicity. One barrier to understanding and addressing agency, vulnerability, and disparity is the lack of specificity and the quality of data across a range of variables, including race, religious affiliation, and socioeconomic status/poverty, and how researchers define and operationalize health indicators (e.g., stress, violence, well-being). These factors are inconsistently conceptualized and difficult to measure within the United States, and they are even less valid for cross-cultural application. As a result, one-size-fits-all solutions remain illusive.

Despite these challenges, it is possible for women to enjoy the benefits of biomedical advances and still assert individual agency. Studies have shown that women amass both confidence and authoritative knowledge during their first pregnancy and begin to rely on their own experience for subsequent pregnancies (Browner & Abel, 1998). The natural childbirth movement has gained credence among physicians and communities, and technology holds the promise of furthering women's agency by providing a global network of social support and information. However, the uneven quality and sheer volume of advice available online has thus far prevented the technology from fulfilling its full potential to advance reproductive justice.

Reproductive justice demands more than mere funding of biomedical care. Women must be empowered to choose among multiple explanatory health care models and service providers. They also require access to multiple levels of authoritative knowledge and resources (e.g., insurance coverage for complementary and alternative providers). Moreover, all women should live in an environment that provides genuine access to alternative choices. Most important, women's ability to act as their own agent requires legal, economic, educational, and psychosocial support. All of this hinges on successfully addressing the value of women and reducing global social and economic disparities. Only then is reproductive justice possible.

REFERENCES

Afsana, K., & Rashid, S. (2009). Constructions of birth in Bangladesh. In H. Selin & P. Stone (Eds.), *Childbirth across cultures* (pp. 55–69). Dordrecht, the Netherlands: Springer.

Amery, J. (2009). Safe motherhood case studies: Learning from south Asia. *Journal of Health, Population, and Nutrition, 27,* 87–88.

Arizmendi, T. G., & Affonso, D. D. (1987). Stressful events related to pregnancy and postpartum. *Journal of Psychosomatic Research, 31,* 743–756.

Ayres, B. (1967). Pregnancy magic: A study of food taboos and sex avoidances. In C. Ford (Ed.), *Cross-cultural approaches* (pp. 111–125). New Haven, CT: Yale University, Human Relations Area Files.

Bailey, B. A. (2006). Factors predicting pregnancy smoking in southern Appalachia. *American Journal of Health Behavior, 30,* 413–421.

Barker, K. K. (1998). A ship upon a stormy sea: The medicalization of pregnancy. *Social Science and Medicine, 47,* 1067–1076.

Beard, J. R., Lincoln, D., Donoghue, D., Taylor, D., Summerhayes, R., Dunn, T. M., . . . Morgan, G. (2009). Socioeconomic and maternal determinants of small-for-gestational age births: Patterns of increasing disparity. *Acta Obstetricia et Gynocologica Scandinavica, 88,* 575–583.

Bechtold, B., & Graves, D. (2010). The ties that bind: Infanticide, gender, and society. *History Compass, 8,* 704–717.

Beck, N., Siegel, L., Davidson, W., Kormeier, J., Breitenstein, A., & Hall, D. (1980). Prediction of pregnancy outcome: Maternal preparation, anxiety, and attitudinal sets. *Journal of Psychosomatic Research, 24,* 343–351.

Begay, C. (2009). Navajo birth: A bridge between the past and the future. In H. Selin & P. Stone (Eds.), *Childbirth across cultures* (pp. 245–254). Dordrecht, the Netherlands: Springer.

Beim, K., Fullerton, J., Palinkas, L., & Anders, B. (1995). Conceptions of prenatal care among Somali women in San Diego. *Journal of Nurse-Midwifery, 40,* 376–381.

Belote, J., & Belote, L. (1984). Suffer the little children: Death, autonomy, and responsibility in a changing "low technology" environment. *Science, Technology, & Human Values, 9,* 35–48.

Biro, F. M., Galvez, M. P., Greenspan, L. C., Succop, P. A., Vangeepuram, N., Pinney, S. M., . . . Wolff, M. S. (2010). Pubertal assessment method and baseline characteristics in a mixed longitudinal study of girls. *Pediatrics, 126,* 1–8.

Black, R. E., Allen, L. H., Bhutta, Z. A., Caulfield, L. E., de Onis, M., Ezzati, M., . . . Rivera, J. (2008). Maternal and child undernutrition: Global and regional exposures and health consequences. *Lancet, 371,* 243–260.

Blake, S. M., Kiely, M., Gard, C. C., El-Mohandes, A.A.E., & El-Khorazaty, M. N. (2007). Pregnancy intentions and happiness among pregnant Black women at high risk for adverse infant health outcomes. *Perspectives on Sexual and Reproductive Health, 39,* 194–205.

Braveman, P., Marchi, K., Egertr, S., Kim, S., Metzler, M., Stancil, T., & Libet, M. (2010). Poverty, near-poverty, and hardship around the time of pregnancy. *Maternal Child Health Journal, 14,* 20–35.

Browner, C., & Abel, E. (1998). Selective compliance with biomedical authority and the uses of experiential knowledge. In M. Lock & P. Kaufert (Eds.), *Pragmatic women and body politics* (pp. 310–326). Cambridge: Cambridge University Press.

Browner, C., & Press, N. (1995). The normalization of prenatal diagnostic screening. In F. Ginsburg & R. Rapp (Eds.), *Conceiving the new world order: The global politics of reproduction* (pp. 307–322). Berkeley: University of California.

Burgard, S. (2004). Race and pregnancy-related care in Brazil and South Africa. *Social Science and Medicine, 59,* 1127–1146.

Burk, M., Wieser, P., & Keegan, L. (1995). Cultural beliefs and health behaviors of pregnant women. *Advances in Nursing Science, 17,* 37–52.

Button, T. M., Thapar, A., & McGuffin, P. (2005). Relationship between antisocial behaviour, attention-deficit hyperactivity disorder, and maternal prenatal smoking. *British Journal of Psychiatry, 187,* 155–160.

Cahill, H. A. (2001). Male appropriation and medicalization of childbirth: An historical analysis. *Journal of Advanced Nursing, 33,* 334–342.

Callahan, G. (2003). Eating dirt. *Emerging Infectious Diseases, 9,* 1016–1021.

Campbell, J. C., Oliver, C. E., & Bullock, L.F.C. (1998). The dynamics of battering during pregnancy: Women's explanations of why. In J. C. Campbell (Ed.), *Empowering survivors of abuse: Health care for battered women and their children* (pp. 81–89). Thousand Oaks, CA: Sage.

Campbell, J. C., Soeken, K., McFarlane, J., & Parker, B. (1998). Risk factors of femicide among pregnant and nonpregnant battered women. In J. C. Campbell (Ed.), *Empowering survivors of abuse: Health care for battered women and their children* (pp. 90–97). Thousand Oaks, CA: Sage.

Campbell, J. C., Torres, S., Ryan, J., King, C., Campbell, D. W., Stallings, R. Y., & Fuchs, S. C. (1999). Physical and nonphysical partner abuse and other risk factors for low birth weight among full term and preterm babies. *American Journal of Epidemiology, 150,* 714–726.

Centers for Disease Control and Prevention. (2006). Recommendations to improve preconception health and health care—United States: A report of the CDC/ ATSDR Preconception Care Work Group and the Select Panel on Preconception Care. *Morbidity and Mortality Weekly Report, 55* (No. RR-6).

Centers for Disease Control and Prevention. (2007a). *HIV/AIDS fact sheet: Mother-to-child (perinatal) HIV transmission and prevention.* Retrieved from http://www.cdc.gov/hiv/topics/perinatal/resources/factsheets/pdf/perinatal.pdf.

Centers for Disease Control and Prevention. (2007b). *Preventing smoking and exposure to secondhand smoke before, during, and after pregnancy.* Retrieved from http://www.cdc.gov/nccdphp/publications/factsheets/prevention/pdf/ smoking.pdf.

Centers for Disease Control and Prevention. (2009, November). *Sexually transmitted disease surveillance, 2008.* Atlanta, GA: U.S. Department of Health and Human Services.

Centers for Disease Control and Prevention. (2010). *Behavioral risk factor surveillance system; PeriStats: Obesity among women of childbearing age: US, 1999–2009.* As cited by March of Dimes (2010). Retrieved from http://www.modimes.org/ Peristats/level1.aspx?reg=99&top=17&stop=350&lev=1&slev=1&obj=1.

Chang, B. (1974). Some dietary beliefs in Chinese folk culture. *Journal of the American Dietetics Association, 65,* 436–438.

Chapman, R. (2003). Endangering safe motherhood in Mozambique: Prenatal care as pregnancy risk. *Social Science and Medicine, 57,* 355–374.

Chavkin, W. (2001) Cocaine and pregnancy—time to look at the evidence. *Journal of the American Medical Association, 285,* 1626–1628.

Chisholm, J., & Coall, D. (2008). Not by bread alone: The role & psychosocial stress in age at first reproduction and health inequalities. In W. Trevathan, E. O. Smith, & J. J. McKenna (Eds.), *Evolutionary medicine: New perspectives* (pp. 134–148). Oxford: Oxford University Press.

Christensen, K. Y., Maisonet, M., Rubin, C., Holmes, A., Flanders, W. D., Heron, J., . . . Marcus, M. (2010). Pubertal pathways in girls enrolled in a contemporary British cohort. *International Journal of Pediatrics, 2010,* 1–10.

Chung, T.K.H., Lao, T. K., Yip, A.S.K., Chiu, H.F.K., & Lee, D.T.S. (2001). Antepartum depressive symptomatology is associated with adverse obstetric and neonatal outcomes. *Psychosomatic Medicine, 63,* 830–834.

Cokkinides, V. E., & Coker, A. L. (1998). Experiencing physical violence during pregnancy: Prevalence and correlates. *Family and Community Health, 20,* 19–37.

Conde-Agudelo, A., Rosas-Bermúdez, A., & Kafury-Goeta, A. (2007). Effects of birth spacing on maternal health: A systematic review. *American Journal of Obstetrics and Gynecology, 196,* 297–308.

Cooper, E. R., Charurat, M., Mofenson, L. M., Hanson, I. C., Pitt, J., Diaz, C. . . . Blattner, W. (2002). Combination antiretroviral strategies for the treatment of pregnant HIV-1–infected women and prevention of perinatal HIV-1 transmission. *Journal of Acquired Immune Deficiency Syndromes, 29,* 484–494.

Corbett, R. W., Ryan, C., & Weinrich, S. P. (2003). Pica in pregnancy: Does it affect pregnancy outcomes? *American Journal of Maternal Child Nursing, 28,* 183–189.

Counihan, C., & Kaplan, S. (2004). *Food and gender: Identity and power.* London: Routledge.

Cunningham, M., & Zayas, L. H. (2002). Reducing depression in pregnancy: Designing multimodal interventions. *Social Work, 47,* 114–123.

Dabelea, D., Snell-Bergeon, J., Hartsfield, C., Bischoff, K., Hamman, R., & McDuffie, R. (2005). Increasing prevalence of gestational diabetes mellitus (GDM) over time and by birth cohort. *Diabetes Care, 28,* 579–584.

DaCosta, D., Larouche, J., Dritsa, M., & Brender, W. (1999). Variations in stress levels over the course of pregnancy: Factors associated with elevated hassles, state anxiety, and pregnancy-specific stress. *Journal of Psychosomatic Research, 47,* 609–621.

Daniels, P., Noe, G. F., & Mayberry, R. (2006). Barriers to prenatal care among Black women of low socioeconomic status. *American Journal of Health Behavior, 30,* 188–198.

da Veiga, P. V., & Wilder, R. P. (2008). Maternal smoking during pregnancy and birthweight: A propensity score matching approach. *Maternal and Child Health Journal, 12,* 194–203.

Davis-Floyd, R., & Sargent, C. (Eds.). (1997). *Childbirth and authoritative knowledge.* Berkeley: University of California Press.

de Boer, H., & Lamxay, V. (2009). Plants used during pregnancy, childbirth, and postpartum care in Lao PDR: A comparative study of the Brou, Saek, and Kry ethnic groups. *Journal of Ethnobiology and Ethnomedicine, 5,* 25.

Dick-Read, G. (1933). *Natural childbirth.* London: Heinemann.

Dietz, P. M., England, L. J., Shapiro-Mendoza, C. K., Tong, V. T., Farr, S. L., & Callsghan, W. M. (2010). Infant morbidity and mortality attributable to prenatal smoking in the US. *American Journal of Preventive Medicine, 39,* 45–52.

Dominguez, T. P., Dunkel-Schetter, C., Mancuso, R., Rini, C. M., & Hobel, C. (2005). Stress in African American pregnancies: Testing the role of various stress concepts in prediction of birth outcomes. *Annals of Behavioral Medicine, 29,* 12–21.

Donner, H. (2004). Labour, privatisation, and class: Middle-class women's experience of changing hospital births in Calcutta. In M. Unnithan-Kummar (Ed.), *Reproductive agency, medicine, and the state* (pp. 137–160). New York: Berghahn.

Dove, N. (2010). A return to traditional health practices: A Ghanaian study. *Journal of Black Studies, 40,* 823–834.

Dudgeon, M., & Inhorn, M. (2009). Men's influences on women's reproductive health: Medical anthropological perspectives. In M. Inhorn, T. Tjørnhøj-Thomsen, H. Goldberg, & M. L. Mosegaard (Eds.), *Reconceiving the second sex: Men, masculinity, and reproduction* (pp. 103–136). New York: Berghahn.

Dugal, R. (2004). The political economy of abortion in India. *Reproductive Health Matters, 12,* 130–137.

Dunkel-Schetter, C. (1998). Maternal stress and preterm delivery. *Prenatal and Neonatal Medicine, 3,* 39–42.

Dunkel-Schetter, C., Gurung, R.A.R., Lobel, M., & Wadhwa, P. D. (2001). Stress processes in pregnancy and birth: Psychological, biological, and sociocultural influences. In A. Baum, T. A. Revenson, & J. E. Singer (Eds.), *Handbook of health psychology* (pp. 495–518). Mahwah, NJ: Erlbaum.

Dunkel-Schetter, C., Sagrestano, L. M., Feldman, P., & Killingsworth, C. (1996). Social support and pregnancy: A comprehensive review focusing on ethnicity
and culture. In G. R. Pierce, B. R. Sarason, & I. G. Sarason (Eds.), *Handbook
of social support and family relationships* (pp. 375–412). New York: Plenum.

Egerter, S., Braveman, P., & Marchi, K. (2002). Timing of insurance coverage and
use of prenatal care among low-income women. *American Journal of Public
Health, 92*, 423–427.

Engel, G. L. (1977). The need for a new medical model: A challenge for biomedicine. *Science, 196*, 129–136.

Engel, G. L. (1980). The clinical application of the biopsychosocial model. *American
Journal of Psychiatry, 137*, 535–544.

Espy, K. A., Francis, D. J., & Riese, M. L. (2000). Prenatal cocaine exposure and prematurity: Neurodevelopmental growth. *Developmental and Behavioral Pediatrics, 21*, 262–270.

Espy, K. A., Kaufmann, P. M., & Glisky, M. L. (1999). Neuropsychologic function
in toddlers exposed to cocaine in utero: A preliminary study. *Developmental
Neuropsychology, 15*, 447–460.

Fantahun, M., Berhane, Y., Wall, S., Byass, P., & Högberg, U. (2007). Women's involvement in household decision-making and strengthening social capital—
crucial factors for child survival in Ethiopia. *Acta Pædiatrica, 96*, 582–589.

Farmer, P. (1996). On suffering and structural violence: A view from below. *Journal
of the American Academy of Arts & Sciences, 125*, 261–283.

Feldman, P. J., Dunkel-Schetter, C., Sandman, C. A., & Wadhwa, P. D. (2000). Maternal social support predicts birth weight and fetal growth in human pregnancy. *Psychosomatic Medicine, 62*, 715–725.

Ferrara, A. (2007). Increasing prevalence of gestational diabetes mellitus. *Diabetes
Care, 30*(Suppl. 2), 141–146.

Field, T., Diego, M., Hernandez-Reif, M., Deeds, O., & Figereido, B. (2009). Pregnancy massage reduces prematurity, low birthweight, and postpartum depression. *Infant Behavior & Development, 32*, 454–460.

Finer, L. B., & Henshaw, S. K. (2006). Disparities in rates of unintended pregnancy
in the United States, 1994 and 2001. *Perspectives on Sexual and Reproductive
Health, 38*, 90–96.

Finerman, R. (1982). Pregnancy and childbirth in Saraguro: Implications for
healthcare delivery in southern Ecuador. *Medical Anthropology, 6*, 269–278.

Finerman, R. (1984). A matter of life and death: Health care change in an Andean
community. *Social Science and Medicine, 18*, 329–334.

Finerman, R. (1987). Inside-out: Women's world view and family health in an Ec-
uadorian Indian community. *Social Science and Medicine, 25*, 1157–1162.

Fiorini, G. T. (1969). The inflammatory theory of pregnancy. *Canadian Family Physician, 15*, 55–59.

Food, Agriculture, and Natural Resources Policy Analysis Network. (2010). Retrieved from http://www.fanrpan.org/news/7635.

Food and Agriculture Organization of the United Nations. (2009). *1.09 billion people
hungry*. Retrieved from http://www.fao.org/news/story/0/item/20568/icode/en/.

Food and Agriculture Organization of the United Nations. (2010). *The state of insecurity in the world: Addressing food insecurity in protracted crisis*. Retrieved
from http://www.fao.org/publications/sofi/en/.

Gadsby, R., Barnie-Adshead, A. M., & Jagger, C. (1993). A prospective study of nausea and vomiting during pregnancy. *British Journal of General Practice, 43,* 245–248.

Ghalioungui, P., Khalil, S., & Ammar, A. R. (1963). On an ancient Egyptian method of diagnosing pregnancy and determining foetal sex. *Medical History, 7,* 241–246.

Gielen, A. C., O'Campo, P. J., Faden, R. R., Kass, N. E., & Xue, X. (1994). Interpersonal conflict and physical violence during the childbearing year. *Social Science and Medicine, 39,* 781–787.

Giscombe, C. L., & Lobel, M. (2005). Explaining the disproportionately high rates of adverse birth outcomes among African Americans: The impact of stress, racism, and related factors in pregnancy. *Psychological Bulletin, 131,* 662–683.

Glinoer, D. (2001). Pregnancy and iodine. *Thyroid, 11,* 471–481.

Glynn, L. M., Wadhwa, P. D., Dunkel-Schetter, C., Chicz-DeMet, A., & Sandman, C. A. (2001). When stress happens matters: Effects of an earthquake timing on stress responsivity in pregnancy. *American Journal of Obstetrics and Gynecology, 184,* 637–642.

Gotlib, I. H., Whiffen, V. E., Mount, J. H., Miline, K., & Cordy, N. I. (1989). Prevalence rates and demographic characteristics associated with depression in pregnancy and the postpartum. *Journal of Consulting and Clinical Psychology, 57,* 269–274.

Greenhalgh, S. (2008). *Just one child: Science and policy in Deng's China.* Berkeley: University of California Press.

Greenhalgh, T. (1987). Drug prescription and self-medication in India: An exploratory survey. *Social Science and Medicine, 25,* 307–318.

Gregory, J. (2010). (M)Others in altered states: Prenatal drug-use, risk, choice, and responsible self-governance. *Social and Legal Studies, 19,* 49–66.

Han, S. (2009). Men's "belly talk" in the contemporary United States. In M. Inhorn, T. Tjørnhøj-Thomsen, H. Goldberg, & M. L. Mosegaard (Eds.), *Reconceiving the second sex* (pp. 305–326). New York: Berghahn.

Harvey, T., & Buckley, L. (2009). Childbirth in China. In H. Selin & P. Stone (Eds.), *Childbirth across cultures* (pp. 55–69). Dordrecht, the Netherlands: Springer.

Hayman, L. (2009). Assessment of social psychological determinants of satisfaction with childbirth in a cross-national perspective. *American Journal of Maternal Child Nursing, 34,* 70.

Hellerstedt, W. L., Pirie, P. L., Lando, H. A., Curry, S. J., McBride, C. M., Grothaus, L. C., & Nelson, J. C. (1998). Differences in preconceptional and prenatal behaviors in women with intended and unintended pregnancies. *American Journal of Public Health, 88,* 663–666.

Henderson, H., & Henderson, R. (1982). Traditional Onitsha Ibo maternity beliefs and practices. In M. Kay (Ed.), *Anthropology of human birth* (pp. 175–192). Philadelphia: Davis.

Henry, J., & Kwong, A. (2003). Why is geophagy treated like dirt? *Deviant Behavior, 24,* 353–371.

Heyd, D. (2009). Male *or* female we will create them: The ethics of sex selection for non-medical reasons. In F. Simonstein (Ed.), *Reprogen-ethics and the future of gender* (pp. 161–173). New York: Springer.

Hobel, C. J., Dunkel-Schetter, C., Roesch, S. C., Castro, L. C., & Arora, C. P. (1999). Maternal plasma corticotropin-releasing hormone associated with stress at

20 weeks' gestation in pregnancies ending in preterm delivery. *American Journal of Obstetrics and Gynecology, 180,* S257–S263.

Hobfoll, S. E., Ritter, C., Lavin, J., Hulsizer, M. R., & Cameron, R. P. (1995). Depression prevalence and incidence among inner-city pregnant and postpartum women. *Journal of Consulting and Clinical Psychology, 63,* 445–453.

Hogan, M. C., Foreman, K. J., Naghavi, M., Ahn, S. Y., Wang, M., Makela, S. M., . . . Murray, C. J. (2010). Maternal mortality for 181 countries, 1980–2008: A systematic analysis of progress towards millennium development goal 5. *Lancet, 375,* 1609–1623.

Hubbard, R. (1995). Genomania and health. *American Scientist, 83,* 8–11.

Hunsberger, M. (2010). Racial/ethnic disparities in gestational diabetes mellitus: Findings from a population-based survey. *Women's Health Issues, 20,* 323–328.

Hunter, J. (1993). Macroterme geophagy and pregnancy clays in southern Africa. *Journal of Cultural Geography, 14,* 69–92.

Ivry, T. (2010). *Embodying culture: Pregnancy in Japan and Israel.* New Brunswick, NJ: Rutgers University Press.

Jasinski, J. L., & Kantor, G. K. (2001). Pregnancy, stress, and wife assault: Ethnic differences in prevalence, severity, and onset in a national sample. *Violence and Victims, 16,* 219–232.

Johnson, K., Posner, S. F., Biermann, M. S., Cordero, J. F., Atrash, H. K., Parker, C. S., . . . Curtis, M. G. (2006). Recommendations to improve preconception health and health care—United States. [A report of the CDC/ATSDR preconception care work group and the select panel on preconception care.] *Morbidity and Mortality Weekly Report, 55*(RR06), 1–23.

Johnson, S. (2010). Discursive constructions of the pregnant body: Conforming to or resisting body ideals? *Feminism & Psychology, 20,* 249–254.

Jordan, B. (1993). *Birth in four cultures* (4th ed.). London: Waveland.

Jordan, B. (1997). Authoritative knowledge and its construction. In R. Davis-Floyd & C. Sargent (Eds.), *Childbirth and authoritative knowledge* (pp. 55–79). Berkeley: University of California Press.

Kahn, R. S., Certain, L., & Whitaker, R. C. (2002). A reexamination of smoking before, during, and after pregnancy. *American Journal of Public Health, 92,* 1801–1808.

Kaiser Commission on Medicaid and the Uninsured. (2007). *The uninsured: A primer—Key facts about Americans without health insurance* [p. 30, Table 1]. Retrieved from http://www.kff.org/uninsured/upload/7451-03.pdf.

Kuhnlein, M., & Receveur, O. (1996). Dietary change and traditional systems of indigenous peoples. *Annual Review of Nutrition, 16,* 417–442.

Kyomuhendo, G. B. (2009). Culture, pregnancy and childbirth in Uganda: Surviving the women's battle. In H. Selin & P. Stone (Eds.), *Childbirth Across Cultures* (pp. 229–234). New York: Springer.

Layne, L. (2009). The home pregnancy test: A feminist technology? *Women's Studies Quarterly, 37,* 61–79.

Lefèber, Y., & Voorhoeve, H. (1997). Practices and beliefs of traditional birth attendants: Lessons for obstetrics in the north? *Tropical Medicine & International Health, 2,* 1175–1179.

Lefèber, Y., & Voorhoeve, H. (1998). *Indigenous customs in childbirth and child care.* Assen, the Netherlands: Van Gorcum.

Liamputtong, P. (2009). Pregnancy, childbirth, and traditional beliefs and practices in Chiang Mai, Northern Thailand. In H. Selin, & P. Stone (Eds.), *Childbirth across cultures* (pp. 175–184). New York: Springer.

Lipsky, S., Holt, V. L., Easterling, T. R., & Critchlow, C. W. (2003). Impact of police-reported intimate partner violence during pregnancy on birth outcomes. *Obstetrics and Gynecology, 102,* 557–564.

Lock, M., & Nguyen, V. K. (2010). *An anthropology of biomedicine.* Chichester, UK: Wiley-Blackwell.

Loudon, I. (1991). On maternal and infant mortality 1900–1960. *Social History of Medicine, 4,* 29–73.

Lu, M. C. (2007). Recommendations for preconception care. *American Family Physicians, 76,* 397–400.

MacDonald, L. D., Peacock, J. L., & Anderson, H. R. (1992). Marital status: Association with social and economic circumstances, psychological state, and outcomes of pregnancy. *Journal of Public Health Medicine, 14,* 26–34.

Malinowski, B. (1916). Baloma: Spirits of the dead in the Trobriand Islands. *Journal of the Royal Anthropological Institute, 46,* 354–430.

March of Dimes. (2008). *Fact sheet.* Retrieved from http://www.marchofdimes.com/professionals/14332_65760.asp.

March of Dimes. (2010). *Fact sheet.* Retrieved from http://www.marchofdimes.com/pnhec/173_769.asp.

Marcus, S. M., Flynn, H. A., Blow, F. C., & Barry, K. L. (2003). Depressive symptoms among pregnant women screen in obstetric settings. *Journal of Women's Health, 12,* 373–380.

Martin, D. (2001). Food restrictions in pregnancy among Hong Kong mothers. In D. Wu & R. Tan (Eds.), *Changing Chinese foodways in Asia* (pp. 97–122). Hong Kong: Chinese University of Hong Kong Press.

Martin, L. T., McNamara, M., Milot, A., Bloch, M., Hair, E. C., & Halle, T. (2008). Correlates of smoking before, during, and after pregnancy. *American Journal of Health Behavior, 32,* 272–282.

Martin, S. L., Mackie, L., Kupper, L. L., Buescher, P. A., & Moracco, K. E. (2001). Physical abuse of women before, during, and after pregnancy. *Journal of the American Medical Association, 285,* 1581–1584.

Mattson, S., & Rodriguez, E. (1999). Battering in pregnant Latinas. *Issues in Mental Health Nursing, 20,* 405–422.

Maynard, S., & Thadhani, R. (2009). Pregnancy and the kidney. *Journal of the American Society of Nephrology, 20,* 14–22.

McBride, C. M., & Pirie, P. L. (1990). Postpartum smoking relapse. *Addictive Behavior, 15,* 165–168.

McCool, W. F., & Simeone, S. A. (2002). Birth in the United States: An overview of trends past and present. *Nursing Clinics of North America, 37,* 735–746.

McGilvray, D. B. (1994). Sexual power and fertility in Sri Lanka: Batticaloa Tamils and Moors. In C. MacCormack (Ed.), *Ethnography of fertility and birth* (pp. 15–63). London: Waveland.

Meilaender, G. (1998). The fetus as parasite and mushroom. In S. Lammers & A. Verhy (Eds.), *On moral medicine* (pp. 612–617). Grand Rapids, IA: Eerdmans.

Meyer-Rochow, V. (2009). Food taboos: Their origins and purposes. *Journal of Ethnobiology and Ethnomedicine 5,* article 18.

Miller, B. (1993). Female infanticide and child neglect in rural north India. In N. Scheper-Hughes (Ed.), *Child survival* (pp. 93–112). Dordrecht, the Netherlands: Kluwer.

Mohamed, A., Kishk, N., Shokeir, N., & Kassem, M. (2006). Role of antenatal care in toxemia of pregnancy in Alexandria. *Journal of the Egyptian Public Health Association, 81,* 1–28.

Morsy, S. (1982). Childbirth in an Egyptian village. In M. Kay (Ed.), *Anthropology of human birth* (pp. 147–174). Philadelphia: Davis.

Mullen, P. D., Quinn, V. P., & Ershoff, D. H. (1990). Maintenance of nonsmoking postpartum by women who stopped smoking during pregnancy. *American Journal of Public Health, 80,* 992–994.

Munroe, R. L., Munroe, R. H., & Whiting, J. (1973). The couvade: A psychological analysis. *Ethos, 1,* 30–74.

Nichter, M., Greaves, L., Block, M., Paglia, M., Scarinci, I., Tolosa, J., & Novotny, T. (2010). Tobacco use and secondhand smoke exposure during pregnancy in low-and middle-income countries: The need for social and cultural research. *Acta Obstetrica, 89,* 465–477.

Nichter, M., & Nichter, M. (1983). The ethnophysiology and folk dietetics of pregnancy: A case study from south India. *Human Organization 43,* 235–246.

Nichter, M., Nichter, M., Muramoto, M., Adrian, S., Goldade, K., Tsler, L., & Thompson, J. (2007). Smoking among low-income pregnant women: An ethnographic analysis. *Health Education & Behavior, 34,* 748–764.

Norbeck, J. S., & Anderson, N. J. (1989). Psychosocial predictors of pregnancy outcomes in low-income Black, Hispanic, and White women. *Nursing Research, 38,* 204–209.

Nordentoft, M., Lou, C., Hansen, D., Nim, J., Pyrds, O., Rubin, P., & Hemmingsen, R. (1996). Intrauterine growth retardation and premature delivery: The influence of maternal smoking and psychosocial factors. *American Journal of Public Health, 86,* 347–354.

Norton, M. (2005). New evidence on birth spacing: Promising findings for improving newborn, infant, child, and maternal health. *International Journal of Gynecology and Obstetrics, 89,* S1–S6.

Núñez-de la Mora, A., & Bentley, G. (2008). Early life effects on reproductive function. In W. Trevathan, E. O. Smith, & J. J. McKenna (Eds.), *Evolutionary medicine: New perspectives* (pp. 149–168). Oxford: Oxford University Press.

Obermeyer, C. (2003). Culture, maternal health care, and women's status: A comparison of Morocco and Tunisia. *Studies in Family Planning, 24,* 354–365.

Obeyesekere, G. (1963). Pregnancy cravings (dola-duka) in relation to social structure and personality in a Sinhalese village. *American Anthropologist, 65,* 323–342.

Ogden, C. (2009). Disparities in obesity prevalence in the United States: Black women at risk. *American Journal of Clinical Nutrition, 89,* 1001–1002.

Omran, A. R. (1977). A century of epidemiologic transition in the United States. *Preventive Medicine, 6,* 30–51.

Parker, B., McFarlane, J., & Soeken, K. (1994). Abuse during pregnancy: Effects on maternal complications and birth weight in adult and teenage women. *Obstetrics & Gynecology, 84,* 323–328.

Petchesky, R. P. (2000). Sexual rights: Inventing a concept, mapping an international practice. In R. Parker, R. Barbosa, & P. Aggleton (Eds.), *Framing the sexual subject: The politics of gender, sexuality, and power* (pp. 81–103). Berkeley: University of California Press.

Pollan, M. (2006). *The omnivore's dilemma: A natural history of four meals.* Berkeley: University of California Press.

Pollard, T., & Unwin, N. (2008). Impaired reproductive function in women in Western and "Westernizing" populations. In W. Trevathan, E. O. Smith, & J. J. McKenna (Eds.), *Evolutionary medicine: New perspectives* (pp. 169–180). Oxford: Oxford University Press.

Ramsey, C. N., Abell, T. D., & Baker, L. C. (1986). The relationship between family functioning, life events, family structure, and the outcome of pregnancy. *Journal of Family Practice, 22,* 521–527.

Rapp, R. (1999). *Testing women, testing the fetus: The social impact of amniocentesis in America.* New York: Routledge.

Rapp, R. (2001). Gender, body, biomedicine: How some feminist concerns dragged reproduction to the center of social theory. *Medical Anthropology Quarterly, 15,* 466–477.

Reed, R. (2005). *Birthing fathers: The transformation of men in American rites of birth.* New Brunswick, NJ: Rutgers University Press.

Rini, C. K., Dunkel-Schetter, C., Wadhwa, P. D., & Sandman, C. A. (1999). Psychological adaptation and birth outcomes: The role of personal resources, stress, and sociocultural context in pregnancy. *Health Psychology, 18,* 333–345.

Ritter, C., Hobfoll, S. E., Lavin, J., Cameron, R. P., & Hulsizer, M. R. (2000). Stress, psychosocial resources, and depressive symptomatology during pregnancy in low-income, inner-city women. *Health Psychology, 19,* 576–585.

Roelands, J., Jamison, M. G., Lyerly, A. D., & James, A. H. (2009). Consequences of smoking during pregnancy on maternal health. *Journal of Women's Health, 18,* 867–872.

Rogers, D. (1992). Rockabye lady: Pregnancy as punishment in popular culture. *Journal of American Studies 26,* 81–83.

Rondo, P.H.C., Ferreira, R. F., Nogueira, F., Ribeiro, M.C.N., Lobert, H., & Artes, R. (2003). Maternal psychological stress and distress as predictors of low birth weight, prematurity, and intrauterine growth retardation. *European Journal of Clinical Nutrition, 57,* 266–272.

Sable, M. R., & Wilkinson, D. S. (2000). Impact of perceived stress, major life events, and pregnancy attitudes on low birth weight. *Family Planning Perspectives, 32,* 288–294.

Sagrestano, L. M., Feldman, P., Rini, K.C.K., Woo, G., & Dunkel-Schetter, C. (1999). Ethnicity and social support during pregnancy. *American Journal of Community Psychology, 27,* 869–898.

Sahin, G. (2003). *Incidence, morbidity and mortality of preeclampsia and eclampsia.* Retrieved from http://www.gfmer.ch/Endo/Course2003/Eclampsia.htm.

Schultz, T. (1997). Demand for children in low income countries. In M. Rosensweig (Ed.), *Handbook of population and family economics* (pp. 349–430). Dordrecht, the Netherlands: Elsevier.

Selin, H., & Stone, P. (Eds.). (2009). *Childbirth across cultures.* Dordrecht, the Netherlands: Springer.

Sesia, P. (1997). "Women come here on their own when they need to": Prenatal care, authoritative knowledge, and maternal health in Oaxaca. In R. Davis-Floyd & C. Sargent (Eds.), *Childbirth and authoritative knowledge* (pp. 397–420). Berkeley: University of California Press.

Shah, A. (2010). *Poverty around the world.* Retrieved from http://www.globalissues.org/article/4/poverty-around-the-world.

Sonfield, A. (2007). More reproductive-age women covered by Medicaid—but more are also uninsured. *Guttmacher Policy Review, 10.* Retrieved from http://www.guttmacher.org/pubs/gpr/10/1/gpr100124.html.

Sonfield, A. (2010). The potential of health care reform to improve pregnancy-related services and outcomes. *Guttmacher Policy Review, 13.* Retrieved from http://www.guttmacher.org/pubs/gpr/13/3/gpr130313.html.

Stenson, K., Sidenvall, B. B., & Heimer, G. (2005). Midwives' experiences of routine antenatal questioning relating to men's violence against women. *Midwifery, 21,* 311–321.

Steverson, J., & Rieckmann, W. (2009). Legislating for the provision of comprehensive substance abuse treatment programs for pregnant and mothering women. *Duke Journal of Gender Law and Policy, 1,* 315–346.

Stone, H. (2009). A history of Western medicine, labor, and birth. In H. Selin & P. Stone (Eds.), *Childbirth across cultures* (pp. 41–54). Dordrecht, the Netherlands: Springer.

Taylor, S. E. (1990). Health psychology: The science and the field. *American Psychologist, 45,* 40–50.

Thornton, P., Kieffer, E., & Salbarria-Pena, Y. (2006). Weight, diet, and physical activity-related beliefs and practices among pregnant and postpartum Latino women: The role of social support. *Maternal and Child Health Journal, 10,* 95–104.

Tomlinson, C. J., & Ellis, J. (2008). Comparison of accuracy and certainty of results of six home pregnancy tests available over-the-counter. *Informa, 24,* 1645–1649.

Torres, S., Campbell, J., Campbell, D. W., Ryan, J., King, C., Price, P., . . . Laude, M. (2000). Abuse during and before pregnancy: Prevalence and cultural correlates. *Violence and Victims, 15,* 303–321.

Turner, B., Maes, K., Sweeney, J., & Armelagos, G. (2008). Human evolution, diet, and nutrition: When the body meets the buffet. In W. Trevathan, E. O. Smith, & J. McKenna (Eds.), *Evolutionary medicine and health: New perspectives* (pp. 55–71). Oxford: Oxford University Press.

Uberti, O. (2011). *The cost of care* [Information graphic]. Retrieved from http://thesocietypages.org/graphicsociology/2011/04/26/cost-of-health-care-by-country-national-geographic/.

UNICEF. (2009). *The state of the world's children, 2009.* Retrieved from http://www.unicef.org/sowc09/report/report.php.

UNIFEM. (2010). *Women, poverty, and economics.* Retrieved from http://www.unifem.org/gender_issues/women_poverty_economics.

Unnithan-Kumar, M. (2004). Reproductive agency, medicine, and the state. In M. Unnithan-Kumar (Ed.), *Reproductive agency, medicine, and the state: Cultural transformations in childbearing* (pp. 1–23). New York: Berghahn.

U.S. Census Bureau. (2008). Age and sex of all people, family members, and unrelated individuals iterated by income-to-poverty ratio and race: 2007—

Below 100% of poverty. *Current population survey, 2008 Annual Social and Economic Supplement.* Retrieved from http://www.census.gov/hhes/www/macro/032008/pov/new01_100_01.htm.

Vermeer, D., & Frate, D. (1975). Geophagy in a Mississippi county. *Annals of the Association of American Geographers, 65,* 414–424.

Victora, C., Matijasevich, A., Silveira, M., Santos, I., Barros A., & Barros, F. (2010). Socio-economic and ethnic group inequities in antenatal care quality in the public and private sector in Brazil. *Health Policy and Planning, 25,* 253–261.

Wadhwa, P. D., Sandman, C. A., Porto, M., Dunkel-Schetter, C., & Garite, T. J. (1993). The association between prenatal stress and infant birth weight and gestational age at birth: A prospective investigation. *American Journal of Obstetrics and Gynaecology, 169,* 858–865.

Wakschlag, L. S., Pickett, K. E., Cook, E., Jr., Benowitz, N. L., & Leventhal, B. L. (2002). Maternal smoking during pregnancy and severe antisocial behavior in offspring: A review. *American Journal of Public Health, 92,* 966–974.

Wheatley, R., Kelley, M., Peacock, N., & Peacock, J. (2008). Women's narratives on quality in prenatal care: A multicultural perspective. *Qualitative Health Research, 18,* 1586–1598.

Wiley, A., & Katz, S. (1998). Geophagy in pregnancy: A test of a hypothesis. *Current Anthropology, 39,* 523–545.

Wolbring, G. (2001). Where do we draw the line? Surviving eugenics in a technological world: Disability and the life course. In M. Priestly (Ed.), *Global perspectives* (pp. 38–49). Cambridge: Cambridge University Press.

Woliver, L. (2002). *The political geographies of pregnancy.* Champaign: University of Illinois Press.

World Health Organization. (2004). *Global database on iodine deficiency.* Retrieved from http://whqlibdoc.who.int/publications/2004/9241592001.pdf.

World Health Organization. (2006a). *World health statistics.* Retrieved from http://www.who.int/whosis/whostat2006.pdf.

World Health Organization. (2006b). *Why does childhood overweight and obesity matter?* Retrieved from http://www.who.int/dietphysicalactivity/childhood_consequences/en/index.html.

World Health Organization & Centers for Disease Control and Prevention. (2008). *Worldwide prevalence of anemia 1993–2005.* Retrieved from http://whqlibdoc.who.int/publications/2008/9789241596657_eng.pdf.

World Health Organization & UNICEF. (2010). Joint United Nations programme on HIV/AIDS. *Towards universal access: Scaling up priority HIV/AIDS interventions in the health sector: Progress report,* released September 28, 2010. Retrieved from http://www.who.int/hiv/pub/2010progressreport/en/index.html.

Zwart, J., Jonkers, M., Richters, A., Öry, F., Bloemenkamp, K., Duvekot, J., & van Roosmalen, J. (2011). Ethnic disparity in severe acute maternal morbidity: A nationwide cohort study in the Netherlands. *European Journal of Public Health, 21,* 229–234.

Chapter 10

Birthing across Cultures: Toward the Humanization of Childbirth

Sayaka Machizawa and Kayoko Hayashi

There has been a global struggle between the medicalization and humanization of childbirth for the last several decades (Wagner, 2007). The humanized birth movement aims to empower women; respect their decisions, values, beliefs, and feelings; and reduce overly medicalized childbirth (e.g., Behruzi et al., 2010; McKay, 1982, 1991; McKay & Philips, 1984).

Wagner (2007) listed four characteristics of humanized birthing: (1) an environment in which women giving birth can make the decisions involved in the process of childbirth; (2) community-based, instead of hospital-based, maternity services; (3) harmonious collaboration among midwives, nurses, and doctors; and (4) evidence-based and scientifically solid maternity services. It should be noted, however, that humanized birth is not limited to a specific definition or criteria. Rather it is a transitioning process for women, their families, and professional providers (Behruzi et al., 2010). In this chapter, we explore birthing practices across cultures and the global movement toward humanized childbirth in relation to power and sociocultural and socioeconomic factors.

Humanization of childbirth is closely related to, and should be incorporated into, reproductive justice. Diaz-Tello and Paltrow (2010) emphasized that reproductive justice is not just about women's power to make decisions about whether and when to have children, but also about how they are treated during the process of labor and childbirth. They used the term *birth justice* to highlight women's right to humanized childbirth:

> It (birth justice) is, at minimum, having access to evidence-based maternity care, accurate information about pregnancy, the risks and benefits of medical procedures, and the agency to choose whether or not to undergo those medical procedures. It is having the power to make those choices and give birth free from fear of intimidation or interference from the state due to "noncompliance" with medical advice, or because of poverty, race or ethnicity, or immigration status. It is also having access to competent and culturally respectful labor support. (pp. 2–3)

VARIABILITY IN MATERNITY SERVICES ACROSS CULTURES

Whereas medicalization of maternity services has been a global phenomenon since World War II (e.g., Wagner, 2007), practices of birthing, including the place of birth (i.e., home vs. hospital), use of technologies and medications, supports in labor, and mother-infant contact after birth, are different across cultures. In addition, even within the same country different practices are observed between different regions, hospitals, and obstetricians (Chalmers, 1996). Wagner (2007) divided maternity services into three categories based on the medicalization-humanization spectrum: (1) the highly medicalized approach, (2) the humanized approach, and (3) the mixture of both approaches. The *highly medicalized approach* is characterized by high technology, doctor-centered care, and marginalization of midwives. This approach is common in countries such as Russia, the United States, and eastern European countries and the urban areas of developing countries. The *humanized approach* is characterized by more natural and holistic methods, woman-centered care, and a stronger role for midwives. This approach is often seen in the Netherlands, New Zealand, and the Scandinavian countries. Lastly, the *mixture of both approaches* is often found in Australia, Canada, Germany, Japan, and the United Kingdom (Wagner, 2007). It should be noted, however, that medicalized and humanized approaches are not necessarily exclusive to each other, and there is a remarkable heterogeneity of maternity care within cultures.

Place of Birth

In countries where the highly medicalized approach to maternal care is common, most childbirth takes place in hospitals. In the United States, the hospital birth rate was less than 5 percent at the turn of 20th century (Wertz & Wertz, 1977, as cited in Mathews & Zadak, 1991). However, this rate has climbed rapidly since World War II with the advancement of medicine and nursing, proliferation of hospitals, and emergence of the specialty of obstetrics (Mathews & Zadak, 1991). By 1969 a rate of hospital births reached 99 percent, and it has remained stable since then (MacDorman, Menacker, & Declercq, 2010). Around the mid 1960s, the home birth movement emerged along with the feminist movement. Feminists often advocated home birth as a way for women to have control over their birthing experience (e.g., Arms, 1977.

Hospital-based and free-standing alternative birth centers emerged in the United States in the late 1960s for women who do not want to give birth at home but prefer a natural and woman-centered labor experience (Mathews & Zadak, 1991). Alternative birth centers are different from hospital birth or home birth in that they are medically supervised but dedicated to providing a natural birthing experience for women and avoiding unnecessarily invasive procedures. Alternative birth settings provide a woman with a single room that is a home-like environment (e.g., carpeting, artwork, refrigerators, television) for labor, delivery, and recovery. A woman is minimally intruded upon by health professionals. This self-contained environment allows the mother, infant, and other loved ones to stay together during the delivery and recovery process. In alternative birth centers, women are involved in the decision-making process about, for example, medications, support persons, and labor positions, and family members are encouraged to participate throughout the experience.

Mathews and Zadak (1991) suggested that some political and financial factors among childbirth professionals have played roles in the movement for alternative childbirth in the last two decades in the United States. For instance, although the statistics support the safety of home birth, obstetricians have discouraged this method of delivery by highlighting its potential risks and dangers. In 1977, the executive director of the American College of Obstetricians and Gynecologists (ACOG) referred to home birth as a form of child abuse and maternal trauma (ACOG Official, 1977, as cited in Mathews & Zadak, 1991). Mathews and Zadak (1991) suspected that strong opposition to home birth by medical professionals stems from their fear of economic competition and desire to retain control over obstetrical practice.

In southern Africa, most rural births take place at home, although *home* usually does not mean the laboring women's home but her mother's (Chalmers, 1996). The community reveres grandmother's hut as the "dwelling place of the ancestral spirits" (p. 13), and thus it is considered as the safest place in the homestead. It is also notable that the grandmother's hut is different from the Western concept of home in that it is the equivalent of a hospital or clinic, rather than a house. In most home births in Western countries, women are usually given a certain degree of decision-making authority over their birth experience. However, in rural African cultures, the grandmother, who is also the traditional birthing attendant, has more initiative than the laboring woman does. The Western medical approach and traditional healing are simultaneously accepted and coexist in many African cultures (Chalmers, 1991, 1996). Thus, the Western view of home birthing as a way to empower women in childbirth may not transfer to the African setting (Chalmers, 1996). Furthermore, whereas the conflict for control over birth in the West usually takes place between the mother and the obstetrician, in rural Africa, if conflict occurs, it is between the traditional birth attendant (e.g., grandmother) and the midwife at the clinic or hospital (Chalmers, 1996).

Place of birth does not only relate to sociocultural factors but also to geographic and socioeconomic factors. In remote areas of China, more than 80 percent of births still take place at home where women have no access to obstetric emergency services, although there has been a strong shift toward hospital birth with the Decrease Project, a national project to decrease home birth (Harris et al., 2007). There is also an association between insurance status and location of birth. Chinese women who are not insured, or have just recently become insured, tend to give birth at home, as hospital birth is more costly (Harris et al., 2007). An increase in the hospital birth rate has resulted in more access to medical care for women, thus the reduced maternal mortality in China.

In the United States, there are socioeconomic and psychological differences between women who choose to have or not to have home birth. Toepke and Albers (1995) reported that women who choose home as the place of birth tend to be older, married, and more socially advantaged than their counterparts. They are also more likely to have higher education, better social support, and healthier habits (e.g., better nutrition). Furthermore, they have less traditional attitudes toward gender roles and childbirth. In their study, women listed the following reasons for choosing home birth over hospital birth: relaxed environment, greater privacy, greater control over delivery procedures, presence of companions, less medication, no restrictions on breastfeeding, no separation of mother and infant after delivery, and lower costs.

Home birth is more common in the Netherlands than in other Western countries. In the period 2005–2008, 29 percent of deliveries in the Netherlands occurred at home. This number was even higher, about 35 percent, in the period 1997–2000 (CBS, 2009). As in the United States, women with higher education are more likely to choose home birth. Over the period

1997–2008, an average of 35 percent of college-educated women gave birth at home, as opposed to 27 percent of their less educated counterparts (CBS, 2009).

These examples show that various factors play roles in determining the place of birth, and common reasons women choose home birth may differ across cultures and countries. In addition, there are cross-cultural difference in the concept of home birth, as well as the quality and safety of home birth.

Cesarean Section

The World Health Organization (WHO) has expressed concerns about the increasing rate of cesarean section in both developed and developing countries (Betra et al., 2007). More than two decades ago, WHO cautioned that cesarean section rates should not be higher than 10–15 percent in any region of the world. Nevertheless, currently about 15 percent of births worldwide occur by cesarean section, although there is great variability in the rate across countries and regions (Betra et al., 2007).

Cesarean section is most commonly performed in Latin America and the Caribbean countries where the proportion of cesarean births is 29.2 percent on average. Within this region, national rates range from below 10 percent in Haiti (1.7%) and Honduras (7.9%) to above 30 percent in Mexico (39.1%), Brazil (36.7%), the Dominican Republic (31.3%), and Chile (30.7%). In contrast, cesarean section is generally low in Africa, ranging from below 2 percent in the Central African Republic, Burkina Faso, Mali, Nigeria, and Chad to above 10 percent in South Africa (15.4%) and Egypt (11.4%). The average cesarean section rate in Asia is 15.9 percent, and in Europe it is 19 percent, although there are unequal distributions across countries within the same region (Betra et al., 2007).

There is also a large discrepancy in the cesarean section rate between developed and developing countries. Whereas the average cesarean birth rate is about 21.1 percent in developed countries, the rate is only 2 percent in the least developed countries. Underuse of cesarean section in emergency or birth complications results in high maternal and perinatal mortality (Weil & Fernandez, 1999). In fact, in countries with high mortality rates, the cesarean section rate has a negative correlation with mortality. However, this correlation is not observed in the countries where the average rate is above the recommended range of 10–15 percent (Betra et al., 2007), where an excessive use of cesarean section is associated with increased health risks for both mothers and infants (Villar et al., 2005).

The high cesarean rate indicates that it is performed not only for medical reasons but also as a result of women's requests and at doctors' discretion. Women's preference for cesarean section seems to be associated not only with available information on different birthing procedures but also with sociocultural factors including common perceptions of different birthing procedures, social class and power, and the intersections of these factors (e.g., Béhague, Victora, & Barros, 2002; Hurst & Summey, 1984).

In Brazil where the cesarean section rate is very high, many women prefer cesarean section because they consider medical intervention to be superior and to represent better quality care. Béhague et al. (2002) used a linked ethnographic and epidemiological approach to investigate the reasons many Brazilian women seek out cesarean section. They found that women with higher incomes and educational levels were more likely than their counterparts to have had a cesarean section. In addition, many lower-and middle-class women also sought medical interventions, especially when they had more decision-making power in their household. Many women considered a cesarean section to be the best medical care and vaginal birth as a risky and negative experience. In addition, some women believed that a traumatic vaginal birth is associated with substandard medical care based on socioeconomic prejudice against poor, uneducated, or young women or those with many children or little prenatal care. As there are class-based differences in the quality of care provided in Brazil, women tend to choose cesarean section because they fear receiving substandard care. The researchers concluded that Brazilian women tend to prefer cesarean section, not only because of a lack of information on how to prepare for a vaginal birth and about the risks associated with cesarean sections, but also because of the different maternity care provided to women based on their socioeconomic status. They emphasized that, when interventions for reducing unnecessary cesarean sections are being developed, it is important to consider issues related to social power and unequal health care provision in addition to educating professionals and patients about different birthing procedures and outcomes.

A relationship between social class and cesarean section has been also reported in the United States. According to Hurst and Summey (1984), cesarean section is more likely to be performed among middle-and upper-class women who actually have lower medical risks than poor women do. These data indicate that different cesarean rates among socioeconomic groups are better explained by factors associated with social class than medical need. Thus, there is a higher risk of unnecessary medical intervention during labor for middle-or upper-class women than for their poorer counterparts in the United States. One obvious factor that would explain the strong relationship between social class and cesarean section rate is the relatively high expense of a cesarean delivery. A cesarean section seems to be consistently more costly than a vaginal delivery across countries. According to International Federation of Health Plans (2010), total average payments for vaginal birth in the United States are $8,435, whereas those for cesarean birth are $13,016. Similarly, in Switzerland, total average payments for cesarean birth are $5,192, nearly 50 percent higher than those for vaginal birth ($3,485). Due to the high expense, a cesarean is not an easy option for women with no health insurance. Threats of malpractice suits are also linked to the social class difference in cesarean deliveries because lower-class women are less likely than middle-or upper-class women to be able to afford malpractice suits.

Morris and McInerney (2010) pointed out the roles of the media in women's choice of their birthing method in the United States. They performed a content analysis of reality-based pregnancy and birth television shows that were broadcast in November 2007. They found that risks associated with a cesarean section were misrepresented in these shows where it was portrayed as the safest way to deliver breech-presenting babies. In fact, they reported that "women's bodies were typically displayed as incapable of birthing a baby without medical intervention" (p. 134). Given that 68 percent of pregnant women in the United States reported having watched reality shows on pregnancy and childbirth on a regular basis, media representations of birthing are no doubt influential in their perceptions of childbirth and their choice of medical procedures (Morris & McInerney, 2010).

In China, some women choose cesarean section to avoid giving birth on inauspicious dates. Furthermore, due to the one-child policy, Chinese women attempt to minimize any maternal or fetal risk of not having a quality child by seeking technological and specialized interventions. Hospitals also promote cesarean deliveries and other costly interventions to generate revenues, which may subject Chinese women to unnecessary medical interventions (Harris et al., 2007).

The rate of cesarean delivery in Japan is much lower than in Western countries, primarily because it is not covered by medical insurance except for high-risk and complicated pregnancy cases (Suzuki, 2008). The relatively low cesarean rate and lesser use of technological interventions in Japan may also be related to cultural views of birth. For example, Engel (1989) stated that Japanese women and health care providers, unlike their Western counterparts, see birth as being primarily physiological, rather than pathological.

Pain Management

There are remarkable cross-cultural differences in approach to pain management during labor and birth. For instance, many women in the Netherlands believe that the use of pain medication is not necessary because women's bodies are capable of regulating the pain of birth (Jordan, 1978). In contrast, in the United States, where about 71 percent of women with vaginal births receive anesthetics to reduce pain (Declercq, Sakala, Corry, & Applebaum, 2006), women tend to hold beliefs that the use of anesthetics is necessary, as pain is undesirable (Jordan, 1978). Morris and

McInerney (2010) found that media representations of pregnancy and birth in the United States tend to convey a message that medication is the only effective way to manage pain. Furthermore, a positive childbirth experience is often linked to the use of pain medication. Women who do not use anesthetics are often portrayed in the media as hysterical and out of control. The researchers stressed that these media representations reflect women's inferior status and the devaluation of female body in American culture. The negative view of pain during birthing may be shared by health care providers as well, as a small portion of North American women reported that they were pressured by their doctors to use pain medication during labor (Declercq et al., 2006).

In Japan, pain medication, such as epidural analgesia, is not commonly used. According to the survey conducted by the Ministry of Health, Labor, and Welfare, the rate of analgesics use in Japan is as low as 2.6 percent, whereas in the United States it is about 60 percent (Press Net Japan, 2011). In Morsbach's (1983) study, nearly one-half of the Japanese mothers interviewed were against the use of pain medication during labor or birth. Many Japanese women expect to confront pain rather than to control it. They tend to believe that natural birth is preferable because childbirth is not a sickness that needs medical interventions (Behruzi et al., 2010). In addition, they expect that enduring pain nurtures a sense of motherhood in women and strengthens the early mother-infant bond. One might suspect that the infrequent use of pain medications is associated with Japanese cultural values that encourage enduring pain (*gaman*) and discourage controlling the body's natural reactions with artificial measures. Japanese women prefer natural methods for pain relief such as massage, breathing techniques, thermo therapy, birth pools (pools for water birth), aromatherapy, warm blankets, and social support (Behruzi et al., 2010). However, it is important to note that the infrequent use of pain medication in Japan does not necessarily mean that Japanese women choose not to use them in birthing. Use of anesthetics is often not an option for Japanese woman because many maternity hospitals and clinics do not have an anesthetist. According to the study by Oishi, Saito, and Shibata (2003), only 22.5 percent of maternity hospitals and clinics they surveyed offered analgesics use in labor and childbirth.

In addition to the cross-cultural variation in use of pain medication, there are also differences in expressions and perceptions of pain. Scopesi, Zanobini, and Carossino (1997) stated that pain perception depends on expectations regarding labor and childbirth. In cultures where severe pain in childbirth is seen normal and expected, women perceive the pain as bearable. Scopesi et al. (1997) reported that there is no association between pain perception and women's emotional responses to their birthing experience, and thus reducing pain does not necessarily ensure a more positive and satisfactory birthing experience. There are also concerns about negative effects of a pain medication on women and their infants. It has been reported that pharmacologic methods of pain relief result in a greater likelihood of respiratory and central nervous system depression in newborn babies (Toepke & Albers, 1995).

AVERAGE COSTS FOR CHILDBIRTH

Average costs for childbirth and the amount covered by health insurance varies across cultures, countries, and regions. In Japan, according to the national survey conducted by Health, Labor, and Welfare Ministry (HLWM) in 2010, the national average cost for uncomplicated childbirth is 473,626 yen, which was equivalent to US$5,757 at the time (US$1 = 82.25 yen; the Gross National Income in Japan was US$38,210 in 2008 per United Nations International Children's Emergency Fund [UNICEF]). There were significant discrepancies between the cost of childbirth in metropolitan and rural areas. The most expensive area was Tokyo, where the average cost of childbirth was about 560,000 yen, the equivalent of US$6,811. The least expensive area was Tottori prefecture, where the average cost of childbirth was about US$4,743. The cost of childbirth includes fees for hospitalization and assessment, medication, and other expenses. The survey also reported that, in Japan, public medical insurance covers 420,000 yen, the equivalent of US$5,108, for childbirth and childcare (HLWM, 2010).

A survey conducted by the U.S. Department of Health and Human Services (USDHHS) revealed that the average medical cost for prenatal care and uncomplicated childbirth is about US$7,600 (the Gross National Income in the United States was US$47,580 in 2008 per UNICEF). The report stated that the average childbirth cost was US$6,520, and the average cost for prenatal care was US$1,962 for women with private insurance. Private health insurance covered 87 percent of the expenses of insured women, who paid 8 percent of the remaining costs out-of-pocket and 5 percent from other sources. Medicaid covered 92 percent of expenses for recipients, who paid less than 1 percent out-of-pocket and 8 percent from other sources (USDHHS, 2010).

Liamputtong (2005) conducted interviews with 30 women about their experiences of childbirth in Chiang Mai and its rural area in northern Thailand. Vaginal birth in a private hospital cost 17,000 Baht, which was the equivalent of US$ 472 (1US$ = 36 Baht) at the time, and cesarean birth cost 30,000 Baht (US$ 833; the Gross National Income of Thailand was $2,840 in 2008 per UNICEF). In Thai culture, women who give birth in a hospital pay an additional gratitude fee (*Bun Khun* in Thai) to the doctors who provide special or private care during pregnancy and birthing. The gratitude fee is negotiated between a woman and her doctor, and it can be either cash or a gift. The cash may range from 2,000 Baht (US$56) for vaginal delivery to 3,000 Baht (US$83) for a cesarean section. The private doctors earned more with a cesarean birth. Many rural poor women in Thailand receive services from public doctors at public hospitals, and most do not have the same access to continuing care as do middle-class women due to their financial constraints.

Perkins et al. (2009) recently conducted representative population-based surveys in three African countries: Burkina Faso, Kenya, and Tanzania. A total of 13,861 women were interviewed in 2003, and 18,525 women were interviewed in 2006. A total of 6,345 in 2003 and 8,302 in 2006 had given birth within the preceding two years. In 2006, 56 percent of births in Tanzania, 45 percent in Burkina Faso, and 33 percent in Kenya occurred in health facilities. The average out-of-pocket medical costs related to non-complicated childbirth were US$4.50, US$6.60, and US$14.20 in Tanzania, Burkina Faso, and Kenya, respectively (the Gross National Income of Tanzania, Burkina Faso, and Kenya was $430, $480, and $770, respectively, in 2008 per UNICEF). In Kenya, the cost of birthing at government hospitals was US$26, US$68.70 at private facilities, and US$6.70 at health centers. The majority of nonfacility births occurred at home, and their costs were much lower than the cost at facilities: US$0.40, US$4.10, and US$3.60 in Burkina Faso, Tanzania, and Kenya, respectively.

Harris et al. (2007) conducted a study in Sichuan (southwest) and Shanxi (northern) Provinces in China from 2005 to 2007, where the cases of 889 normal births and 456 cesarean sections were audited. The results showed that vaginal births in county hospitals cost between 200 and 1,000 yuan, and births in provincial hospitals cost 2,000 or more yuan. Harris et al. noted that annual household income in the areas of their study ranged from 2,200 to 3,500 yuan. A cesarean section cost 8,000–10,000 yuan in one major hospital in the capital city, and 1,000–2,000 in county hospitals. Harris et al. reported that it has been a custom in Shanxi province for women to offer a *red bag* (i.e., an informal payment or gift) to doctors with whom they worked in birthing process, and the cost of the red bag often amplified financial difficulty for patients and their families.

The description of overall costs of childbirth in different countries shows that there is significant variance in price between vaginal births and cesarean sections. It is also notable that, in some countries, medical costs in capital hospitals were much higher than in community hospitals, and hospital care was much more costly than nonhospital care. These differences suggest that women who have financial restrictions also have limited access to medical care that they may need to receive.

EMOTIONAL CARE THROUGH SOCIAL SUPPORT

Numerous reports provide evidence that emotional support during childbirth results in positive outcomes after birth. It has been reported, for example, that support during pregnancy correlates with a higher APGAR index for infants and lower incidence of postpartum depression for mothers (Collins, Dunkel-Schetter, Lobel, & Scrimshaw, 1993). According to Sosa, Kennell, Klaus, Robertson, and Urrutia (1980), presence of a doula (i.e., an experienced woman who provides support during labor) is associated with fewer complications during childbirth and shorter duration of labor. Similarly, when husbands or other family members were not allowed to accompany them, women who received continuous emotional support from trained-volunteer women expressed significantly less pain, required less analgesia, and expressed a greater sense of positive coping during labor than did those who received care only from busy medical professionals in hospitals (Abramson, Breedlove, & Isaacs, 2007). Furthermore, mothers who received continuous labor support more frequently showed increased alertness after birth, breastfed more, and reported less postpartum depression, and mothers' sense of control and positive perception of labor were higher when they had labor support (Abramson et al., 2007). Butler, Abrams, Parker, and Laros (1993) reported that women who received support from a midwife had a lower risk of cesarean section.

Many researchers have investigated the effects of the presence of a husband during childbirth, but the findings have been contradictory. Whereas some studies show positive effects of a husband's presence, such as reduced perceived pain and more satisfaction (e.g., Henneborn & Cogan, 1975), other studies did not detect such effects. These inconsistent findings seem to be because there are factors that moderate the effect of a husband's presence (e.g., Keinan, 1997; Scopesi et al., 1997). For instance, Scopesi et al. (1997) stated that the effect of social support during labor is moderated by different factors, such as biomedical risk, culture, and the women's personality. In addition, it appears that the ideal support person for birthing depends on both cultural and individual factors. In many Western countries, the presence of a spouse or partner is considered important. However, in Africa there are traditional taboos against the spouse's presence during labor. Thus, Chalmers (1996) cautioned that advocating spousal support for African women in childbirth could be counterproductive.

According to a large survey conducted in the United States, 82 percent of women responded that they had received emotional and physical support from their husband or partner while in labor, followed by support from nursing staff (56%), a family member or friend (38%), and a doctor (32%) (Declercq et al., 2006). Only a minority of women had received support from a midwife (8%) or doula (3%). Whereas 100 percent of women who received support from a doula and 87 percent of those who had received support from their husband or spouse felt that they had received quality care during their labor, less than one-half of women who received support only from an obstetrician (37%) or a family physician (44%) reported that they had received quality and supportive care.

The percentage of women who have their husband present during childbirth in Japan seems to range from 30 percent to 60 percent (e.g., Baby Weekly Research, 2010; Benesse Jisedai Ikusei Kenkyujo, 2010), which is lower than that in most Western countries. The majority (96%) of Japanese women who had had their husband or partner present during labor reported that they were happy with this arrangement. More than 70 percent of pregnant women reported that they hope to have their spouse or partner present during childbirth, and about 60 percent of men expressed a desire to attend their wife's childbirth. Those women who do not want their spouse with them often worry that seeing their wife giving birth may be too shocking or that their spouse may become unable to see them as sexual beings. Some reported that labor and birthing should be a private experience in which husbands should not be allowed to participate.

Barriers seem to exist that may prevent Japanese women from receiving their preferred social support during labor. A qualitative field study in Japan (Behruzi et al., 2010) indicates that there is often a restriction on the number of attendees allowed during labor. For example, many hospitals do not allow women's children, parents, or friends to be present. This implies that Japanese women often have limited power to choose their companions during labor.

Peterson (1996) asserted that it is important to embrace childbirth as an empowering feminine experience and that it is important to receive emotional support during this process. She also stated that it is important for women to have a safe space to talk about and process their experiences of birthing as well as the prenatal period, so that they are able to integrate birthing experiences into their sense of self and to develop their new identity as a mother. Peterson suggested the following six areas to explore in helping women to prepare for their birthing experiences: (1) She has the power to engage in decision-making process during birthing. (2) She believes that her emotional experiences during birthing are acceptable and that she will have opportunity to express her feelings. (3) She is informed and feels prepared for the laboring process, and she is able to cope with the distress. (4) In case she needs or wants surgical or other intervention, she is able to receive services in response to her physical and emotional needs. (5) She has opportunities to explore her feelings about motherhood. (6) She has opportunities to explore her feelings about her birthing and any of her previous pregnancy and childbirth experiences. It should be noted, however, that, whereas the above suggestions are ideal for all women, they may not be realistic for disadvantaged or underprivileged women who have limited financial and/or other resources. For instance, they may not be able to afford surgical or other services, even if there is a medical need.

Page (2001b) reported that some countries utilize the midwifery system to provide individual support and care for women. In Canada, New Zealand, and the United Kingdom, action has been taken to develop a system for midwives to provide quality care for women. In these countries, midwives are highly educated and skilled professionals who practice on their own in the community and provide primary care. They have a referral network with hospitals and have the right to transfer laboring women to the hospital if requested or necessary. Most important, they develop personal relationships with women and provide sensitive and individual care in response to women's needs. The Netherlands seems to have the most developed midwifery system where family doctors, obstetricians, and midwives have clear and distinguished roles and responsibilities in the health care system. In the United Kingdom, midwives play important roles in the provision of community services for women. There is a system called *continuity of care,* in which a midwife maintains a consistent relationship and provides care for the same woman both in community and hospital settings throughout the birthing process. In New Zealand, women can choose to work with either midwives or family doctors depending on the quality of care that they wish to receive. In the United States, doctors and nurses usually provide care for women, and only a small number of people receive services from midwives. In Brazil, due to its high rate of cesarean section, the number of professional midwives is very small.

Abramson et al. (2007) wrote about another supportive resource for women in the community: *doulas,* individuals who are trained to accompany mothers during labor and birth to provide continuous presence and support. Doulas generally are considered to be effective resources for mothers who have insufficient support from family and friends because of immigration, social isolation, or difficult family lives. Support and care from women within a similar culture and community empower birthing women and strengthen the community (Abramson et al., 2007). Community-based doulas tend to stay in the communities where they have worked, and they continue to help families and build relationships with other professionals in those communities. These community-based doulas may develop intense and intimate relationships with birthing women, and they, in turn, help to build a nurturing environment for the newborn baby.

CONTINUOUS SUPPORT FOR WOMEN

Martis (2007) reported on the benefit of practicing continuous one-to-one support for women during childbirth. Women who receive continuous one-to-one support are less likely to have regional analgesia/anesthesia, operative vaginal birth, or cesarean section. They are also more likely to have a spontaneous vaginal birth, a shorter labor, and greater satisfaction with their childbirth experience. This phenomenon was observed in Belgium, Botswana, Canada, Guatemala, Mexico, South Africa, the United Kingdom, and the United States. The positive effect was stronger when (1) other sources of support were not available, (2) epidural anesthesia was not routinely used, (3) one-to-one support was provided by someone who was not an employee at the hospital, and (4) the support started early in labor.

Martis (2007) asserted that one-to-one continuous support can be offered at low cost in communities in both developing and developed countries. The support person does not need to have sophisticated training; some training sessions provided by the hospital are sufficient. It is recommended that support persons have had their own birthing experiences. The training at hospitals may include an information session and a walk through the birthing facility. Martis stated that this system of volunteer lay support persons is particularly helpful when women do not have sufficient support from their families. As noted earlier, women who are in the labor process are in need for one-to-one psychological support and care from others (Peterson, 1996). Martis's (2007) emphasis on the utilization of community resources allows the community to provide more intimate and individually focused care for birthing women.

POWER TO MAKE DECISIONS

One of the important goals of humanizing childbirth is to increase women's control over their birthing process and experience. This includes decisions about labor positions, pain management methods (e.g., use of anesthetics or more holistic strategies such as massages), obstetric procedures (e.g., cesarean section, use of enema, induction of labor), mother-infant contact after delivery, and companions and support during delivery. The amount of control held by laboring women is influenced by various factors such as birth setting and participants (e.g., McKay, 1991), as well as cultural practices (e.g., Behruzi et al., 2010).

Scopesi et al. (1997) examined women's childbirth experience at different hospital settings in Europe and the United States and found significant variability among these hospitals in women's ability to exert control over their childbirth experience. They also found that different areas of control were emphasized at different hospitals. For instance, a hospital that encourages women to make decisions about support and company during labor may still have a restrictive policy about their choice of obstetric procedures.

Behruzi et al. (2010) noted that women's lack of full participation in the decision-making process is a barrier to humanized birth care in Japan. Japanese women tend to take a passive role in medical settings, which might be related to power dynamics between genders and between patients and care providers. For instance, in Japan, physicians' authority is assumed, and patients are often expected to obey their physician and not question his or her decisions. In addition, because of gender bias, women may be seen as less capable of making competent decisions. Thus, often women cannot make decisions because they are not given adequate and accurate information by their health care providers (Behruzi et al., 2010).

In traditional African cultures where male dominance pervades, women are often expected to hold the responsibility for the outcomes of labor, yet they do not have the power to make decisions about delivery procedures and care (Chalmers, 1996). For example, women are blamed when the birth requires medical interventions, when the baby is lost, or when the birth is difficult. Furthermore, pregnancy is regarded as unclean, and women need to go through a purification ritual before reuniting with their partner or husband.

In the United States, where maternal care tends to be highly medicalized, the majority of women appear to have knowledge of their legal rights and control in the birth process. According to the large-scale survey by Declereq et al. (2006), about three of four women reported that they were aware of their rights to receive a clear and full explanation of medical procedures and options. Similarly, about three of four women were aware that they have the right to refuse or accept medical procedures, tests, or drugs that are offered to them. Regarding decisions about labor and childbirth, about three-quarters of women believed that they should be the one who makes decisions after consulting health care providers, and slightly less than one-quarter believed that decisions should be made collaboratively by mothers and their health care providers. It is interesting, however, that understanding the legal rights of laboring women does not necessarily translate into the ability to exert these rights. Only 10 percent responded that they have refused or accepted interventions that were offered to them or to their baby during their hospital stay. In addition, only 18 percent of those who had received an episiotomy reported that they had had a choice about this procedure. Whereas about 80 percent of women believed that they should be informed about every possible complication associated with common medical interventions, the majority of women (more than 60%) had incorrect knowledge about or were unsure of the adverse effects of cesarean section. These results indicate that, in reality, women may not receive clear and accurate information about medical interventions and the potential adverse effects associated with them. Their lack of information or knowledge may hinder them from making effective decisions.

McKay (1991) stressed the importance of proactive information sharing in empowering women. When women are not given accurate and adequate information, they cannot fully participate in the decision-making process. She referred to Kirkham's research that identified problems with health providers' information-giving behavior. Some examples of these problems are: (1)Women of lower social class tend to receive less information based on the assumption that they are incapable of understanding medical information. (2) Professionals block conversation by silence and changing the subject and do not listen to women's concerns or complaints.

(3) Providers ask routine questions that may limit women's choices.
(4) Professionals respond to women's concerns with empty reassurance
such as "don't worry." (5) Providers do not necessarily consider omitting
to give information as poor-quality care.

TOWARD HUMANIZED CHILDBIRTH

Despite the variability in birthing practices across cultures, the movement toward humanized childbirth has been observed around the world.
In some countries, this movement has led to new social and political reforms for the medical profession. For example, in 1993, the British government incorporated the concept of humanized childbirth in its policy for
maternity services based on the following three principles:

1. Maternity care should focus on women. The care should enable a
   woman to feel that she is in control of what is happening to her and
   to make decisions about her care. She should be able to discuss matters fully with the professionals who are involved in her care.
2. All women should have easy access to maternity services. Maternity
   services need to be locally based and culturally sensitive to service
   recipients.
3. Maternity services need to be monitored and planned in the community so that the services address communities' needs. The care
   should be effective, and the resources need to be used efficiently (Department of Health, 1993).

Page (2001a) asserted that this policy is relevant to the provision of maternity care anywhere in the world. We agree, and so we conclude this
chapter with several implications of promoting the humanization of childbirth and enhancing the safety and quality of women's birthing experience
around the world.

First, it is imperative to recognize that there is no universal definition of
humanized birth. Desirable and effective maternity care appears to be different for different cultures and individuals. Therefore, caregivers should
listen to the voice of the laboring woman and continuously make an effort
to understand her preferences and concerns and to meet her needs with
a flexible and personalized approach. Women's needs should be defined
by the women who receive maternity care, not by the professionals who
provide the care. Respectful and woman-focused care is the key to ensure
women's rights to autonomous decision making and to promote culturally
sensitive maternity care.

Second, although unnecessary medical interventions may hinder humanized birth, we should keep in mind that medicalized and humanized
approaches are not necessarily opposites or exclusive of each other. For ex-

ample, many women desire personalized and humanistic maternity care, yet they accept and trust technology (Mathews & Zadak, 1991). In fact, the humanization of birth has the potential to combine the advantages of medicalized birth with those of holistic and traditional approaches. Many women's lives have been saved by medical advances. The humanized birth movement should not be confused with the anti-technological movement, and traditional birthing should not be romanticized. Scientifically solid and evidence-based care is an essential component of humanized childbirth (Wagner, 2007).

In order to utilize advanced medical knowledge and technology for humanized childbirth, it is crucial for health professionals, including midwives and doulas, to build respectful relationships with each other. The respectful relationships among professionals involved in childbirth can promote efficient referrals upon medical necessity or women's requests, and a smooth referral process among professionals will expand the possibilities and accessibility of services that women are able to receive (Page, 2001a). Another issue to address here is the importance of utilizing community resources when we promote humanization of birth. Partners in Health (PIH) was cofounded by medical doctors in Boston, Massachusetts, in 1987 to improve the accessibility, quality, and affordability of medical services for the poor in Guatemala, Haiti, Malawi, Mexico, Peru, Russia, Rwanda, and the United States (PIH, 2010). One of the five principles of the PIH model asserts that health programs should involve community members in all of the processes of assessment, design, implementation, and evaluation. By training and hiring health workers from the local communities, the programs become community run, are self-sustainable, and address needs that are unique to each community. The implication of this PIH principle for the humanization of birth is that program developers are encouraged to use human resources in their own community/society, which allow them to develop systems that address individuals' needs in an attentive, personalized, culturally sensitive, continuous, and affordable manner.

There are always power dynamics that interplay between all parties involved in birthing. For example, the hierarchal structure of medical settings may hinder women from fully participating in the decision-making process, even if the health professionals provide clear explanations of women's legal rights and the options and interventions that are offered to them. Professional providers should strive to develop a collaborative relationship with a laboring woman and her family or significant others. Nevertheless, it is unrealistic to expect that this effort can eliminate the power differential between providers and laboring women. Therefore, it is important for health providers to be aware of the power dynamics that exist in their relationship with a laboring woman and to consider how these dynamics may impact the woman throughout her birthing experience.

Last, as we discussed earlier, women's ability to make decisions about their labor and childbirth are influenced and limited by various social and cultural factors, such as race, ethnicity, gender, age, class, sexual orientation, disability, and immigration status. In other words, reproductive oppression is an *intersectional* issue. In order to maximize women's control over their reproductive lives and ensure their birthing rights regardless of their social positions, issues such as socioeconomic disadvantage, racial discrimination, inequalities in wealth and power, and differential access to resources and services need to be addressed (Ross, 2006). Diaz-Tello and Paltrow (2010) highlighted the importance of academic and grassroots activism to combat birthing injustices and promote women's birthing rights. Coalition and collaborative efforts between professional providers, scholars, individual activists, and activist organizations are necessary to advocate for women's right to humanized childbirth and to reproductive justice in all regards.

REFERENCES

Abramson, R., Breedlove, G., & Isaacs, B. (2007). Birthing support and the community-based doula. *Zero to Three, 27*, 55–59.

Arms, S. (1977). *Immaculate deception: A new look at women and childbirth.* Boston: Houghton-Mifflin.

Baby Weekly Research. (2010). Retrieved from http://www.babycome.ne.jp/online/research/detail.php?vol=115_1.

Béhague, D. P., Victora, C. G., & Barros, F. C. (2002). Consumer demand for caesarean sections in Brazil: Population based birth cohort study linking ethnographic and epidemiological methods. *British Medical Journal, 324*, 942–945.

Behruzi, R., Hatem, M., Fraser, W., Goulet, L., Li, M., & Misago, C. (2010). Facilitators and barriers in the humanization of childbirth practice in Japan. Retrieved from http://www.ncbi.nlm.nih.gov/pmc/articles/PMC2889847/.

Benesse Jisedai Ikusei Kenkyujo. (2010). Retrieved from http://www.benesse.co.jp/jisedaiken/research/index.html#link1.

Betra, A., Merialdi, M., Lauer, J. A., Bing-Shun, W., Thomas, J., Look, P. V., & Wagner, M. (2007). Rates of cesarian section: Analysis of global, regional, and national estimates. *Paediatric and Perinatal Epidemiology, 21*, 98–113.

Butler, J., Abrams, B., Parker, J., & Laros, R. (1993). Supportive nurse-midwife care is associated with a reduced incidence of cesarean section. *American Journal of Obstetrics and Gynecology, 168*, 1407–1413.

CBS. (2009). Statistics Netherland. Retrieved from http://www.cbs.nl/en-GB/menu/themas/gezondheid-welzijn/publicaties/artikelen/archief/2009/2009-2696-wm.htm.

Chalmers, B. (1991). Changing childbirth customs. *Pre-and Peri-Natal Psychology, 5*, 221–232.

Chalmers, B. (1996). Cross-cultural comparisons of birthing: Psycho-social issues in Western and African birth. *Psychology and Health, 12*, 11–21.

Collins, N. L., Dunkel-Schetter, C., Lobel, M., & Scrimshaw, S. C. (1993). Social support in pregnancy: Psychosocial correlates of birth outcomes and postpartum depression. *Journal of Personality and Social Psychology, 65,* 1243–1258.

Declercq, E. R., Sakala, C., Corry, M. P., & Applebaum, S. (2006). Listening to mothers II: Report of the Second National U.S. Survey of Women's Childbearing Experiences. *Journal of Perinatal Education, 16,* 9–14.

Department of Health. (1993). *Changing childbirth: The report of the Expert Maternity Group.* London: Stationary Office Books.

Diaz-Tello, F. & Paltrow, L. M. (2010). *Birth justice as reproductive justice* [NAPW Working Paper January 2010 Draft]. Retrieved from http://advocatesfor pregnantwomen.org/BirthJusticeasReproRights.pdf.

Engel, N. S. (1989). An American experience of pregnancy and childbirth in Japan. *Birth, 16*(2), 81–86.

Harris, A., Gao, Y., Barclay, L., Belton, S., Yue, Z. W., Min, H., et al. (2007). Consequences of birth policies and practices in post-reform China. *Reproductive Health Matters, 15*(30), 114–124.

Health, Labor, and Welfare Ministry in Japan [HLWM]. (2010). *National survey 2010.* Retrieved from http://www.mhlw.go.jp/toukei/itiran/index.html.

Henneborn, W. J., & Cogan, R. (1975). The effect of husband participation in reported pain and the probability of medication during labor and birth. *Journal of Psychosomatic Research, 19,* 215–222.

Hurst, M., & Summey, P. (1984). Childbirth and social class: The case of cesarean delivery. *Social Science and Medicine, 18,* 621–631.

International Federation of Health Plans. (2010). *2010 comparative price report: Medical and hospital fees by country.* Retrieved from http://ifhp.com/documents/ IFHP_Price_Report2010ComparativePriceReport29112010.pdf.

Jordan, B. (1978). *Birth in four cultures.* Montreal, Quebec, Canada: Eden Press.

Keinan, G. (1997). Social support, stress, and personality: Do all women benefit from husbands' presence during childbirth? In G. R. Pierce, B. Lakey, I. G. Sarason, & B. R. Sarason (Eds.), *Sourcebook of social support and personality* (pp. 409–427). New York: Plenum.

Liamputtong, P. (2005). Birth and social class: Northern Thai women's lived experiences of caesarean and vaginal birth. *Sociology of Health and Illness, 27,* 243–270.

MacDorman, M. F., Menacker, F., & Declercq, E. (2010). Trends and characteristics of home and other out-of-hospital births in the United States, 1990–2006. *National Vital Statistics Reports, 58*(11), 1–15.

Martis, R. (2007). Continuous support for women during childbirth: RHL commentary. In World Health Organization (Ed.), *The WHO reproductive health library.* Retrieved from http://apps.who.int/rhl/pregnancy_childbirth/childbirth/ routine_care/rmcom/en/print.html.

Mathews, J., & Zadak, K. (1991). The alternative birth movement in the United States: History and current status. *Women & Health, 17*(1), 39–56.

McKay, S. (1982). Humanizing services through family-centered care. *Contemporary OB/GYN, 22,* 241–248.

McKay, S. (1991). Shared power: The essence of humanized childbirth. *Pre-and Peri-Natal Psychology, 5,* 283–295.

McKay, S. & Philips, C. (1984). *Family-centered maternity care: Implementation strategies.* Rockville, MD: Aspen.

Morris, T., & McInerney, K. (2010). Media representations of pregnancy and childbirth: An analysis of reality television programs in the United States. *Birth, 37,* 134–140.

Morsbach, G. (1983). Attitudes and experiences of Japanese mothers concerning the period of childbirth. *Psychologia, 26,* 73–85.

Oishi, T., Saito, E., & Shibata, F. (2003). Nihon no masuibunben no jittai to sono mondaiten. *Boseieisei, 44,* 409–414.

Page, L. (2001a). The humanization of birth. *International Journal of Gynecology & Obstetrics, 75,* 55–58.

Page, L. (2001b). Human resources for maternity care: The present system in Brazil, Japan, North America, western Europe, and New Zealand. *International Journal of Gynecology & Obstetrics, 75,* 81–88.

Partners in Health. (2010). *The PIH model of care.* Retrieved from http://www.pih.org/pages/what-we-do/.

Perkins, M., Brazier, E., Themmen, E., Bassan, B., Diallo, D., Mutunga, A., et al. (2009). Out-of-pocket costs for facility-based maternity care in three African countries. *Health Policy and Planning, 24,* 289–300.

Peterson, G. (1996). Childbirth: The ordinary miracle: Effects of devaluation of childbirth on women's self-esteem and family relationships. *Pre-and Perinatal Psychology Journal, 11,* 101–109.

Press Net Japan. (2011). Uman ai. Mutsu bunben naze kokunaide hirogaranai? Retrieved from http://www.47news.jp/CN/201101/CN2011011901000393.html

Ross, L. (2006). Understanding reproductive justice. *SisterSong.* Retrieved from http://www.sistersong.net/publications_and_articles/Understanding_RJ.pdf.

Scopesi, A., Zanobini, M., & Carossino, P. (1997). Childbirth in different cultures: Psychophysical reactions of women delivering in US, German, French, and Italian hospitals. *Journal of Reproductive and Infant Psychology, 15,* 9–30.

Sosa, R., Kennell, J., Klaus, M., Robertson, S., & Urrutia, J. (1980). The effect of supportive companion in perinatal problems, length of labor, and mother-infant interacting. *New England Journal of Medicine, 303,* 597–600.

Suzuki, S. (2008). Mutsubunben ga fukyusinai Nippon. *Ishimanabu.* Retrieved from https://ishimanabu.jp/column/?task=detail&id=46.

Toepke, M., & Albers, L. (1995). Neonatal considerations when birth occurs at home. *Journal of Nurse-Midwifery, 40,* 529–533.

United Nations International Children's Emergency Fund. (2008). Retrieved from http://www.unicef.org/.

U.S. Department of Health & Human Services. (2010). *Agency for Healthcare Research and Quality.* Retrieved from http://www.hhs.gov/.

Wagner, M. (2007). Global midwifery—traditional and official—and humanization of birth. *Midwifery Today, 83,* 55–57.

Weil, O., & Fernandez, H. (1999). Is safe motherhood an orphan initiative? *Lancet, 354,* 940–943.

Villar, J., Valladares, E., Wojdyla, D., Zavaleta, N., Carroli, G., Velazco, A., et al. (2005). Caesarean delivery rates and pregnancy outcomes: The 2005 WHO global survey on maternal and perinatal health in Latin America. *Lancet, 367,* 1819–1829.

Chapter 11

Female Feticide and Infanticide: Implications for Reproductive Justice

Ramaswami Mahalingam and Madeline Wachman

Many demographers and journalists have noted the rising disparity in sex ratios in various Asian countries, such as China, India, and Korea (Croll, 2000; Das Gupta & Shuzhuo, 1999). Some scholars predict that, in the next few decades, this disparity will result in approximately 90 million men from India and China who will not be able to marry (Hudson & den Boer, 2004; Hutchings, 1997). These alarming sex-ratio disparities and the missing girls concern many demographers, planners, and economists. To develop meaningful interventions, we need to understand the cultural psychology of son preference and extreme neglect of girls. In this chapter, we argue that structural and cultural factors shape attitudes toward female infants, the most vulnerable members of society. We also explore the complex consequences of extreme neglect of girls in the form of sex-selective abortion and female infanticide and their impact on the lives of the men and women in these communities.

Our purpose here is threefold. First, we review the relevant literature on neglect of girls and infanticide in general, and then focus on India, which has a long history of neglect of girls that includes infanticide and sex-selective abortion. Second, we explore the complex consequences of systemic neglect of girls with respect to reproductive justice based on a cultural–ecological framework. Finally, we discuss the significance of these findings for combating extreme forms of neglect of girls (e.g., female infanticide, feticide) in places (e.g., Tamilnadu and Punjab, India) with a documented history of extreme sex discrimination and consider the implications for reproductive justice from a cultural-psychological perspective.

FEMALE INFANTICIDE AND
SEX-SELECTIVE ABORTION

The female infanticide phenomenon is as old as many cultures. In many countries, governments have allowed, and sometimes encouraged, the killing of female, handicapped, or other unwanted children. Gender-specific infant mortality varies across cultures and regions of a country. Theories of why sex differentials in infant mortality occur also vary across and within countries. Although it is well known that sex ratios have historically been substantially higher in many Asian countries, the cultural and psychological reasons behind these differences have not been sufficiently explored (Mahalingam, 2007). Most of the ethnographic and demographic research on sex determination has focused on the low status and oppression of women (see Hrdy, 1999, for a review). Female oppression is manifested in various forms. Female infanticide and sex-selective abortion are examples of an extreme form of neglect of girls, and gender inequality is one of its major contributing factors.

Sex determination is a dominant and persistent theme in countries with disproportionate sex ratios. Unequal power structures and gender relations are at the core of sex discrimination in cultural practices. Additional socioeconomic factors that contribute to female infanticide include irrational national population control policies and the unethical use of reproductive technology. In China, for example, the government implemented the one-child policy in 1979. This policy has achieved its objective of decreasing the country's fertility rate, but it also has provoked citizens to practice sex-selective abortion. The 2000 Chinese census indicated that, at birth, there are 100 girls for every 120 boys This number remained the same in the 2005 intercensus, and it left China with an estimated 32 million fewer female citizens under 20 years old (Zhu, Lu, & Hesketh, 2009). Moreover, the 2005 intercensus also reported more than 1.1 million more births of boys. Experts predict that the sex ratio in China will steadily worsen over the next two decades (Zhu et al., 2009).

According to Oster (2005), women who carry Hepatitis B are more likely to give birth to sons than to daughters. Based on census data from Tamilnadu, India, Srinivasan and Bedi (2008) argued that the Hepatitis B infection rate does not account for the disparity in the sex ratios in higher birth order (i.e., girls with more older siblings). They found that there were more late-born boys than girls, which could not be explained by the prevalence of Hepatitis B. Srinivasan and Bedi (2008) have also noted that the bulk of sex determination happens before birth and that cultural preference and access to sex-determination technologies are major proximal causes for the disparity in the sex ratio.

Improved ultrasound technology has allowed parents to determine the sex of the fetus. Increased access to this technology has led to increased rates of female infanticide, and thus the male-to-female ratio in many countries has become increasingly disproportionate (Das Gupta & Shuzhuo, 1999; Hesketh, Lu, & Xing, 2005). Sex-selective abortion was first documented in India in the 1970s. One of the first studies on sex-selective abortion in India showed that, in an urban clinic, 430 of the 450 women who were told that the sex of the baby was female went on to have an abortion, whereas 250 of the 700 who were told they had male fetuses went on to give birth, despite the risk of genetic disorders (Ramanamma & Bambawale, 1980). At the time of the study, sex-detection was done with amniocentesis at around 18–20 weeks of gestation. Now, modern technologies allow sex-selection to occur prior to conception, via in vitro fertilization and artificial insemination. However, most sex-elective abortion (i.e., female feticide) is a result of ultrasound imaging because the other techniques are more expensive. Though improvements in health care and conditions for pregnant women have resulted in reductions in infant mortality, advancements in technology to find the sex of the fetus have offset all of that progress.

Sharma (2008) noted that assisted reproductive technology has facilitated female feticide, which has contributed to 100 million girls missing from the world's population and led to a gendercide. Gender inequality and discrimination are problems of global importance, and extreme neglect of female infants underscores the various forms of sex determination over a woman's lifetime. In many cultures, women are blamed for not producing sons, despite the fact that women cannot control the sex of their children. Mothers whose children are only, or predominantly, female are blamed for the rest of their lives, and they are abused or mistreated for not producing sons. Such mistreatment affects the physical and mental health of mothers of daughters for the rest of the mothers' life. Thus, giving birth to daughters itself could lead to the maltreatment of mothers, and it is a potential risk factor that could seriously affect the health of mothers living in communities with extreme son preference (Shyama, 1996).

Few studies have been conducted to examine differences in infanticide rates across various cultural conditions; thus far, most hypotheses about neglect of girls and infanticide are relatively global (Keller,

Nesse, & Hofferth, 2001). In order to mitigate sex determination and subsequent female infanticide and feticide, it is important first to understand the unique complexities of each community that has had a long history of infant gender disparities. We focus on India, but we also call for the need to identify culture-specific factors and psychological antecedents for female infanticide and feticide in other countries. Here we provide a cultural–ecological framework for the study of neglect of girls, and we also discuss how extreme neglect of girls could affect the psychological well-being of both men and women in communities with a long history of neglect of girls, as well as the social consequences of those "missing" girls.

THE PROBLEMS OF FEMALE INFANTICIDE AND NEGLECT OF GIRLS IN INDIA

During the 19th century, the colonial British government formed a committee to investigate the prevalence of female infanticide (Panigrahi, 1972). Fanny Parks (as cited in Panigrahi, 1972), a British traveler in the northern part of India, reported that she had never seen so few women as during her 4 years in India. The British government responded to reports about villages or tribes without even a single female child by enacting the Female Infanticide Act in 1870, which was intended to abolish the practice of killing female infants (Miller, 1981). Although the colonial government claimed that they had abolished female infanticide in northwestern India, subsequent census records revealed enduring male-biased sex ratios over the next several decades (Miller, 1981). A century later, detailed ethnographic reports (e.g., Muthulakshmi, 1997; Shyama, 1996; Srinivasan, 1992; Venkatachalam & Srinivasan, 1993) left little doubt that female infanticide and feticide still exist today in Tamilnadu, India.

NEGLECT OF GIRLS: THEORETICAL PERSPECTIVES

To prevent female infanticide, one needs to understand the conditions under which it is likely to occur. Most of the research on neglect of girls and infanticide is primarily focused on explicating the structural and cultural reasons for differential treatment of girls. Two complementary perspectives dominate the current discussion of female infanticide: (1) the structural perspective and (2) the cultural-practices perspective. The structural perspective focuses on the contribution of structural factors (e.g., women's literacy, public policies) to the practice of neglect of girls. The cultural-practices perspective focuses on the role of cultural practices (e.g., the need to have son to perform funeral rituals) in fostering an unfavorable attitude toward girls. Below, we examine these perspectives in more detail.

Structural Perspective

Feminists have argued that women's low status and the structural differences between society's treatment of women and men are the main causes of neglect of girls and female infanticide (e.g., Dube, Dube, & Bhatnagar, 1999; Hegde, 1999; Muthulakshmi, 1997; Srinivasan, 1992). They advocate developmental programs geared toward improving women's educational and employment opportunities. Consequently, interventions by development agencies in India have been based on the assumption that improving women's literacy will lead to their empowerment and, subsequently, to declines in extreme forms of neglect of girls. However, recent demographic reports suggest that when women's status improves, preferential allocation of resources to sons also increases, which is the opposite of the desired outcome (Das Gupta & Visaria, 1996; Premi, 2001). It seems paradoxical that women's empowerment and status mobility result in increased investment in boys (Das Gupta & Visaria, 1996). In some parts of India, education of women correlates *positively* with neglect of girls (Das Gupta & Visaria, 1996). In Punjabi villages, for example, discrimination against girls and the "child mortality rate of higher-parity daughters" remains similar for educated and uneducated women (Das Gupta & Visaria, 1996, p. 124). Anderson and Romani (1997) found that, in Korea, although low infant mortality generally correlates with higher socioeconomic status (also see Anderson, Kim, & Romani, 1997), there is a greater differential between male and female infant mortality even in families of higher socioeconomic status. Therefore, when families have discretionary resources, they invest differentially in their sons and daughters. Therefore, it remains unclear that raising women's status *alone* will protect female infants; discrimination against daughters might actually *increase* with the upward mobility of women's status in India (Das Gupta & Visaria, 1996; also see Anderson & Romani, 1997; Anderson et al., 1997, for similar findings in China and Korea).

Ethnographers have pointed out that literacy is only one of several factors in women's decisions to keep a female child (Jeffery & Jeffery, 1997; Seymour, 1999). Other structural factors (e.g., federal policy that promoted smaller families, the easy availability of reproductive technologies) also contribute to the increase in male-biased sex ratios. During the early 1970s, the federal government of India promoted birth control programs and targeted women to implement various birth control methods (e.g., sterilizations; Ramasubban & Jejeebhoy, 2000). The Indian government also launched an advertisement campaign that emphasized the benefits of smaller families and depicted an ideal family with two children, a son and a daughter. Rarely did they present two daughters in any picture. Media theorists have argued that these implicit messages about gender shape and reinforce existing biases (Rosengren & Windahl, 1989). The Chinese government also used similar strategies to promote its one-child policy. Researchers have reported that, after China's introduction of the one-child policy, the abandonment of girls, female infanticide, and female feticide all increased dramatically (Hudson & den-Boer, 2004; Hutchings, 1997).

The easy availability of reproductive technologies to determine the sex of a fetus (e.g., ultrasound) has also contributed to the practice of female feticide. Noninvasive ultrasound tests cost as little as $10 (about 500 rupees) in India, and ultrasound clinics can be found even in small Indian towns. These technologies encourage people to achieve the ideal combination of one son and one daughter by aborting unwanted female fetuses; couples rarely abort male fetuses. In the government hospital of Amristar, in Punjab, for example, only one female child is born for every two male children (Natarajan, 1997). The technological control of achieving an ideal sex ratio for a family now affects even caste groups that did not originally practice female infanticide. Clinics offer their services to couples from all social strata, and, consequently, couples from any caste group can use technology to achieve an ideal gender composition (i.e., one boy and one girl) among their offspring. In sum, the structural perspective states that the increase in male-biased sex ratios is caused by a combination of structural factors (e.g., the low status of women, federal policies that promote small families, easy access to reproductive technologies).

Cultural-Practices Perspective

The cultural-practices perspective considers more context-specific reasons that might contribute to extreme forms of neglect of girls (i.e., female infanticide, female feticide). Some anthropologists (e.g., Gregor, 1988; Picone, 1998; Sargent, 1987; Scheper-Hughes, 1992) have suggested that female infanticide is tied to cultural practices and folk beliefs about what counts as a human being, such as questioning whether a baby should be considered a human being. Such folk beliefs exist cross-culturally (see Hrdy, 1999, for a review). Scheper-Hughes (1992) noted that, in poverty-stricken northeastern Brazil, people do not consider killing babies to be infanticide. Instead, they view babies as the *other*, and, because they are not truly human, babies might be left to die; therefore, mothers are discouraged from bonding with newborns. In other societies, children are not believed to be human beings until they reach school age (Hrdy, 1999). Picone (1998) found that, in parts of pre-World War II Japan, parents who had children with visible birth defects considered those children shameful and often killed them.

Scheper-Hughes (1992) examined the systemic nature of infanticide in Brazil. She argued that the social construction of mothers is always dichotomized between a *caring* mother and a *killer* mother. Based on her ethnographic work in poverty-stricken areas of northern Brazil, where there had been a high incidence of infanticide but no gender difference in infant mortality, Scheper-Hughes (1992) examined how material conditions shape maternal behavior. She reported that women often engaged in various discursive practices (e.g., not naming the child) to distance themselves from being mothers, and she argued that these impoverished mothers, who themselves needed nourishment, could not care for their newborns, who would often die from starvation. Examples of infanticide in Brazil and India call into question the universality of the notion of mothers as essentially "caring and benevolent" because of their dominant role in bearing children (Scheper-Hughes, 1992). Whereas abject poverty diminished Brazilian mothers' ability to nurture, there could be other factors and beliefs about gender that play a major role in the case of Tamil mothers. A key difference to note is that, in Brazil, infanticide remains gender blind, whereas, in Tamilnadu and elsewhere in India and Asia, it is almost exclusively female infants and fetuses that are killed (Harriss-White, 2001). In Tamilnadu, ethnographic reports provide graphic details about the various means used to kill a newborn female infant (e.g., Muthulakshmi, 1997; Venkatachalam & Srinivasan, 1993). In most of the cases, women (i.e., mothers, grandmothers, midwives) do the killing.

Ethnographic reports often suggest that, in India, the practice of giving a dowry to marry off a daughter remains a major stressor for parents, and it is a common form of transfer of marital goods (Murdock, 1967, 1981). Thus, each daughter represents a drain on family resources because the parents have to pay a dowry to arrange her marriage, and poorer families must pay proportionately more than wealthier families for a particularly desirable husband. As a result, spousal abuse is frequent when daughters of poorer families marry wealthier men (Rao, 1993a, 1993b, 1997). Most analyses attribute spousal abuse to the low status of women in a patriarchal culture (Dube et al., 1999; Muthulakshmi, 1997).

Neglect of girls is also related to religious and cultural practices that mandate the need for a son. Miller (1981) argued that Hindu beliefs and practices (e.g., only sons can perform funeral rites) contribute to neglect of girls. In the Hindu death ceremony, or *pind daan*, performed to ensure that the parent reaches heaven, only a son may set fire to the funeral pyre. According to the 1991 Indian census, the sex ratio of children under the age of six in the state of Tamilnadu is 945 girls to every 1,000 boys. Venkatachalam and Srinivasan (1993) described the various methods used to kill a newborn female infant. These range from starving the infant to feeding it paddy (i.e., rice with its outside husk) with milk or milk with a mixture of poisonous herbs (also see Vasanthi, 1995; Venkataramani, 1986). The cultural-practices perspective highlights the underlying social and cultural reasons for son preference that lead to extreme forms of son preference. The undervaluing of daughters due to various cultural practices, such as dowry and patrilocal system (where the woman has to relocate and live with her husband's family and become a member of her husband's clan), contribute to differential investment in daughters and sons.

Although several cultural psychologists have studied infanticide, very few of them examined the antecedents of female infanticide. Most of the psychological studies on infanticide were based on clinical cases conducted in the United States and Europe with mothers who had committed infanticide, and the researchers documented the women's underlying depression and other related psychopathology as major reasons for their infanticidal behavior (for a review see Spinelli, 2001; also see Chandra, Venkatasubramanian, & Thomas, 2002, for a similar study conducted in India). These researchers examined only the cases of infanticide that were clinically documented in relation to maternal depression or other severe mental illness. Although their studies help us to understand the psychopathology of infanticide, they may not help us to understand the cultural-psychological basis of the *systematic* and *gender-specific* nature of the female infanticide practiced in Asia. An understanding of the culture-specific moral underpinnings of female infanticide is of great importance as policy makers consider ways to combat female infanticide.

Despite the overwhelming evidence of the male-biased sex-ratio (see Harriss-White, 2001) in several communities in India, few cultural psychologists have examined the psychological consequences of neglect of girls. Mahalingam (2007) argued that cultural–ecological factors play a critical role in extreme neglect of girls. Based on field-based behavioral-ecological research on communities with extreme neglect of girls, he discovered that land-owning and warrior communities tend to practice extreme sex discrimination for very different ecological reasons. Agricultural communities tend to be patrilocal (i.e., women after marriage become part of their husband's family, and wealth is transferred from father to sons). Having more daughters depletes the land resources of a family because land would be given away as dowry, and fragmenting land depletes its value. In contrast, warrior communities need more sons to protect the community during inter-communal conflicts. Women are viewed as a liability in these communities because of the patriarchal notion that the purity of women holds the honor of the community. Mahalingam (2007) conducted a study in a caste group that is predominantly agricultural and a warrior caste group, both of which have a documented history of extreme neglect of girls where only about 750 girls survive for every 1,000 boys between the ages of zero and five years. He found that, in the warrior caste, the culture of honor plays a critical role in shaping attitudes toward women. In contrast, members of the land owning caste, when given a hypothetical situation about a patriarch has to decide between dividing his land and cash resources of equal value between a son who has three sons and a son who has three daughters, were significantly more likely to choose the option that the son who has only sons should get the ancestral land and the son who has only daughters should get the cash. Thus, ecological factors, such as the economic nature of a community (e.g., agricultural, warrior) play a vital role in shaping their attitude toward sex discrimination and determination. A confluence of cultural–ecological factors, cultural practices (e.g., patrilocal arrangement, funeral rites), and social factors (e.g., dowry, availability of ultrasound technologies) contribute to extreme neglect of girls (i.e., female feticide/infanticide).

EXTREME NEGLECT OF GIRLS: IMPLICATIONS FOR WOMEN'S PSYCHOLOGICAL WELL-BEING AND REPRODUCTIVE JUSTICE

Hudson and den Boer (2004) proposed that excessive men in a community accentuate the need to establish idealized traditional gender norms that value hyper-femininity and hyper-masculinity. Mahalingam, Haritatos, and Jackson (2007) conducted a study in Tamilnadu, India in a community with a history of neglect of girls. They proposed a dual pathway model that predicts that idealized beliefs about masculinity and femininity, although positively related to self-esteem, are also related to shame. The pressure to live up to idealized expectations would also be positively related to depression. Tests of their dual pathway model showed that idealized beliefs about masculinity were positively related to both self-esteem and shame for both women and men. In another study conducted in Punjab, which also a history of extreme neglect of girls, Yim and Mahalingam (2006) found that idealized beliefs about the divine power of chaste women were positively related to the psychological well-being of men. Traditional gender beliefs about chastity were positively related to life satisfaction for men. Mahalingam and Haritatos (2006) found that, in communities with a history of extreme neglect of girls, essentialist beliefs about women were positively related to attitudes toward violence against women, and Mahalingam and Balan (2008) found that adolescent girls who endorsed traditional gender beliefs scored high on measures of life satisfaction and low on measures of academic achievement. Women who pursue life goals that are congruent with traditional gender-role expectations scored higher on life satisfaction than did those who pursue life goals that are incongruent with traditional gender-role expectations (Balan & Mahalingam, 2008).

Preferential treatment toward sons persists even among highly educated women (Das Gupta & Visaria, 1996). One could argue that, if women were given the opportunities, they would like to treat their sons and daughters equally, but obligations and pressures from their husbands' families could override such desires. To preserve family unity and avoid conflicts, women seemed to make a mother's ultimate sacrifice and killed their own daughters (Hrdy, 1999). Many cultural narratives valorize women as self-sacrificing arbiters of family unity, which makes them silent partners in the perpetuation of neglect of girls and feticide. It is imperative that men change their view of daughters as a drain on family resources. For instance, when the state government offered to take female infants and put them up for adoption, there were not many volunteers. Instead, villagers reasoned that these girls might come back as adults and seek the family's resources (Natarajan, 1997).

In addition, the more educated daughters are, the more expensive it becomes to arrange their marriage to men who are either equally or better educated. Behavioral ecologists have argued that hypergyny (i.e., the preference to marry up) is also linked to neglect of girls and infanticide (e.g., Dickeman, 1979, 1981). Women's empowerment and mobility could contribute to an additional problem, that of finding a qualified bridegroom, and parents have to pay more for an expensive marriage on top of the expenses incurred in educating their daughters. In the patrilocal marriage system, a woman is expected to shift her affiliation and loyalty to her husband's family after marriage, which is regarded as a depletion of her natal family's resources. Women's empowerment should be linked to shifts in societal values, such as the abolition of dowry, patrilocal practices, and the arranged marriage system. Instead of exclusively contributing to their husbands' family resources, employed and educated women should have more freedom to care for their own parents so that parents who have daughters also believe that they can depend upon their daughters for help when they are old. This is important because India does not have a social security system that provides financial and health care benefits for senior citizens.

COMPLEX CONSEQUENCES OF EXTREME NEGLECT OF GIRLS: IMPLICATIONS FOR REPRODUCTIVE JUSTICE

Reproductive justice research is primarily focused on women's right to make decisions that matter to their health. Recently, several scholars have argued that research on reproductive justice must be broadened in scope to be sensitive to the lives of women from various cultural and social contexts (Luna, 2009; Oomman & Ganatra, 2002; Rahman, 1994). It is interesting that, in many countries (e.g., India, China), the reproductive rights of women (i.e., the right to make reproductive decisions and the right of access to health services) are guaranteed through various legal means. However, on closer examination, one finds that it is not clear whether the formal laws and governmental policies of a country indeed "restrict or enhance women's reproductive health and rights" (Rahman, 1994, p. 982). In countries with a long history of discrimination against girls, women's right to have a son or daughter is hampered by a variety of cultural, social, and ecological factors. Women may be forced to abort female fetuses, as many women in India and China do not have the freedom to give birth to daughters. Cultural factors that favor and value women who give birth to sons puts women under undue stress, which affects their physical and mental health. Often pressured to abort a female fetus or to commit female infanticide, women silently endure the shame and trauma of losing a child just because she is a girl. For example, in India, cultural–ecological factors restrict women's agency to make informed decisions about their reproductive rights.

We argue that women's right to give birth to a daughter or a son (not just to a son) needs to be understood within the cultural–ecological context where giving birth to a daughter greatly undermines the woman's authority and power within her household. For instance, based on the results of China's Health and Nutrition Survey, Li and Wu (2011) found that a woman with a first-born son has a 3.9 percent greater role in household decision making than a woman with a first-born daughter. In addition, a first-born son improves the mother's nutritional intake and decreases her likelihood of being underweight. Thus, producing a son improves the intrahousehold bargaining power of women. Ebenstein and Sharygin (2009) observed that the "missing" girls of China also contribute to the prevalence of prostitution and sexually transmitted infections that adversely affect the physical and psychological well-being of women in these communities. Hence, the reproductive justice perspective needs to be sensitive to the culture-specific production of patriarchal norms and values that greatly restrict women's capacity to exercise their agency in making decisions about whether to have a boy or girl despite the fact that they technically have the right to make reproductive choices.

We propose a cultural–ecological model where a confluence of ecological, cultural, and social factors contributes to extreme neglect of girls. Ecological factors include agricultural communities' preference to have more sons so that ancestral land is not fragmented as a result of daughters' dowries, cultural practices (e.g., patrilocal marriage arrangements) underscore the need to produce a male heir, and social factors (e.g., dowry, viewing sons as means to support parents during old age) foster a cultural logic that justifies and perpetuates the need to have more sons.

As a consequence of a systemic historical preference for sons, communities end up with excessive men/boys. Hudson and den Boer (2004) argued that male-biased sex ratios affect community mental health in complex ways. Male-biased sex ratios have contributed to cultures that valorize hyper-feminine and hyper-masculine expectations. Both women and men believe in culturally valued, idealized representations of men and women. In communities where extreme forms of sex determination persist, endorsing such idealized beliefs about gender positively relates to lower levels of anxiety and higher levels of self-esteem for women (Mahalingam & Balan, 2008; Mahalingam & Jackson, 2007). However, endorsing such idealized beliefs also negatively predicts academic achievement for adolescent girls (Mahalingam & Balan, 2008). For men, endorsing hyper-masculine ideals relates to both higher levels of shame and self-esteem. Also men who endorse idealized beliefs about masculinity and feminin-ity also endorse positive attitudes toward violence against women. Thus, idealized essentialist representations about gender negatively shape the psychological well-being of men and the academic achievement of women in communities with surplus men.

The paucity of women in these communities has serious consequences. As noted by Hudson and den Boer (2004), the excessive men in the com-munity contribute to a cultural milieu that fosters intra-and intergroup competition among men for resources and academic success because only successful men are likely to find a suitable bride from their own caste group. In addition, the cultural practice of patrilocality puts the women at a greater disadvantage in several ways. Mothers are under enormous pressure to produce a son. Inability to produce a son adversely affects the social status of a woman in her husband's family, which could also contribute to domestic violence and abuse of women by her husband and his relatives. Thus, patrilocal arrangements put the woman who has given birth only to daughters at additional risk of emotional and physical abuse.

Hudson and den Boer (2004) have discussed the various implications of surplus men, including the phenomenon of single men in China who are called *bare branches* (the Chinese term is *guang gun-er*). Hudson and den Boer (2004) observed that bare branches contribute to increased inter-group conflicts and global instability. They have examined the relationship between surplus men and wars, and concluded that sex-ratio disparity is a critical factor in the escalation of international armed conflicts between countries with surplus men.

The shortage of marriageable women also contributes to the prolif-eration of sex trafficking, as women from other countries are smuggled into China (see chapter 5, "Reproductive Injustice"). China has already witnessed a high incidence of kidnapping and selling of women in prov-inces where there is a shortage of women (Sharma, 2008). A kidnapped bride can be bought for $600 in Hebei province (see Lai-wan, Eric, & Hoi-yan, 2006, for a review). The sex industry is also rampant in these communities, and prostitution proliferates in many Chinese cities. It is estimated that there at least there are six million prostitutes in China, and the sex industry's annual income is estimated to be three billion dollars (see Lai-wan et al., 2006). In these communities safe sex prac-tices (e.g., condom use) are perceived to be in opposition to dominant masculine norms, and the lack of motivation to adopt these practices contributes to the spread of HIV and other STIs in communities with male-biased sex ratios.

Another social consequence of sex-selective abortion is the practice of fraternal polyandry, where a woman is married to a group of brothers, usually legally married to the oldest brother. All younger brothers can have sexual intercourse with the wife of their oldest brother. Occasionally, a younger brother is the one who gets married, and older brothers can have sexual intercourse with their younger brother's wife. The disparity in the sex ratio has contributed to the culture of fraternal polyandry in Punjab, particularly in the rural areas (Garg, 2005). Sharma (2008) has also noted this trend among Indian and Chinese immigrant communities in North America where the cultural preference for sons persists. Communities in Canada with a concentration of Chinese and Indian immigrants have census-documented, male-biased sex ratios. Sharma (2008) also noted that south Asian and Chinese immigrants are the major clients who use more advanced technologies to predetermine the sex of the fetus, and these parents rarely desire to have a girl. Typically, they use these clinics to conceive a boy (see Sharma, 2008, for a review). Thus, there is a cultural continuity in the preference for sons among Asian immigrants to Western countries. It is unclear to what extent the preference for sons affects the psychological well-being of daughters in immigrant communities. In a study of Punjabi second-generation daughters from immigrant families in the United States, Mahalingam and Haritatos (2006) found no evidence of extreme sex discrimination. However, they noted that sex discrimination occurred in parental expectations in different domains. The daughters were expected to uphold cultural values and expectations; idealized beliefs about ethnic gender representations were common, and daughters often felt pressure to embody those representations.

Some demographers and public-health researchers have argued that sex-selective abortion may actually reduce postnatal discrimination against girls (see Oomman & Ganatra, 2002). Such arguments fail to notice the systemic pressures on women to abort a female fetus for the sake of the family and to uphold the patriarchal values of the community. Although laws have been enacted in countries to ban tests specifically for sex-determination, the laws do not ban abortions subsequent to a test that provides evidence of the sex of a fetus (Oomman & Ganatra, 2002). It is important to develop a reproductive justice framework that is sensitive to the experience of women living in communities that value mothers only when they give birth to sons. We need to challenge the patriarchal norms that are embedded in the cultural–ecological context of sex discrimination and devaluation of daughters. Women are often forced to do female feticide because of the pressures from the society as well as from the family. Such cultural ethos greatly restricts women's ability to exercise their reproductive rights. Empowerment of women in these communities may help women to contest the cultural practices that devalue girls and to articulate the complex consequences of devaluing girls on the community's mental and physical health in a culturally sensitive way. Reproductive justice perspectives need to be sensitive to the issue that "an abortion for sex selection is inherently different from other abortions. Indeed in these situations, the pregnancy is wanted, not unwanted, provided it can result in the outcome perceived as valuable—a male child" (Oomman & Ganatra, 2002, pp. 186–187). In addition, women in these contexts are also likely to lack agency. So the cultural context of reproductive rights where the right to have an abortion is discriminately applied only when the fetus is female indicates the patriarchal values and norms that undermine women's agency and empowerment. Our research shows that certain specific ecological factors (e.g., land-owning caste, culture of honor) facilitate the "reproduction" of these patriarchal values. Hence, a reproductive justice framework must focus on specific forms of agency where women can have the right *not* to abort a female fetus yet retain the general right to terminate unwanted pregnancies. Any discussion on reproductive justice in this cultural context must rethink reproductive agency to encompass women's right to *resist* sex-selective abortion so that a healthy balance in the sex-ratio will ultimately improve the physical and psychological well-being of both women and men in their communities. The promotion of reproductive empowerment should be grounded in the cultural realities of women's lives so that the policy decisions and interventions are sensitive to the everyday realities of women at various identity intersections.

CONCLUSIONS

In this chapter, we offer a cultural–ecological framework to identify the various antecedents to extreme neglect of girls, which leads to communities with surplus men and millions of missing girls. We argue that a confluence of cultural, ecological, and social factors contribute to extreme son preference. Systematic historical sex discrimination contributes to male-biased sex ratios, and communities with male-biased sex ratios face complex predicaments. Idealized beliefs about femininity and masculinity are valued in these communities. Endorsing such idealized cultural beliefs about gender adversely affects both women's and men's psychological well-being and the social mobility of women. The paucity of women also contributes to the proliferation of sex industry, kidnapping and trafficking, and fraternal polyandry, which all affect the freedom, reproductive rights, and physical and psychological well-being of women and girls.

Cultural psychologists and policy makers need to consider disparities in sex ratios as a critical variable in any examination of how cultural–ecological factors shape beliefs about gender and their impact on the psychological well-being of women and men. We need an interdisciplinary approach to study the complex consequences of male-biased sex ratios in any culture. Extreme sex determination in the form of sex-selective abortion that leads to surplus men is a growing trend in many parts of the world (Sharma, 2008). Male-biased sex ratios need to be identified as a major risk factor for the psychological well-being and reproductive rights of women. Social and cultural interventions to combat female infanticide and feticide need to highlight the impact of male-biased sex ratios on the community's mental health. Social changes that encourage flexible arrangements for parental care (i.e., by daughters as well as by sons) and inter-caste marriages might change societal attitudes toward daughters. In addition to providing financial incentives to keep daughters and public policy that supports the empowerment of women, governments should invest in social programs that advocate practices that promote gender-egalitarian values (e.g., school curricula). Reproductive justice perspectives should be sensitive to the cultural–ecological factors that shape and constrain women's agency and pressure them to abort female fetuses. Culturally sensitive reproductive-justice perspectives will help us to understand the unique challenges of combating the practice of sex-selective abortions in various Asian countries. Successfully combating female infanticide and feticide is necessary to achieve reproductive justice for the women and girls who live in these communities and for those missing girls, who never had a chance to live.

REFERENCES

Anderson, B. A., Kim, D. & Romani, J. H. (1997). *Health personnel, son preference and infant mortality in China* [Research Report No. 97–401]. Ann Arbor: Population Studies Center, University of Michigan.

Anderson, B. A., & Romani, J. H. (1997). *Socioeconomic characteristics and excess female infant mortality in Jilin province, China* [Research Report No. 97–409]. Ann Arbor: Population Studies Center, University of Michigan.

Balan, S., & Mahalingam, R. (2008). *Culture, ecology, and lifegoals.* Unpublished manuscript, University of Michigan.

Chandra, P., Venkatasubramanian, G., & Thomas, T. (2002). Infanticidal ideas and infanticidal behavior in Indian women with severe postpartum psychiatric disorders. *Journal of Nervous and Mental Diseases, 190,* 457–461.

Croll, E. (2000). *Endangered daughters: Discrimination and development in Asia.* New York: Routledge.

Das Gupta, M., & Shuzhuo, L. (1999). Gender bias in China, South Korea, and India 1920–1990: Effects of war, famine, fertility decline. *Development and Change, 30,* 619–652.

Das Gupta, M., & Visaria, L. (1996). Son preference and excess female mortality in India's demographic transition. In Korea Institute for Health and Social Affairs and United Nations Population Fund (Eds.), *Sex preference for children and gender discrimination in Asia* (pp. 96–102). Seoul, Korea: KIHASA.

Dickeman, M. (1979). Female infanticide, reproductive strategies, and social stratification: A preliminary model. In N. A. Chagnon & W. Irons (Eds.),

Evolutionary biology and human social behavior: An anthropological perspective (pp. 321–368). North Scituate, MA: Duxbury Press.

Dickeman, M. (1981). Paternal confidence and dowry competition: A biocultural analysis of purdah. In R. D., Alexander & D. W., Tinkle (Eds.), *Natural selection and social behavior* (pp. 417–438). New York: Chiron Press.

Dube, R., Dube, R., & Bhatnagar, R. (1999). Women without choice: Female infanticide and the Rhetoric of the over population in postcolonial India. *Women's Studies Quarterly, 27,* 73–86.

Ebenstein, A. Y., & Sharygin, E. J. (2009). The consequences of the "missing girls" of China. *World Bank Economic Review, 23,* 399–425.

Garg, B. (2005, July 16). Draupadis bloom in rural Punjab. *Times of India*. Retrieved from http://articles.timesofindia.indiatimes.com/2005-07-16/india/27861707_1_agrarian-crisis-family-farm-punjab (page no longer available).

Gregor, T. (1988, November). *Infants are not precious to us: The psychological impact of infanticide among Mehinaku Indians*. Paper presented in the meeting of the American Anthropological Association, Phoenix, AZ.

Harriss-White, B. (2001). Gender-cleansing: The paradox of development and deteriorating female life chances in Tamilnadu. In R. Sunderrajan (Ed.), *Signposts: Gender issues in post-independence India* (pp. 125–154). New Brunswick, NJ: Rutgers University Press.

Hegde, R. (1999). Making bodies, reproducing violence. *Violence Against Women, 5,* 507–524.

Hesketh, T., Lu, L., & Xing, Z. W. (2005). The effect of China's one-child family policy after 25 years. *New England Journal of Medicine, 353,* 1171–1176.

Hrdy, S. B. (1999). *Mother nature: A history of mothers, infants, and natural selection.* Pantheon: New York.

Hudson, V. M., & den Boer, A. M. (2004). *Bare branches: The security implications of Asia's surplus male population.* Cambridge, MA: MIT Press.

Hutchings, G. (1997, April 11). Female infanticide will lead to an army of bachelors. *London Telegraph*. Retrieved from http://www.telegraph.co.uk/htmlContent.jhtml?html=/archive/1997/04/011/wchi11.html.

Jeffery, R., & Jeffery, P. (1997). *Population, gender, and politics.* Cambridge: Cambridge University Press.

Keller, M. C., Nesse, R. M., & Hofferth, S. (2001). The Trivers–Willard hypothesis of parental investment: No effect in the contemporary United States. *Evolution and Human Behavior, 22,* 343–360.

Lai-wan, C. C., Eric, B., & Hoi-yan, C. C. (2006). Attitudes and practices toward sex selection in China. *Prenatal Diagnosis, 26,* 610–613.

Li, L., & Wu, X. (2011). Gender of children, bargaining power, and intrahousehold resource allocation in China. *Journal of Human Resources, 46,* 295–316.

Luna, Z. (2009). From rights to justice: Women of color changing the face of US reproductive rights organizing. *Societies Without Borders, 4,* 343–365.

Mahalingam, R. (2007). Culture, ecology, and beliefs about gender in son preference caste groups. *Evolution and Human Behavior, 28,* 319–329.

Mahalingam, R., & Balan, S. (2008). Culture, son preference and beliefs about masculinity. *Journal of Research on Adolescence, 18,* 541–554.

Mahalingam, R., & Haritatos, J. (2006). Culture, gender, and immigration. In R. Mahalingam (Ed.), *Cultural psychology of immigrants* (pp. 259–278). Mahwah, NJ: Erlbaum.

Mahalingam, R., Haritatos, J., & Jackson, B. (2007). Essentialism and the cultural psychology of gender in extreme son preference communities in India. *American Journal of Orthopsychiatry, 77,* 598–609.

Mahalingam, R., & Jackson, B. (2007). Idealized cultural beliefs about gender: Implications for mental health. *Social Epidemiology and Social Psychiatry, 42,* 1012–1023.

Miller, B. D. (1981). *The endangered sex: Neglect of female children in rural north India.* Ithaca, NY: Cornell University Press.

Murdock, G. P. (1967). *Ethnographic atlas.* Pittsburgh, PA: University of Pittsburgh Press.

Murdock, G. P. (1981). *Atlas of world cultures.* Pittsburgh, PA: University of Pittsburgh Press.

Muthulakshmi, R. (1997). *Female infanticide: Its causes and solutions.* New Delhi, India: Discovery.

Natarajan, S. (1997). *Watering the neighbor's plant: Media perspectives on female infanticide in Tamilnadu,* [Monograph no. 6]. Chennai, India: M. S. Swaminathan Research Foundation.

Oomman, N., & Ganatra, B. R. (2002). Sex selection: The systemic elimination of girls. *Reproductive Health Matters, 10,* 184–188.

Oster, E. (2005). Hepatitis B and the case of the missing women. *Journal of Political Economy, 113,* 1163–1216.

Panigrahi, L. (1972). *British social policy and female infanticide in India.* New Delhi, India: Munshiram Manoharlal.

Picone, M. (1998). Infanticide, the spirits of aborted fetuses, and the making of motherhood in Japan. In N. Scheper-Hughes & C. Sargent (Eds.), *Small wars: The cultural politics of childhood* (pp. 37–57). Berkeley: University of California Press.

Premi, M. K. (2001, May 26). The missing girl child. *Economic and Political Weekly,* 1875–1880.

Rahman, A. (1994). A view towards women's reproductive rights perspective on selected laws and policies in Pakistan. *Whittier Law Review, 15,* 981–1001.

Ramanamma, A., & Bambawale, U. (1980). The mania for sons: An analysis of social values in South Asia. *Social Science & Medicine, 14,* 107–110.

Ramasubban, R., & Jejeebhoy, S. (2000). *Women's reproductive health in India.* Jaipur, India: Rawat.

Rao, V. (1993a). Dowry "inflation" in rural India: A statistical investigation. *Population Studies, 47,* 283–293.

Rao, V. (1993b). The rising price of husbands: A hedonic analysis of dowry increases in rural India. *Journal of Political Economy, 101,* 666–677.

Rao, V. (1997). Wife-beating in rural south India: A qualitative and econometric analysis. *Social Science & Medicine, 44,* 1169–1180.

Rosengren, K. E., & Windahl, S. (1989). *Media matter: Childhood and adolescence.* Norwood, NJ: Ablex.

Sargent, C. (1987). Born to die: The fate of extraordinary children in Bariba culture. *Ethnology, 23,* 79–96.

Scheper-Hughes, N. (1992). *Death without weeping: The violence of everyday life in Brazil.* Berkeley: University of California Press.

Seymour, S. (1999). *Women, family, and child care in India: A world in transition.* Cambridge: Cambridge University Press.

Sharma, M. (2008). Twenty-first century pink or blue: How sex selection technology facilitates gendercide and what we can do about it. *Family Court Review, 46*, 198–215.

Shyama. (1996). *Tamizaga gramangalil pen sisu kolai*. Chennai, India: Manimekalai.

Spinelli, M. G. (2001). A systematic investigation of 16 cases of neonaticide. *American Journal of Psychiatry, 126*, 325–334.

Srinivasan, S., & Bedi, A. S. (2008). Daughter elimination in Tamilnadu, India: A tale of two ratios. *Journal of Development Studies, 44*, 961–990.

Srinivasan, V. (1992, October 9). Death for the female-foeticide and infanticide in Salem District. *Frontline*, 82–84.

Vasanthi. (1995, September 30). Salem, the killing goes on. *India Today*, 83.

Venkatachalam, R., & Srinivasan, V. (1993). *Female infanticide*. New Delhi, India: Har-Anand.

Venkataramani, S. H. (1986, June 15). Born to die. *India Today*, 26–33.

Yim, J., & Mahalingam, R. (2006). Culture, masculinity, and psychological well-being in Punjab, India. *Sex Roles, 55*, 715–724.

Zhu, W. X., Lu, L., & Hesketh, T. (2009). China's excess males, sex selective abortion, and one child policy: Analysis of data from 2005 national intercensus survey. *British Journal of Medicine, 338*, 920–923.

Chapter 12

Reproductive Justice for Women and Infants: Restoring Women's Postpartum Health and Infant-Feeding Options

Ingrid Johnston-Robledo and Allison Murray

Women face many challenges after giving birth, yet their needs during this time are often underestimated and neglected (Borders, 2006; Cheng & Li, 2008). During the postpartum period, which is typically conceptualized as the first six weeks after the birth of an infant, first-time mothers adjust to infant care, breastfeeding, physical and emotional changes, and the transition to the maternal role (Borders, 2006; Cheng & Li, 2008). Clearly, the nature of women's challenges and their means of coping with stress vary a great deal depending on the cultural context and the resources to which they have access. In developed nations, a primary challenge may be the absence of sufficient structural support to assist women in their efforts to breastfeed and work outside the home (Chrisler & Johnston-Robledo, 2011; Chuang et al., 2010), whereas women from developing nations may be at risk for severe postpartum morbidity (Miller, Lester, & Hensleigh, 2004) or face difficult decisions about infant feeding if they are infected with HIV (Coutsoudis, 2005). Women's postpartum health is a matter of reproductive justice because, without resources and support during this vulnerable time, women's well-being, social status, economic security, and the health of their infants can be jeopardized. In this chapter, we use a reproductive justice framework to discuss breast-feeding and two threats to women's physical well-being in the immediate postpartum period (i.e., postpartum hemorrhage and obstetric fistula) and pay particular attention to women in resource-poor countries. We describe the efficacy of various programs and policies that have been designed to optimize women's experiences within these two broad domains as well as challenges to their implementation.

POSTPARTUM MORBIDITY

Postpartum Hemorrhage

Improvement of maternal health is one of the eight Millennium Development Goals (MGDs) articulated and adopted by a UN General Assembly in September 2000 (Shaw, 2006). The primary target of this goal is the reduction in maternal mortality rates. According to the World Health Organization (WHO, 2010a), 99 percent of all deaths due to pregnancy or childbirth complications occur in developing nations. One-half of those deaths occur in sub-Saharan African nations, and one-third in south Asia (WHO, 2010c). One of the most common causes of maternal mortality during the immediate postpartum period (24 hours after birthing) is severe postpartum hemorrhage (PPH). Without proper treatment, women can die from uncontrolled bleeding within 2 hours after childbirth. In developing countries, PPH can occur as a result of uterine atony (i.e., the uterus does not contract or assume proper muscle tone in the immediate postpartum), vaginal and cervical lacerations due to improper use of interventions or premature pushing, and placental abruption (i.e., the separation of the placenta from the uterus before the infant is born; Miller et al., 2004). In developed countries (e.g., Australia, Belgium, France, United Kingdom, United States) PPH is more likely to be caused by uterine atony, and it occurs primarily among women who have experienced induced and/or prolonged labor and those who birthed multiple infants (Knight et al., 2009).

Factors that can contribute to postpartum hemorrhage in resource-poor countries include birthing with an unskilled attendant, lack of sufficient transportation or access to emergency care, high rates of anemia that place women at higher risk for PPH, and difficulties with accurate estimates of blood loss (Geller, Adams, Kelly, Kodkany, & Derman, 2006). Cultural beliefs and customs can also result in risk for PPH; for example, Nigerian women told researchers that they had avoided early care for their PPH because they were afraid of forced tubal ligation (Geller et al., 2006). In their review of the anthropological literature on the meaning of childbirth blood across cultures, Thaddeus and Nangalia (2004) reported that PPH may not be recognized readily or treated properly because postpartum blood is viewed as cleansing (e.g., Benin), powerful (e.g., Morocco), or polluting (e.g., Indonesia).

Lack of knowledge can also serve as a barrier to treatment. Thaddeus and Nanglia (2004) noted that, in parts of Egypt, women did not recognize PPH as a life-threatening complication of childbirth, whereas women in Nepal and India who had been exposed to educational interventions were able to list PPH as a major postpartum danger sign. However, knowledge of PPH as life threatening was not associated with northern Indian women's ability to recognize or seek treatment for PPH (Sibley et al., 2005). In a study conducted in Bangladesh (Sibley et al., 2007), only 42 percent of participants mentioned severe bleeding as a dangerous postpartum problem. The elders who were interviewed attributed excessive bleeding to evil spirits, and they believed that a spiritual healer was most appropriate to consult about this problem. In interviews with poor Muslim women in Pakistan, 13 percent of those who had experienced severe postpartum blood loss did not perceive the problem as serious, and, of those who did, 68 percent initially sought treatment from family members (Fikree, Ali, Durocher, & Rahbar, 2004). Clearly interventions involving education and training to address PPH must be sensitive to cultural beliefs that influence and impede treatment-seeking behavior.

Potential solutions for addressing PPH include training for attendants, increased availability and acceptance of skilled care, community education, uterotonic medications such as misoprostol and Uniject (synthetic oxytocin), anemia detection, and improved emergency care and transportation (Geller et al., 2006; Miller et al., 2004; Thaddeus & Nangalia, 2004; Tsu, Langer, & Aldrich, 2004). However, there are significant structural and cultural barriers to the implementation of these solutions. Breastfeeding in the immediate postpartum period can facilitate uterine contraction, but, in many countries, women may avoid immediate breastfeeding due to cultural beliefs about the dangers of colostrum (Geller et al., 2006), the yellow fluid rich with protein and antibodies that precedes the flow of breastmilk in the first three days after birthing.

Obstetric Fistula

Another highly preventable and treatable cause of maternal morbidity that impacts women's quality of life is unrepaired obstetric fistula, a highly prevalent but neglected problem in developing countries in Africa and south Asia (Wall, 2006). This worldwide public health issue affects between 50,000 and 100,000 women each year (WHO, 2010d). Fistulas are openings between the vagina and bladder or vagina and rectum due to tissue necrosis (Steiner, 1996). Although fistulas can occur as a result of forced intercourse and female genital cutting, the primary cause of fistulas in resource-poor countries is obstructed labor (i.e., labor that does not progress due to the position of the fetus or its size in relation to the mother's pelvis; Wall, 2006); obstructed labor occurs in approximately 5 percent of live births (WHO, 2010d). Obstetric fistulas can also form as a result of vaginal deliveries that are botched by instruments such as forceps (Steiner, 1996). From their meta-analysis of the literature on obstetric fistulas in developing countries, Ahmed and Holtz (2007) found that 85 percent of the women who had developed obstetric fistulas had also experienced a stillbirth. The deceased fetus can take several days to emerge from the vagina, thus the necrosis of tissue is exacerbated by the pressure of the deceased fetus on the vaginal tissue (Wall, 2006). Fistulas occur most commonly in remote or rural areas in countries without sufficient emergency obstetric care, such as Afghanistan, Bangladesh, India, Pakistan, and sub-Saharan African countries (Shefren, 2009). Women who are prone to obstetric fistulas are lower income, younger, and shorter in stature than those who are less prone (Zheng & Anderson, 2009). In countries where girls marry and become pregnant at a young age, as young as 13 or 14, the rate of fistulas is much higher (Wall, 2006). Many girls experience obstetric fistulas because their pelvises are not fully developed, especially if they are undernourished (Wall, 2006). It was estimated that rates of obstetric fistulas would fall by more than 10 percent in Niger, Nigeria, and Tanzania if risks due to young maternal age were eliminated or childbearing were delayed (Tsui, Creanga, & Ahmed, 2007).

Obstetric fistulas often go untreated, which results in devastating psychosocial, economic, and physical health consequences for girls and women. According to the WHO (2010d), 2 million women in Asia and sub-Saharan Africa suffer from untreated obstetric fistulas. Urinary and/or fecal incontinence and a very strong odor occur as a result of the damage, which render the girls and women highly stigmatized. As a result, they are often isolated and deprived of proper nutrition and resources for personal hygiene (Ahmed & Holtz, 2007). From their meta-analysis, Ahmed and Holtz (2007) concluded that 36 percent of women are divorced or abandoned as a result of their obstetric fistulas. They also found that 22 percent of Ethiopian women resorted to begging for food and that Nigerian women must live with their parents, but they are unable to cook or participate in social or religious events (Ahmed & Holtz, 2007). In Bangladesh, women with obstetric fistulas reported depression, embarrassment, and painful sex, and 52 percent of their husbands reported a marked decrease in their sexual pleasure with their wives (Ahmed & Holtz, 2007). Fistulas can also lead to miscarriage and perinatal mortality in future pregnancies.

Simple surgical procedures can cure up to 90 percent of uncomplicated obstetric fistulas; however, only 12,000 women since 2003 have received treatment in 45 different countries (WHO, 2010d). Some research suggests that, once their fistulas are repaired, women are able to reintegrate into their communities (Ahmed & Holtz, 2007). Fistulas can be prevented by delayed childbearing, increased access to maternal health care with skilled birth attendants, increased access to emergency obstetrical care, and better or increased resources for family planning (WHO, 2010d). Continued neglect of obstetric fistulas, in the form of inadequate preventive care and surgical treatment, is a serious violation of women's human rights (Cook, Dickens, & Syed, 2004). After their extensive literature review, Zheng and Anderson (2009) concluded that this public health issue is receiving increased international attention, but additional research is needed in order to develop and implement effective interventions. Ahmed and Holtz (2007) called for more long-term research on the prognosis of surgery to repair fistulas and the surgery's impact on women's well-being and quality of life. Unrepaired fistulas have a deleterious impact on women's lives, economic well-being, and future reproductive health. Future research, clinical attention, and policy development that will help prevent and treat obstetric fistulas are critical to a global reproductive justice agenda. Nonprofit organizations, such as the World Wide Fistual Fund (http://www. worldwidefistulafund.org/) contribute to the development of hospitals specifically designed for obstetric fistula surgery.

BREASTFEEDING

Feminist scholars have neglected breastfeeding as a political and reproductive health issue (Hausman, 2003; Labbok, Smith, & Taylor, 2008). Within a global context, unique dilemmas surface, such as concerns that breastfeeding recommendations can be interpreted as imperatives that prioritize the rights of infants over women's rights (Kent, 2006; Labbok & Nakaji, 2010; Latham, 1997) or that international breastfeeding initiatives are paternalistic (Jansson, 2009). Recently, however, some feminist scholars have begun to examine breastfeeding from a human/reproductive rights perspective (Labbok, 2006). Given the documented direct and indirect benefits of breastfeeding to both women and their infants, access to the resources necessary to make an informed choice about infant feeding and to succeed and persist with breastfeeding is a reproductive justice issue. For example, scholars have conceptualized barriers to breastfeeding as human rights violations in countries where safe alternatives to breastmilk are largely unavailable (Kent, 2006; Latham, 1997).

Breastfeeding Patterns

Breastfeeding rates are increasing in both developed and developing countries in response to various international breastfeeding initiatives (Labbok & Nakaji, 2010; Walker, 2007). The WHO (2011) recently issued a recommendation that all mothers breastfeed their babies exclusively for the first 6 months in an effort to promote optimal health and development of infants. The American Academy of Pediatrics' (2005) official policy statement on breastfeeding also recommends exclusive breastfeeding for the first 6 months postpartum.

According to statistics from the WHO (2010a), only 35 percent of all infants less than 6 months of age are breastfed exclusively. This figure ranges a great deal depending on the cultural context. A comprehensive study of breastfeeding practices and programs was recently conducted in 33 different countries by the World Breastfeeding Trends Initiative (2010). The researchers concluded that 46 percent of infants in those countries were breastfed exclusively for the first 6 months and that the median duration of breastfeeding was 18 months. The country with the lowest rate of exclusive breastfeeding was Mexico (5.5%), whereas Afghanistan had the highest rate (83%). In approximately one-half of the countries studied (e.g., Cape Verde, Indonesia, Peru, Uganda), the rate was 50 percent or higher. In addition to Mexico, the countries with the lowest rates of exclusive breastfeeding were Costa Rica and the Dominican Republic. According to a United Nations Children's Fund (UNICEF) report (2011), exclusive breastfeeding rates increased substantially between 1995 and 2008 in the developing world. Based on an analysis of breastfeeding rates in 86 countries, it was determined that rates have increased from a mean of 26 percent of infants to a mean of 46 percent of infants. Regions with the highest exclusive breastfeeding rates were south Asia (45%) and eastern and southern Africa (47%), whereas the regions with the lowest rates were western and central Africa (23%). In three different regions, women in poorer households were more likely to initiate breastfeeding than were those with more household wealth (Latin America/Caribbean, east Asia and Pacific, Middle East and North Africa).

In the United States, 74 percent of mothers initiate breastfeeding at birth, but only 43 percent are still breastfeeding at six months postpartum (Centers for Disease Control and Prevention, 2010). In a comprehensive review of the literature on breastfeeding patterns in Australia, Canada, Europe, and the United States, Callen and Pinelli (2004) found that European and Australian women were more likely to initiate and persist with breastfeeding than were women in Canada and the United States. In all four geographic locations, women with the highest incidence and duration of breastfeeding were more likely to be married, older, and of higher socioeconomic levels than women with lower rates.

Benefits of Breastfeeding

The benefits of breastfeeding to infant and maternal health are established and well documented. The WHO (2010a) estimated that breastfeeding and appropriate complementary feeding could save the lives of approximately 1.5 million children under the age of five every year.

A meta-analysis of studies on breastfed infants from a variety of developing countries concluded that breastfeeding protects infants' health during the first six months, especially from diarrhea and respiratory infections such as pneumonia, the two primary causes of child mortality (Collaborative Study Team on the Role of Breastfeeding on the Prevention of Infant Mortality, 2000). Furthermore, the WHO estimated that approximately two-thirds of deaths due to malnutrition among children under the age of five years are due to bottle-feeding and inadequate complementary feeding (i.e., supplementing breastmilk with solid foods after six months). After a comprehensive, albeit dated, review of studies on causes of infant mortality in developing countries, it was concluded that infants who were not breastfed are six times more likely to die before two months of age than are those who were breastfed (Collaborative Study Team on the Role of Breastfeeding on the Prevention of Infant Mortality, 2000). Female infants may suffer disproportionately from inadequate breastfeeding. For example, Graham, Larsen, and Xu (1998) found that female infants from rural China were less likely than male infants to be breastfed, and Guilmoto (2009) argued that this form of systematic neglect of female infants may contribute to the imbalance in the sex ratio in several Asian countries. In developed countries, breastfed infants are less likely than formula-fed infants to experience gastrointestinal infections, respiratory diseases, and type 1 diabetes (Ip et al., 2007).

Although benefits of breastfeeding to mothers are not as unequivocal as benefits to infants, breastfeeding may contribute to postpartum weight loss as well as lower rates of breast and other reproductive cancers, type 2 diabetes, and coronary heart disease (Godfrey & Lawrence, 2010). Women, particularly those with insufficient access to contraceptives, benefit from the delayed resumption of menstrual cycles, which allows for the spacing of children through the lactation amenorrhea method (Labbok, 2008; WHO, 2010a), thereby indirectly improving maternal nutrition and reducing reproductive stress (Labbok, 2006). There are also many economic benefits of breastfeeding associated with reduced morbidity rates for children (Weimer, 2001), such as avoidance of the high cost of breastmilk substitutes (United States Breastfeeding Committee, 2002).

Shaw (2006) argued that the benefits of breastfeeding extend beyond maternal and infant health to sustainable development worldwide. She noted that breastfeeding is critical to the attainment of four of the eight UN MDGs, yet breastfeeding was not identified among the original list of health targets or indicators. For example, breastfeeding can contribute to the eradication of hunger, environmental sustainability, reduced child mortality, and lower infectious disease rates among children. Labbok (2006) indicated that breastfeeding has implications for the other four MDGs as well: universal primary education, empowerment of women, improved maternal health, and the formation of global partnerships. However, neither of those authors argued for a breastfeeding imperative nor that women have a unique responsibility for sustainable development.

Barriers to Breastfeeding and Healthy Breastmilk Substitutes

As noted earlier, barriers to women's right to breastfeed, whether personal or structural, can be considered violations of women's and children's human rights. Yet, national and international recommendations for women's breastfeeding behavior are problematic when women are not provided with sufficient resources to adhere to them. A comprehensive review of barriers to breastfeeding is beyond the scope of this chapter. However, the barriers most relevant to a reproductive justice framework are those that threaten resources required for breastfeeding and infringe on the well-being of women and infants. For example, Latham (1997) discussed four barriers to breastfeeding that are common and currently being addressed across countries. These include medicalization of infant feeding, marketing of breastmilk substitutes, lack of resources available to assist women in their efforts to continue breastfeeding once they return to work, and the absence of community support for breastfeeding women. He argued that women in resource-poor countries are slowly shifting away from breastfeeding due to modernization, and his claim is borne out by available data. For example, in a study of 1,600 women from the Philippines (Abada, Trovato, & Lalu, 2001), the mean duration of breastfeeding was 7.5 months. Predictors of early termination were early introduction of formula, higher levels of maternal education, exposure to prenatal care, a hospital birth, and larger families. The researchers concluded that modernization is contributing to an overall decline in breastfeeding, which may threaten children's health and survival. Many of their suggestions for promoting breastfeeding among professional women are similar to those necessary in Western countries, such as flexible hours and breaks from work to breastfeed. A small sample of women from Hong Kong who had breastfed longer than 6 months reported that they were discouraged from breastfeeding by both elder family members and health care providers and that they thought breastfeeding was inconsistent with the image of a professional woman (Tarrant, Dodgson, & Choi, 2004).

Work-related barriers figure prominently in women's breastfeeding behavior in both developed and developing countries. Obstacles include lack of sufficient maternity leave (Baker & Milligan, 2008; Chuang et al, 2010; Latham, 1997; Mandal, Roe, & Fein, 2010), lack of on-site childcare, and work schedules that do not permit breaks to breastfeed or express breastmilk (Chrisler & Johnston-Robledo, 2011). In the United States, women who work part time are more likely both to initiate breastfeeding and to breastfeed for longer periods of time than women who work full time (Mandal et al., 2010). In a sample of working women in Thailand, approximately one-half of the participants identified psychosocial barriers related to work (e.g., exhaustion, lack of time, return to work) as their primary reasons for weaning their infants, which typically occurred at five months (Kaewsarn & Moyle, 2000). Kakute et al. (2005) examined barriers to exclusive breastfeeding among a sample of 320 women from rural villages in Cameroon. Participants identified farm work and lack of assistance with household labor as reasons for mixed feeding. One-third of the women had given their infants water to drink within the first months of life, and 84 percent had exposed their infants to solid foods before six months.

Cultural beliefs about breastmilk, breastfeeding, and colostrum are varied, and they can serve as barriers to breastfeeding (Baumslag & Michels, 1995). In the study of rural Cameroonian women's reasons for mixed feeding, Kakute et al. (2005) found that the most common reasons for initiating mixed feeding were family/community pressure (45%) and perceptions that their babies were not satisfied by breastmilk alone (20%). Fifty-two percent of the mothers did not believe that colostrum was healthy or necessary for newborns. Instead, they were often given cow's milk or *viindi*, a type of sacred water. These practices deter early initiation of breastfeeding and can threaten infants' health. Seventy-six percent of a sample of pregnant Nigerian women indicated that they would express and discard their colostrum because it was viewed as dirty and harmful to newborns (Davies-Adetugbo, 1997). In Nigeria, infants are fed a watery porridge along with breastmilk as young as two months of age, a practice that can lead to severe diarrhea and, ultimately, infant mortality. In northern Malawi, paternal grandmothers are centrally involved in early childcare and strongly influence new mothers to supplement breastmilk, which they perceive to be inadequate, within the first six months with water, root and herbal infusions, and porridge (Kerr, Dakishoni, Shumba, Msachi, & Chirwa, 2008). From their focus group of women in Hong Kong, Tarrant et al. (2004) learned that women were often discouraged from breastfeeding by their in-laws. Their breastfeeding behavior led to disruptions in family harmony, which caused the mothers a great deal of distress. Programs designed to promote breastfeeding must be culturally sensitive and take into account the important role that extended family members play in women's breastfeeding behavior and decisions.

In addition to holding beliefs about the inadequacy of exclusive breastfeeding, women may also believe that their own milk supply is insufficient. Gatti (2008) reviewed 20 studies of maternal perceptions of insufficient milk supply during the first six months postpartum in a variety of countries (e.g., Australia, Canada, Hong Kong, Mexico, New Zealand, Thailand, Turkey, and the United States). On average, 35 percent of women reported early weaning, and thus supplementation, due to assumptions that their milk supply was insufficient, and most of them named infant fussiness as their rationale for this assumption. Women whose infants were fed for-mula while in the hospital were more likely than other women to perceive that their milk supply was insufficient. Most women had weaned after one to four weeks of breastfeeding, and all studies that explored various rea-sons for early weaning revealed that perception of insufficient milk was listed as one of the top reasons. Although maternal malnutrition is a prev-alent problem in the developing world, it does not influence the quantity or quality of women's breastmilk unless they are severely malnourished (Black et al., 2008).

Women from resource-poor countries face a variety of barriers to se-curing healthy substitutes for breastmilk, such as infant formula, which further complicates choices about infant feeding. Formula-fed infants are at a higher risk of infant mortality due to both deprivation of benefits from breastfeeding and exposure to pathogens in formula that is not prepared properly (Marino, 2007). The cost of ready-made formula or powdered formula is prohibitive for many women in resource-poor countries. For example, in rural South Africa, one container of powdered formula (which weighs one kilogram) costs the equivalent of 25 hours of pay (Dorosko & Rollins, 2003). Other requisite resources for safe replacement feeding are clean water, clean containers, and adequate refrigeration. Marino (2007) argued that early mixed feeding and weaning among infants in develop-ing countries leads to significant health risks because of the myriad bar-riers to resources necessary for safe food preparation (e.g., clean water, cooking fuel). Based on their observational study of a small sample of women in rural and semirural South Africa, Dorosko and Rollins (2003) concluded that it was time consuming for women to obtain water for for-mula preparation and that the surfaces they used to prepare the formula were unsanitary.

The safety of breastmilk substitutes is especially critical to the infant-feeding options and decisions of women infected with HIV. Women in resource-poor countries who test positive for HIV face a difficult choice between potentially transmitting the virus to their infants via breastmilk or formula feeding, which increases the risk for intestinal and respiratory diseases (Wright, 2004). Intrauterine or intrapartum vertical transmission of HIV is much more likely to occur than transmission through breast-milk. According to a survival analysis study conducted in Zambia (Fox et al., 2008), infants who were infected postpartum had one-quarter of the mortality rate of infants who were infected at earlier stages, and weaning increased mortality within the first year for both groups of infants. Ex-clusive breastfeeding is very beneficial to HIV-infected infants (Coovia & Kindra, 2008; Fox et al. 2008). Thus, in developing countries, the bene-fits of breastfeeding may outweigh the risk of HIV transmission (Cook & Dickens, 2002; Kuhn & Stein, 1997). The WHO/UNICEF (2004) guidelines for breastfeeding among HIV-positive women recommended that women avoid breastfeeding only if replacement feeding met certain conditions (e.g., safe, affordable, feasible). Doherty et al. (2007) concluded that the vague nature of these conditions may have contributed to ineffective implementation of these guidelines among a large sample of HIV-positive South African women, as many of them fed their infants formula even when these conditions were not met (e.g., insufficient supply of fuel and clean water). That group of infants was more likely than the infants who were breastfed to contract HIV and/or die.

After their comprehensive review of the literature concerning breastfeeding among HIV-infected women in a variety of African countries, Coovia and Kindra (2008) concluded that exclusive breastfeeding for six months led to the most positive infant health outcomes and the lowest risk of vertical transmission. Others (Becquet et al., 2008; Coutsoudis, 2005) have also argued that the risk of vertical transmission is higher among infants who are fed both breastmilk and formula than among those who are breastfed exclusively. For example, Wright (2004) indicated that mixed feeding can place infants at risk for HIV because contaminants can irritate infants' gastrointestinal tracts and render them more susceptible to the virus. HIV-infected women in developing countries may be encouraged to mix-feed or formula-feed their babies through the introduction of free infant formula, but this can backfire and undermine efforts to encourage safe, exclusive breastfeeding and to optimize infant health (Coutsoudis, Goga, Rollins, & Coovia, 2002).

The most effective method of preventing vertical transmission is antiretroviral therapy (ARV; Coovia & Kindra, 2008). In a study of the 25 countries with the highest HIV rates among pregnant women (Mahy et al., 2010), there was a 24 percent reduction in the incidence of infant infection, due to the use of ARVs, between 2000 and 2009. Unfortunately, levels of access to ARV vary a great deal. For example, in Nigeria, the country with the highest number of HIV-positive mothers, only 22 percent were estimated to have had access to ARV, whereas in South Africa, the country with the second-highest HIV rate among mothers, 88 percent were estimated to have access to ARV. In a recent study (Homsy et al., 2010) of the efficacy of ARV for preventing vertical transmission, none of the infants born to 102 HIV-infected mothers in rural Uganda contracted HIV within the seven-month follow-up period. However, 19 percent of the infants died at a median age of three months, primarily due to severe diarrhea and/or vomiting. This outcome was six times more likely among infants who were not exclusively breastfed.

The availability and efficacy of ARV for pregnant and postpartum women led to a modification of the WHO (2010b) breastfeeding guidelines for HIV-positive women. They now recommend that all HIV infected women receive lifelong antiretroviral therapy so that they will be able to breastfeed safely, if they so choose. Exclusive breastfeeding for 6 months is still recommended unless mothers have access to a replacement that is safe, affordable, feasible, and sustainable. If they do not have access to safe replacements for breastmilk, mothers are encouraged to breastfeed, despite their HIV status, for their infants' first 12 months of life. Mothers of infants known to be HIV-infected are strongly encouraged to breastfeed exclusively for 6 months and then supplement for two years.

Breastfeeding Initiatives and Programs

In their comprehensive chapter on breastfeeding and human rights, Labbok and Nakaji (2010) reviewed many different international policies and programs designed to promote breastfeeding. For example, WHO/ UNICEF (1989) established *The 10 Steps for Successful Breastfeeding* to guide health care providers' efforts to encourage new mothers to breastfeed. Examples of some of the steps included the development of a written breastfeeding policy, initiation of breastfeeding within the first hour of birth, the avoidance of infant formula unless medically indicated, training of health care providers in implementation of the steps, and assisting women with, and educating them about, breastfeeding. Labbok (2007) indicated that the efficacy of the *Baby-Friendly Hospital Initiative,* the program designed to implement the 10 steps, has been demonstrated empirically, thus the program should continue to be supported and implemented.

That kind of program, which provides women with the tools they need to make informed decisions about infant feeding, aligns with basic health care ethical principles such as respect for patient autonomy and promotion of patient welfare and, therefore, promotes women's basic human rights (Gillis & Sigman-Grant, 2010). Researchers and practitioners should routinely revisit those 10 steps, consider their cultural sensitivity and relevance, and determine ways to expand their reach beyond formal health care settings.

Another international policy of note is the *International Code of Marketing of Breast-milk Substitutes,* which was adopted in 1981 by the World Health Assembly. This code, which had only been implemented in 86 countries as of 2005 (Labbok & Nakaji, 2010), prohibits the advertising of breastmilk substitutes and distribution of free samples and requires that information about infant formula proclaim the benefits of breastfeeding and disclose the costs and dangers of substitutes. Eighteen of the 24 countries in west and central Africa have either adopted or drafted laws or regulations designed to implement the provisions of the code, which is central to children's survival in these regions (Sokol, Clark, & Aguayo, 2008).

Although the cultural context, women's lived experiences, and their life circumstances differ across countries, Walker (2007) noted that many of the policies and programs designed for women in developing countries would assist American women in their ability to reach the breastfeeding goals established by the U.S. government, yet the United States has not implemented many of them. However, programs such as the *Baby Friendly Hospital Initiative* that have altered hospital protocols regarding breastfeeding through the WHO's 10 steps have been the most effective means of promoting early breastfeeding among American women (Shealy, Li, Benton-Davis, & Grummer-Strawn, 2005). Further, in the United States, there is now a federal law that requires employers to provide breastfeeding women with sufficient breaks from work and a comfortable space to allow for the expression of breastmilk for up to one year postpartum (U.S. Government, 2010). Although this is a landmark piece of legislation, time and space to express breastmilk may not assist American women in their breastfeeding goals as well as do policies and programs that keep women with their infants. In fact, the language of this new law does not suggest that women can use this break time to breastfeed their infants. Flexible working hours, part-time options, and on-site childcare may be more effective means of encouraging sustained breastfeeding among employed women (Grummer-Strawn & Shealy, 2009).

From a large meta-analysis of the efficacy of breastfeeding interventions in developed countries, Chung, Raman, Trikalinos, Lau, and Ip (2008) concluded that those programs that promote breastfeeding during both pregnancy and the postpartum period lead to the highest increases in short-and long-term breastfeeding rates. They also found that programs involving peer or lay support have been found to be especially effective.

The WHO 2004 guidelines for infant feeding among HIV-infected mothers are another important advancement in international breastfeeding promotion (Labbok & Nakaji, 2010). However, there are myriad barriers to the implementation of these breastfeeding guidelines (Doherty et al., 2007; Mahy et al., 2010; Ramdhial & Coovia, 2010). For example, the newest set of guidelines (WHO, 2010b) recommended that HIV-infected mothers receive counseling that will help them to make their choices through an analysis of the costs and benefits within their socioeconomic and cultural contexts. Research has demonstrated, however, that in resource-poor countries, such as Cambodia, Cameroon, and Kenya, the quality of counseling varies a great deal across countries and settings, and health workers' priorities and values may clash with those of their clients (Desclaux & Alfieri, 2009), thereby limiting the level of informed choice for HIV-infected mothers. Clearly, reproductive justice for HIV-infected women, whether or not they choose to breastfeed, involves access to quality prenatal and postpartum health care; family planning resources; accurate, culturally sensitive counseling; and ARV. These resources would optimize both maternal and infant health and well-being. Research designed to address and remove barriers to these resources should be an international priority

Jansson (2009) critiqued many of these international breastfeeding programs as paternalistic, individualistic, and depoliticized. Analyses such as hers are important tools necessary to develop and implement effective, transnational, feminist, reproductive health agendas and to reveal the inherent complexities involved. In the face of these complexities, scholars (Labbok, 2006; Labbok et al., 2008) have begun to consider the relevance of a reproductive justice framework to breastfeeding, an issue that is all too often ignored by both feminist theorists and international assemblies. Labbok (2006) argued that women deserve the information, resources, and support necessary to make an informed decision about how to feed their infants and to succeed with breastfeeding, should they make that choice. Further, moving from an individualistic paradigm that conceptualizes breastfeeding as a lifestyle choice to one that emphasizes breastfeeding as a reproductive justice issue encourages an examination of structural constraints on breastfeeding (Labbok et al., 2008; Smith, 2008). Thus the responsibility for supporting women in their choice to breastfeed rests with institutions, such as families, workplaces, governments, communities, and hospitals (Labbok, 2008; Labbok et al., 2008).

CONCLUSION

Clearly, women living in resource-poor countries are still denied the basic health care, information, and resources they need to survive the postpartum period, let alone to achieve optimal postpartum health. Barriers to quality care must be recognized as violations of women's fundamental right to health and addressed as such via broad-based international coalitions. The inclusion of improvements in maternal health and the empowerment of women as two of the eight MDGs (Shaw, 2006) are examples of a collective approach to these human rights violations that prioritize women's health and well-being. Worldwide, maternal mortality rates are staggering, but they could be reduced significantly by improved maternal nutrition, delayed childbearing, and the prevention of postpartum hemorrhage. Increased access to treatments for obstetric fistulas would also be an important step toward reproductive justice for women in developing countries.

Although much progress has been made to help women overcome powerful barriers to breastfeeding, a practice that is embraced and pursued by many women in developing countries, new issues have surfaced, such as pressures to modernize, women's increasing labor role in the global economy, cultural beliefs about breastfeeding and breastmilk, and concerns about the transmission of HIV to infants. Women must be given the tools and resources necessary to make informed and authentic choices about infant feeding. Labbok (2008) argued that future efforts to promote breastfeeding must be transdisciplinary and include various coalitions (e.g., family and community, health systems, legislators) in order to be sustainable and effective. A reproductive justice framework that recognizes and optimizes interconnections among reproductive health, economic justice, and clinical practice (Gilliam, Neustadt, & Gordon, 2009; Petchesky, 2000) holds a great deal of promise as a means to shape research, clinical, educational, and policy agendas that will eliminate threats to women's postpartum health and breastfeeding options.

REFERENCES

Abada, T.S.J., Trovato, F., & Lalu, N. (2001). Determinants of breastfeeding in the Philippines: A survival analysis. *Social Science & Medicine, 52,* 71–81.

Ahmed, S., & Holtz, S. A. (2007). Social and economic consequences of obstetric fistulae: Life changed forever? *International Journal of Gynecology and Obstetrics, 99,* 510–515.

American Academy of Pediatrics. (2005). Breastfeeding and the use of human milk. *Pediatrics, 115,* 496–506.

Baker, M., & Milligan, K. (2008). Maternal employment, breastfeeding, and health: Evidence from maternity leave mandates. *Journal of Health Economics, 27,* 871–877.

Baumslag, N., & Michels, D. L. (1995). *Milk, money, and madness: The culture and politics of breastfeeding.* Westport, CT: Bergin & Garvey.

Becquet, R. Ekouevi, D. K., Menan, H., Amani-Bosse, C., Bequet, L., Viho, I. . . . Leroy, V. (2008). Early mixed feeding and breastfeeding beyond six months increase the risk of postnatal HIV transmission: ANRS 1201/1202 Ditrame Plus, Abidjan, Cote d'Ivoire. *Preventive Medicine, 47,* 27–33.

Becquet, R., Ekouevi, D. K., Arrive, E., Stringer, J. S., Meda, N., Chaix, M. L. . . . Dabis, F. (2009). Universal antiretroviral therapy for pregnant and breast-feeding HIV-1-infected women: Towards the elimination of mother-to-child transmission of HIV-1 in resource-limited settings. *Clinical Infectious Diseases, 49,* 1936–1945.

Black, R. E, Allen, L. H., Bhutta, Z. A., Caulfield, L. E., de Onis, M., Ezzati, M. . . . Rivera, J. (2008). Maternal and child undernutrition: Global and regional exposures and health consequences. *Lancet, 371,* 243–260.

Borders, N. (2006). After the afterbirth: A critical review of postpartum health relative to method of delivery. *Journal of Midwifery & Women's Health, 51,* 242–248.

Callen, J., & Pinelli, J. (2004). Incidence and duration of breastfeeding for term infants in Canada, United States, Europe, and Australia: A literature review. *Birth, 31,* 285–292.

Centers for Disease Control and Prevention. (2010). *Breastfeeding report card— United States 2010.* Retrieved from http://www.cdc.gov/breastfeeding/pdf/ BreastfeedingReportCard2010.pdf.

Cheng, C-Y., & Li, Q. (2008). Integrative review of research on general health status and prevalence of common physical health conditions of women after childbirth. *Women's Health Issues, 18,* 267–280.

Chrisler, J. C., & Johnston-Robledo, I. (2011). Pregnancy discrimination. In M. A. Paludi, C. Paludi, Jr., & E. DeSouza (Eds.), *Praeger handbook on understanding and preventing workplace discrimination: Legal, management, and social science perspectives* (pp. 105–132). Santa Barbara, CA: Praeger.

Chuang, C-H., Chang, P-J., Chen, Y-C., Hsieh, W-S., Hurng, B-S., Lin, S-J., & Gen, P-C. (2010). Maternal return to work and breastfeeding: A population co-hort study. *International Journal of Nursing Studies, 47*, 461–474.

Chung, M., Raman, G., Trikalinos, T., Lau, J., & Ip, S. (2008). Interventions in pri-mary care to promote breastfeeding: An evidence review for the U.S. Pre-ventive Services Task Force. *Annals of Internal Medicine, 149*, 565–575.

Collaborative Study Team on the Role of Breastfeeding on the Prevention of Infant Mortality. (2000). Effect of breastfeeding on infant and child mortality due to infectious diseases in less developed countries: A pooled analysis. *Lancet, 355*, 451–455.

Cook, R. J., & Dickens, B. M. (2002). Human rights and HIV positive women. *Inter-national Journal of Gynecology and Obstetrics, 77*, 55–63.

Cook, R. J., Dickens, B. M., & Syed, S. (2004). Obstetric fistulae: The challenge to human rights. *International Journal of Gynecology and Obstetrics, 87*, 72–77.

Coovia, H., & Kindra, G. (2008). Breastfeeding, HIV transmission, and infant sur-vival: Balancing pros and cons. *Current Opinions in Infectious Diseases, 21*, 11–15.

Coutsoudis, A. (2005). Breastfeeding and the HIV positive mother: The debate con-tinues. *Early Human Development, 81*, 87–93.

Coutsoudis, A., Goga, A. E., Rollins, N., & Coovia, H. M. (2002). Free formula milk for infants of HIV-infected women: Blessing or curse? *Health Policy and Plan-ning, 17*, 154–160.

Davies-Adetugbo, A. A. (1997). Sociocultural factors and the promotion of exclu-sive breastfeeding in rural Yoruba communities of Osun State, Nigeria. *So-cial Science & Medicine, 45*, 113–125.

Desclaux, A., & Alfieri, C. (2009). Counseling and choosing between infant-feeding options: Overall limits and local interpretations by health care providers and women living with HIV in resource-poor countries. *Social Science & Medicine, 69*, 821–829.

Doherty, T., Chopra, M., Jackson, D., Goga, A., Colvin, M., & Persson, L-A. (2007). Effectiveness of the WHO/UNICEF guidelines on infant feeding for HIV-positive women: Results from a prospective cohort study in South Africa. *AIDS, 21*, 1791–1797.

Dorosko, S., & Rollins, N. (2003). Infant formula preparation by rural and semi-rural women in South Africa. *Food Policy, 28*, 117–130.

Fikree, F. F., Ali, T., Durocher, J. M., & Rahbar, M. H. (2004). Health service utili-zation for perceived postpartum morbidity among poor women living in Karachi. *Social Science & Medicine, 59*, 671–694.

Fox, M. P., Brooks, D., Kuhn, L., Aldrovandi, G., Sinkala, M., Kankasa, C., . . . Thea, D. M. (2008). Reduced mortality associated with breast-feeding-acquired HIV infection and breastfeeding among HIV-infected children in Zambia. *Epidemiology and Social Science, 48*, 90–96.

Gatti, L. (2008). Maternal perceptions of insufficient milk supply in breastfeeding. *Journal of Nursing Scholarship, 40*, 355–363.

Geller, S. E., Adams, M. G., Kelly, P. J., Kodkany, B. S., & Derman, R. J. (2006). Post-partum hemorrhage in resource-poor settings. *International Journal of Gynecology and Obstetrics, 92,* 202–211.

Gilliam, M. L., Neustadt, A., & Gordon, R. (2009). A call to incorporate a reproductive justice agenda into reproductive health clinical practice and policy. *Contraception, 79,* 243–246.

Gillis, M., & Sigman-Grant, M. J. (2010). Principles of health care ethics and the WHO/UNICEF 10 steps to successful breastfeeding. *Journal of Human Lactation, 26,* 11–16.

Godfrey, J. R., & Lawrence, R. A. (2010). Toward optimal health: The maternal benefits of breastfeeding. *Journal of Women's Health, 19,* 1597–1602.

Graham, M. J., Larsen, U., & Xu, S. (1998). Son preference in Anhui Province, China. *International Family Planning Perspectives, 24,* 72–77.

Grummer-Strawn, L. M., & Shealy, K. R. (2009). Progress in protecting, promoting, and supporting breastfeeding: 1984–2009. *Breastfeeding Medicine, 4,* S31–S41.

Guilmoto, C. Z. (2009). The sex ratio transition in Asia. *Population and Development Review, 35,* 519–549.

Hausman, B. L. (2003). *Mother's milk: Breastfeeding controversies in American culture.* New York: Routledge.

Homsy, J., Moore, D., Barassa, A., Were, W., Likicho, C., Waiswa, B. . . . Mermin, J. (2010). Breastfeeding, mother-to-child HIV transmission, and mortality among infants born to HIV-infected women on highly active antiretroviral therapy in rural Uganda. *Journal of Acquired Immune Deficiency Syndromes, 53,* 28–35.

Ip, S., Chung, M., Raman, G., Chew, P., Magula, N., DeVine, D. . . . Lau, J. (2007). *Breastfeeding and maternal and infant health outcomes in developed countries.* [Evidence Report/Technology Assessment No. 153.] Rockville, MD: Agency for Healthcare Research and Quality.

Jansson, M. (2009). Feeding children and protecting women: The emergence of breastfeeding as an international concern. *Women's Studies International Forum, 32,* 240–248.

Kaewsarn, P., & Moyle, W. (2000). Breastfeeding duration of Thai women. *Australian College of Midwives Journal, 13,* 21–25.

Kakute, P. N., Ngum, J., Mitchell, P., Kroll, K. A., Forgwei, G. W., Ngwang, L. K., & Meyer, D. J. (2005). Cultural barriers to exclusive breastfeeding by mothers in a rural area of Cameroon, Africa. *Journal of Midwifery and Women's Health, 50,* 324–328.

Kent, G. (2006). Child feeding and human rights. *International Breastfeeding Journal, 27,* 1–27.

Kerr, R. B., Dakishoni, L. Shumba, L., Msachi, R., & Chirwa, M. (2008). "We grandmothers know plenty": Breastfeeding, complementary feeding, and the multifaceted role of grandmothers in Malawi. *Social Science & Medicine, 66,* 1095–1105.

Knight, M., Callaghan, W. M., Berg, C., Alexander, S., Bouvier-Colle, M-H., Ford, J. B. . . . Walker, J. (2009). Trends in postpartum hemorrhage in high resource countries: A review and recommendations from the International Hemorrhage Collaborative Group. *BMC Pregnancy and Childbirth, 9,* 55–65.

Kuhn, L., & Stein, Z. (1997). Infant survival, HIV infection, and feeding alternatives in less-developed countries. *American Journal of Public Health, 87,* 926–931.

Labbok, M., & Nakaji, E. (2010). Breastfeeding: A biological, ecological, and human rights imperative for global health. In P. Murthy & C. L. Smith (Eds.), *Women's global health and human rights* (pp. 421–436). Sudbury, MA: Jones and Bartlett.

Labbok, M. H. (2006). Breastfeeding: A woman's reproductive right. *International Journal of Gynecology and Obstetrics, 94,* 277–286.

Labbok, M. H. (2007). Breastfeeding and the Baby-Friendly Hospital Initiative: More important and with more evidence than ever. *Journal of Pediatrics, 83,* 99–101.

Labbok, M. H. (2008). Transdisciplinary breastfeeding support: Creating program and policy synergy across the reproductive continuum. *International Breastfeeding Journal, 3,* 3–16.

Labbok, M. H., Smith, P. H., & Taylor, E. C. (2008). Breastfeeding and feminism: A focus on reproductive health, rights, and justice. *International Breastfeeding Journal, 8,* 1–6.

Latham, M. C. (1997). Breastfeeding—A human rights issue? *International Journal of Children's Rights, 5,* 397–417.

Mahy, M., Stover, J., Kiragu, K., Hayashi, C., Akwara, P., Luo, C. . . . Shaffer, N. (2010). What will it take to achieve virtual elimination of mother-to-child transmission of HIV? An assessment of current progress and future needs. *Sexually Transmitted Infections, 86*(Suppl. 2), ii48–ii55.

Mandal, B., Roe, B. E., & Fein, S. B. (2010). The differential effects of full-time and part-time work status on breastfeeding. *Health Policy, 97,* 79–86.

Marino, D. D. (2007). Water and food safety in the developing world: Global implications for health and nutrition of infants and young children. *Journal of the American Dietetic Association, 107,* 1930–1934.

Miller, S., Lester, F., & Hensleigh, P. (2004). Prevention and treatment of postpartum hemorrhage: New advances for low-resource settings. *Journal of Midwifery & Women's Health, 49,* 283–292.

Petchesky, R. P. (2000). Human rights, reproductive health, and economic justice: Why they are indivisible. *Reproductive Health Matters, 8,* 12–17.

Ramdhial, M., & Coovia, H. (2010). The new WHO recommendations on HIV and infant feeding: Bridging the gap between training, learning, and doing. *South African Journal of Child Health, 4,* 62–64.

Shaw, D. (2006). Women's right to health and the Millenium Development Goals: Promoting partnerships to improve access. *International Journal of Gynecology and Obstetrics, 94,* 207–215.

Shealy, K. R., Li, R., Benton-Davis, S., & Grummer-Strawn, L. M. (2005). *The CDC guide to breastfeeding interventions.* Atlanta, GA: U.S. Department of Health and Human Services, Centers for Disease Control and Prevention.

Shefren, J. M. (2009). The tragedy of obstetric fistula and strategies for prevention. *American Journal of Obstetrics & Gynecology, 7,* 668–671.

Sibley, L. M., Blum, L. S., Kalim, N., Hruschka, D., Edmonds, J. K., & Koblinsky, M. (2007). Women's descriptions of postpartum health problems: Preliminary findings from Matlab, Bangladesh. *Journal of Midwifery & Women's Health, 52,* 351–360.

Sibley, L. M., Caleb-Varkey, L., Upadhyay, J., Prasad, R., Saroha, E., Bhatla, N., & Paul, V. K. (2005). Recognition of and response to postpartum hemorrhage in rural northern India. *Journal of Midwifery & Women's Health, 50,* 301–308.

Smith, P. H. (2008). "Is it just so my right?": Women repossessing breastfeeding. *International Breastfeeding Journal, 3,* 12–18.

Sokol, E., Clark, D., & Aguayo, V. M. (2008). Protecting breastfeeding in west and central Africa: Over 25 years of implementation of the International Code of Marketing of Breastmilk Substitutes. *Food and Nutrition Bulletin, 29,* 159–162.

Steiner, A. K. (1996). The problem of postpartum fistulas in developing countries. *Acta Tropica, 62,* 217–223.

Tarrant, M., Dodgson, J. E., & Choi, V. W. (2004). Becoming a role model: The breastfeeding trajectory of Hong Kong women breastfeeding longer than 6 months. *International Journal of Nursing Studies, 41,* 535–546.

Thaddeus, S., & Nangalia, R. (2004). Perceptions matter: Barriers to treatment of postpartum hemorrhage. *Journal of Midwifery & Women's Health, 49,* 293–297.

Tsu, V. D., Langer, A., & Aldrich, T. (2004). Postpartum hemorrhage in developing countries: Is the public health community using the right tools? *International Journal of Gynecology and Obstetrics, 85,* S42–S51.

Tsui, A. O., Creanga, A. A., & Ahmed, S. (2007). The role of delayed childbearing in the prevention of obstetric fistulas. *International Journal of Gynecology and Obstetrics, 99*(Suppl. 1), S98–S107.

United Nations Children's Fund. (2011). *Exclusive breastfeeding rates have increased in most regions.* Retrieved from http://www.childinfo.org/breastfeeding_progress.html.

United States Breastfeeding Committee. (2002). *Economic benefits of breastfeeding.* Retrieved from http://www.usbreastfeeding.org/LinkClick.aspx?link=publications%2FEconomic-Benefits-2002-USBC.pdf&tabid=70&mid=388.

United States Government. (2010, December). *Break time for nursing mothers under the FLSA* [Fact Sheet #73]. Retrieved from http://www.dol.gov/whd/regs/compliance/whdfs73.htm.

Walker, M. (2007). International breastfeeding initiatives and their relevance to the current state of breastfeeding in the United States. *Journal of Midwifery & Women's Health, 52,* 549–555.

Wall, L. L. (2006). Obstetric vesicovaginal obstetric fistula as an international public-health problem. *Lancet, 368,* 1201–1209.

Weimer, J. P. (2001). The economic benefits of breastfeeding. *Food Review, 24,* 23–26.

World Breastfeeding Trends Initiative. (2010). *The state of breastfeeding in 33 countries.* Retrieved from http://www.ibfanasia.org.

World Health Organization. (2010a). *Breastfeeding key to saving children's lives.* Retrieved from http://www.who.int/mediacentre/news/notes/2010/breastfeeding_20100730/en.

World Health Organization. (2010b). *Guidelines on HIV and infant feeding: Principles and recommendations for infant feeding in the context of HIV and a summary of evidence.* Retrieved from http://www.who.int/child_adolescent_health/documents/9789241599535/en/.

World Health Organization. (2010c). *Maternal mortality fact sheet.* Retrieved from http://www.who.int/mediacentre/factsheets/fs348/en/index.html.

World Health Organization. (2010d). *10 facts on obstetric fistula*. Retrieved from http://www.who.int/features/factfiles/obstetric_fistula/en/.

World Health Organization. (2011). *Exclusive breastfeeding for six months best for babies everywhere*. Retrieved from http://www.who.int/mediacentre/news/statements/2011/breastfeeding_20110115/en/.

World Health Organization/United Nations Children's Fund. (1989). *Protecting, promoting, and supporting breastfeeding: The special role of maternity services*. Geneva, Switzerland: Author.

World Health Organization/United Nations Children's Fund. (2004). *HIV and infant feeding: A guide for health care managers and supervisors*. Geneva, Switzerland: Author.

Wright, H. (2004). Breastfeeding and the transmission of HIV. *British Journal of Midwifery, 12*, 88–92.

Zheng, A. X., & Anderson, W. J. (2009). Obstetric fistula in low-income countries. *International Journal of Gynecology and Obstetrics, 104*, 85–89.

Chapter 13

Conclusion: An International View of Public Policy for Reproductive Justice

Janet Sigal, Florence L. Denmark, Amy Nadel, and Rebecca A. Petrie

The UN Millennium Development Goal (MDG) 5 addresses the need to alleviate maternal mortality and provide universal access to reproductive health care. As part of this initiative, the International Conference on Population Development (ICPD) was held in 1994, in Cairo, Egypt, in an effort to encourage national leaders to recognize and address each individual's right to reproductive health. At this meeting it was acknowledged that population is not purely about numbers, but about people; this stance marked women's health, education, employment, and empowerment as issues that should be at the forefront in plans for a sustainable future. During this meeting, a Programme of Action was laid out to prioritize individual needs, such as the right to sexual and reproductive health, access to family planning, and women's empowerment. The ICPD Programme of Action also called for the collection and analysis of population data to inform national and international policy decisions (General Assembly, 2009).

The Commission on Population and Development has led the initiative to achieve the ICPD goals and objectives. The commission has en-

couraged governments and development partners to improve maternal
health, reduce maternal and infant mortality, and prevent and address
the HIV/AIDS epidemic through strengthening health systems and ensuring health care services. Family planning, prenatal and postnatal
care, safe delivery, treatment for fertility and sexually transmitted diseases, sex education, availability of contraception, safe access to abortion
(where legal), and management of complications due to abortion are all
areas that require a response from nation-states. Governments were
called on to provide financial and technical support to prevent pregnancy-related deaths and complications (Economic and Social Council,
POP/975, 2009).

Then in 2009, to commemorate the 15th anniversary of the ICPD, the
United Nations held a conference in New York to urge renewed commitment to gender equality and reproductive health rights. UN Secretary-
General Ban Ki-Moon praised the Cairo Programme of Action and urged
development partners to recommit to it until it is fulfilled. International
leaders reported on their own efforts to achieve the ICPD goals, which are
to be fulfilled before 2015. Some of their efforts included making family
planning universally available, meeting agreed goals in education, and
reducing infant, child, and maternal mortality rates (General Assembly,
2009).

One of the primary MDGs is to reduce maternal mortality by three-
fourths by 2012. This goal was to be accomplished through the provision
of universal access to reproductive health care services. Currently, there
are approximately 500,000 deaths each year for mothers, due to pregnancy-related causes. An even larger number, anywhere between 10 and
15 million women, incur severe health problems as a result of pregnancy
and childbirth. Some steps to provide broader health care services include
offering family planning services, skilled obstetrical care, and trained prenatal and postnatal care for both mother and baby. Access to contraception alone would have an enormous effect by preventing approximately
188 million unintended pregnancies each year, which in turn would lead
to fewer abortions and unplanned births and therefore save nearly 200,000
mothers from dying of pregnancy-related causes, according to the United
Nations Population Fund (UNFPA) and the Guttmacher Institute (Scherer,
2010).

AGENCIES THAT ADDRESS REPRODUCTIVE HEALTH

The UNFPA is a leader in addressing reproductive justice. The UNFPA
is concerned with raising awareness of gender perspectives on reproductive rights; it provides technical support and developmental frameworks
at a national level on which governments can build health policies and
programs (United Nations, 2010). The UNFPA (2009, p. ii) states their mis-

sion as follows: promotes "the right of every woman, man and child to enjoy a life of health and equal opportunity and supports countries in using population data for policies and programmes to reduce poverty and to ensure reproductive rights and gender equality." Recently the UNFPA has focused closely on the reproductive rights of indigenous women. This group can derive particular benefit from relevant policies, services, and the support for HIV/AIDS. UNFPA has conducted research studies with ethnic minorities in Latin American and Asia to increase public knowledge and create culturally sensitive programming (Economic and Social Council, E/C.19/2009/3, 2009).

UNFPA targets local and national authorities, leaders, and health providers and helps them to integrate financial, programmatic, and technical support. Furthermore, building women's organizations and networks is key in fostering ownership within these countries. A related focus has been the empowerment of women to demand sexual and reproductive health care policies and information. UNFPA has tailored its interventions in a nation-by-nation approach and taken particularly careful consideration of rural areas where maternal mortality is highest. UNFPA has furthered the study of HIV/AIDS in these indigenous areas by examining people's related knowledge, attitudes, and practices (Economic and Social Council, E/C.19/2009/3, 2009).

Women Deliver is a global advocacy organization dedicated to taking action against maternal death. They work internationally to gain political commitment and financial investment for attainment of MDG 5. Women Deliver is founded on the idea that entire societies benefit when their resources and money are spent on improving the lives of women, children, and families, which is summed up in their slogan: "Invest in Women—It Pays!" (Women Deliver, 2010).

Another international organization that supports the right to a healthy reproductive life is Pathfinder International. This organization affirms that, in addition to being a fundamental human right, health care is necessary for expanding opportunities for women, families, communities, and nations. Pathfinder works in more than 25 countries to provide health services, including contraception, maternal care, HIV prevention, and AIDS care and treatment to all who need it (Pathfinder International, 2010).

Although the UN generally sets standards and develops conventions or treaties that hold member nations accountable for human rights protections, including reproductive rights, the World Health Organization (WHO) is its empirical research agency. WHO specializes in monitoring health globally, collecting accurate data regarding reproductive health and other health issues, and assisting countries to achieve high standards of health by providing resources and expert consultants. The UN sets standards such as the MDGs, and WHO guides nations to implement policies and best practices to achieve those goals.

An example of the involvement of WHO in guiding and monitoring reproductive rights and health was described by Cottingham et al. (2010). The authors discussed WHO's efforts to link reproductive rights and human rights through a WHO tool to improve conditions for women. This tool involves "examining the legal/policy and public health data alongside the country's human rights commitments. The latter consist of international and regional human rights treaties ratified . . . and country-specific concluding observations of the treaty monitoring bodies, as well as states' own national constitutions and human rights laws" (p. 552). In other words, the tool compares the human rights guarantees integral to signed international treaties with actual data and governments' laws to determine whether each country is adhering to its international commitments to protect reproductive rights. Cottingham et al. suggested that, for many governments, there is an inconsistency between commitments and national laws and policies. Recommendations to close the observed gaps must emanate from diverse national groups including government officials from various branches (e.g., education, justice), nongovernmental groups (e.g., particularly those involved in women's advocacy efforts), researchers from universities, health professionals, and other members of civil society (e.g., family planning organizations). In particular, these groups must focus on categories of women who face persistent barriers to sexual and reproductive health rights.

This approach by WHO has been tested in a number of locations including Brazil, Indonesia, and Mozambique, where WHO personnel have assisted governments in conducting such investigations. Even if this tool proves to be successful in guiding nations to assess reproductive justice and issue recommendations to improve conditions for women, the next step, according to Cottingham et al. (2010), will be to make certain that these recommendations are implemented.

CHALLENGES, EXPLANATIONS, AND RECOMMENDATIONS

In this section, we examine some explanations for why gaps exist in the protection of reproductive rights globally and then consider some recommendations for international improvement in reproductive health standards.

Barriers and Explanations

Generally, reproductive rights are more strongly protected in developed than in developing nations. However, there is considerable variation in these protections within each group, and there is an ongoing struggle to protect these rights by international organizations such as the UN and WHO and by nongovernmental organizations (NGOs) in civil societies.

One explanation for barriers against full access to reproductive rights is poverty (e.g., Ndaruhuye, Broekhuis, & Hooimeijer, 2009). If a nation is impoverished, there will not be funds available for family planning, free contraceptives, or comprehensive care for women during pregnancy. One version of this explanation suggests that population density (associated in part with a lack of family limitation services) contributes to poverty, which can then lead to an increase in the number of unsafe abortions. However, one weak point of this explanation is that it does not appear that an increase in family planning services necessarily reduces the number of induced abortions (e.g., Zhu et al., 2009).

A second explanation is that there is a lack of understanding and awareness, as well as misconceptions about emergency contraception (EC) and other forms of family size limitation (Center for Reproductive Rights, 2001, 2004). Even in countries where EC is freely available or accessed over the counter (e.g., South Africa; Maharaj & Rogan, 2008), there is considerable variability in the use of EC. Simply increasing awareness and knowledge of EC among women and health providers does not automatically translate into increased use of this effective prevention of pregnancy approach (Bildircin & Sahin, 2005). Misconceptions about the timing of usage (within 72 hours of unprotected sex), possible side effects (Will it have a negative impact on future births or fertility?), and perceived effectiveness have prevented many health professionals from recommending the process to their clients and stopped many women from using EC. The other misconception, that EC is a form of abortion, prevents its wider usage in many developing and developed countries (Center for Reproductive Rights, 2004).

A third barrier that has been identified as a problem with EC is limited access to it and inability to pay for it, which is associated with its low level of use in some countries. In particular, rural women often are not even aware of EC as a prevention-of-pregnancy pill.

Negative and even hostile attitudes of government officials and health professionals toward family planning, as well as incompetence of professional health workers in some countries (e.g., Pakistan) contribute to the high level of maternal and child mortality (Ali, Ahmed, & Kuroiwa, 2008). Privacy issues both in family planning and purchase of contraceptives and EC are problems in some countries (e.g., Center for Reproductive Rights, 2004; Okonofua et al., 2009).

Another barrier is that, at times, national health systems and health providers are also hesitant to incorporate cultural perspectives into their reproductive program planning (Okonofua et al., 2009). Furthermore, UNFPA believes that MDG 5 could better recognize the need for an intercultural approach to maternal health and pay more respect to indigenous and ethnic minority women (Economic and Social Council, E/C.19/2009/3, 2009).

According to Pillai and Wang (1999), the most significant barrier to global protection of reproductive rights is the unequal power balance between men and women (see chapter 3 "Women's Power in Relationships"). This inequality is strongest in patriarchal societies where men are the heads of government and other institutions, as well as the family, which causes women to be totally dependent on their male family members. The male head of the family makes all the decisions, and, in extreme cases (e.g., Afghanistan), women are not permitted to go outside the home unless accompanied by a male relative. In some societies (e.g., Nigeria; Okonofua et al., 2009), women are not even permitted to seek the services of a male doctor. If a wife is experiencing complications from pregnancy or birth, her husband will go to the hospital to consult with the medical personnel. Pillai and Wang (1999) concluded that "gender equality has positive effects on women's reproductive rights" (p. 275). If women are educated, gender equality is more likely to occur. In addition to patriarchal societies, other fundamentalist religious groups may adversely affect women's control over their reproductive rights.

Although certain threats to women's reproductive health are being tackled head-on and public awareness of the injustice is growing, other issues are not as visible or have not been approached systematically. Human trafficking is a horrific and widespread industry that claims more and more victims each year, yet it is relatively unknown to the general public (see chapter 5, "Reproductive Injustice"). In fact, it is the fastest-growing criminal enterprise in the world. Kevin Bales (as cited in Fischer, 2010, p. 133), president and cofounder of Free the Slaves, recently said that "there are more people in slavery today than at any other time in human history." There are roughly 27 million victims in 47 nations. In the United States alone, there are approximately 15,750 men, women, and children trafficked each year. Rates of human trafficking in India and Asia are estimated to be in the millions. These individuals are often forced into sexual slavery, held captive, drugged, and threatened with physical harm to themselves and their families' lives to keep them quiet about their experiences. Organizations in the United States, such as the Immigration and Customs Enforcement and the Coalition to Abolish Slavery & Trafficking, and international organizations, such as the UN, are working to raise awareness and, ultimately, to terminate this underrecognized, modern form of slavery (Fischer, 2010).

Recommendations

Perhaps the most significant and difficult approach to achieving MDGs concerning women and children is to change the culture in certain countries. When women are valued, are educated, contribute economically to the family, and become full partners in family decision making, their potential to achieve reproductive justice will increase. The ability to control the number and spacing of children will enable women to lead fulfilling and satisfying lives. Therefore, gender equality (as measured by international databases) should be the focus of plans to reduce maternal mortality and improve child health.

Increased awareness of, knowledge about, and understanding of the effective use of contraceptives and EC, by both the public and health professionals, should improve reproductive health globally. In addition, health professionals must be trained in comprehensive obstetric care, particularly in emergency situations, and careful medical records should be kept in health institutions. Furthermore, as indicated by Cali, Kalaca, and Sarikaya (2004), the linking of family planning to broader health care facilities would encourage greater utilization and normalization of these services as standard medical interventions.

Reproductive rights must be recast in terms of human rights, and the United Nations and other international organizations must make their member nations accountable for reaching the mandated relevant MDGs. Beyond simply encouraging nations to achieve MDGs, such as reducing maternal mortality by 2015, organizations such as WHO must provide resources and experts to assist member nations to meet these goals.

Another recommendation is that all relevant interventions should occur at early ages, particularly sex education in the schools and prevention programs for adolescents, who represent a general at-risk group for unplanned pregnancies. In support of this recommendation, Arisi (2003) reported that in the Netherlands, where early interventions are the norm, the rate of abortion is very low. In addition, Pinter et al. (2005) reported that close to 80 percent of women in the Netherlands use contraceptives, a further indication that early sex education is effective.

It is important to involve men in family planning and throughout the pregnancy process. Men should not demand sexual relations when the decision is consensual. In China, when men were involved in the planning process, contraceptives were used more effectively by couples (Zhu et al., 2009).

WHO (2010) has published a manual on programs for safe motherhood and child health. The interventions in the manual include universal access to family planning as well as comprehensive care for women during pregnancy and for infants and children. According to the introduction to the manual, the recommendations protect the human rights of partners and are culturally sensitive. Specific means of implementing WHO standards of care are described and discussed in the manual. Health professionals across the globe should be aware of and follow the recommended interventions described in the WHO manual.

There has been some progress in building awareness of women's reproductive rights as related to specific at-risk populations. On May 3, 2008,

the first global treaty was put into place to address the needs of persons
with disabilities, as the Convention on the Rights of Persons with Disabilities, produced by the UN. The overall purpose of this convention was to
address the fundamental freedoms and human rights of all persons with
disabilities and to promote respect for them, and it specifically addressed
their reproductive rights. Persons with disabilities are up to three times
more likely than others to be the victims of physical and sexual abuse,
which puts them at greater risk of contracting HIV and other STIs. This
historic document is the first universal human rights treaty to mention
sexual and reproductive health overtly (Department of Public Information, 2008).

The United States has made progress in working toward the MDGs
for reproductive health. When President Barack Obama assumed office, his first step was to rescind the Mexico City Policy, which made
it easier for women in developing countries to receive assistance from
the United States to gain access to reproductive health information
and services. The President's Emergency Plan for AIDS Relief supports
confidential HIV counseling and testing, links HIV+ women with care
and treatment, and provides referrals to family planning programs for
women in these treatment programs. The Obama administration has
created the White House Council on Women and Girls to provide leadership in the areas of women's and girls' health, empowerment, and
human rights, and the administration would like to ratify the Convention on the Elimination of Discrimination against Women. Furthermore,
the United States has been generous in funding the UNFPA, and the
U.S. Congress has approved additional funds for assistance for family
planning (Pollak, 2009).

A final suggestion concerns the importance of ending conflict within
and between nations and its concomitant violence. Rape is a common consequence of war and civil conflict, and many of the victims are women and
children (see chapter 4, "Sexual Assault"). The eastern Congo is a horrible
example of this association. Unsafe and unsanitary conditions, as well as
poor or nonexistent health care, often occur in refugee camps that house
individuals who have fled from conflict. Such terrible situations and conditions must be eradicated from our modern world.

Only now that the public is making connections between the reproductive years of women's lives and their long-term health, well-being,
safety, and the economic security of the generations to come is reproductive justice getting the attention it deserves. Reproductive rights represent
a fundamental human right, and every woman is entitled to control her
reproductive life. Therefore, governments should be held accountable for
ensuring comprehensive reproductive health care and the public safety of
all of their women citizens.

REFERENCES

Ali, M., Ahmed, K. M., & Kuroiwa, C. (2008). Emergency obstetric care in Punjab, Pakistan: Improvement needed. *European Journal of Contraception and Reproductive Health Care, 1*(2/3), 201–207.

Arisi, E. (2003). Changing attitudes towards abortion in Europe. *European Journal Contraception and Reproductive Health Care, 8*(2), 109–121.

Bildircin, M., & Sahin, N. H. (2005). Knowledge, attitudes, and practices regarding emergency contraception among family-planning providers in Turkey. *European Journal of Contraception and Reproductive Health Care, 10*(3), 151–156.

Cali, S., Kalaca, S., & Sarikaya, O. (2004). Minimizing missed opportunities: An approach to decrease the unmet need for family planning. *European Journal of Contraception and Reproductive Health Care, 9*(4), 285–289.

Center for Reproductive Rights. (2001, December). *Trends in reproductive rights: East central Europe* [Briefing Paper]. Retrieved from http://reproductiverights. org/en/document/trends-in-reproductive-rights-east-central-europe.

Center for Reproductive Rights. (2004, September). *Governments worldwide put emergency contraception into women's hands: A global review of laws and policies* [Briefing Paper]. Retrieved from http://reproductiverights.org/en/ document/governments-worldwide-put-emergency-contraception-into-womens-hands.

Cottingham, J., Kismodi, E., Hilber, A. M., Lincetto, O., Stahlohofer, M., & Gruskin, S. (2010). Using human rights for sexual and reproductive health: Improving legal and regulatory frameworks. *Bulletin of the World Health Organization, 88,* 551–555.

Department of Public Information. (2008, May). *Disability treaty closes a gap in protecting human rights: United Nations Enable: Rights and Dignity of Persons with Disabilities.* Retrieved from http://www.un.org/disabilities/defeault. asp?id=476 (page no longer available).

Economic and Social Council, E/C.19/2009/3. (2009, May). *Information received from the United Nations system and other intergovernmental organizations: United Nations Population Fund.* Paper presented at the Permanent Forum on Indigenous Issues, New York.

Economic and Social Council, POP/975. (2009, April). *Commission on Population and Development concludes session by adopting guideline for international action over the next five years.* Paper presented at the Commission on Population and Development. New York: Department of Public Information, News and Media Division.

Fischer, M. A. (2010, October). Freedom fighter. *Readers Digest,* 128–141.

General Assembly, GA/10869. (2009, October). *Secretary-general urges renewed commitment to gender equality, reproductive health rights, marking the 15th anniversary of Cairo Population and Development Conference.* Remarks presented at the 64th Sixty-fourth General Assembly Plenary Session. New York: Department of Public Information, News and Media Division.

Maharaj, P., & Rogan, M. (2008). Emergency contraception in South Africa: A literature review. *European Journal of Contraception and Reproductive Health Care, 13*(4), 351–361.

Ndaruhuye, D. M., Broekhuis, A., & Hooimeijer, P. (2009). Demand and unmet need for means of family imitation in Rwanda. *International Perspectives on Sexual and Reproductive Health, 35*(3), 122–130.

Okonofua, F. E., Hammed, A., Nzeribe, E., Saidu, B., Abass, T., Adeboye, G., . . . Okolocha, C. (2009). Perceptions of policymakers in Nigeria toward unsafe abortion and maternal mortality. *International Perspectives on Sexual and Reproductive Health, 35*(4), 194–202.

Pathfinder International. (2010, September 17). *USA Today* (Mediaplanet; independent supplement), p. 4.

Paul, A. M. (2010, September 22). The first nine months. *Time,* 50–55.

Pillai, V. K., & Wang, G-Z. (1999). Women's reproductive rights, modernization, and family planning programs in developing countries: A causal model. *International Journal of Comparative Sociology, 40,* 270–292.

Pinter, B., Aubeny, E., Bartfai, G., Loeber, O., Ozalp, S., & Webb, A. (2005). Accessibility and availability of abortion in six European countries. *European Journal of Contraception and Reproductive Health Care, 10*(1), 51–58.

Pollack, M. J. (2009, March 31). *Statement by Margaret J. Pollack, Acting Deputy Assistant Secretary of State for the Bureau of Population, Refugees, and Migration, and Head of the United States Delegation to the United Nations Commission on Population and Development.* New York: USUN Press Release #064.

Scherer, W. Y. (2010, September 17). Maternal mortality. *USA* Today (independent supplement), p. 4.

United Nations. (2010, September 8). Countries committed to strengthen the rights of persons with disabilities. *DESA News.* Retrieved from http://un.org/en/developemtn/desa/news/social/disabilities-conference.shtml.

United Nations Population Fund. (2009). *UNFPA annual report.* New York: United Nations.

Women Deliver. (2010, September 17). *USA Today* (Mediaplanet; independent supplement), p. 4.

World Health Organization. (2010). *Packages of interventions for family planning, safe abortion care, and maternal, infant, and newborn health.* Geneva: Author.

Zhu, J. L., Zhang, W-H., Cheng, Y., Xu, J., Xu, X., Gibson, D., & Temmerman, M. (2009). Impact of post-abortion family planning services on contraceptive use and abortion rate among young women in China: A cluster randomised trial. *European Journal of Contraception and Reproductive Health Care, 14*(1), 46–54.

Afterword

What Can We Do to Help the World's Women Achieve Reproductive Justice?

Joan C. Chrisler

Reading about the injustice that women and girls face every day can be depressing, and readers may find themselves wondering if the problems are too big to solve and wishing there were some way that they could help. Yes, the problems are huge, but progress is being made, and all of us can help. Here are some things that any of us can do.

First, we should know our rights and exercise them. Everyone should be familiar with the laws of their country and the resources available in their communities for sex education, family planning, and reproductive health care. Educating ourselves and those around us is important.

Second, we should all vote for candidates for political office who support reproductive justice in all its forms. Politicians at all levels make public policy that affects the lives of women and girls, and they can fund initiatives at home and abroad to bring women closer to reproductive justice. Even more important, we could run for office ourselves and support women's rights!

Third, we can support nonprofit organizations that advocate for reproductive justice and/or provide direct health care and legal services to the world's women. We can support these groups in whichever way is best for us: by donating our time to their work, by seeking employment in their office where our skills can be utilized every day, by donating money to assist in their work, by raising money from our friends and family to support these organizations, and by using social networking to let others know about the work these organizations do and how important we think it is. Some of these organizations have action alerts that tell us when we can take simple, concrete actions (e.g., writing to our legislators, attending a meeting or demonstration). Others provide opportunities for volunteers to work on the ground in developing countries for long or short periods of time (e.g., vacations, semester breaks, internships). Below are some groups that work on the topics discussed in this book. Check out their websites, and think about what you could do to support their work.

Family Planning

- International Planned Parenthood Federation (http://www.ippf. org)—provides low-cost reproductive health services and family planning education in 180 countries around the world.
- The Guttmacher Institute (http://www.guttmacher.org)—promotes sexual and reproductive health through research, policy analysis, and public education.
- Americans for UNFPA (http://www.americansforunfpa.org)— supports the work of the United Nations Population Fund.
- Center for Reproductive Rights (http://www.reproductiverights. org)—wages legal battles to promote reproductive rights as a fundamental human right.

Sex Education and Prevention of STIs

- Engender Health (http://www.engenderhealth.org)—works to improve the sexual health and well-being of people around the world, especially in developing countries.
- Pathfinder International (http://www.pathfind.org)—provides educational and health care services related to all aspects of reproductive health, especially HIV and AIDS prevention.

Pregnancy Care and Maternal Mortality

- Women Deliver (http://www.womendeliver.org)—global advocacy organization that calls for action to reduce maternal and infant mortality.

- The White Ribbon Campaign for Safe Motherhood (http://www. whiteribbonalliance.org)—international advocacy group that raises awareness about mortality from pregnancy-related conditions.

Postpartum Health

- The Fistula Foundation (http://www.fistulafoundation.org)—funds surgery to repair fistulas and other childbirth-related injuries.
- The Worldwide Fistula Fund (http://www.worldwidefistulafund. org)—funds surgery to repair obstetric fistulas in developing countries.

Menstrual Hygiene Supplies

- Days for Girls (http://www.daysforgirls.org)—organizes volunteers to sew and gather menstrual hygiene supplies and distributes them free to girls and women worldwide who cannot afford or access them.
- Sustainable Health Enterprises (http://she28.sheinnovates.com)— teaches women in developing countries to produce and sell afford-able, sustainable menstrual hygiene supplies.

Antitrafficking

- Love 146 (http://www.love146.org)—raises awareness about, and res-cues and rehabilitates victims of, child sex trafficking.
- Coalition to Abolish Slavery and Trafficking (http://www.castla. org)—provides advocacy, outreach, and client services (e.g., legal, mental health) to survivors.

Index

About the Editor and Contributors

EDITOR

JOAN C. CHRISLER, PhD is the Class of 1943 Professor of Psychology at Connecticut College, where she teaches courses on health psychology and the psychology of women. She has published extensively on the psychology of women and gender and is especially known for her work on women's health, attitudes toward menstruation, premenstrual syndrome, women and weight, and body image. She has served as Chair of APA Division 52's (International Psychology) International Committee for Women and has been president of several professional associations, including APA Division 35 (Psychology of Women) and the Society for Menstrual Cycle Research. She is a past editor of *Sex Roles* and has also served on the editorial boards of *Fat Studies, Psychology of Men & Masculinity, Psychology of Women Quarterly,* and *Teaching of Psychology.* She has edited or coedited a number of other books, most recently *Handbook of Gender Research in Psychology* (2010, Springer), *Lectures on the Psychology of Women* (4th ed., 2008, McGraw-Hill), *Women over 50: Psychological Perspectives* (2007, Springer), and *From Menarche to Menopause: The Female Body in Feminist Therapy* (2004, Haworth). Dr. Chrisler has won many awards for her scholarship, teaching, leadership, service, and mentoring.

CONTRIBUTORS

VIRGINIA BRAUN, PhD is Senior Lecturer in Psychology at the University of Auckland. Her research has focused on women's bodies, gendered bodies, and sex and sexuality, particularly the intersections between sociocultural meanings and individuals' desires, experience, and practices. Her main focus of research has been meanings and practices associated with female genitalia, including female genital cosmetic surgery.

THEMA BRYANT-DAVIS, PhD is Associate Professor of Psychology and Director of the Culture and Trauma Research Laboratory at Pepperdine University. She has served as president of APA Division 35 (Psychology of Women) and chair of its Global Issues Committee and formerly represented the American Psychological Association at the United Nations. She has studied and written about sexual assault and is the author of the book *Thriving in the Wake of Trauma: A Multicultural Guide.*

PAMELA A. COUNTS, BA is a PsyD candidate in clinical psychology at Pepperdine University. She has conducted several research projects on multicultural approaches to interpersonal trauma recovery; her research and clinical interests include spirituality and religion, sexual assault, human sex trafficking, dehumanization, and natural disaster response. She has also presented talks on African American women's approaches to coping with and surviving the aftermath of sexual assault.

FLORENCE L. DENMARK, PhD is the Robert Scott Pace Distinguished Research Professor of Psychology at Pace University. She is an internationally recognized scholar, researcher, and policy maker, who has served as president of several professional associations, including the American Psychological Association. Her research interests are women's leadership and leadership styles, the rights of women, aging women in cross-cultural perspective, and the history of women in psychology. She is currently the main NGO representative to the United Nations for the International Council of Psychologists.

RUTHBETH FINERMAN, PhD is Professor of Medical Anthropology and Chair of the Department of Anthropology at the University of Memphis. She also holds an adjunct appointment in the Department of Preventive Medicine at the University of Tennessee Health Sciences Center and is affiliated with the University of Memphis Center for Research on Women, where she collaborates on studies of reproductive health among underserved populations in the U.S. mid-South region. She has worked extensively on reproductive and maternal-child health in Central and South America.

KAYOKO HAYASHI, MA is a PsyD candidate in clinical psychology at the Chicago School of Professional Psychology. Her expertise and interests include cultural psychology, cross-cultural research, issues of expats, existential theory, psychoanalysis, couple therapy, and trauma.

INGRID JOHNSTON-ROBLEDO, PhD is Associate Professor of Psychology and Assistant Dean of Arts and Sciences at the State University of New York, College at Fredonia. Her primary area of expertise is reproductive and sexual health, and she has published widely on psychosocial aspects of menstruation, breastfeeding, postpartum adjustment, and motherhood.

MAKIKO KASAI, PhD is a member of the faculty of the School of Education at Naruto University of Education. Her areas of research include sexual minorities, cross-cultural counseling, international psychology, and school counselor training. She is in the process of developing an LGBT affirmative counseling program and research center in Japan.

SAYAKA MACHIZAWA, PsyD is Associate Director of the Community Partnerships Department at the Chicago School of Professional Psychology, where she coordinates and oversees community-based research activities. She also maintains an independent practice in clinical psychology as a specialist in neuropsychological, psychological, and fitness-for-duty evaluation. As a consultant, she facilitates seminars on cross-cultural issues and corporate wellness. Her interests include disaster psychology, cross-cultural psychology, and feminist psychology.

RAMASWAMI MAHALINGAM, PhD is Associate Professor of Psychology at the University of Michigan. His research concerns the cultural psychology of gender, with a particular focus on gender discrimination in India. He has also used an intersectionality framework to examine the impact of perceived discrimination on the psychological well-being of Asian Americans, and he developed a Critical Intersectional Awareness scale to measure beliefs about intersectional identities.

MARGARET A. MCLAREN, PhD is the Harriet W. and George D. Cornell Professor of Philosophy at Rollins College. She has published in a wide range of areas including feminist theory, 20th-century French philosophy, virtue ethics, and women's rights and empowerment in a global context. Her current research addresses issues at the intersection of gender, culture, and human rights. She is the author of *Feminism, Foucault, and Embodied Subjectivity.*

ALLISON MURRAY, BA is an MS candidate in the nurse practitioner program at the University of Rochester. She majored in psychology and women's studies at the State University of New York, College at Fredonia, where she developed her interest in women's reproductive health.

AMY NADEL, BA is a PhD candidate in clinical psychology at Fairleigh Dickinson University. She has conducted research on sexual assault and domestic violence. Recently she presented the results of her work on the effects of perpetrator status and victim's behavior on perceptions of date rape.

KATHRYN L. NORSWORTHY, PhD is Professor of Counseling Psychology at Rollins College, and she maintains an independent psychotherapy practice. Since 1997, she has been engaged in activist research and practice projects on trauma, feminist counseling, women's leadership, and peace building in Thailand, Cambodia, and northern India, with refugee and internally displaced communities of Burma, and with international groups. She is a coeditor of the *International Handbook of Cross-Cultural Counseling: Cultural Assumptions and Practices Worldwide.*

VRUSHALI PATIL, PhD is Assistant Professor of Sociology and Women's Studies at Florida International University. She uses a transnational feminist perspective to explore how people in the Global South negotiate collective identities in the context of global/transnational power relations. Her work also addresses the current phase of neoliberal globalization's impact on racial, gender, and sexual politics, particularly in relation to global processes associated with tourism and diaspora.

REBECCA A. PETRIE, MSEd is a PsyD candidate in school-clinical psychology at Pace University, where she recently received the Ted Bernstein Award for excellence in school psychology. She has conducted research on gender-based violence throughout the life cycle.

ALIZA PHILLIPS, MA is a PhD candidate in clinical psychology at the New School for Social Research. Her current research interest is the psychology of doctor-patient relationships.

JOY K. RICE, PhD is Clinical Professor of Psychiatry and Professor Emerita of Educational Policy Studies and Women's Studies at the University of Wisconsin–Madison. She has been recognized nationally and internationally for her research and professional work on gender equity, psychotherapy, and social justice and for her advocacy for and promotion of the welfare and status of disadvantaged women and their families.

S. CRAIG ROONEY, PhD is a licensed clinical psychologist at the Center for Family and Individual Counseling in Columbia, Missouri. His previous publications have been on lesbian, gay, and bisexual issues and on multicultural practice and education.

LISA R. RUBIN, PhD is Assistant Professor of Psychology and Assistant Director of Clinical Training at the New School for Social Research. Her current work addresses the objectification and medicalization of the female body in medical contexts, including pregnancy, breast cancer, hereditary breast cancer risk, and infertility. Her most recent work concerns attitudes toward preimplantation genetic diagnosis for the BRCA (breast cancer) gene mutation among BRCA mutation carriers and attitudes toward anonymity among oocyte donors and recipients.

NANCY FELIPE RUSSO, PhD is the Regents Professor Emerita of Psychology and Gender Studies at Arizona State University. She has worked on international issues related to women's reproductive rights and unwanted childbearing around the world as a researcher and policy advocate for more than four decades. She is the author or editor of more than 200 publications related to the psychology of women and gender, and she has won many awards for her work.

LYNDA M. SAGRESTANO, PhD is Associate Professor of Psychology and Director of the Center for Research on Women at the University of Memphis. Her research interests include maternal and prenatal health, adolescent sexual behavior, HIV prevention, sexual harassment in school, domestic violence, and barriers to economic self-sufficiency for women. She currently serves on the Board of Directors of the National Council for Research on Women.

NANCY M. SIDUN, PsyD, ABPP, ATR is a Supervising Clinical Psychologist at Kaiser Permanente-Hawaii Region and maintains an independent clinical practice in Honolulu. She previously chaired a Task Force on Human Trafficking for APA Division 52 (International Psychology) and is currently a member of the American Psychological Association's Task Force on Trafficking of Women and Girls. She has presented and published widely in the area of human trafficking, especially as it relates to the sexual exploitation of women and girls.

JANET SIGAL, PhD is Professor Emerita of Psychology at Fairleigh Dickinson University. Her research interests include perceptions of domestic violence, sexual harassment, and cross-cultural and international psychology. She currently represents the American Psychological Association at the United Nations.

JULIA R. STEINBERG, PhD is Assistant Professor of Health Psychology in the Department of Psychiatry at the University of California, San Francisco, where she completed the Charlotte Ellertson Postdoctoral Fellowship in Abortion and Reproductive Health. Her research is at the intersection of psychology and reproductive health, and she has published several articles on the relationship of abortion and mental health.

DIONNE P. STEPHENS, PhD is Assistant Professor of Psychology at Florida International University. Her research concerns sociocultural factors that shape sexual health processes of women of color, with emphasis on gender and ethnic/racial identity development. Her current research is on the influence of sexual scripts on diverse Black and Hispanic populations' sexual risk outcomes (including STI acquisition, intimate violence, and HPV vaccination).

TAMI L. THOMAS, PhD, CPNP, RNC is Assistant Professor of Nursing at Emory University. She is a board-certified pediatric nurse practitioner and was awarded a Robert Wood Johnson Foundation Fellowship for her research on population-specific risk factors for sexually transmitted infections. Her current research concerns interventions to disseminate health care innovations, such as the HPV vaccine, to rural adolescent and pediatric populations who experience health disparities.

SHAQUITA TILLMAN, MA is a PsyD candidate in clinical psychology at Pepperdine University. She is a research assistant in the Culture and Trauma Research Laboratory at Pepperdine, where she is studying human trafficking, genocide, intimate partner abuse, sexual assault, and child sexual abuse. She is especially interested in the ethnocultural context of recovery following traumatic experiences.

MADELINE WACHMAN, BA and MA is a research assistant in the Division of General Pediatrics at Children's Hospital/Harvard University Medical School. She is currently working on an HIV-medication adherence intervention for young adults in Boston and also assists with a work-site-based parenting program in Cape Town, South Africa. Her primary research interest is lay theories of health and health behavior.

LAURA D. WATERFIELD, MA is a mental health intern at the Center for Drug Free Living in Orlando, Florida. Her research and clinical interests include feminist psychology, mindfulness, and women's rights. She is an advocate for equality, who infuses justice and equality in her work with her individual clients, families, and groups, and in social change work in her local and global communities.

CPSIA information can be obtained at www.ICGtesting.com
Printed in the USA
BVOW06*0039160916

462272BV00007B/43/P